HE CAME DOWN FROM HEAVEN

*The Preexistence of Christ
and the Christian Faith*

DOUGLAS MCCREADY

InterVarsity Press
Downers Grove, Illinois

Apollos
Leicester, England

InterVarsity Press, USA
P.O. Box 1400, Downers Grove, IL 60515-1426, USA
World Wide Web: www.ivpress.com
Email: mail@ivpress.com

APOLLOS (an imprint of Inter-Varsity Press, England)
38 De Montfort Street, Leicester LE1 7GP, England
Website: www.ivpbooks.com
Email: ivp@ivp-editorial.co.uk

InterVarsity Press®, USA, is the book-publishing division of InterVarsity Christian Fellowship/USA®, a student movement active on campus at hundreds of universities, colleges and schools of nursing in the United States of America, and a member movement of the International Fellowship of Evangelical Students. For information about local and regional activities, write Public Relations Dept., InterVarsity Christian Fellowship/USA, 6400 Schroeder Rd., P.O. Box 7895, Madison, WI 53707-7895, or visit the IVCF website at <www.intervarsity.org>.

Inter-Varsity Press, England, is the publishing division of the Universities and Colleges Christian Fellowship (formerly the Inter-Varsity Fellowship), a student movement linking Christian Unions in universities and colleges throughout Great Britain, and a member movement of the International Fellowship of Evangelical Students. For information about local and national activities write to UCCF, 38 De Montfort Street, Leicester LE1 7GP, email us at email@uccf.org.uk, or visit the UCCF website at www.uccf.org.uk.

All Scripture quotations, unless otherwise indicated, are taken from the Holy Bible, New International Version®. NIV®. Copyright © 1973, 1978, 1984 by International Bible Society. Used by permission of Zondervan Publishing House. Distributed in the U.K. by permission of Hodder and Stoughton Ltd. All rights reserved. "NIV" is a registered trademark of International Bible Society. UK trademark number 1448790.

Design: Cindy Kiple

Images: Adam Woolfitt/CORBIS

USA ISBN-10: 0-8308-2774-9
*   ISBN-13: 978-0-8308-2774-9*

UK ISBN-10: 1-84474-104-4
*   ISBN-13: 978-1-84474-104-5*

Printed in the United States of America ∞

Library of Congress Cataloging-in-Publication Data

McCready, Douglas, 1947-
  He came down from heaven: the preexistence of Christ and
  Christian
 faith / Douglas McCready.
    p. cm.
  Includes bibliographical references.
  ISBN 0-8308-2774-9 (pbk.: alk. paper)
  1. Jesus Christ—Pre-existence—History of doctrines. I.
  Title.
  BT203.M3385 2005
  232'.8—dc22

                            2005018541

British Library Cataloguing in Publication Data

A catalogue record for this book is available from the British Library.

| **P** | 18 | 17 | 16 | 15 | 14 | 13 | 12 | 11 | 10 | 9 | 8 | 7 | 6 | 5 | 4 | 3 | 2 | 1 |
| **Y** | 18 | 17 | 16 | 15 | 14 | 13 | 12 | 11 | 10 | 09 | 08 | 07 | 06 | 05 | | | | |

To my wife, Dianne,

whose continued support and encouragement

helped the dream become reality

CONTENTS

PREFACE

I began this study with the intention of writing an article about the changes and challenges that have appeared in the doctrine of the preexistence of Jesus Christ. I first thought seriously about the matter in a graduate seminar on Christ's preexistence led by Karl-Josef Kuschel at the University of Tübingen's Institute for Ecumenical Studies in 1985. Kuschel and I disagreed sharply on the subject. Eight years later, I picked up a copy of his *Born Before All Time?* and decided it needed a response.

As I organized my research and the reading list swelled, I gained a deeper appreciation of how all the areas of Christian theology are closely connected. Preexistence is linked with the incarnation and other christological studies as well as the Trinity. It then links to soteriology and pneumatology. In order to keep this book manageable in length and complexity, I have tried to stay focused on the preexistence of Christ and only refer to the other issues as they affect my theme. One concern that did become increasingly important as I reflected on the doctrine is its practical application in the life of the believer. This was Paul's great concern and that of the theologians of the early church. It should be ours as well. My hope in writing this book is that people might gain a greater appreciation of the immensity of God's love for us in Jesus Christ. But that can't happen until we know Jesus Christ as the preexistent Son of God who became incarnate for us and our salvation.

Initially, my response was a paper at a regional meeting of the American Academy of Religion; then it became a journal article; and finally I decided it would take a book to adequately address the subject. I wanted to emphasize the church's early and sustained belief in Christ's preexistent deity, and my work on the manuscript was advanced through the greater availability of patristic sources thanks to InterVarsity Press's Ancient Christian Commentary on Scripture series. The move from presentation and article to book can be quite daunting, especially in this case. I realized this more and more as I worked through the various aspects of Christ's preexistence. Fortunately, there was a lot of encouragement along the way. Especially important has been the help from InterVarsity Press during the revision and rewriting process.

The work has also been delayed because I have been activated as an Army Reserve chaplain three times since 2000. I completed the editing of the text in Germany, where I spent fifteen months as a community chaplain, less than two hundred miles from Tübingen. I am grateful for the patience of Gary Deddo, my editor, and InterVarsity Press as I worked through a major rewriting and expansion of the initial manuscript. Thanks to Gary and two anonymous readers, this is a much better book than the first and much-revised second versions that went to InterVarsity Press.

I also owe thanks to my family, especially my wife, Dianne, who put up with my many days in the stacks at Princeton and Westminster Theological Seminaries, followed by hours of reading, note taking, and writing. Despite this, she has encouraged me in the project and prayed faithfully for its successful conclusion.

In chapter nine particularly, I criticize important modern biblical scholars and theologians. My criticisms of their scholarly conclusions should not be construed as a questioning of their Christian commitment. I have studied under some of those I criticize and have heard from their own lips their sense of commitment. I confess my mystification at the disconnect I see there between faith and scholarship, something Roger Nicole and I have discussed several times. I hope this book displays the continuity between faith and theology that is lacking in so much modern theology.

1

THE SETTING

I t has been said that without belief in the preexistence of Christ, Christianity would no longer be recognizable.[1] The doctrine of Christ's personal preexistence as the second person of the Trinity is taken for granted by most orthodox Christians and has been since New Testament times. For more than a century, however, biblical scholars and theologians have increasingly questioned the teaching. This contrasts with previous challenges to the doctrine of Christ's preexistence that have come primarily from outside Christianity. The result, however, is the same: a god who differs radically from the biblical God. This has ruinous consequences for Christian faith and practice. As Werner Löser notes, "The way that the pre-existence of Christ is understood determines how one speaks about the theology of God and of human salvation."[2]

The doctrine of Christ's preexistence did not result from theological curiosity or speculation. As early as the first decade of the church, Christians saw preexistence as necessary for understanding Christ's person and significance in human salvation. What is probably the earliest statement of his preexistence (Phil 2:5-11) was not written to teach us about who Jesus is, but to exhort its readers about their behavior. As Dick France has written:

> The basic fact which lies behind all the theological terms and titles is the worship of the carpenter. This is a phenomenon sufficiently arresting to require explanation, even if they had never progressed to the stage of openly calling him "God." This worship was no easy option for pious Jews.[3]

---

[1]Bruce A. Demarest, *Jesus Christ* (Wheaton, Ill.: Victor, 1978), p. 20.

[2]Werner Löser, "Jesus Christus: Gottes Sohn, aus dem Vater geboren vor aller Zeit: Zur Deutung der Präexistenzaus sagen in der gegenwärtigen Theologie," *Internationale Katholische Zeitschrift* 6 (1977): 45.

[3]R. T. France, "The Worship of Jesus," in *Christ the Lord,* ed. H. H. Rowdon (Downers Grove, Ill.: InterVarsity Press, 1982), p. 35.

So the doctrine of Christ's preexistence is not an end in itself; it is a means of understanding what it is about this man Jesus that has led Christians to conclude he is more than a man. This does not mean, however, that the doctrine of Christ's preexistence is merely about the role he plays in God's plan; it has to do with who Christ is, something we must establish before we can concern ourselves about what he does.[4] It also is about what God is like, because denial of Christ's preexistence entails denial of the trinitarian nature of God. At a minimum the doctrine of Christ's preexistence speaks to who Jesus Christ is and what he has accomplished, and to the nature of God himself.

In a world where many search for meaning and significance, having a sense of what existentialism has called "thrownness" into the world—a world where people are appalled at human brutality to others and the power of nature to wreak havoc, where people wonder if they must make their way alone through life—the cry rings out, "Does anyone know? Does anyone care?" The doctrine of Christ's preexistence answers yes to both questions, affirming that God has not abandoned us in our sin and misery. And he did not merely send an agent to tell us how to make everything OK or a repairman to perform some fixes— he came himself. The doctrine of preexistence reminds us forcefully that God himself has entered into our circumstance in order to redeem and restore his human creatures along with the rest of his creation. This is the truth that gives meaning and power to Jesus' affirmation that God so loved the world that he sent his Son to save it. If preexistence is mythical or of some other nonfactual nature, then Jesus is not deity and this affirmation of God's love for and intervention on behalf of his creatures becomes an empty promise.

The Term *Preexistence*

Some have suggested we need to find a better term than *preexistence*, one that better explains what we mean. This suggestion usually comes from those who understand Christ's preexistence as a mythological or metaphorical concept, however. One writer who does not think in this way has suggested a replacement that would not satisfy those who most object to the original: eternal existence. It is true this language describes the reality of Christ as believed by historic Christianity, but I do not believe it distinguishes adequately between what we are trying to say about the incarnate Son and what we believe about the Father and the Holy Spirit. All are eternally existent, but only the Son has changed

---

[4]H. E. W Turner notes Christ's preexistence has always had an ontological role in the church's doctrine of the incarnation (*Jesus the Christ* [London: Mowbrays, 1976], p. 15).

his situation in such a way that the term *preexistence* is helpful. While it may not be the best term for what we mean, no one has yet suggested an adequate alternative. And what we are talking about is so important that we cannot remain silent. As Fred Craddock writes:

> To drop the term "pre-existence" without an adequate replacement would be to run the risk of being left with no larger frame of reference for understanding the event of Jesus Christ. This is another way of saying we would be left without a larger frame of reference for understanding human history. The result is almost predictable. Without the overarching (or permeating) presence of the transcendent, created values cease to be regarded as created; relative values cease to be relative.[5]

Craddock makes three extremely important points in this brief paragraph. First, we can only correctly understand Jesus Christ if we understand him as one who transcends this world. Second, our history makes sense only when seen against the transcendent reality of Jesus, who entered that history. Third, when we remove from our world the transcendent that we know through Jesus, we abandon the absolute values inherent in God's universe and replace them with our created and relative values, which we then make absolute. So the preexistence of Christ is not a private dispute among theologians who maintain no contact with the real world (as many of the medieval theological disputes have been portrayed); it has implications for how we live our lives day by day and whether our universe has any meaning or purpose beyond our immediate concern for survival.

Is Jesus Christ the preexistent Son of God become incarnate in space and time for our salvation, or was Jesus an exceptionally good man who caught God's eye and was selected to become a son of God? Everything hangs on our answer to this question, because there is no middle path.[6] Either Jesus is the God-man or he was merely a human being.[7] Only one of these could be our savior. That is why the matter of Jesus' origin is so crucial. Although he does not use the language of preexistence here, Brian Hebblethwaite has stated the issue clearly:

---

[5]Fred Craddock, *The Pre-existence of Christ in the New Testament* (Nashville: Abingdon, 1968), p. 185.

[6]I am ignoring the view that Jesus was less than a good person primarily because it does not appear to fit the evidence, but also because it is neither a widely held view nor one in any way compatible with Christianity. Further, such an individual would not have received the adulation that preexistence seeks to explain in regard to Jesus.

[7]The idea that Jesus could have been some third kind of being was suggested by Arius and rejected at Nicea in A.D. 325 as incompatible with his role as Savior. Today, the Jehovah's Witnesses are the best-known representatives of this view.

It is the internal, christological debate, presupposing belief in God, between those who hold that Jesus Christ was and is God made man and those who believe him to have been a, perhaps the, chosen, spirit-filled yet purely human, representative of God to man, that is the crucial debate over what precisely the specifically Christian religion is all about.[8]

The language of incarnation presupposes Christ's personal or real preexistence; otherwise there was no one to *become* incarnate.[9] Many, but not all, of those who do not accept the doctrine of preexistence as taught by historic Christianity also reject belief in Christ's incarnation in favor of some form of adoptionism.[10]

The modern objections to belief in Christ's preexistence as historically understood are several. For some the doctrine of Christ's preexistence appears to denigrate his humanity. For those who are receptive to the Enlightenment's skepticism about the supernatural, preexistence is incompatible with their belief in a closed universe. A third objection comes from those who believe functional language is truer to the biblical witness than is ontological. They correctly consider the traditional language of preexistence to be making an ontological statement, a statement about who Jesus is rather than what role he plays. These theologians often say the concept of preexistence is a late addition to the early church's understanding of Jesus and came from Hellenistic sources. A fourth group charges that belief in Christ's preexistence removes Christianity to a realm above all other religions as the only religion founded by God personally, thus making all other religions false. Some critics belong to more than one of these groups, but all agree the doctrine of Christ's preexistence is incompatible with their view of the world and their understanding of Christianity. In later chapters we will examine their arguments in more detail.

Difficulty in accepting or clearly understanding the incarnation—as exemplified, for example, by *The Myth of God Incarnate*—requires rejection of Christ's

---

[8]Brian Hebblethwaite, *The Incarnation* (Cambridge: Cambridge University Press, 1987), p. 155.
[9]In Christian theology, *incarnation* is understood literally as enfleshment of that which previously was without flesh. Current dictionary definitions are less specific, expanding the meaning to making manifest or giving form to (see, e.g., *Merriam Webster's Collegiate Dictionary*). Unlike the technical meaning, this popular sense does not require preexistence.
[10]See, e.g., Francis Watson, "Is John's Christology Adoptionist?" in *The Glory of Christ in the New Testament: Studies in Christology,* ed. L. D. Hurst and N. T. Wright (Oxford: Oxford University Press, 1987), pp. 112-24, and G. B. Caird, "Son by Appointment," in *The New Testament Age,* ed. William C. Weinrich (Macon, Ga.: Mercer University Press, 1984): 1:73-81. Both argue the New Testament presents Jesus as Son of God by adoption rather than by nature. Interestingly, both authors have chosen to make their arguments from books generally considered to present most clearly the position contrary to their own (i.e., the Gospel of John and the letter to the Hebrews, respectively).

preexistence if one is to reject incarnational teaching successfully.[11] If "God incarnate" is problematic language, it is easier to attack the *God* part of the phrase than the *incarnate* part since Jesus' historical existence scarcely can be doubted today. This appears symptomatic of many current attempts to reformulate difficult Christian doctrines in order to make them more easily understood and accepted by modern minds. The great risk involved is that in making doctrine simpler, theologians often distort it, and no theological persuasion is exempt. Doctrines can be changed subtly or not so subtly (deliberately or not) into something other than what Christians have historically affirmed by either oversimplifying complex issues or removing the tension inherent in many Christian doctrines due to our finite perspective. In this new, rational neatness and tidiness, these doctrines lose their historic meaning. This is precisely what I believe is happening with the doctrine of Christ's preexistence.

THREE INTERPRETATIONS OF *PREEXISTENCE*

Not everyone who discusses the doctrine of preexistence understands it in the same way. Neither is there universal agreement as to who is the subject of this preexistence. There appear to be at least three interpretations of *preexistence.* The first and classic meaning can be called real or personal preexistence. This means the one who became incarnate as Jesus of Nazareth truly and personally existed as the Son of God, the second person of the Trinity before his incarnation. (Most theologians hold that the incarnated one did not become coextensive with the Son of God because some of the attributes of deity and humanity differ significantly.) From this perspective the incarnation would not have been possible without a preexistent Christ. The one who was preexistent was the Son of God, not the humanity of Jesus which came into existence at a particular time and place. So the orthodox Christian understanding of Christ's real preexistence requires no less than a binitarian God of whom one person entered time and space as a particular human being. I specify *orthodox* because in the fourth century Arius denied Christ's deity while accepting his preexistence as the first among the created order. Gerald O'Collins suggests the language of personal preexistence not only means Christ existed before

---

[11]John Hick, ed., *The Myth of God Incarnate* (Philadelphia: Westminster Press, 1977). Brian Daley makes explicit the link between the incarnation and preexistence in the following definition of the incarnation: "The Christian doctrine of the Incarnation: the fundamental conviction of Christian faith that in Jesus of Nazareth God's eternal, personally substantial Word 'became flesh and dwelt among us.' " (See Brian E. Daley, "Nature and the 'Mode of Union': late Patristic Models for the personal Unity of Christ," in *The Incarnation*, ed. Stephen T. Davis et al. (Oxford: Oxford University Press, 2002), pp. 164-65.

the incarnation; it means that he has never not existed.[12]

In this discussion I use Christ's *preexistence* as shorthand for what is more accurately termed the *personal* or *real* preexistence of the Son of God. It is personal because the Son of God preexisted as the second person of the triune God; it is real because he actually existed and was not merely an intention in the mind of God.[13] This is to distinguish the one who is preexistent from the *man* Jesus, who generally has not been held to be preexistent.[14] Actually, any teaching of the preexistence of Jesus that includes in any measure a preexistent human nature detracts from the impact of the incarnation and would seem to contradict John's proclamation that the Word who is God *became* flesh, a condition that had not existed prior to his incarnation. O'Collins offers a succinct statement of what Christ's preexistence means in theological terms: "The christological doctrine of pre-existence maintains that Christ's personal existence is that of an eternal Subject within the oneness of God, and hence cannot be derived from the history of human beings and their world. His personal being did not originate when his visible history began."[15] The preexistence of the Son of God is not simply a mat-

---

[12]Gerald O'Collins, *Christology* (New York: Oxford University Press, 1995), p. 238. He says because preexistence has to do with being part of an uncreated, nontemporal order, it might better be called eternal existence.

[13]A third term used to describe this is *divine preexistence*. The three terms are only synonymous if they include personhood and eternal preexistence. Otherwise, they could be descriptive of creatures or things rather than of the Creator. This was demonstrated in the Arian controversy of the fourth century. I will use *Christ* for the preexistent One and *personal preexistence* for the position I am arguing. Although technically incorrect, the *preexistence of Christ* is the conventional term used; to use another more theologically accurate term could be confusing since many of those I will interact with speak of the preexistence of Christ. I will use *personal* preexistence instead of *real* preexistence to emphasize the personhood of the preexistent One. Personal preexistence will be shorthand for personhood, eternal existence and deity.

[14]I am here not separating the preexistent Son from Jesus. My point is that the God-man Jesus is a divine-human being whose divine person and nature are eternal but whose humanity had a beginning in time. This is what the incarnation is about, and what I believe John 1:14 and Philippians 2:7 say: without ceasing to be God, the Son took to himself humanity and became a man. This was possible without incoherence because humanity has been created in the divine image and this provides a point of contact between Creator and creation. As H. R. Mackintosh wrote, "The Church has never affirmed that the humanity of Christ was real prior to the birth in Bethlehem" (*The Doctrine of the Person of Jesus Christ*, 2nd ed. [Edinburgh: T & T Clark, 1913], p. 457). Origen is the major Christian theologian who taught Jesus had a preexistent soul, but in his Platonism he taught that everyone has a preexistent soul. This teaching on preexistent souls was not well-received by the church. John Balchin notes only God can properly be described as preexistent because everything else is part of creation (John F. Balchin, "Paul, Wisdom and Christ," in *Christ the Lord*, ed. H. H. Rowdon [Downers Grove, Ill.: InterVarsity Press, 1982], p. 209). This shows that to call the Son of God preexistent is to make an ontological statement. Only one who is preexistent can be God, although preexistence alone is insufficient to make one God.

[15]O'Collins, *Christology*, p. 237.

ter of chronology, that he was before his incarnation, but is also qualitative, the one who was incarnated as Jesus of Nazareth is eternally existent as deity.

There is a danger in presenting Christ's preexistence in a way that denigrates or denies Jesus' real and full humanity. This has occurred often enough in the history of the doctrine to encourage others to shy away from the doctrine altogether, but it lacks any biblical justification. The clear witness of the New Testament writers is that the preexistent Son of God took to himself a full and real humanity. Later theologians stated that he did so without any detriment to either his deity or his humanity.

The second understanding is called *ideal preexistence.* This means Christ existed in the mind of God prior to the incarnation, but did not exist personally prior to that same incarnation. This view claims, "There was no time when Christ was not in the Father's purpose. He is as old as the saving love of God: His mission, embracing life and death and triumph, formed eternally an integral and cardinal element of the divine plan."[16] This sounds good, but as it stands it can be said as much of you and me as of Christ. It is not that it is untrue but rather that it is insufficient. An equally good term for ideal preexistence is *election.*

Some advocates of this position claim support from ideas found in intertestamental Judaism.[17] Christ's ideal preexistence would be a preexistence of divine intention but would have no reality until intention became actualized in time. This interpretation has consequences for the Christian understandings of the triunity of God and the person of Christ. Both are devastating to historic Christianity, destroying the biblical presentation of God and any hope we might have for salvation. Ideal preexistence is trivial because if existence in the mind of God qualifies as preexistence, everything and everyone must be described as preexistent. Ideal preexistence does not necessarily reject trinitarian teaching, but those who accept the doctrine of the Trinity and teach the ideal preexistence of Christ generally separate Jesus Christ from the second person of the Trinity. This allows them to preserve Christ's full humanity (including a point of origin in time and space), but does not require a fundamental change in God from unitary being to triunity. In so doing, it empties of all content John's words that God loved the world enough to send his Son to save it. More radical theologians, however, are willing to suggest such a drastic change in the essence of

---

[16]Mackintosh, *Doctrine of the Person of Christ,* pp. 454-55.
[17]I will take this up in greater detail in chapter six. O'Collins says, however, that Christian understanding of the preexistence of a divine person is distinct from such ideas as the preexistence of Torah in intertestamental Judaism and the preexisting ideas of Platonism (O'Collins, *Christology,* p. 237).

God. P. T. Forsyth once described ideal preexistence as "quite inadequate" to the New Testament and Christian experience because it is "too remote and pale" to be the source of Christian faith. He continued, "If you reduce the Eternal Sonship to an idea you will reduce the eternal Fatherhood to the same tenuity," a consequence he rightly considered unacceptable.[18]

In a recent book, Karl-Josef Kuschel uses the term "eschatological preexistence."[19] What he appears to mean by this is that "the Easter experience" requires some sort of preexistence as its justification. He thus conceives of Christ's preexistence as a theological construct or etiological myth added before Jesus' earthly life to balance and justify the resurrection and his postexistence. Kuschel's position appears to be a restatement of Harnack's conclusion that "this post-existence of his gave to the ideas of his pre-existence a support and concrete complexion which the earlier Jewish theories lacked."[20] Kuschel's standing as a Catholic theologian requires he maintain some concept of Christ's preexistence while his theology of world religions leads him to modify the traditional Christian statement. C. Stephen Evans has suggested the incarnation might be understood to include such mythic concepts, but only if the reality of God and God's actions that comprise the incarnation account is acknowledged, and the points where divine reality intersects human history are acknowledged as historical.[21]

Some who follow some sort of etiological understanding of Christ's preexistence see it as merely myth or metaphor, a scheme designed to give Jesus standing at least equal to contemporary religious leaders. Klaas Runia says, "The first presupposition [of certain forms of historical criticism] is the idea that it was customary in the first century to represent one's religious ideas in the form of myths or mythological concepts."[22] John Hick may be the best known and most prolific advocate of this mythical understanding. It does not appear necessary that one accept a position similar to Hick's in order to hold some sort of eschatological

[18]P. T. Forsyth, *The Person and Place of Christ* (Boston: Pilgrim, 1909), p. 286.

[19]Karl-Josef Kuschel, *Born Before All Time?* trans. John Bowden (New York: Crossroad, 1992), p. 363. He also discussed this concept in a preliminary form in his seminar on the preexistence of Christ at the University of Tübingen during the spring of 1985.

[20]Adolf von Harnack, *History of Dogma,* trans. Neil Buchanan (New York: Dover, 1961), 1:325. Kuschel does not describe his approach as mythic, but, as I understand it, the approach seems to be intended to explain the Christian interpretation of certain events of Jesus' life and death without necessarily granting the status of history to them.

[21]C. Stephen Evans, *The Historical Christ and the Jesus of Faith* (Oxford: Clarendon, 1996), pp. 50ff.

[22]Klaas Runia, *The Present-Day Christological Debate* (Downers Grove, Ill.: InterVarsity Press, 1984), p. 90. John Hick certainly operates by this presupposition, as we will see in chapter nine, but so do others like Rudolf Bultmann who reach very different theological conclusions from Hick about the impact of myth on christology and Christianity.

preexistence, however. Kuschel's position may well be similar to the one Forsyth described as "conceiving Christ as the realization of the divine purpose."[23]
Unlike ideal preexistence, this view relates Christ's existence to God's will and
action, not only his thought. Christ here is the supreme object of God's election,
but still lacks a personal preexistence.

These three understandings of preexistence differ from each other in important ways, but the fault line lies between real or personal preexistence and the
other two. Only personal preexistence seems compatible with traditional Christian teachings about the nature of God and the person of Jesus Christ. Changes
in these teachings will affect all other key Christian doctrines. I only mention
these consequences now because they cannot determine our decision about
whether or what kind of preexistence of Christ is true. That decision must await
an examination of the New Testament evidence, its Jewish and Hellenistic background, and a review of the nature and interconnectedness of theology. Nonetheless, theology and biblical study go hand-in-hand, each influencing and en-
riching the other. To pretend these preliminary comments and biblical survey
are possible apart from theology is just that—pretense—and such pretense will
only make our journey more difficult.

WORLDVIEWS AND THEIR PRESUPPOSITIONS

As important as the evidence will prove to be, even more important is the
worldview, with its presuppositions and prejudices, each of us brings to our investigation. Worldviews are all-encompassing understandings of reality that govern how we think and act, what evidence we accept, and how we interpret it.
It is the strength and durability of our worldviews that lead to the common advice not to discuss politics or religion at social gatherings. Our positions on
these subjects are so deeply entrenched in our thinking that any perceived challenge to them becomes a challenge to who we are. Worldviews not only affect
how we interpret our universe, they even influence what information from that
universe reaches our minds so that it can be interpreted at all. Because our
worldviews are such powerful instruments governing our perception of reality,
it is essential we recognize the worldview we live by and be able to justify our
decision to do so.

Unfortunately, many people do not know what a worldview is and so are
unaware they have one themselves or of the reasons behind the one they have.
Os Guinness bemoans what he describes as the failure of English-speaking
evangelicals to recognize the importance of presuppositions; instead they are

---

[23]Forsyth, *Person and Place of Christ,* p. 286.

overimpressed by data, statistics, and "facts."[24] None of us comes to the study of Christ's preexistence neutral, and none of us can remain utterly objective during the course of this study. I write because I believe the doctrine of Christ's personal preexistence is justified by the evidence, is theologically and philosophically coherent, and is essential to Christian faith and practice. Others have written on the subject because they have reached contrary conclusions. In later chapters I will enter into conversation with many of them.

While all humans have had and continue to have worldviews, the one I am particularly concerned about here has dominated Western culture for more than two hundred years, arising out of the Enlightenment of the seventeenth and eighteenth centuries. All of us living in societies influenced by Western thinking have appropriated this worldview to some extent—even those of us who challenge its key presuppositions as they affect theology, philosophy and ethics.

The philosophical and theological understanding of reality that came out of the Enlightenment was human-centered, rationalistic, naturalistic and anti-authority. Incorporating the scientific theories of Descartes and Newton, it pictured the universe as an enormous machine. All the parts work together to keep the whole functioning, and the way to understanding is through investigation using the scientific method of Francis Bacon. This method incorporates observation and reasoning to decipher the universe and all that is in it. The goal of Bacon's scientific method, however, was to understand the world in order to control it. As this method became normative, some reached two conclusions. First, if something is not susceptible to such investigation, it does not exist (or it is nonsense). Out of this came the religious view known as deism. It was an attempt to maintain the reality of God in a universe where his existence could not be demonstrated. For deists, long ago God created the universe and set everything in motion. He also ordained the physical laws that make the universe run according to plan. But with all this accomplished, there was nothing more for God to do. So, in a sense, God has become superfluous because the world can exist and function without him. Second, this method resulted in the exaltation of human reason. This was the age that truly believed "man is the measure of all things" and concluded everything must be susceptible to human understanding because human reason is sufficient to comprehend the universe. This confidence in human reason still drives some scientists, although many recognize that, despite its power and value, human reason is a finite and not always reliable tool. The one great difficulty with the requirement that some thing or some belief be empirically demonstrable in or-

[24]Os Guinness, *Dining with the Devil* (Grand Rapids: Baker, 1993), p. 44.

der to be accepted as real or true is that the requirement itself is not open to empirical verification.

This worldview is not only the source of liberal theology; it has also influenced evangelical Protestantism to a surprising degree. In fact, as modern theology increasingly becomes postmodern, evangelicals and fundamentalists may find themselves the last remaining defenders of key Enlightenment presuppositions. Regarding modernist theology, this worldview believes in a god that is too small, at least too small to be the God of the Bible. Because its ultimate authority is human reason, anything that seems incompatible with the conclusions of human reason must be wrong, no matter how well attested. It often boils down to the conclusion that whatever does not match *my* reasoned conclusions is suspect. It is rather like the bumper sticker I recently saw on the back of a Volkswagen in a campus parking lot: "Question authority."

Maurice Wiles notes Christian incarnational teaching has "always run counter to the most natural lines of approach to theological knowledge."[25] It is something the church has affirmed because that has been where the evidence leads, even if it does not neatly conform to the canons of human reason. The apostle Paul said something similar in 1 Corinthians 1 when he called God's foolishness wiser than human wisdom. Modern critical thinking wants a world where everything is open to human reason. Such a world lacks any sense of mystery or the transcendent. It is a bland, boring world with no room for wonder or worship. Bernard Ramm has said of such a mentality that it

> focuses its attention on problems, difficulties, and improbables. It desires a religion which has no mystery, no supernatural, and nothing transcendental. Therefore the incarnation is not a magnificent drama to be affirmed in joy but a doctrine too imponderable to believe. . . . It is a modernized, secularized, positivistic mentality which has lost the capacity to wonder. It reflects the human effort to reduce a three dimensional universe to one of two.[26]

For those who consider themselves Christian theologians, and even those theologians who just happen to be Christians (these two groups are not necessarily the same), the authoritative source by which all claims are measured must be the Bible.[27] The question each of us needs to ask is whether we hear

---

[25]Maurice Wiles, *The Remaking of Christian Doctrine* (London: SCM Press, 1974), p. 44.
[26]Bernard L. Ramm, *An Evangelical Christology* (Nashville: Thomas Nelson, 1985), p. 52.
[27]This is not as clear-cut as it sounds here, but we will look at the implications of and difficulties in application of that statement about ultimate authority in the next chapter when we begin to consider what Scripture has to say about our topic.

and seek to understand the Bible or sit in judgment of it on the basis of our
own preexisting criteria. I do not direct this question only to liberal theologians; conservative theologians are no less at risk of unwittingly acting in
this way.

MODERNISM AND POSTMODERNISM

During the past several decades, a new outlook has arisen to challenge the op-
timism of Enlightenment modernism. A conglomeration of different attitudes
displaying a common skepticism about the key aspects of Enlightenment
thought, this approach goes by the name of postmodernism. It began in literary
studies but has spread into philosophy, theology and most other disciplines
outside the natural sciences. Postmodernism rejects the existence of absolutes,
or at least the possibility of ever knowing them. As expressed by the American
philosopher Richard Rorty, the measure of a belief or practice is not its truth
but its effectiveness in accomplishing what we want to do. So Rorty offers prag-
matism as the method of knowing. Other postmodernists have focused on Bacon's belief that knowledge is power and on Nietzsche's "will to power" to
charge that all belief systems incorporate an oppressive power relationship intended to keep one group in power and others subservient. This is the proximate source of modern claims that Christianity is a force for oppression of
women, minorities, non-Western and non-Christian people, lesbians and ho-
mosexuals, and others. The Christian teaching about the preexistence of Christ
will certainly be viewed by some of these groups as foundational to what they
consider Christianity's oppressive intent. Nonetheless, by its challenge to many
of the Enlightenment's comfortable and unexamined premises, postmodernism, if handled cautiously, offers a new possibility for theology that could re-
invigorate Christian thinking.

Enlightenment thought in its liberal form has had a problem accepting both
incarnation and atonement as taught by traditional Christianity. This has been
due in no small measure to its difficulty in accepting the reality of the supernatural. Incarnation certainly has to do with the preexistent One, and, I would argue, atonement in any meaningful sense does as well. Historic Christianity has
taught that atonement, in whatever version we conceive it, is the work of the
God who has entered into our history. Only the moral theory, where Jesus
serves solely as our example, does not require an incarnation (though it permits
one), but the moral theory fails by virtue of its neglect of the depth and perva-
siveness of human sin.

Considering God's work of salvation apart from the preexistent Son raises
more difficulties than viewing it in terms of the incarnation of the Son. And *in-*

carnation is a meaningful term only when there is a preexisting person to become incarnate. Some who object to the teaching that Jesus Christ preexisted as the Son of God do so because they believe the teaching compromises Jesus' full humanity. Their concern is well-founded to the extent that many who historically have accepted the doctrine of preexistence have in practice downplayed Jesus' real and full humanity, but not all have done so. In their attempt to preserve Jesus' humanity, these objectors to preexistence have frequently downplayed or denied his deity. Yet both Christ's deity and his humanity are necessary if Jesus is to be our savior according to historic doctrine.

What is involved here is not some Hellenistic corruption of early Christian teaching, but the effect of the Enlightenment's faith that human reason can comprehend all that is. Because the related doctrines of Christ's two natures and his preexistence are beyond the capacity of the human mind to fully understand, something has to go. It is much easier to understand Jesus as a human and to deemphasize or ignore his deity. But if God is God in any meaningful sense, and we are humans—not sinful humans, just humans—then it makes perfectly good sense that there are things about God and what he does that will be beyond our understanding. Stephen Evans writes, "Though we must not be too quick to appeal to mystery, it would be arrogance to assume that finite, sinful humans can always understand the actions of God."[28] What Evans says about God's works applies no less to his person.

As we continue to look at the effect on our thinking of worldviews and the presuppositions that constitute them, we need to consider the role these presuppositions play. They provide boundaries and direction to our thought by filtering out some of the data that continually bombard us, and focusing our minds on other of those data that are compatible with our worldview. So our presuppositions act as a filter to block information incompatible with our worldview. This filter is not always successful (for various reasons having to do with the strength of the message coming to us, the completeness and coherence of our worldview, or the work of the Holy Spirit), but when it is, its success is unobtrusive—we do not even notice the force of the data that does not agree with our outlook on the world. Our presuppositions allow, preclude, or sometimes force us to believe certain things and perform certain actions. Apart from a transformation of worldviews, a process akin to a religious conversion, we remain unreceptive to information and opinions that do not fit within the worldview we have accepted.

Modern culture, building on the Enlightenment model of a mechanical uni-

[28]Evans, *Historical Christ,* p. 91.

verse, has opted for what is called a closed universe. At the popular level this is contradicted by interest in angels, horoscopes, fortunetelling and the like (although all but the angels presume a deterministic understanding of reality). This means everything must be explainable in terms of what we can know through scientific study; there can be no appeal to divine intervention or any form of the supernatural. To speak of a closed universe is to say everything can be explained solely in terms of material reality and physical processes with no remainder. Despite his commitment to Christianity, Rudolf Bultmann exemplifies this view with his famous statement that "it is impossible to use electrical light and the wireless and to avail ourselves of modern medical and surgical discoveries, and at the same time to believe in the New Testament world of spirits and miracles."[29]

Although I believe he is quite wrong in what he says (and doubt he intended this consequence), Bultmann has stated clearly the implications of a closed view of the universe. In a closed universe there is no room for the biblical God. If God exists, as Bultmann surely believed he does, then God must be beyond the universe and cannot meaningfully affect what happens in the universe. This worldview influences our understanding of every facet of Christian doctrine and must, in the end, be considered inconsistent with Christian faith. Commitment to belief in a closed universe shuts off even the possibility of there being anything other than material reality before any consideration of evidence. In addition to those who have committed themselves to such a materialist ontology, there are others who live out this view of reality even as they profess otherwise. This is rarely a matter of hypocrisy but rather of muddled thinking.

Can the preexistent Son of God become human? That has been the basic question Christian thinkers have had to consider for nearly two thousand years. But it is a question that contains a number of other questions. What do we mean by preexistent? Does God have a Son? If so, how does God have a Son? Do God and humans have enough in common that God can become human? If so, *how* could such a thing occur? How could deity and humanity coexist in one person in a way that each retains its integrity? Behind these questions are still others that involve interpreting the relevant biblical passages, the Jewish and Hellenistic background and alleged parallels to pre-

---

[29]Rudolf Bultmann et. al., *Kerygma and Myth,* ed. Hans Werner Bartsch, trans. Reginald H. Fuller (New York: Harper & Row, 1961), p. 5. The concurrent existence (sometimes in the same person) of belief in a closed universe and in angels, horoscopes, and the like may itself be evidence of the poverty of a secular, mechanistic worldview.

existence and incarnation, and modern metaphysical concerns. Muslims and Jews are appalled at any suggestion that God has a Son in any nonmetaphorical sense. John Knox answers all my questions with a resounding "no!" when he writes:

> Not only is it impossible, by definition, that God should become a man, it is also impossible, by definition, that he should "make" one. A true human being could not be freshly created. Such a creation might look like a man and a man's faculties, but he would not *be* a man.[30]

Knox's firm conclusion is built on his presupposition and nothing more. He has a certain sense of what it means to be a human, and incarnate deity does not fit. As far as he is concerned, his understanding of what it means to be human is the only valid one. Knox has defined deity and humanity in such a way that they are incompatible. He has not allowed for even the possibility he might be wrong. This is an example of thinking that is driven by presuppositions.

Knox is not the only person who thinks this way, and one need not share his conclusion to be guilty of such thinking. Any view that limits consideration of an issue solely on the basis of one's presuppositions runs great risk of being wrong because it is immune from correction by evidence it cannot recognize. As R. G. Hamerton-Kelly has pointed out, this approach expresses a fundamental attitude toward reality that defines the discussion out of existence:

> Recent attempts to define pre-existence agree that it involves and presupposes a whole view of reality. . . . Where there is no clear understanding of existence as temporal, and as distinct from a non-temporal essence, there can be no idea of pre-existence. It would appear, therefore, that pre-existence belongs in the realm of discourse which is concerned with the world of reality other than the sense-perceptible world, namely in the realm of metaphysical discourse. Contemporary Protestant Biblical scholarship, however, seems, on the continent at least, to interpret pre-existence in such a way as to minimize its reference to a metaphysical realm.[31]

Gregory Boyd echoes Hamerton-Kelly's conclusion when he writes, "The control-beliefs of a scholar determine what kind of Jesus he or she is looking

---

[30]John Knox, *The Humanity and Divinity of Christ* (Cambridge: Cambridge University Press, 1967), pp. 67-68.

[31]R. G. Hamerton-Kelly, *Preexistence, Wisdom, and the Son of Man* (Cambridge: Cambridge University Press, 1973), pp. 5-6. The only point where I would change what Hamerton-Kelly has written is to add that this attitude has infected some Roman Catholic biblical scholars as well.

for by defining what kind of Jesus is and is not possible."[32] George Tyrrell and Albert Schweitzer said something similar early in the twentieth century when they criticized the liberal Protestant search for the historical Jesus as an attempt to create Jesus in our image.

Most theologians and biblical scholars work in the academic world, a world predominantly secular and skeptical of the supernatural. Being intellectually respectable in that environment too often requires accommodating a naturalistic worldview, not necessarily as a personal commitment but as the controlling method by which one does scholarly work. This often results in scholars producing "naturalistic explanations of the primordial Christian events which, purely as arguments, are less coherent and plausible than the traditional supernatural ones."[33] Some say it is more scholarly and open-minded to bracket the supernatural or reject it unless evidence compels us to acknowledge it. I contend that such an a priori decision is neither scholarly nor open-minded, but is instead dogmatism. It is not a matter of evidence but of philosophical and theological presuppositions about how the world *must* be. Such a decision is not open-mindedness. At best, it means the supernatural is irrelevant to the subject at hand. As long as one holds on to these suppositions, no amount of evidence is likely to be convincing.

My concern is with Christ's preexistence, but the incarnation keeps intruding itself into the discussion. It can be no other way. Incarnation is meaningless apart from the preexistent Christ, and Christ's preexistence is irrelevant apart from the incarnation of the Son to save us and to reveal God to us. These teachings cannot stand in isolation. They *are* distinct—that is, each serves its own purpose, and each has its own justification and place in the fabric of Christian theology—but they are interconnected in such a way that if one fails, the other must fail too. This means while my focus will be on Christ's preexistence, I will necessarily be considering aspects of the incarnation as well. Considered in isolation, Christ's preexistence becomes abstract and speculative, but that is pre-

---

[32]Gregory Boyd, quoted in Jeffery L. Sheler et al., "In Search of Jesus," *U. S. News and World Report,* April 8, 1996, p. 47. What I call "worldview," Boyd calls "control-beliefs." Both terms indicate the power of these often preconscious understandings. Sheler goes on from this point to examine the lives of various leaders of the group calling itself the Jesus Seminar because he believes their lives are key to understanding their belief systems. While such an approach probably has value, it is much more a psychological interpretation of individual theologians than a theological evaluation of their work.

[33]Eric L. Mascall, *Theology and the Gospel of Christ* (London: SPCK, 1977), p. 1. Mascall says intellectual respectability is not in and of itself bad, merely that it becomes a danger when we allow the dominant mindset of academia to determine our conclusions despite the strength of alternate conclusions.

cisely what Christian theology must not become. Thus the doctrine of Christ's personal preexistence should be understood as part of a web of beliefs that are interconnected and have practical implications for our lives.

CHALLENGES TO THE DOCTRINE OF CHRIST'S PREEXISTENCE

There are at least six major challenges to the traditional doctrine of Christ's personal preexistence. These are not generally independent, but in most cases they are mutually supporting. We will look at each of these in detail in chapter nine, but now is a good time to introduce them and identify some of their leading advocates. The first challenge is *exegetical*. To different degrees, both James Dunn and G. B. Caird have challenged the traditional belief that many of the New Testament authors taught the personal preexistence of Christ before his incarnation. According to Dunn, only the Fourth Gospel, which he dates among the latest New Testament books, explicitly teaches Christ's preexistence. Paul and Hebrews do not. Caird, on the other hand, says Paul is alone among New Testament writers in teaching Christ's personal preexistence. Dunn and Caird are leading twentieth-century New Testament scholars, but their conclusions regarding Christ's personal preexistence have been widely criticized by their peers for being incompatible with each other. This then is a limited challenge in that those with exegetical concerns do not absolutely deny the doctrine of preexistence, and it is weakened by the inability of scholars to agree on which New Testament books they think do or do not teach preexistence.

The second challenge differs from the first in that it is *presuppositional*, although its leading spokesmen are New Testament scholars. Both John Knox and Rudolf Bultmann reject a priori the possibility that Christ could have preexisted his earthly life. For Bultmann this is because the teaching must have been mythological; for Knox it is because one individual cannot at the same time and in the same way be fully God and fully human. The humanity inevitably ends up being submerged in the deity. I will deal with Knox's legitimate concern about affirming Christ's full humanity in chapter nine, but I note here that Bultmann's Gnostic redeemer myth has been rejected by most New Testament scholars as anachronistic. The causal relation, if any, is more likely to have gone from Christianity to Gnosticism rather than the reverse.

The third challenge is *philosophical and ecumenical*. John Hick is the best-known representative of this position. I call this view philosophical because Hick is a philosopher of religion rather than a theologian (this differentiates it from the next challenge). It is ecumenical in the broadest sense because Hick sees Christianity as only one way of getting in touch with what he calls the Real, something that transcends the attempts of all religions and philosophies to understand what is and what stands behind all religions, whatever their apparent differences. If the doctrines of preexistence and the incarnation are right about Jesus, then Hick recognizes Christianity must be the unique vehicle of God's dealings with humanity. Because this conclusion is incompatible with his ecumenical concerns, Hick rejects it.

Hans Küng, Karl-Josef Kuschel and Paul Knitter represent the fourth challenge, one that is *theological and ecumenical.* All three theologians are Roman Catholics, and this makes their challenge somewhat more nuanced than it might otherwise be due to the normative status of church council decisions within Roman Catholicism. This position advocates soteriological pluralism—each religion is the valid way of salvation for its adherents. As with Hick's position, this view does not fit well with traditional christological doctrine, including the teaching of Christ's personal preexistence.

The fifth challenge responds to the all-too-common problem within Christian orthodoxy of emphasizing Christ's deity as the expense of his humanity. This has been true of many traditional Catholics and Protestants, although both verbally affirm the creedal teaching that Christ is fully God and fully human. Scholars like John Knox and John Macquarrie raise this challenge with their concern to affirm Christ's full humanity. Unfortunately, they do so to the detriment of his deity. There is an inherent tension in the doctrine of the person of Christ; we relax or remove it in either direction at our peril. This tension is contrary to our rationalistic desire to have everything neat and clear, but we have no orthodox alternative. To a very great extent, this challenge overlaps the presuppositional one. The conclusion that God cannot become human without submerging the humanity implies the bold claim to know God so comprehensively that one can be certain what God can and cannot do. It claims no less than to know what it means to be human, even though this is a matter of continued debate in the relevant disciplines and Christian orthodoxy declares Jesus Christ to be the measure of true humanity.[34]

The sixth challenge comes from the *adoptionist* understanding of Jesus. This sees Jesus not as the Son of God become human but as the man Jesus who by God's plan or his own merit was adopted to be the son of God. Friedrich Schleiermacher represents this view as does much of the liberal

---

[34]"We must not form a conception of Humanity and either ask if Christ is Human or insist on reducing Him to the limits of our conception; we must ask, 'What is Humanity?' and look at Christ to find the answer." (William Temple, "The Divinity of Christ," in *Foundations,* ed. B. H. Streeter [London: Macmillan, 1920], pp. 258-59).

Christianity that owes its origin to him. Jesus' role in this view is exemplary and inspirational rather than mediatorial and salvific. This was approximated in early Christianity by Ebionitism, surfaced intermittently in succeeding centuries and reappeared in strength in Europe during the eighteenth century.

Each of these challenges to the classic teaching of Christ's preexistence derives from a legitimate concern for balanced Christian theology or the recognition of other religions and disbelief in religion in the modern world. Each challenge, however, deviates to some degree from the biblical witness as developed by Christians of the first five centuries. I will try to demonstrate this in later chapters by first examining the biblical evidence and then describing how early church theologians interpreted this evidence.

How Do We Proceed from Here?

As we have begun considering Christ's preexistence, the impact of our presuppositions and their resulting worldview has become evident. If we reject beforehand God's ability to interact with the order he created, we will find it difficult accept evidence or arguments to the contrary.[35] Unless someone can demonstrate that the concept of Christ's preexistence is incoherent, however, I believe the proper course is to accept the possibility of such preexistence and then see what evidence is available to us and is relevant to the question. Only then should we reach a conclusion.[36]

The closed-universe understanding that makes the supernatural impossible a priori is not the product of scientific study but a tentative working hypothesis that enables much scientific study, although many scientists would remind us that it applies only to our study of the physical realm through the natural sciences. Even at this level it is a philosophical, not a scientific, premise. The method of presuming a closed universe is far more acceptable in the natural sciences with their subject matter than it is in theology, which by its very nature ought to presume the opposite. In science the presumption is reasonably con-

---

[35]John Robinson says, "Presumptions can have a binding or blinding effect on what one is able to 'see' in a situation or in the data before one" (J. A. T. Robinson, *The Priority of John,* ed. J. F. Coakley [London: SCM Press, 1985], p. 2).

[36]C. Stephen Evans suggests this is the proper way to examine the possibility of the incarnation (Evans, *Historical Christ,* pp. 125-28). Because incarnation and preexistence are interwoven teachings and because of the arguments Evans makes in support of the coherence of the doctrine of the incarnation, I conclude the doctrine of Christ's preexistence as I have defined it is coherent. That does not mean it is necessarily true—that is the issue before us. But before we can investigate it, we need to assure ourselves we are not wasting our time, that the question is even open to consideration.

sistent with the nature of the discipline (although some modern scientific discoveries have raised questions about this presumption); to understand theology in terms of a closed universe, however, is virtually to deny the nature of the discipline. Thus I suggest we should begin by acknowledging the possibility of a universe open to divine activity. No other possibility is consistent with historic Christianity. This is not to say we are required to begin our investigation by accepting the reality of the supernatural, only that we must be ready to acknowledge it if that is where the evidence points.

All humans have been raised and live within one tradition or another. These traditions certainly influence how we think and act. The question is how completely our context determines our thought. In writing about the background to the Johannine prologue, Rudolf Bultmann wrote:

> And the exegesis has as its first task to discover what *possible forms of expression were open to the author; the possibilities being those he has inherited with the tradition in which he stands.* What the author intends to say here and now, is of course not simply to be deduced from these possibilities: but they have given a particular direction to what he intends to say, and have imposed particular limits.[37]

Despite the qualification in the second sentence, Bultmann's method is unduly restrictive in that he understands one's tradition as imposing limits that cannot be transcended rather than serving as a starting point and guide to understanding an author's thought. It is difficult to see how the position Bultmann represents allows for any possibility of progress in human thought if the only way we can express ourselves is in terms of those forms of expression we have inherited from our tradition.

Bultmann at least retains a concern for the meaning and intent of the author. The more recent phenomenon called postmodernism rejects the normativity of authorial intent in favor of allowing each reader to interpret the text in accord with her or his understanding. Postmodernists reject any claim to objectivity, normativity or authoritative reading of a text. This differs from the biblical hermeneutics of *sensus plenior,* or belief that a biblical text may contain meaning beyond that which the original author intended. The latter, while denying the author's meaning is exhaustive, nonetheless recognizes that what is stated is true even if it is not the complete truth.

One important question that has received renewed attention from philosophers and theologians deals with our knowing. As this applies to Christ's pre-

---

[37]Rudolf Bultmann, *The Gospel of John,* trans. G. R. Beasley-Murray et al. (Philadelphia: Westminster Press, 1971), p. 20.

existence, there seem to be three questions: What can we know? How can we know? What do we need to know?[38]

Most human knowledge comes through observation and experimentation. We see certain actions and conclude one or another event has occurred. Involved in this process is the interpretation that a relation exists between cause and effect that is more than chronological coincidence. For scientific events, part of knowing comes about through being able to replicate an experiment or observation. For historical events, such replication is not possible, so we use other ways to evaluate our experiences and observations, seeking external confirmation and checking our purported experience against commonly accepted understandings of what can happen. Even for scientists, observation and experimentation are not self-evident or self-justifying. But there is another important way both scientists and historians obtain knowledge. Both infer events from consequences that can be observed even though for some reason the original event is not observable. No human was around to see the beginning of the physical universe, but from various residual effects still open to observation scientists are confident the big bang is the best explanation of the universe's beginning.

Christians also believe knowledge comes through the work of the Holy Spirit.[39] This is not experiential in the sense of being the result of either observation or inference, but it is not for that reason any less real. Empirical study has value and validity within its proper sphere, which is material reality, but material reality is only a part of reality. And some aspects of material reality are not susceptible to empirical study. In the theological realm, some subjects can be studied empirically (e.g., did Jesus really live? did he rise from the dead?), but other subjects, even related subjects, are not open to empirical study (e.g., how did the resurrection happen? is God triune or unitary? does God exist?). These questions lie outside our ability to scientifically or historically investigate. If we are to have answers, they must come by revelation. Christianity (as well as other religions) believes revelation is possible, even necessary, for humans to understand the most important truths about material and immaterial reality. According to historic Christian teaching, this revelation comes through the Holy Spirit.

Christology studies both the person and the work of Christ. From the earliest

---

[38]There are other and more fundamental issues than these in the field of epistemology, but this is not the place and I am not the one best qualified to discuss them. I suggest C. Stephen Evans's *Historical Christ and the Jesus of Faith,* particularly its bibliography, as a resource to guide interested readers into the current discussion dealing with the possibility and limits of human knowledge.

[39]See, for example, Jn 16:13, where Jesus tells his disciples that the Holy Spirit will lead them to all truth after he has gone. In Mt 16:17, Jesus attributes Peter's confession that Jesus is the Messiah to divine revelation, not human insight.

days of Christianity, people have realized that for Jesus to have accomplished what the New Testament writers attribute to him, certain things about Jesus had to be true. Not all these truths would be open to human observation. Christ's preexistence is a truth humans have to infer because we did not see it (and could not have seen it). The evidence with which to evaluate this inference comes from the New Testament and, according to most patristic theologians and exegetes, from a small number of passages in the Old Testament. What is important to remember, however, is that not all the evidence we accept as leading to knowledge need come from direct observation; some will come indirectly. This is true whether we are talking about chemistry, history or theology.

As we consider whether the doctrine of Christ's preexistence is meaningful and true, we have to ask what constitutes a sufficient ground to accept or reject this teaching. Direct evidence of Christ's preexistence is unavailable to us, so we can neither prove nor disprove it empirically. Instead, we have to approach it indirectly, which is the way we approach most subjects. We should look at this doctrine as one part of a network of mutually supporting beliefs. A surprising number of Christian beliefs relate in one way or another to the doctrine of Christ's preexistence. Some of these are open to investigation and confirmation in ways that the doctrine of preexistence is not. For instance, few today would deny Jesus of Nazareth lived some two thousand years ago in Palestine and died by crucifixion at the hand of the Romans. Many recognize some measure of truth in the Christian doctrine of universal human sinfulness, even though they might not use the language of sin in their description. In addition to empirical evidence, there is what I will call logical evidence. If what Christianity says about God, the world, humanity and Jesus is true, then certain other things follow necessarily. This has been the historical process Christians have used to argue for the atonement and the two natures of Jesus. It is also the process that leads us to the doctrine of Christ's preexistence. The necessity of the doctrine flows from its role in grounding key christological and soteriological teachings. Its truth must finally be a matter of faith, however.

I will conclude this chapter by considering how we can pull all this together and reach the conclusion I have suggested is the correct one. Writing more broadly about christology, Maurice Wiles presents the issue this way:

> How can this Jesus, with all the marks of manhood upon him, be the one in whom God saves the world? But we have to learn to struggle with it in our terms and not theirs. We have to use in the struggle, as for the most part they tried to do, all the insights of contemporary philosophy and psychology without becoming the slave of any.[40]

---

[40]Maurice Wiles, *The Christian Fathers* (New York: Oxford University Press, 1982), p. 82.

Wiles was contrasting the modern task with the patristic one, but his broader question leads directly to the very subject I am considering. But Wiles and those who share his view cannot accept the answer I am proposing precisely because they have made contemporary philosophy and psychology normative.

We cannot investigate Christ's preexistence directly, but that does not mean we cannot reach legitimate conclusions about the claim that Christ preexisted personally as the Son of God. This approach is not unique to matters of religion; scientists often reach conclusions on similar grounds. This does not mean ancient events did not leave evidence people can find, analyze and draw conclusions about. I am thinking more along the lines of the big bang theory of the origin of the universe. This theory has received support not from evidence uncovered prior to the theory but from observations that confirmed what the theory said would be true of the universe if the theory was correct. This is how I intend to proceed in looking at the evidence and arguments regarding Christ's preexistence. In doing so, I will operate along the lines of Sherlock Holmes's famous dictum that what remains when you have eliminated the impossible, however improbable it might seem, must be the truth.[41] So we will consider various possible explanations for who Jesus Christ is and how the doctrine of his preexistence as the Son of God came to be. This will involve not only biblical evidence, possible influence from Hellenistic and other sources, and the thinking of early church fathers, but also examining how the various alternatives fit into Christian theology.

This undertaking is more complex than it first appears. It also requires me to state at the outset the premises I will be working from. The most important of these, apart from accepting the reliability of the Bible as a source, is that if Jesus is fully God, there could never have been a time when he was not. The basis for this premise is twofold. First, the God of the Bible is one God; for him to adopt a human into the Godhead appears to require God to become plural or for the adopted Jesus to be significantly less than the original God. This premise has nothing to do with divine impassibility or the influence of Greek thought on Christianity. It is about the nature of God as we find it in the Old Testament (which also has no room for the idea of humans becoming God).[42] The second matter deals with human sinfulness as the Bible presents it. Simply stated, I see no way any human being who is merely a human being can live a life so free

---

[41]Arthur Conan Doyle, *The Sign of the Four*, in *The Complete Sherlock Holmes* (Garden City, N.Y.: Doubleday, 1927), 1:111. The complete quotation actually is a question: "How often have I said to you that when you have eliminated the impossible, whatever remains, *however improbable,* must be the truth?"

[42]See, for example, Is 42:8; 43:11; 44:6, 8; 45:5-6, 14, 18, 21, 22; 46:9 (and compare with Jn 17:5).

of sin, can demonstrate such great God-consciousness, can make himself so pleasing to God, that God elevates that person to deity or that God would do such a thing even if a person did lead a sinless life. That is neither biblical religion nor a biblical understanding of human nature.

WHAT YOU SEE IS WHAT YOU GET?

I also assume that the existence of the supernatural must be more than a formal possibility. It must receive more than lip service or it is no possibility at all. While I accept the reality of the supernatural, I ask only that evidence for the supernatural be admitted into court and considered on its merits. Unless we are willing to leave open the possibility of the supernatural pending our consideration of the evidence, we will never be able to recognize favorable evidence, much less evaluate it. The situation today, however, is not one of rampant credulity, believing any and all religious claims no matter how weakly attested, but unvarnished skepticism, doubting religious claims simply because they are religious, no matter how strongly they are attested. This attitude is not a scholarly presumption; it is simple prejudice.[43] Markus Bockmuehl writes:

> Open historical and philosophical questions about Jesus and Christianity have too often been declared closed in ways which amputate the former from the latter and in effect *preclude* faith. Hatched in ivory towers and reared in theological colleges, these ideas have sometimes seemed to lay observers to show the academics fiddling while the Church burns.[44]

The question confronting us is clear. By asking, "How can this Jesus, with all the marks of manhood upon him, be the one in whom God saves the world?" Maurice Wiles shows our subject is a matter of practical concern, and not merely academic. Having stated the challenge we face, Wiles suggests a response. He says we must struggle with the question on our terms, not those of the early church. And in our struggle we should emulate the early church fathers who used the insights of contemporary philosophy and psychology without becoming their slaves. This is good advice, but it is difficult to follow. We tend either to ignore contemporary thought forms or to allow them to dictate our conclusions.

Much of the modern rejection of the traditional teaching about Christ's preexistence presumes the normativity of post-Enlightenment philosophy and psychology, and rejects classical Christian doctrine because it does not; defenders

---

[43]I owe this distinction between presupposition and presumption and the willingness to label academic prejudice for what it is to John A. T. Robinson. See his *Priority of John,* p. 1.
[44]Markus Bockmuehl, *This Jesus* (Downers Grove, Ill.: InterVarsity Press, 1996), p. 168.

of the doctrine often are guilty of the reverse. In every age it is the responsibility of theologians to consider the intellectual contribution of their contemporaries, appropriating or adapting what they can without compromise and rejecting everything incompatible with Christian faith. The failure to do the second is what Bockmuehl criticizes. It is no less important to recognize the philosophical and psychological premises the biblical and early Christian authors wrote from, neither dismissing them because they are two thousand years old nor enshrining them for all time. That too is not presupposition but prejudice. Yet we cannot struggle with the question of who Jesus is on our terms until we have understood who he is on the early church's terms and why they reached the conclusion they did. We may even find their questions are not all that different from our own. While I believe Wiles is too eager to reformulate traditional concerns in modern terms, he shows a good understanding of the original context and how earlier Christians reached the conclusions they did.

WHERE DOES SKEPTICISM FIT?

Probably the most serious consequence of appropriating modern philosophical ideas is an inability or unwillingness to accept the God of the Bible as he presents himself to us. Bruce Vawter expresses my concern this way:

> We must accustom ourselves to a God, if we would have the God of the New Testament, who occasionally affronts our rationalism. This is easier said than done, since man is innately rationalistic and theology, which is the creation of man, has been tenaciously rationalistic from its inception.[45]

Vawter is saying there is a difference between rationality and rationalism. Humans are basically rational beings (although Freud reminded us we are not as rational as we like to think we are), but one of the consequences of sin is that our rationality can become distorted into rationalism, the belief that our minds are the measure of everything. Rationalism thus denies human finitude and tries to put the human creature in the place of the divine Creator. It results in a reductionistic understanding of Christianity, especially of Jesus Christ. It gives us only a human Jesus of whom Brian Hebblethwaite writes, "The purely human Christ, however open to the will of God, cannot possibly carry the weight of significance which is attributed to him."[46]

The incarnation and the preexistence of Christ that must logically precede it ultimately outstrip our capacity to fully understand them. H. E. W. Turner says

---

[45]Bruce Vawter, *This Man Jesus* (Garden City, N.Y.: Doubleday, 1973), p. 150.
[46]Brian Hebblethwaite, "The Appeal to Experience in Christology," in *Christ, Faith and History,* ed. S. W. Sykes and J. P. Clayton (Cambridge: Cambridge University Press, 1972), p. 264.

that is why we cannot do away with terms like *paradox* and *mystery,* even if they are out of favor in our culture. He adds, "It is not a direct appeal to the irrational, otherwise Christology could not have got started at all, but a realistic assessment that there are limits beyond which human thought cannot carry us. . . . It is not the 'murder of logic' but an admission that human logic is not omnicompetent in the expression of divine truth."[47] Nearly a century ago, Mackintosh noted that

> we need have no hesitation in confessing that the pre-existence of Christ outstrips our faculty of conception, and that no theoretic refinements alter this in the very least. Not merely are we faced here by the impossibility of beholding the life of God on its inward side, which means that thought is working altogether apart from experience, but in addition we encounter once more the haunting and insoluble enigma of time as ultimately related to eternity. . . . We cannot think eternity crudely as equivalent to time without beginning and without end; and the chronological quality of pre-existence is therefore fatal to its adequacy as a final or coherent representation of what, *ex hypothesi,* is above time. Christ cannot after all be pre-existent in any sense except that in which God Himself is so relatively to the incarnation.[48]

Some think it scholarly to approach a subject with an initial skepticism. I think this approach derives from the attitude toward things religious engendered by those masters of suspicion, Marx, Nietzsche and Freud. Skepticism is not a neutral approach. It runs contrary to how humans approach most other matters. We cannot exclude a priori any aspect of what Christianity claims God has done or can do by requiring those claims to meet some artificial standard that is probably beyond the possibility that anyone or anything can meet. Evans argues "scepticism about accepting material in the Gospels as authentic cannot be justified on the grounds that it is a more 'cautious' policy that is less likely to lead to mistakes."[49] If we err on the side of caution (or skepticism), we err no less than if we err on the side of credulity and the consequences are no less serious.[50]

This is an important consideration for our investigation of Christ's preexistence because the evidence supporting that teaching comes predominantly from the New Testament, some even coming from Gospel reports of what Jesus said about himself (especially in John's Gospel). Many New Testament scholars to-

---

[47]Turner, *Jesus the Christ,* pp. 130-31.
[48]Mackintosh, *Doctrine of the Person of Jesus Christ,* p. 457.
[49]Evans, *Historical Christ,* pp. 338-39.
[50]John Robinson opens *The Priority of John* by criticizing this attitude, which he calls uncritical skepticism. See pp. 2-3.

day believe the Johannine witness to be a creation of one early church community rather than reflective of the teaching of the early church in general. Nevertheless, Evans says:

> One simply cannot begin by ruling out as impossible any supernatural knowledge or insight on the part of Jesus, if one wishes to test the claim that God was at work in Jesus in a special way, or that Jesus was actually God incarnate. . . . A refusal to take this possibility seriously is just as "dogmatic" and "uncritical" as is the view of the narrative taken by a theologian who refuses to consider the possibility that Luke invented the prophecy [of the destruction of Jerusalem] after the fact.[51]

This is not to challenge historical criticism—that is another matter altogether—but simply to say the presuppositions used by many such critics stack the deck against an objective answer. And it leaves unanswered (perhaps even unasked) the question whether it is possible to investigate religious subjects using purely secular criteria. Evans's conclusion, and this comes from a philosopher rather than a theologian, reminds us of the profound skepticism of some scholars that John's Gospel accurately reflects Jesus' self-understanding is not a consequence of scholarly study of the text, but a presupposition brought to the text from outside. Recognizing this frees us to let John speak and to evaluate carefully what he has to say.[52] None of this is to deny that the content of John's gospel raises legitimate questions because of its differences from the Synoptic Gospels, particularly Jesus' explicit expressions of divine self-consciousness.

BEING VERSUS FUNCTION

One other major issue in christology remains for us to consider. This is the claimed antithesis between being and function. I say claimed because the way the question has often been posed creates a false dilemma. We need not choose between being and doing. Actually, thinking we need to choose is itself the source of error. To understand Jesus, we need to link who he was with what he did. Each throws light on the other. We cannot understand Jesus' mission without considering where he came from and what the nature of his relationship with God was—and we recognize more easily who he is by seeing what he has said and done.

It has become fashionable to think we should understand people in terms of

[51]Evans, *Historical Christ*, pp. 333-34.

[52]For a recent study of John's reliability by a New Testament scholar, see Craig L. Blomberg, *The Historical Reliability of John's Gospel* (Downers Grove, Ill.: InterVarsity Press, 2001). Blomberg discusses authorship, dating, audience, authorial intent and genre as well as reviewing specific texts throughout the Gospel before concluding in favor of John's reliability.

what they do. For example, when two people meet, the conversation turns quickly to the work each does. What kind of work we do ranks us relative to other people who do different kinds of work. Those who are unemployed thus become social nobodies and have learned to think of themselves in that way. The mentally retarded, mentally ill and those with serious physical handicaps who perform no obvious function in society are marginalized. Their lack of evident function detracts from their perceived being. But this contradicts the Bible's affirmation that our worth derives from our having been created in the image of God, not from our actions, and that we have worth despite our actions! By the same analogy, it is Jesus' existence as God the Son that is ultimate; his miracles and words of wisdom are secondary.

So, as we consider Jesus, the first question is, In what way is God in Jesus? This is logically prior to the question, What has God done in Jesus? The two questions are closely related because different ways God could be present in Jesus set different limits to what he could accomplish in and through him. So our first question must be ontological. Despite claims to the contrary, granting being precedence over function is not some strange idea unique to Greek thought. It is the general conclusion of the multiple strands of Western thought that the world makes much better sense when we place being before function. Christian theologians during the early centuries of the church, but especially in the Nicene and immediately post-Nicene period, stressed that Jesus' role as Savior requires he first exist as both God and human. No one emphasized this more than Athanasius.

Functional statements always presume (even if unconsciously) some ontological understanding. This is not less true for us today than it was for biblical or classical writers. Therefore, to explain functional statements in an exclusively functional context is impossible. This means those who say that because New Testament christological language is functional, early Christians could not have considered Jesus in ontological terms are wrong. When in the Gospels people asked, "What kind of man is this that [does this act or speaks this way]?" they were asking ontological questions and expecting ontological answers—even if they were Jews who had never studied an iota of Greek philosophy and had never heard the word *ontology*.

Discussion of Christ's preexistence moves our study into the arena of ontology. The doctrine of Christ's personal preexistence makes a clear statement about who Christ is, thereby enabling the doctrines of the incarnation and atonement to make clear statements about what he did. So if Jesus spoke or acted as one who had enjoyed life with God the Father prior to his earthly existence, or others reliably concluded this to have been true, we must consider the possibility that he had done so. The experience of such a Jesus is what led early Christians to shift their focus from what Jesus had done to who he was, although even the earliest documents about Jesus have something to say about Jesus' person. The shift came early (before A.D. 50), and by the time of Paul's letter to the Philippian church, it meant he could offer guidance on how Christians should behave toward one another based on their common belief in Christ's preexistence.

Our primary source for studying the doctrine of Christ's preexistence is the New Testament. In the next four chapters we will look further at hermeneutical issues involved in interpreting New Testament texts and then examine a number of texts in approximately the order they were written. I believe this will show belief in Christ's preexistence appeared early enough in Christian thought that the New Testament authors were able to assume their readers knew of and accepted the teaching. Next, we will look at possible influences from the Old Testament, intertestamental Judaism and Hellenistic thought. Then, I will survey the development of the doctrine in the history of Christian thought (emphasizing the patristic witness), examine where the doctrine fits into the entire fabric of Christian theology and evaluate some modern theological attempts to deal with the doctrine.

2

THE NEW TESTAMENT WITNESS

The earliest and preeminent source for considering Christ's preexistence is the New Testament. This same New Testament reflects what Bauckham calls "the highest possible Christology, the inclusiveness of the unique divine identity, [which] was central to the faith of the early church even before any of the New Testament writings were written, since it occurs in all of them."[1] An essential part of that christology was belief in Christ's personal preexistence.

Prior to the twentieth century, few doubted that Paul's letters, John's Gospel and letters, and the letter to the Hebrews clearly teach Christ's preexistence; a case can also be made that the Synoptic Gospels, 1 Peter, and even Jude affirm this teaching. I. Howard Marshall says of this:

> In the writers who are concerned with theological reflection about the person of Jesus, incarnational thinking is of central importance and forms indeed the organizing principle of their Christology. Moreover, in the case of these writers we have found good reason to believe that for them the son of God who becomes incarnate was a pre-existent Being. . . . Such incarnational thinking begins with the preexistent Son of God and states that he became man or became flesh. It thus deals with the question of how the Son of God became man rather than how a particular man, Jesus, could be the Son of God. . . . In incarnational theology the Son of God is the subject and Jesus is, as it were, the predicate.[2]

If the path of New Testament incarnational thought starts with the preexistent Son and assumes a real incarnation, then modern concerns about how Jesus could be both human and the Son of God entirely miss the point of New Testament christology.

In any case, the concept of Christ's preexistence appears in many of the

---

[1]Richard Bauckham, *God Crucified* (Grand Rapids: Eerdmans, 1998), p. 27.
[2]I. Howard Marshall, "Incarnational Christology in the New Testament," in *Christ the Lord,* ed. H. H. Rowdon (Downers Grove, Ill.: InterVarsity Press, 1982), p. 13.

books of the New Testament, even if none of them uses the term itself. It remains, however, to consider how the New Testament authors understood this concept, because those modern scholars who believe the New Testament teaches Christ's preexistence cannot agree on the meaning of the term even though they claim the support of the New Testament authors for their interpretations. George Caird describes as unquestioned the assumption that Paul, John and Hebrews, at a minimum, teach Christ's preexistence. The problem, he says, is most scholars assume the term *preexistence* is self-explanatory.[3] (This has recently begun to change as writers have recognized they need to interact with others who hold different views.) Mackintosh concludes that the New Testament understanding of the term required it be both real and personal: "The only pre-existence in which the apostolic writers are interested in is not ideal but real and personal. The love which entered history in Jesus could come only through a personal channel."[4] Mackintosh says too that the New Testament writers present the doctrine as "a fundamental certainty." It is significant that Mackintosh discusses the doctrine in terms of its soteriological importance, not as a speculative theme.

No less important than the meaning of the term is the authority we as exegetes grant to the biblical text. It means little to acknowledge particular New Testament writings teach Christ's preexistence if we grant those writings no more authority than the op-ed page of our local newspaper.

In no small measure, what we conclude about the New Testament teaching concerning Christ's preexistence and even whether various New Testament books do discuss it depends on how we approach the text.[5] Our conclusion depends on where we enter the hermeneutical circle. If we begin believing much of the New Testament language is a mythical way of expressing some eternal truth and that language has nothing to do with history, then we are unlikely to find preexistence, incarnation, atonement or resurrection in the documents. We will be much more likely to see ourselves and our world staring back at us from the mirror, because our interpretive tool will turn out to be a mirror rather than a looking glass. Regarding this perspective, Bernard Ramm writes:

---

[3]G. B. Caird, "Son by Appointment," in *The New Testament Age,* ed. William C. Weinrich (Macon, Ga.: Mercer University Press, 1984), 1:74.

[4]H. R. Mackintosh, *The Doctrine of the Person of Christ,* 2nd ed. (Edinburgh: T & T Clark, 1913), p. 447.

[5]John Robinson writes, "It makes a considerable difference whether one regularly approaches a saying of Jesus with the question, Is there any reason why he should not have said this? or Is there any reason why he should? Since there is often no decisive evidence to the contrary, the answer you get will be determined by the question you ask" (J. A. T. Robinson, *The Priority of John,* ed. J. F. Coakley [London: SCM Press, 1985], p. 2).

Such a mentality focuses its attention upon problems, difficulties, and imponderables. It desires a religion which has no mystery, no supernatural, and nothing transcendental. Therefore the incarnation is not a magnificent drama to be affirmed in joy but a doctrine too imponderable to believe. . . . It is a modernized, secularized, positivistic mentality which has lost the capacity to wonder.[6]

Markus Bockmuehl says the academic attempt of the past one hundred years to understand Jesus has prematurely declared open historical and philosophical questions to be closed in ways that irreparably divide the two fields and preclude the possibility of faith.[7] Many modern scholars are so uncomfortable with questions of faith, both their own and that of the New Testament authors, that they try to do their work without regard for matters of faith, a task predestined to failure. I think it is probably correct to acknowledge, however, such approaches are often attempts to preserve and present Christianity in a world recognized as fundamentally hostile to and skeptical of traditional Christianity. Although I consider such a compromising approach unsound and self-defeating, I cannot fault the motivation behind it.

Our attitude toward Scripture colors our respect for its authority and our confidence in its reliability. It is a waste of time and effort to consider whether the New Testament teaches some doctrine or records some fact if we are unwilling to accept the Bible's authority when we conclude it does so. Or, to put it another way, it really does not mean much if we agree certain New Testament books teach Christ's preexistence, even if they do so in great detail and with clarity, if we then say, "So what? It is only a book some people wrote a long time ago, and what did they know?" Even after we recognize the New Testament does teach Christ's preexistence and acknowledge its authority as God's Word to us, it remains for us to consider how and why the different writers teach this doctrine. We need to be ready to see the different emphases and rationales they offer for their teaching.

One issue we cannot avoid is the claim by some biblical scholars and theologians that the biblical language of preexistence is myth or metaphor intended to express Christ's significance (in terms contemporary pagans would have understood) rather than statements about Christ's objective reality. The evidence and conclusions these scholars offer are important to our investigation, but I will delay considering them until chapter six, when we look at possible Jewish and Hellenistic background to the preexistence teaching, since this is usually considered to be the source of those myths. My examination of the argument that preexistence is the language of myth will conclude in chapter nine when we

[6]Bernard L. Ramm, *An Evangelical Christology* (Nashville: Thomas Nelson, 1985), p. 52.
[7]Markus Bockmuehl, *This Jesus* (Downers Grove, Ill.: InterVarsity Press, 1996), p. 168.

consider the modern critiques of and alternatives to the traditional teaching.

If we grant that the New Testament books do teach Christ's preexistence (a conclusion I argue in chapters two through five), what is the relationship between these books? Does the nature of Scripture allow us to draw from several books, even from books by different writers, to develop a comprehensive sense of what is being affirmed and of what is being denied? Can we presuppose the teaching of earlier books when we read later ones? While some have argued it is improper to synthesize the evidence from different writers and some consider certain evidence to be highly suspect (primarily John's Gospel), I am working from the premise that while the New Testament has many human authors, it has but one divine Author. The presence of this divine Author ensures consistency and continuity between the thoughts of the human authors and allows me to synthesize the words of Paul, John, the writer to the Hebrews, and other New Testament writers. It remains my task to do this synthesis intelligently and honestly.

The path I intend to follow in considering what the New Testament writers have to say about Christ's preexistence begins with the earliest materials (Paul's letters) and moves chronologically through the other relevant writings. In doing this, I accept the traditional attribution of Pauline authorship, dating his letters from about A.D. 50 to the early 60s and including the pastoral letters. I accept the traditional claims regarding authorship of the Gospels and date the Synoptics (and the anonymous letter to the Hebrews) prior to the destruction of the temple in Jerusalem, while John probably wrote in the late 80s or early 90s. Given Peter's authorship of the two letters attributed to him, both must come from the early to mid-60s. In reading the New Testament books, we need, as James Dunn says, to allow the meaning intended by the authors and heard by the original audience to "exercise a critical function in relation to the use subsequently made of what they wrote."[8]

Dating and authorship of the New Testament documents are controversial and the conclusions we reach have important consequences for how we interpret the documents. Regarding the late dating of New Testament books containing incarnational language, Dunn warns:

> The later we have to postpone the emergence of the Christian doctrine of incarnation the more real becomes the possibility that the doctrine is the product not of organic growth ("development" as from seed to plant), but of grafting of a different growth onto the earlier (non-incarnational) stock, or of transformation into a different species (by "Hellenization," philosophization, or whatever).[9]

---

[8]James D. G. Dunn, *Christology in the Making* (Philadelphia: Westminster Press, 1980), p. xvi.
[9]Ibid., p. xiv.

Stephen Davis observes, "Though some comparative datings are based on carefully crafted linguistic arguments, others seem based more substantially on critical assumptions about what sorts of things might have been expressed by 'early' believers and what could have been expressed only by 'later' believers."[10] What Dunn and Davis are warning against is the tendency to bring to one's study presuppositions about what New Testament authors could have known and must have thought—particularly belief that theology must have evolved along a particular trajectory—to conclude particular beliefs could not have been early or that certain beliefs were derived from certain other sources. Often, this is simply an inadvertent smuggling of one's conclusion into the premise.

If we accept traditional authorship of the Gospels, Pastoral Letters and Petrine letters, at least two consequences follow.[11] First, the documents carry the authority of the individual credited with their authorship, in each case an apostle or the

---

[10]Stephen T. Davis, *Risen Indeed* (Grand Rapids: Eerdmans, 1993), p. 70.

[11]I accept traditional dating and authorship for the New Testament documents because modern critics have not offered what I consider convincing arguments for later dates or against traditional authorship. Claims that the earliest Christians considered pseudepigraphic writings acceptable are arguments from silence and use contemporary pagan and later Christian pseudepigraphic documents to derive a first-century Christian practice. Because of its significance for Christian apologetics, I consider the destruction of the temple in Jerusalem a key to dating the Synoptics and Hebrews. The Synoptics' inclusion of Jesus' prophecy of the temple's destruction and Hebrews' presentation of Jesus as replacing the temple sacrifice lead me to conclude that if the temple had been destroyed when the books were written, the authors would have used that event in support of their message. Luke and Acts constitute a two-part account, but Acts ends its account of Paul in Rome without reaching a conclusion. I surmise that this was because Paul had not yet been executed. If I am correct, then Luke must date from the early 60s and Mark and Matthew earlier. A common argument for dates after 70 is that Jesus' prophecies of the destruction of the temple in the Synoptics constitute "prophecies after the fact." Until I am convinced this conclusion is something more than a prejudice against the supernatural and the prophecy it makes possible, I cannot credit the argument. In any event, experts on the first third of the first century tell us Palestine was in such ferment that despite the absence of open rebellion an insightful person could forecast serious trouble ahead. Moreover, Jesus' prophecy sounds similar to descriptions of the Babylonian destruction of Jerusalem found in the Old Testament prophets. So even a merely human Jesus could have foretold the destruction of the First Jewish War; if we grant Jesus was as the New Testament writers present him, prophecy would create no barrier nor present a difficulty to dating the Synoptics prior to the war. Many New Testament scholars caution us that our knowledge of the early church and of the environment it existed in is incomplete. In fact, this knowledge appears sufficiently incomplete that it is risky to offer conclusions about dates of New Testament books on the basis of how things must or must not have been. Specifically, to say such books as the Pastorals are later than Paul because church organization was too primitive for a date in Paul's lifetime seems to go beyond the evidence. This is particularly the case when the argument becomes circular in deriving claims about development based on the supposedly late date of the books. The attempt to portray christology as developing from "low" to "high" has been discredited by the reality that Paul's christology is no lower than John's, and the Synoptics are much higher than some critical scholars are willing to admit.

associate of an apostle, and the credibility of their content is greater than if they were the product of some other writer. Second, accepting traditional authorship means the documents must be dated earlier rather than later because we know when some of the authors died, and for others the normal human lifespan places an upper limit on when they could have written. The earlier the New Testament books are dated, the earlier it is certain such teachings as Christ's preexistence were accepted within the early church. Late dating of the Gospels and letters does not necessarily mean the doctrines were late. This is especially true of preexistence since key statements about it are found in what have been widely described as hymns. These hymns may predate the documents we find them in (some of which are undeniably very early), and it is possible their use in the form we find them is evidence not only that they are earlier than the documents but that their use and acceptance were sufficiently widespread that the New Testament writers could quote them as reminders of a faith held in common.

Many New Testament documents contain elements of what scholars have concluded were hymns to Jesus.[12] There is no agreement these hymns were written prior to or by persons other than the New Testament authors, however. Some have concluded the fragments were earlier because they believe they have identified places where the authors have inserted their own material into the hymns to clarify or make an additional point. Martin notes all the hymns deal with Christ's person and mission, including his enjoyment of preexistent glory with God the Father and participation in creation.[13] Witherington concludes the fragments in Paul, John and Hebrews reflect a Wisdom christology dating from early Jewish Christianity. This means the hymns reflect a very early christology that is also a very "high" christology. He concludes, "Indeed, it was a Christology which ultimately led to a full-blown doctrine of the pre-existence of the Son and in due course when the logical implications of that idea sank in, to a doctrine of the incarnation."[14] If the hymns do predate the New Testament books containing them, this would mean the earliest expression of Christ's preexistence appeared in the context of worship and mission, not theological speculation, and the formal doctrine was a considered response to an undeveloped sense of Jesus' uniqueness and his deity. This would be a significant conclusion, to say the least.

Why the New Testament books were written is important to our investigation of what they say about Christ's preexistence. It is not always easy to determine

---

[12]Ralph Martin identifies the following as christological hymn fragments: 1 Tim 3:16; Phil 2:6-11; Heb 1:3; Jn 1:1-14; 1 Pet 1:18-21; 2:21-25; 3:18-22; Rev 5:9-10; 12:10-12; 19:1ff.

[13]Ralph P. Martin, *Worship in the Early Church* (Grand Rapids: Eerdmans, 1974), pp. 51-52.

[14]Ben Witherington III, *Jesus the Sage* (Minneapolis: Fortress, 1994), p. 249.

this purpose, but it certainly was *not* to convince readers of Christ's preexistence. Particularly in Paul's letters, Christ's preexistence served as an assumption he held in common with his audience that was used to justify some other belief or practice. As we consider the texts that somehow deal with Christ's preexistence, it will be necessary to keep in mind why preexistence is in the text, how it is in the text, and what the implications of this are or should be. So if Paul assumes Christ's preexistence in making an argument that Christians ought to behave in a certain way, it is legitimate to conclude he is not offering Christ's preexistence as a new doctrine but is presuming his audience not only knows the doctrine but accepts it as true. Otherwise, Paul's argument would fall on deaf ears.

Hermeneutical Issues

Once we have made a decision about the author, date and purpose of the New Testament books, we are in a position to determine what these books are saying. This raises several additional questions. Do we examine the texts for their meaning independently, or should we act in terms of a web of beliefs where the whole may be greater than the sum of the parts and where the meanings of the texts are interdependent? The tendency of New Testament scholars has been to examine texts regarding Christ's preexistence atomistically and then total up their findings to reach a conclusion. I believe a better way requires we work back and forth between each text and the broader context, recognizing that if there is a general sense Christ preexisted his earthly life, then some texts must be understood differently than if there was no such sense (on the ground most authors do not waste time proving what their audience already accepts). Perhaps the best analogy for this is a detective story where clues are discovered one by one, and each affects how we should interpret the other clues.

Part of the mindset of many who have lived after the Enlightenment is a conceit that we are wise and rational, but ancients were naive and credulous—an attitude Thomas Oden calls modern chauvinism.[15] I suggest the historical evi-

---

[15]Marcus Borg, coming at christology from a sharply different perspective than my own, agrees with this concern. He has written, "The primary intellectual objection to [belief in the spiritual realm] flows from a rigid application of the modern worldview's definition of reality. Yet the modern view is but one of a large number of humanly constructed maps of reality" (quoted by Ben Witherington III, *The Jesus Quest* [Downers Grove, Ill.: InterVarsity Press, 1995], p. 99). As a graduate student I asked one of my professors about the way modern scholars unselfcritically assume the naturalistic mindset of the Enlightenment. He acknowledged it was a problem and offered Hegel's master-slave relationship to explain its dominance and lack of self-critical awareness. Oden's comment was made during an interview with Kenneth Myers about the Ancient Christian Commentary on Scripture series Oden is editing. It can be found in the *Mars Hill Audio Journal* 36 (January-February 1999).

dence, including the biblical evidence, shows people two thousand years ago could be quite skeptical. Otherwise, why was "Doubting Thomas" so resistant to the testimony of his fellow disciples, and why was there so much recorded resistance to Jesus' miracles and resurrection? On the other hand, a quick look at most daily newspapers with their horoscope columns, the local supermarket checkout counter with its rack of tabloids reporting all sorts of sensational events, the number of people who play the daily lottery, and the popularity of such television programs as *Touched by an Angel* and *The X-Files* cast doubt on how rational, advanced and secular we post-Enlightenment people really are. The Enlightenment emphasized the place of human reason to the point of believing everything worth knowing can be comprehended in terms of unaided human reason. Bruce Vawter, however, cautions, "We must accustom ourselves to a God, if we would have the God of the New Testament, who occasionally affronts our rationalism. This is easier said than done."[16]

In *Christology in the Making,* James Dunn cautions against reading biblical texts according to their "common sense." In line with this premise, both Dunn and Karl-Josef Kuschel say if readers did not come to the New Testament texts with a belief in preexistence drawn from later theology, they would not find it in the texts. Kuschel argues a metaphysical sonship is no part of the New Testament's concern. With regard to the earliest New Testament formulations, Dunn agrees. His warning about "common sense" is appropriate in those cases where the text requires special knowledge of history, geography or the like for accurate interpretation, and in instances where the text presumes a worldview or perspective alien to that of the reader. But it is inconsistent with Christian tradition (especially Protestant tradition) to deny the average Christian can open the Bible and read from it the key teachings of the faith. I mention Dunn's caution at this point because we later will see he uses this to warn that the meaning of Philippians 2:6-11 is not its common-sense meaning.

Because Christ's preexistence is such a fundamental teaching, evidence for it should not require the specialized skills of modern biblical scholars in order to be found—although such skills should enhance our understanding of what we do find. The work of biblical and theological specialists is essential to the health of the church, but Paul especially cautions us against overemphasizing the role of human knowledge in discerning spiritual truth (an attitude more gnostic than orthodox Christian). So can crucial texts be read in a straightforward manner without misleading the reader? I believe so. As I will argue later, Dunn's admission that Philippians 2:6-11 sounds like it teaches Christ's preexistence is not ne-

[16]Bruce Vawter, *This Man Jesus* (Garden City, N.Y.: Doubleday, 1973), p. 150.

gated by his argument that it does not; instead, it makes his claim sound very much like special pleading.

The current reassessment of Christ's preexistence results from the rejection by some New Testament scholars and theologians of the traditional interpretation of key passages that have been generally held to teach the doctrine.[17] Although this history of interpretation is not rejected out of hand, sound exegetical practice would seem to give the benefit of the doubt to interpretations that have lasted intact from the early church until this century. For some who have argued the need to reinterpret the texts teaching Christ's preexistence, the motivation seems to be skepticism about the supernatural or our ability to recognize it; for others, it seems to be an excessive caution unrelated to any conclusion about the doctrine's truth or falsity; for yet others, it is fear of presumption, arrogance or exclusivism in dealing with people of other faiths or no faith at all. Piet Schoonenberg concludes preexistence plays no essential role in the New Testament message.[18] As will become evident in chapter nine, however, most of the challenges come from those who have serious reservations about Christ's personal preexistence.

From the conservative side, the problem of interpreting the evidence often seems to be one of reading back into the biblical texts the creedal conclusions of early church councils. Because those creeds are considered to have been built on a foundation of biblical evidence, this is illegitimate circular reasoning. The creeds have their proper place in proclaiming Christ's preexistence, but it is not to justify particular interpretations of biblical texts; it is always the biblical texts that must justify the content and wording of the creeds. Moreover, these creeds are not worded in the language of the New Testament but that of Hellenism, although this Hellenistic terminology had been transformed for the purpose of defending New Testament teachings against Hellenistic philosophical concepts. In any case, it is illegitimate to read later theological conclusions back into New Testament texts, tempting as that may be.

The influence of Hellenism on christology (and theology in general) has been debated vigorously for decades. Some see Hellenism and Judaism as belief systems so totally different as to be incompatible in every way. They consider Judaism a dynamic religion concerned only with function whereas Hellenism was a static philosophy that emphasized ontology. In his book *Christianity,*

---

[17]Stephen T. Davis, a professional philosopher who is also a very competent theologian, says about this, "It seems to me that the views of a group of New Testament scholars, even if they constitute a majority, carry little authority for outsiders if respected scholars equally conversant with the facts continue to disagree with that majority" (*Risen Indeed,* p. 325).

[18]Piet Schoonenberg, *The Christ,* trans. Della Couling (New York: Herder & Herder, 1971), p. 99.

Hans Küng said the first paradigmatic change in Christianity occurred when speculative questions about the nature of God and of Jesus replaced the cross and resurrection as the center of Christian thought. The language of Hellenistic metaphysics replaced that of the Bible and christology "from above" replaced christology "from below."[19] Küng ignores that one reason early Christian theologians used Hellenistic language was that it was the language of the culture in which the early church existed and which it was trying to evangelize.

While both heretics and orthodox used biblical language to argue their positions, they read the Bible with sharply different presuppositions. Heretics like Arius operated within a clearly Hellenistic worldview. But the question remains: were Judaism and Hellenism really such incompatible views that one could not influence the other? During the past twenty years New Testament scholars have begun to recognize that, given the Hellenistic cities established there during the first century B.C., Galilee was not immune to Hellenistic influence—it was probably the most Hellenistic area of Palestine.[20] Several scholars have even suggested Jesus may have been bilingual (trilingual?) in Greek and Aramaic (and Hebrew?). My point is not that Hellenism was a major influence in the development of christology—I do not believe it was—but it was neither something novel Christians had to deal with only after Christianity spread beyond Palestine nor that they did so by accommodating it.

MYTH

Although I will deal with the claim that the doctrine of Christ's preexistence is myth in chapters six and nine, I need at least to mention that many modern objections to the supernatural aspects of Christ's life do describe them as myth. Designating preexistence, incarnation, resurrection and similar events as myth allows scholars to acknowledge them as significant for the story of Jesus Christ without accepting them as factual.[21] Küng says we must not take myths literally, but neither may we ignore them—they present truth in a way historical reporting never can. Truth is not the same thing as facticity, he says; neither is it equivalent to historical truth. Sometimes fiction conveys truth better than does history. Implicit in this view is the denial that Christianity is an essentially historical re-

---

[19] Hans Küng, *Christianity*, trans. John Bowden (New York: Continuum, 1994), pp. 166-76.
[20] See, for example, N. T. Wright, *Jesus and the Victory of God* (Minneapolis: Fortress, 1996), 2:74.
[21] As a technical term in literary studies (and theology), *myth* is a matter of genre and says nothing about facticity. Thus it is technically accurate to designate factual literature as myth, but because the common understanding of the term includes a fictional nature, the technical use is confusing for most people and can even be misleading.

ligion and the traditional belief that if claims regarding the historicity of the key events of Jesus' birth, ministry, and death are false, we must also reject Christianity as false. Myth allows uncongenial historical claims to be rejected without thereby repudiating Christianity. The mythic approach to christology also reflects the belief that people of Jesus' day thought in terms of myth and used myths to explain extraordinary occurrences. Küng represents this view when he writes, "With reference to the beginning and ending, to the death and birth of Jesus Christ, insofar as these things transcend sense experience, the formation of myths is to be expected."[22]

Myth allows modern writers to acknowledge that early Christians believed such things about Jesus as his preexistence, incarnation, miracles and resurrection without thereby agreeing these were in any sense objective reality. C. K. Barrett objects that while it is possible the New Testament writers did invent myths, he can find no evidence of such a tendency during the New Testament period:

> What I have not observed in this period is a tendency to make new myths of a historical or quasi-historical kind. To say this is not, of course, to prove that the New Testament writers did not invent such myths, still less to establish the historical accuracy of everything contained in the New Testament. But it does suggest that in the New Testament event and interpretation are related to each other in a different way from that which is suggested by the language of myth. . . . To the New Testament writers, event and interpretation were equally valid and real, and we cannot say that one is primary and the other secondary.[23]

CULTURAL SENSITIVITY

In understanding what people of other times and cultures say, we need to keep in mind not only our context as readers but also their context as writers. We are prone to give verbal assent to this while continuing to understand those writers in terms of *our* worldview. It is difficult to put oneself in the place of people from other times and cultures, even when we know enough about them to understand what is required of us (witness our difficulty in understanding the current Middle Eastern and Balkan conflicts in terms of their histories and cultures—something even more difficult when we are looking at ancient Palestine). Experts in the field warn that what we think we know about the lives and customs of first-century Jews has many gaps and is often simplistic and overgeneralized. This means we far too readily assume what a

[22]Hans Küng, *On Being a Christian,* trans. Edward Quin (Garden City, N.Y.: Doubleday, 1976), p. 419.
[23]C. K. Barrett, "Myth and the New Testament: How Far Does Myth Enter into the New Testament?" *Expository Times* 68 (1957): 361-62.

Jew of that time could or could not know or believe; at the same time, we too facilely assume we know the details of early Christian belief and practice. In saying this, I am not arguing for agnosticism in these matters, because I believe we can know a great deal about the subject; I am only calling for a proper humility. This is especially necessary because too often we who live after the Enlightenment look down on those from antiquity as naive and credulous, people without the benefit of our scientific wisdom, and ready to believe any claim no matter how weak its justification. This conceit is not only a poor attitude with which to approach study of ancient societies—it is untrue. So it becomes necessary to investigate what people really believed and how they really looked at their world. When we fail to do so, we can only impose our worldview on them, saying this is how these people must have seen and done things. In saying this, I am in agreement with the projects of such scholars as N. T. Wright and James Dunn, who seek to understand the New Testament world on its terms (although I do not necessarily agree with all their conclusions), and in complete disagreement with those who deny normative meanings and authorial intent. As Dunn writes:

> The text by itself cannot provide sufficient check on what we hear it saying; for there are so many allusions and taken-for-granteds which depend on the fact that the document is a *historical* document (a document of a particular time and place in history), which would be wholly apparent to writer and reader of the time, and on which much of its meaning depends, but which are now hidden from us by our remoteness from that historical context. The text does provide the check; but it is surely the text set *within its historical context* which can do so adequately.[24]

New Testament scholars disagree whether the New Testament directly calls Jesus God. In terms of first century Judaism, it would be understandable if no New Testament writer described Jesus as God because of the difficulty such language would create for early Christians with a Jewish background, but such an identification would demonstrate clearly that they had understood how radical was the divine in-breaking of the incarnation. It is important to note that every passage that identifies Jesus as *theos* can be translated other ways or has variants that read differently. It is also important to remember that Jesus' deity can be defended quite adequately from the New Testament without identifying him verbally as God.

The argument against the New Testament identifying Jesus as *theos* is nor-

---

[24]Dunn, *Christology in the Making,* p. xiv.

mally formulated in terms of what the writers could have believed and describes the textual evidence as grammatically or textually uncertain.[25] A. T. Wainwright, however, believes the natural construction of the Greek "favors the view that Christ is called God." He cites Romans 9:5; 2 Thessalonians 1:12; Titus 2:13; 2 Peter 1:1; James 1:1; Hebrews 1:8; Matthew 1:23; John 1:1; 17:3; 20:28; and 1 John 5:20 as passages that identify Jesus as God. He also discusses four other passages where such an identification is a variant reading. He argues the correct procedure is to choose the most natural reading of the Greek without regard to what we think the writers could have believed; the factor of psychological probability is appropriate only when linguistic possibilities are equal. Regarding Paul, he says, "The claim is made that, since St. Paul was a man of a particular character, brought up in a particular environment, he could not have made the statement that Christ was God. . . . [But] we are not in a position to say with an air of finality what was psychologically impossible for St. Paul."[26] Wainwright so emphasizes the authority of the text that he says even "if the natural interpretation of the Greek seems to involve the author in an inconsistency, it should nonetheless be accepted. Linguistic arguments should be used to determine the meaning of the language; psychological arguments to explain the development and shape of the thought."[27] While I am sympathetic to Wainwright and agree with his conclusion, some of the texts we will examine as we investigate what the New Testament says about preexistence may not be as clear-cut as he seems to think.

In his book *Jesus*, A. N. Wilson notes that whereas the Gospel writers presented Jesus from a particular point of view, he intends to examine Jesus objectively. Wilson is correct to note that the Gospels were written from particular perspectives and with particular purposes (although he is far from the first to do so), but he is fooling himself when he declares he will write objectively (although again he is far from the first to do so). None of us is entirely objective, and to think we are is to delude ourselves, making us careless about how we are handling our material and causing us to reject too quickly views other than our own because they are "subjective." Recognizing our own subjectivity need not compromise the truth of what we say; actually, it can make our work fairer because we do recognize our own preferences and

---

[25]See, e.g., A. E. Harvey, *Jesus and the Constraints of History* (Philadelphia: Westminster Press, 1982), p. 157. Many of the disputed passages can be read along the line of either "our God and Lord Jesus Christ" or "our God and the Lord Jesus Christ."

[26]A. T. Wainwright, "The Confession 'Jesus Is God' in the New Testament," *Scottish Journal of Theology* 10 (1957): 276.

[27]Ibid., p. 277.

prejudices and thus are able to compensate for them.[28]

All writing involves interpretation simply because when we write about a subject we necessarily select some materials and omit others. Acting in good faith, we make selections of what is important and what is not, what to include and what to ignore. We cannot include everything. Those who openly declare their allegiance and purpose to their audience are less likely to mislead either themselves or their readers, and those who disagree with them are forewarned about where the argument is coming from. For christology, this includes details of authorship, date and authority of New Testament books; differences between Synoptic and Johannine accounts; accuracy and extent of the reported words of Jesus; and the sources of influence on the New Testament authors.

FUNCTIONAL CHRISTOLOGY

Oscar Cullmann and Hans Küng are representative of scholars who understand the New Testament to be concerned with Jesus' function rather than his being. In his study of the Philippians hymn, Ralph P. Martin says a growing consensus holds that the New Testament contains no evidence for metaphysical language in christology: "The modern emphasis rather is upon a functional Christology which is set within the frame work of the Redeemer's saving acts."[29] This means titles used of Jesus and descriptions of his actions are about the role he played, not who he was. Thus, according to some theologians, language about preexistence intends to express Jesus' significance for us in exalted terms, not to say something about his origin or being. These scholars say questions of being were alien to Hebrew thought. Such questions only became part of Christian discussion after Hellenistic thought had entered the church. Leonhard Goppelt goes even further. He argues that especially in Paul, preexistence places Jesus on God's side even before he is on ours. For Hellenists as well as for Jews, such language provided assurance of a basic order to the universe. Thus for Paul preexistence language could only be figurative because God is outside time and space.[30] What the preexistence language of

---

[28]An excellent critique of the claim to "scholarly objectivity" as a possibility or necessity can be found in C. Stephen Evans, *The Historical Christ and the Jesus of Faith* (Oxford: Oxford University Press, 1996). Evans points out our inability to step outside our worldviews and the value they can have in our investigation of Christian claims about Jesus. He adds that although the Enlightenment assumption that beliefs must be constructed on objectively certain foundations has been acknowledged to be naive, it has not been rejected in practice (p. 349).

[29]Ralph P. Martin, *Carmen Christi*, 2nd ed. (Cambridge: Cambridge University Press, 1983), p. 106. Martin does not identify himself with this tendency.

[30]Leonhard Goppelt, *Theologie des Neuen Testaments. Zweite Teil: Vielfalt und Einheit des apostolischen Christuszeugnisses* (Göttingen: Vendenhoeck & Ruprecht, 1976), pp. 399ff.

the New Testament means is that in Jesus we encounter the Creator as Savior.

This understanding does not deal adequately with the fact that New Testament authors clearly seem to describe Jesus in ontological terms and report people asking questions that require ontological answers. Reginald Fuller says, "It is not just a quirk of the Greek mind, but a universal human apperception, that action implies prior being—even if, as is also true, being is only apprehended in action."[31] Fuller's comment explains the New Testament's emphasis on what Jesus said and did because it is through these we come to appreciate who the Jesus who said and did these things was. Even John A. T. Robinson said Paul and the writer of the letter to the Hebrews *combine* preexistence language with "designatory" (or functional) language, language that in terms of later concerns looks very much adoptionistic.[32] Robinson argues, however, that the New Testament writers used preexistence language about Jesus just as it underwent a change in meaning. He says the functional statements they intended about how Jesus acted as God's representative came to be understood instead as ontological statements about who Jesus was.[33]

R. T. France agrees that New Testament christology originally was functional, but adds its ultimate character was ontological: "The truth about Jesus which was first perceived functionally was then necessarily worked out in ontological terms. This was surely inevitable for Jews who could hardly think of a man as exercising divine functions without considering what effect this belief had on their monotheism."[34] He adds that neither approach can exist in isolation, so we should see functional and ontological approaches as complementary: Jesus' ability to fulfill his appointed role depended on who he was, but who he was must be seen primarily through what he did.[35] Brian Hebblethwaite rightly suggests it is impossible to consider a person solely in functional terms: "Whether we speak of God's action in the man Jesus or of God's personal presence *as* the man Jesus, we are using the category of substance. What is at issue is the manner of God's presence."[36] The point is that functional language cannot stand alone but must always be joined with that of substance, in Hebrew thought no less than in Greek. Similarly, substance thought cannot stand alone because we

[31]Reginald H. Fuller, *The Foundations of New Testament Christology* (London: Fontana, 1965), p. 248.
[32]Robinson, *Priority of John*, p. 391.
[33]John A. T. Robinson, *The Human Face of God* (London: SCM Press, 1973), chap. 5. He acknowledges this whole idea is purely hypothetical.
[34]R. T. France, "The Worship of Jesus," in *Christ the Lord,* ed. H. H. Rowdon (Downers Grove, Ill.: InterVarsity Press, 1982), pp. 33-34.
[35]R. T. France, "Development in New Testament Christology," *Themelios* 18 (1992): 5.
[36]Brian Hebblethwaite, *The Incarnation* (Cambridge: Cambridge University Press, 1987) p. 161.

only recognize what someone is through what that person does. Logically, what someone is precedes what that person does because one first must be before one can do.[37] George Lindbeck says:

> It is possible to separate the person from the work of Christ only if one thinks in nonnarrative terms. . . . In the Gospel accounts, accommodated to human understanding as they are, person and work coincide. It is through Jesus' saving work that his personal identity as fully human yet Son of God becomes manifest.[38]

The seeming contradiction between essence and form looks instead like a complementarity, as do most of the other apparent christological contradictions.

CHRISTOLOGICAL TITLES

The New Testament applies a number of titles to Jesus. Most of these come from the Old Testament, but this does not mean they are necessarily to be understood in Old Testament terms, even assuming there was a distinct Old Testament meaning for them. Nineteen centuries after the New Testament was completed, we do not always use the christological titles it contains in the same sense as did the New Testament writers.

Messiah. One title was quickly transformed into part of Jesus' name in the first Christian generation. Jesus himself was very careful to distinguish his use of this term from that of his contemporaries. Jesus the Messiah (or Christ) became Jesus Christ. The Messiah (Hebrew) or Christ (Greek) was the anointed of God, a person commissioned by God for a special task. Thus Jesus was deemed to fulfill an office that required anointing; the primary office in Old Testament Israel requiring anointing was that of king.

In biblical Judaism the term *messiah* did not necessarily carry any connotation of divine status, and Jews of Jesus' day were not expecting their messiah to be other than a human. Actually, many expected their messiah to be a political-military figure who would lead the people of Israel to freedom from foreign rule and establish an earthly theocratic kingdom. There seems, however, to have been no clear and unanimous sense of what the messiah would be like. Different Jewish groups appear to have had different messianic expectations. Some considered the messiah to be preexistent, but this was an ideal rather than a real preexistence.

---

[37]I say this recognizing existentialists argue existence precedes essence, so that what we are comes to be (not merely to be seen) out of what we do.

[38]George Lindbeck, "Atonement and the Hermeneutics of Intratextual Social Embodiment," in *The Nature of Confession,* ed. Timothy R. Phillips and Dennis L. Okholm (Downers Grove, Ill.: InterVarsity Press, 1996), p. 231.

Jesus was reserved in his acceptance of messianic acclaim during his earthly ministry (the "messianic secret"), probably because he feared popular misunderstanding would have interfered with his intent (at several points, the Gospels report what appear to have been popular calls for Jesus to act like a political or military messiah, e.g., Jn 6:15). Only during the last week of his life, and earlier in private to a Samaritan woman, did Jesus acknowledge his messiahship. When he entered Jerusalem at the start of Passion Week, Jesus rode a donkey, presenting himself publicly as king, but a king come in peace. Before the Sanhedrin, Jesus acknowledged being Messiah, but presented this messiahship eschatologically in language drawn from Daniel 7:13. To Pilate he also acknowledged he was king. In these last two cases, however, there was no longer any possibility people might misinterpret his claim in an immediate temporal political and military sense. So Jesus understood himself as Messiah, but he did so on his terms. Jesus understood his messianic role in terms of suffering, death and resurrection (Mt 16); he would accomplish his mission by suffering, not by overpowering. Riesenfeld says this about Jesus' use of Old Testament messianic thought:

> It is obvious the messianic terms used by Jesus are to be found in the Old Testament and in later Jewish literature, and there they have, as a matter of course, to be analyzed in their context. The decisive feature, however, lies in the manner in which certain elements have been taken over, whilst others have been rejected.[39]

Son of God. Mark begins his story of Jesus with the words, "The beginning of the gospel about Jesus Christ, the Son of God" (Mk 1:1). "Son of God" has been a title for Jesus since the writing of the New Testament, although it is not one Jesus himself used (at least not in this complete form). While Christians have used the title to denote Jesus' deity, neither the Judaism nor the paganism of Jesus' day understood the title in this way.[40] Neither did the early church. Pagans used the title to acclaim great humans without implying their deity.

In the Old Testament, kings (especially David), righteous individuals and even Israel are called sons of God. Larry Hurtado notes that "divine sonship did not function to connote divinity, but it certainly indicated a special status and

[39]H. Riesenfeld, "The Mythological Background of New Testament Christology," in *The Background of the New Testament and Its Eschatology,* ed. W. D. Davies and D. Daube (Cambridge: Cambridge University Press, 1956), p. 91.
[40]Cornelius Plantinga says, "The NT scandal is that Jesus Christ differs not only in degree but also in kind from God's other revealers and agents. . . . NT literature pointedly claims that Jesus Christ and the eternal divine Son of God are the same person and that the person is distinct from the Father" (Cornelius Plantinga Jr., "Trinity," in *International Standard Bible Encyclopedia* [Grand Rapids: Eerdmans, 1988], 4:915).

relationship with God."[41] Cullmann says the title indicates a functional rather than an ontological unity between Christ and God, but interestingly in his discussion of the title he calls Christ "the pre-existent one."[42] Peter Hinchliff, however, concludes the title has more than functional significance; it even has an ontological character, because Jesus' sonship was different from that of kings and prophets. He notes the title presents to us a relationship that actually says something about God as well as Jesus, namely, that Jesus' relationship with God was unique and manifested God's concern for and involvement in his creation.[43]

James Charlesworth reminds us that while early Christians may have invested this title with unprecedented significance, they nevertheless inherited the title from Judaism, so Judaism must provide the starting point for any interpretation.[44] This means that Klaas Runia's claim that the title Son of God and the concept of Christ's preexistence cannot be separated in the New Testament overstates the evidence. Similarly, John Robinson's assertion that Son of God has no ontological implications but only "is to allow God wholly and utterly to be the Father" understates the possibilities for understanding the title. Jacques Dupuis links the various understandings of the title by saying it expresses ontologically "the filial consciousness that had been at the centre of Jesus' subjective experience of God during his earthly life."[45] According to Bruce Vawter, to describe Jesus as anything other than God's natural Son during his earthly life is to teach adoptionism.[46] Vawter's claim requires belief in Christ's preexistence, as does any understanding of Son of God that has ontological content. Along the same line, Alan Segal writes that in Paul, Hebrews and the Johannine writings, the term Son of God includes the idea of preexistence, although it did not originate to express that preexistence. He adds that "like *Kyrios* and unlike *Christos,* the term 'Son of God' would have remained meaningful to people who were not aware of its Jewish background."[47]

For Knox, however, the language is functional, not ontological: Jesus was

---

[41]Larry W. Hurtado, *Lord Jesus Christ* (Grand Rapids: Eerdmans, 2003), pp. 23, 103.

[42]Oscar Cullmann, *The Christology of the New Testament,* rev. ed., trans. Shirlie C. Guthrie and Charles A. M. Hall (Philadelphia: Westminster Press, 1963), p. 247.

[43]Peter Hinchliff, "Christology and Tradition," in *God Incarnate: Story and Belief,* ed. A. E. Harvey (London: SPCK, 1981), pp. 94-95. Although Hinchliff never mentions Christ's preexistence specifically, what he says seems to require it.

[44]James Charlesworth, *Jesus Within Judaism* (Garden City, N.Y.: Doubleday, 1988) p. 152. Craig Blomberg says the Qumran scrolls show Son of God was a pre-Christian Jewish messianic title, but did not necessarily imply deity. (See Craig Blomberg, *The Historical Reliability of John's Gospel* [Downers Grove, Ill.: InterVarsity Press, 2001], p. 80.)

[45]Jacques Dupuis, *Who Do You Say I Am?* (Maryknoll, N.Y.: Orbis, 1994), p. 70.

[46]Vawter, *This Man Jesus,* p. 143.

[47]Alan Segal, *Two Powers in Heaven* (Leiden: E. J. Brill, 1977), p. 208 n. 73.

merely designated as Son of God and Christ. Knox's approach to the Gospel material assumes much of the language attributed to Jesus actually came from the Gospel writers. He clearly thinks this is the case with the Son of God language. Jesus could not have thought such things about himself; the early church created these sayings in order to exalt Jesus above contemporary rivals for allegiance. So it is important to decide whether it was Jesus who claimed to be the Son of God or the early church that described him that way for apologetic purposes. Only in the former case is preexistence necessary. But none of this seems terribly important, because Knox considers this all myth and rejects any necessary connection between function and being.

France is uncomfortable about Knox's approach for two reasons. First, to say Jesus never considered himself to be Son of God requires rejecting the general testimony of the Gospels. Second, it focuses too much attention on one title while ignoring the broader witness of the Gospels that Jesus was aware of his "more than human status."[48] In a different context, France reminds us that the strongest evidence of Jesus' claim to deity, and thus also to preexistence, is implicit: the "assumption of a divine role which is all the more impressive because it does not seem to require arguments or defense, and which occurs in a variety of Gospel traditions."[49] Jesus unobtrusively acted as though he were deity, assumed divine authority and applied to himself texts that in the Old Testament clearly referred to God alone. If Jesus was correct in his self-understanding, then he was God incarnate, requiring acceptance of both the implications of this claim and the hints of personal preexistence mingled with it.

For I. Howard Marshall and C. F. D. Moule, the title has ontological implications, but not in an immediate and straightforward way. Moule believes that by itself the title offers no necessary claim to divine status; it is the conjoining of this title with others (especially Son of Man) and its context in the Gospels that indicate "the traditions about Jesus had led to a radical reinterpretation of what it meant to be a son of God."[50] For Marshall, this is a title where "the relation of Jesus to God is especially prominent," and "the concept of deity is present." But it took time for the church to recognize the implications of the title. Elsewhere, Marshall argues this title must encompass more than function or status because "it expresses the hidden relationship with God which enabled Jesus to act as the

---

[48]R. T. France, "Development in New Testament Christology," *Themelios* 18 (1992): 6.

[49]R. T. France, "The Worship of Jesus," in *Christ the Lord,* ed. H. H. Rowdon (Downers Grove, Ill.: InterVarsity Press, 1982), p. 28.

[50]C. F. D. Moule, *The Origin of Christology* (Cambridge: Cambridge University Press, 1977), p. 28.

Revealer" and thus expresses "an essential relationship to God."[51] Quoting Werner Kramer, he also says it describes Jesus' significance not in terms of specific historical actions but in terms of metaphysical and cosmological speculation "by introducing the concept of his pre-existence."[52] The title Son of God certainly appears to describe Jesus as more than a human, but by itself it does not provide sufficient foundation for a doctrine of Christ's preexistence.

Jesus often referred to himself as "the Son" (especially in John's Gospel), generally in a context where he identified God as "the Father" or "my Father." At the least, this language implies a special, even unique, relationship between Jesus and God of which Jesus was aware. Jesus never spoke of God as "our Father" where he was included in the "our." (The Lord's Prayer of Matthew 6 with its "our Father" is a model for how the disciples should pray, not an example of how Jesus prayed.) This demonstrates even more clearly his consciousness of nothing less than a unique filial relationship with God, and certainly encourages belief in his preexistence as the Son. Marshall says Jesus was aware he enjoyed a unique filial relationship to God and this can be seen in his use of "Abba" and "my Father" language and in his self-designation as Son.[53]

Son of Man. Moule associates the Son of God title with Jesus' favorite self-designation, Son of Man. In the New Testament, Jesus is the only one who used this title of himself (eighty-three times), with three exceptions: Acts 7:56, Revelation 1:13 and Revelation 14:14. The latter two texts describe the ascended Jesus in language clearly drawn from Daniel 7:13, where it is a description of a heavenly figure, not a title. In the Gospels, it was Jesus' most frequent way of speaking about himself. Others neither challenged his use of the term nor asked him to explain what he meant by it. Neither his disciples nor the early church used "Son of Man" in affirming their belief about Jesus' person.

New Testament scholars have argued for more than a century over the meaning of this title, whether it even was a title, and of whom Jesus was speaking when he used the title (or term).[54] Whether or not he used it as a title, I am con-

---

[51]I. Howard Marshall, "The Development of Christology in the Early Church," *Tyndale Bulletin* 18 (1967): 83ff.

[52]Werner Kramer, quoted in Marshall, "Development of Christology," p. 85. Marshall adds that the combination of sending and sonship language used to describe Jesus "shows sufficiently that the idea of preexistence was already present in the pre-Pauline church."

[53]Marshall, "Development of Christology," p. 79.

[54]Hurtado says, "In an important sense of the word, 'the son of man' is not a *title*. That is, it does not designate an office or figure previously established and identified by this expression in the speech patterns of pre-Christian Jewish circles/traditions. Nevertheless, in the canonical Gospels the expression is obviously a fixed, formulaic construction with a specific, indeed exclusive, reference" (*Lord Jesus Christ,* p. 305).

vinced Jesus was speaking of himself, and Son of Man was a term whose implications went well beyond its surface meaning. It was not an expression of Jesus'
humanity but rather implied his deity. Hamerton-Kelly says "Son of Man" was
not a defined concept in the Judaism of Jesus' day, although it was a recognized
image that included the idea of preexistence.[55] Segal concludes, "There is no
need to postulate a previous title 'son of man' or even outline a complete model
of the figure. The unity could easily have been achieved in applying all the different traditions to Jesus. The title would then emerge later, as a result of the
exegesis." He adds that even though some sort of "son of man" tradition existed
prior to the Gospels, the New Testament was the earliest document to use "son
of man" as a title.[56]

To say the term contained a *clear* claim to preexistence is to say too much.
I believe Jesus used the term precisely because it did not have a clearly defined meaning. Instead, the self-designation was intended to cause Jesus'
hearers to think about who Jesus was without forcing them prematurely to a
particular conclusion. I think the ultimate source of the title is Daniel 7:13.[57]
This vision of Daniel portrays an exalted being who receives from God power
and authority very much like that which the New Testament writers portray
the risen Jesus as receiving. This "one like a son of man" also receives universal worship in a manner reminiscent of Isaiah 45:23 and anticipatory of
Philippians 2:10-11. Moule shares this conclusion that Daniel 7 is the source
of the Son of Man title (not all instances of "son of man" in the Old Testament
are titular). "I am among those who still believe it is Dan. 7 that gives [the
Son of man title], in the Gospel tradition, its decisive colour." He explains one
reason for this is that the Gospels almost always say "the Son of Man," not
"Son of Man."[58]

"Son of Man" also appears in some extrabiblical literature whose date is uncertain. Their portrayal of the Son of Man as preexistent and divine reinforces
Christian teaching, but if the documents are late, they reflect that teaching rather
than serving as sources for it. The term "son of man" appears ninety-three times

---

[55]R. G. Hamerton-Kelly, *Preexistence, Wisdom, and the Son of Man* (Cambridge: Cambridge
University Press, 1973), p. 100. Hamerton-Kelly considers this an ideal rather than a personal
preexistence, however.

[56]Segal, *Two Powers in Heaven,* pp. xi, 204.

[57]Hurtado, however, sees little evidence in first-century Christian sources that Daniel 7:13-14
played the important role often claimed for it, although he acknowledges the Synoptics and
Revelation probably use Daniel as background for their Son of Man language. Hurtado prefers
Psalms 8; 80; and 110 as sources for most New Testament Son of Man language (*Lord Jesus
Christ,* p. 298).

[58]Moule, *Origin of Christology,* pp. 12-13.

in the Old Testament book of Ezekiel where it emphasizes Ezekiel's humanity in contrast to God's majesty and does not serve as a title. While some have argued this same meaning attaches to the term when Jesus uses it, his use of "Son of Man" does not occur in contexts emphasizing his humanity or a sharp distinction from God. The term also appears in Numbers 23:19; Job 25:6; and Psalms 8:4; 144:3, where it emphasizes humanity's frailty and limitations.[59] Psalm 80:17 presents the son of man in a more positive light, but it also points to a humble human origin. None of these verses offers any thought of preexistence of this son of man; such an idea would seem to be among the last things on the authors' minds, and again none uses the term as a title.

Jesus' use of Son of Man was allusive and meant to encourage people to think not only about what he was saying but who was speaking. In terms of its Daniel 7:13 origin, it implied the preexistence and deity of the one spoken of. Alone, this title is probably not sufficient to affirm Jesus Christ's preexistence simply because of its indefinite and allusive nature.

Wisdom. Marshall associates the Old Testament wisdom theme with the Son of God title. The theme of God's wisdom has received increasing attention in recent years, but conclusions have been far from unanimous. Proverbs, the Wisdom of Solomon and Ecclesiasticus describe the wisdom of God in personified language, yet these personifications do not appear to be or to be intended to be persons or hypostases. The language showed some flexibility in pre-Christian Jewish thought about God but never to the extent that it risked compromising monotheism. Dunn says most Jews would have understood wisdom language as "poetical description of divine immanence, of God's self-revelation and interaction with his creation and his people."[60]

In the Gospels, Jesus used wisdom language about himself and his mission, and Paul used similar language in his letters to describe Jesus. The divine wisdom Dunn describes prepared the way for Jesus' use of wisdom themes for himself, but once again Jesus has transformed an Old Testament concept by giving it a content that goes beyond the original without denying the thrust of the original. His language is no longer a poetical description but the actual coming of God to be among his people. Ben Witherington has crafted his christology around this wisdom theme. This has led him to conclude "the pre-existence issue is raised immediately by the use of wisdom material in the hymns to say things about the career of Christ even before his earthly existence. Only by ig-

---

[59]Lamar Eugene Cooper Sr., *Ezekiel,* The New American Commentary 17 (Nashville: Broadman & Holman, 1994), p. 74.
[60]Dunn, *Christology in the Making,* p. xx.

noring this background can one claim one has to bring the pre-existence idea to the text to find it here."[61]

Wisdom unquestionably introduces preexistence into the discussion about Jesus, but the pre-Christian materials do not present us with a personal preexistence, and they do not require the preexistent one be a divine being, but neither do they preclude such conclusions.

Logos. Alone among the Gospels, John set the stage for Jesus' life prior to creation and tells us of the Word (or Logos) who was before creation, was with God and himself possessed all those attributes of God that make God God. John identified this Word with Jesus, who is the Word incarnate.[62] Cullmann says the Logos title expresses an important aspect of New Testament christology; "the unity in historical revelation of the incarnate and the pre-existent Jesus."[63] This Logos language reflects themes found in such Old Testament books as Genesis, Psalms and Isaiah, where God's word is his active and effectual self-communication. Creating and sustaining, the divine word of the Old Testament also executes divine judgment. Guthrie describes this word as "the powerful agency of God."[64] John used Logos language only in his prologue, but he clearly identified the Logos with Jesus and presented the Word as both the personal agent of God and as deity himself, *and* he did so in a monotheistic Jewish setting. Because Logos was such an important concept in Greek philosophy, many have suggested John drew on this source to show the Logos as the universal principle of reason and coherence either in contrast to Jewish ideas or in some combination with those ideas. For Greek thought, however, Logos was always a principle or power, never personal. William Thompson says that while using Logos with at least some Hellenistic flavor would seem to make good sense in communicating the Gospel, there are in fact no Greek parallels to what John said.[65] Barth has suggested the presence of the Logos only in the prologue to John's Gospel means we must interpret the Word in terms of Jesus and not vice versa. If Barth is correct, this significantly relativizes the influence of both pre-Christian Jewish and Greek concepts in understanding Jesus. Logos christology proclaims the

---

[61]Witherington, *Jesus the Sage*, p. 263 n. 56. In saying this, Witherington calls into question the conclusions of such scholars as Dunn and Kuschel. Witherington offers a clear summary of his wisdom christology in his *The Jesus Quest*, chap. 7.

[62]William M. Thompson offers an extended meditation on John's incarnate Word, interpreting John 1:1 as almost explicitly trinitarian, and thus the Word as divine, personal and preexisting (*The Struggle for Theology's Soul* [New York: Crossroad, 1996], pp. 119-39).

[63]Cullmann, *Christology of the New Testament*, p. 258.

[64]Donald Guthrie, *New Testament Theology* (Downers Grove, Ill.: InterVarsity Press, 1981), p. 324.

[65]Thompson, *Struggle for Theology's Soul*, pp. 120-21.

Word's eternal being, so its assumption of preexistence is undeniable.

Some have acknowledged this preexistence of the Logos yet denied Christ's preexistence by rejecting any identity between the Word and Jesus. I believe John 1:14 renders this move illegitimate, however. Maurice Wiles, following G. B. Caird, offers another rationale for denying Christ's preexistence. He does not necessarily reject an identification of the Word with Christ but contends, "neither the Fourth Gospel nor Hebrews ever speaks of the eternal Word or Wisdom of God in terms which compel us to regard it as a person." It is our reading of the New Testament through Pauline spectacles that leads us to see personhood here (I assume "eternal Word" admits pre existence) because only Paul among New Testament writers affirms belief in the personal preexistence of Christ.[66] Thompson argues that while Old Testament wisdom literature does not teach a personal Wisdom, this is the very point at which it falls short of the Johannine prologue.[67] At issue here is the extent to which the New Testament goes beyond the Old while remaining in essential continuity with it.

Lord. The final christological title I will consider is "Lord" (or *kyrios*). In the Greek of Jesus' day, this word could be anything from "sir" to an indirect way of speaking of the biblical God. By and large, the Gospel use of the term is no more than a polite honorific, but Paul's letters speak repeatedly of the Lord Jesus Christ in a way that requires much more. In Philippians 2, every tongue will confess Jesus is Lord. Given the exalted status described for Jesus (and the Old Testament source for the language used), this title intends to say a great deal. Paul described Jesus as Lord in contexts where he presented him as deity. In Isaiah 45:23, the language Paul applied to Jesus (as Lord) in Philippians 2:10-11 was used self-referentially by God. Given that the Bible the New Testament writers used was probably the Septuagint (a Greek translation of the Old Testament), it is significant that this text uses the term *Lord* to speak of God where the Hebrew has YHWH. Martin Hengel has concluded this transference of the divine name to Jesus occurred very soon after his resurrection by way of the *kyrios* title. Contrary to some who have suggested the use of this title for Jesus arose in a late Hellenistic environment, Hengel says:

> To use "Kyrios" in the absolute as a divine title is essentially un-Greek. . . . The title expresses a personal relationship with the deity, which was so important for the oriental. . . . It is quite mysterious how it could have been possible in terms of the his-

---

[66]Maurice Wiles, "Person or Personification? A Patristic Debate About Logos," in *The Glory of Christ in the New Testament: Studies in Christology,* ed. L. D. Hurst and N. T. Wright (Oxford: Oxford University Press, 1987), p. 281. It is unclear how one can read John's prologue and still reach this conclusion.
[67]Thompson, *Struggle for Theology's Soul,* p. 121.

tory of the tradition for Jesus to be identified with a Hellenistic cult deity. The theory that Gentile Christians alone were responsible for this transference is untenable, because there is early evidence for the title, and "pure" Gentile Christianity is a fiction.[68]

The New Testament titles for Jesus can be questioned one by one and objections can be raised to each individually, but the impact of these titles in understanding who Jesus is comes from their mutual reinforcement. The titles often occur together in the letters, and throughout the New Testament we find them in contexts that point us in a clear direction regarding their meaning. When we consider the titles as a group, we find they either teach or presuppose Christ's deity and his preexistence as the Son of God. Further, I believe it is more legitimate to consider the evidence in toto rather than to make each piece stand on its own without reinforcement from other evidence that can be found in close proximity in the text or in the same author.

THE "SENDING STATEMENTS"

Before looking at some other issues preliminary to exegesis of specific texts, I want to consider briefly what have been called the "sending statements." In the New Testament these take either the form "I have come . . ." or "God sent . . ." Whether these statements about Jesus distinguish him qualitatively from other messengers of God is the subject of heated debate. The question is whether the statements by Jesus in the Gospels and about Jesus in the letters differ in quality from those about Old Testament figures and John the Baptist. In the case of Jesus, the context is important—are the sending statements found in conjunction with such titles as "Son" or "Son of God"? Edouard Schweizer makes precisely this point when he writes that the sending statements by themselves contain no intrinsic sense of Christ's preexistence, but because this sending language occurs only in Paul and John (who presuppose Christ's preexistence on other grounds) the sending language probably reflects belief in Christ's preexistence.[69] Approaching the debate from the other direction, Marshall adds that the Son of God title appears in resurrection or sending contexts. The latter, he says, deal with the preexistent Son as Savior.[70] To state the argument in favor of understanding "sending statements" in terms of Christ's preexistence, "God sent his son into the world" has a different flavor to it than "John the Baptist came . . ." has. DeJonge concludes that both Paul and John regarded the unique rela-

---

[68]Martin Hengel, *The Son of God* (Philadelphia: Fortress, 1976), p. 78.

[69]Eduard Schweizer, "The Sending of the Preexistent Son of God," *Theological Dictionary of the New Testament* (Grand Rapids: Eerdmans, 1971), 8:375.

[70]Marshall, "Development of Christology," p. 85.

tionship between God and the Son to have existed before the Son was sent on his mission. He is unsure what conclusions we can draw from Mark.[71]

The argument against seeing the New Testament sending statements as expressing Christ's preexistence have in common their claim that the language about Jesus is no different in kind from that used of the prophets. They rightly point out Old and New Testament passages speaking about God having sent individuals without any implication beyond the messenger's or prophet's source of authority. There is no indication of place of origin in Psalm 105:26, Jeremiah 1:5, Micah 6:4, Luke 4:25 or 20:13. Fuller makes this clear in his conclusion: "Their intention is not to speculate about the Redeemer's preexistence, but to assert the historical mission of Jesus rests on the divine initiative."[72] With his focus on functional christology, I believe Fuller misses the intent of the New Testament authors. Schweizer compares the New Testament sending statements with statements about Old Testament prophets, angels and John the Baptist.

While it is true that the Old Testament uses sending language in reference to angels and prophets, it never describes those sent as God's sons.[73] John 1:6 speaks of John the Baptist being a man sent from God, and this is consistent with the objection, but John is a *man* sent from God in this pericope whereas Jesus is the Word or light who came into the world. The context places John and Jesus on quite different levels. The Old Testament describes prophets as messengers sent by God, but these prophets were never described as sons of God. In every case, the prophets proclaimed, "The word of the Lord came to me." Jesus never spoke this way; in fact, the evangelists report the people's amazement because Jesus spoke with authority—his own authority.

Markus Bockmuehl says Jesus did not normally discuss his heavenly preexistence, but occasionally he did so in a veiled way, using the language of being sent or having come for some particular purpose.[74] So, for Bockmuehl, the sending statements appear at least some of the time to be statements about Christ's preexistence. Werner Kramer also thinks the sending statements presuppose Christ's preexistence. He adds that this language offers an insight into the pre-Pauline understanding of the Son of God term, which he sees as *initially* having a functional sense. Emil Brunner concludes that the sending language distinguished Jesus qualitatively from the prophets: he spoke of his own coming in a

[71]Martinus DeJonge, *God's Final Envoy* (Philadelphia: Westminster Press, 1988), p. 118.
[72]Fuller, *Foundations of New Testament Christology*, pp. 194-95.
[73]Gerald O'Collins, *Christology: A Biblical, Historical and Systematic Study of Jesus Christ* (New York: Oxford University Press, 1995), p. 128.
[74]Bockmuehl, *This Jesus*, p. 53.

way no prophet had ever done: "I am come," he said, "to call sinners to repentance." The Son of Man "is come" not to be ministered unto but to minister. No
prophet said that *he* had "come"; prophets said that the Word of God has "come"
to them.[75]

Like the christological titles, the sending statements cannot be viewed in isolation. The context of each sending statement is crucial. The prophets of the Old
Testament were messengers sent from God, but Jesus is the *Son* sent from God.
God's word comes to the prophets; Jesus is God's Word come into the world.
The sending statements in isolation do not prove Christ's preexistence. In conjunction with the christological titles and other material, however, they provide
powerful evidence for his preexistence. Once again, the proper method for examining this evidence is not to look at each piece in isolation but to seek the
cumulative weight of the different pieces as they reinforce or counter each
other, just as we do in other disciplines.

RESURRECTION AND PREEXISTENCE

Some who have questioned the classic teaching of Christ's preexistence have
drawn a connection between preexistence and resurrection. They have suggested that somehow the early church hit upon the idea of preexistence in an
attempt to relocate Jesus' significance from postresurrection to before his birth,
thus making him a more imposing figure in contemporary terms. This emphasis
on the resurrection is important, but this is because it validates claims about
who Jesus Christ is and what he came to accomplish, and, in conjunction with
the ascension, it completes the cycle from preexistence through incarnation and
death to resurrection and return to heavenly glory.

The second concern about the place of the resurrection in this discussion
seems to be an expectation that we can and should look at the person of Jesus
in terms of his earthly life apart from any reference to the resurrection. This suggestion is fraught with danger because apart from the resurrection Jesus was no
more than a failed prophet and teacher. Without the resurrection, it is certain
his disciples would have returned to their fishing and other occupations, and
there never would have been a church. Nor would there have been any concern
about preexistence.

Jesus' resurrection was a worldview-shattering event. Not only did it call
into question every materialist understanding of reality, it also forced a new
understanding of all Old Testament prophecies that pointed to Jesus and the

---

[75]Emil Brunner, *The Christian Doctrine of Creation and Redemption: Dogmatics,* trans. Olive
Wyon (Philadelphia: Westminster Press, 1952), 2:350.

terminology associated with them. Nils Dahl says Jesus' life, death and resurrection changed the way we may speak about God, his Messiah and his relation to the world.[76] We cannot go back and act as if the resurrection never happened, because it is the constitutive event of Christian history. To bracket it artificially is fruitless because doing so takes away precisely that which is the key to understanding everything else about Jesus, including his preexistence. The question should not be, How can we understand Jesus apart from the resurrection? but, Why should we seek such an interpretation in the first place?

Something that will be evident in the Pauline material is that discussion of Christ's preexistence is not the focus of the texts but appears instead to be a generally accepted presupposition Paul used to make some other point, usually of Christian practice. Philippians 2:6-11 is probably the best example of this. It is significant that the earliest statements of Christ's preexistence assume its truth in order to make some other point on the basis of the readers' prior acceptance of the truth of preexistence. It is not only important that this is so, but that it is for Paul rather than for John that it is so. What this means, assuming my interpretation of Paul's letters is correct, is that belief in Christ's preexistence was in his personal preexistence, and this belief was early and widespread. It is also significant that while Paul was attacked for many things he said and did, none of his opponents is on record as objecting to any aspect of his christology, a christology that has Christ's preexistence as one of its essential premises.

OLD TESTAMENT BACKGROUND

Before examining the specific New Testament texts that appear to deal with Christ's preexistence, some general comments about the Old Testament context are necessary. We find there an understanding of the nature of God, God's relationship to creation (and especially to humanity), and divine grace that is important in understanding how the early church could come to believe Jesus Christ preexisted his earthly life as the Son of God. Although there is no unanimity among scholars on the subject, it appears the pre-Christian Jewish understanding of God had become much more complex than is popularly be-

---

[76]"Very important rules for christological language were given in the Scripture Christians received from the Jews. Yet the life, death, and resurrection of Jesus changed the rules. Whatever was said about God, or about the world and human existence in it, about sin and salvation, ethical conduct and matters of church, had to be related to Jesus in some way, or at least not contradict the rule of faith in Jesus Christ" (Nils Dahl, *Jesus the Christ,* ed. Donald H. Juel [Minneapolis: Fortress, 1991], p. 133).

lieved without repudiating Old Testament monotheism.[77] Evidence for this
includes the mysterious angel of the Lord who appeared to many Old Testament figures, the visitor to Abraham in Genesis 18, the wisdom passages of
Proverbs and the Old Testament Apocrypha, the one like a son of man of
Daniel 7:13, and even the servant of the Lord of Isaiah. Patristic exegetes understood all these as manifestations of the preincarnate Christ. Extrabiblical material includes various entities considered preexistent (in an ideal sense), a vigorous angelology and speculation about such Old Testament personages as
Enoch, Moses and Elijah.

The Old Testament presents God not only as creating but as actively loving
his creation. When the humans who comprise the crowning glory of that creation turned away in rebellion, God pursued and sought to reclaim his rebellious creatures. Nowhere is this more powerfully presented in the Old Testament than in the prophet Hosea. Isaiah also offers a hint of how much God is
willing to suffer to redeem his fallen and rebellious creatures. And, of course,
the protoevangelium of Genesis 3:15 provides a veiled hint whose scope only
becomes apparent long afterward. What is everywhere clear is that God's concern for his creation is the product not of his need but of his love. What we see
vaguely in the Old Testament becomes clear in the New, and there the teaching
of Christ's preexistence is no small part of the picture of God's love.

The popular image of God in the Old Testament is that of wrathful judge.
This is contrasted with the merciful God of the New Testament. Some heretics
of the first centuries of the church took this caricature so far that they transformed the biblical God into two antagonistic gods. Any serious reading of the
Bible, however, shows the God of both Testaments to be the same God with
the same character. Divine grace is no less evident in the Old than in the New.
The way God showed this grace is different, as is its finality in the New, but in
the Old Testament God called a covenant people whom he redeemed and sanc-
tified as his own. He did not choose these people because they were especially
good or religious; he chose them despite their lack of positive qualities (Deut

---

[77]Jewish concepts of God during the two centuries prior to the destruction of the temple in A.D.
70 seem to have been more flexible than they have been since that time, when God has been
conceived in a strictly unitary sense. Some have suggested this was a response to the growth
and development of the young Christian movement. Blomberg explains that "Larry Hurtado
has demonstrated that the monotheism of first century Judaism allowed for divinity within the
unity of the Godhead in ways that later forms of Judaism did not" (Blomberg, *Historical Reliability*, p. 73). In a later work Hurtado writes, "As has become clearer in recent decades of
scholarly study, the religion of ancient Israel had not always manifested the monotheistic emphasis that was so familiar a feature of Jewish religious teaching and practice by the Roman
era (*Lord Jesus Christ*, p. 29).

9:5-6). Again and again he pulled these people of Israel out of the mess they always seemed to get themselves into. In the New Testament these realities are no less evident in God's dealing with his new covenant people. In fact, the doctrine of Christ's preexistence shows God has taken one very large additional step. Whereas in the Old Testament he repeatedly sent messengers to warn his people, in the New he came himself. When it came time for the most dangerous and difficult task, God did not delegate, he did it himself. That is what the Gospel message that God so loved the world that he sent his Son to be its Savior is all about. Only with a doctrine of preexistence can we affirm this powerful expression of God's love.

CONCLUSION

This survey of biblical thinking about Christ and his preexistence has been necessary, but it is not sufficient. We must go beyond comments about the biblical witness to examine text by text what the Bible itself says about Christ's preexistence. The conflict with Arianism in the fourth century, however, showed the preliminaries are no less necessary than the biblical exegesis. Both sides in that conflict cited Scripture to support their cases. Interestingly, Christ's preexistence was not at issue (both sides readily accepted that), but the conflict revolved around who this one was who could be called the Christ. In other words, who was it who was preexistent and what was the duration of his preexistence? The orthodox party was forced to use Hellenistic language to refute the Hellenistic thought of the Arian party and preserve the biblical worldview.

3

PAUL'S WRITINGS

Apart from James, who did not discuss christology, the earliest books of the New Testament were Paul's letters. Comprising half the New Testament documents, these letters responded to problems in local congregations; they are not treatises in systematic theology. Nonetheless, they are deeply theological. Combining what we now call systematic theology and practical theology, Paul's letters provide clear direction for Christian behavior based on Christian belief (or occasionally Christian belief based on the work of Christ). It is in this context that we find Paul alluding to Christ's preexistence in at least seven of his letters. No less than four—Romans, 1 Corinthians, Galatians and Philippians—speak in terms of Christ's *divine* preexistence (meaning not only that the one born on the first Christmas really existed before that birth, but that he existed as God the Son).[1] Hurtado says, "The overwhelming majority of scholars in the field agree that there are at least a few passages in Paul's undisputed letters that reflect and presuppose the idea of Jesus' pre-existence."[2]

BACKGROUND

One value of Paul's letters is that they date from only twenty to thirty-five years after Jesus' death and appear in some cases to contain even earlier material. Paul's is generally considered a very high christology, affirming in multiple ways Jesus' deity, so this early date is significant. It debunks to the evolutionary interpretation of christology that claims Christian thought began with a good man, Jesus, who slowly came to be considered something more than a human. If Paul,

---

[1]Gerald O'Collins, *Interpreting Jesus* (Ramsey, N.J.: Paulist Press, 1983), p. 16. O'Collins is emphasizing that the Son of God not only preexisted his incarnation, but that in his preexistent state he was deity. His term "divine preexistence" encompasses both the personal preexistence of Christ prior to the incarnation and his eternal preexistence as the second person of the Trinity.
[2]Larry W. Hurtado, *Lord Jesus Christ* (Grand Rapids: Eerdmans, 2003), p. 119. He lists Phil 2:6-11; 1 Cor 8:6; 10:4; 15:47; 2 Cor 8:9; Gal 4:4; Rom 8:3.

writing as the earliest of the New Testament authors, offers as high a christology
as John, who wrote at the end, then apparently low christologies in other authors
need to be explained on other grounds (or the mentality that sees these christologies as low needs to be reconsidered).[3] Paul's contribution to the New Testament probably began about the year A.D. 48 with his letter to the churches in
Galatia and ended some eighteen years later with the Pastoral Letters.

Paul wrote as a Jew, a devout Jew, who had become convinced Jesus was
the Messiah and much more. He emphasized his zeal to preserve Jewish tradition, faithful observance of the law and life as a devout Pharisee. In Acts, Luke
reports Paul's training in Jewish law under Gamaliel in Jerusalem. Paul's conversion occurred during a trip from Jerusalem to Damascus to persecute Jews who
were proclaiming Jesus as Messiah. Although he came from a city in Asia Minor
and was a Roman citizen, it seems the formative influence in Paul's life was traditional Judaism, not Hellenism. Despite the claim Paul was the founder of
Christianity, creating a religious story around an obscure Jewish carpenter, both
chronology and context support Paul's claim that his message was that of Jesus'
original disciples. Martin Hengel describes Paul's christology thus:

> Paul's conception of the son of God, which was certainly not his own creation but
> goes back to earlier community tradition before Paul's letters, thus proves to be
> quite unique. Jesus, the recently crucified Jew . . . is not only the Messiah whom
> God has raised from the dead, but much more. He is identical with a divine being,
> before all time, mediator between God and his creatures.[4]

In his letters Paul barely mentioned Jesus' birth and earthly ministry; he focused instead on Jesus' death and resurrection. These letters unite doctrine and
practice in a way that demonstrates their intimate connection, and shows theology is not an abstract, intellectual pursuit. Nowhere is this more evident than in
his mention of Christ's preexistence. Vincent Taylor calls Paul's ascription of
preexistence to Jesus more significant than the titles he used to describe Jesus
or the functions he attributed to him.[5] Kittel considers Paul's preexistence statements a constituent part of his theology that simply tries to explain what underlies the obvious reality of Jesus Christ. Because Paul's preexistence language al-

---

[3] A high christology is one that teaches Jesus Christ's deity. Orthodox versions such as those found in the Apostles' and Nicene creeds also teach his full humanity. A low christology presents Jesus as a good man, even a spirit-filled man, but no more, who possibly was adopted as God's son during his life or after his death. The Ebionites of the early church and some liberal Protestants have taught such a human Jesus.
[4] Martin Hengel, *The Son of God* (Philadelphia: Fortress, 1976), p. 15.
[5] Vincent Taylor, *The Person of Christ in New Testament Teaching* (London: Macmillan, 1958), p. 53.

ways occurred in the context of explaining something of practical importance to early Christians, Kittel concludes, "It is thus plain that for Paul awareness of the pre-existence of Jesus Christ is a much deeper thing than the statements alone might suggest."[6] For Seyoon Kim, preexistence is "an essential element in Paul's Son-Christology." Kim grounds this belief along with Christ's mediatorship and sending in Paul's Damascus road experience.[7] Herman Ridderbos calls Paul's description of Christ's preexistence unreserved and says Paul considered the teaching "one of the most fundamental and indispensable parts of the faith of the church."[8]

These New Testament specialists could say these things because when Paul discussed preexistence, he never attempted to persuade his readers to accept this doctrine and he never made it the focus of his teaching. He appears to have assumed his readers both understood and accepted the doctrine. Given that Paul wrote only about two decades after Jesus' death, this is extremely significant.[9] If within twenty-five years of Jesus' death, Paul could assume readers of his letters both understood and accepted Christ's preexistence, then the teaching must have arisen very early in the church's history.[10] Goeffrey Lampe, no advocate of orthodox christology, expressed his astonishment at this situation, saying:

The most remarkable fact about the historical Jesus is demonstrably true: that the

---

[6]Gerhard Kittel, "The Distinctiveness of the *Logos* Sayings in Jn 1:1," *Theological Dictionary of the New Testament*, ed. Gerhard Kittel, trans. Geoffrey W. Bromiley (Grand Rapids: Eerdmans, 1967), 4:130.

[7]Seyoon Kim, *The Origin of Paul's Gospel,* 2nd ed. (Tübingen: J. C. B. Mohr, 1984), pp. 111, 114.

[8]Herman Ridderbos, *Paul,* trans. John Richard DeWitt (Grand Rapids: Eerdmans, 1975), pp. 70-71.

[9]John Knox, who rejects the personal preexistence of Christ, writes, "Every allusion [to preexistence] is such as to suggest that Paul is dealing with an idea both familiar and indubitable. The preexistence is taken for granted, needing no emphasis, elaboration, or proof. Paul's references to it are almost casual in manner, usually hints rather than explicit affirmations" (*Jesus Lord and Christ* [New York: Harper & Brothers, 1958], pp. 150-51). H. R. Mackintosh agrees preexistence appears in Paul "incidentally," but says this means "preexistence was an idea so familiar to Christians as to require no explanation or apology" (*The Doctrine of the Person of Christ,* 2nd ed. [Edinburgh: T & T Clark, 1913], p. 66). Thomas Oden writes that allusions to Christ's preexistence "are not presented with baroque flourish or as if they were an elaborated extension added later as a result of subsequent reflection. The attestation is attended with no speculative details or mythic ornamentations but rather presented as an element of faith presumably shared by all who proclaim the gospel of God" (*The Word of Life: Systematic Theology* [San Francisco: Harper & Row, 1989], 2:69).

[10]If this were not the case, Paul's failure to define and defend his belief would be incomprehensible. Gordon Fee concurs, saying, "Although Pauline theology must first of all be based on *explicit* theological data, one must also pay close attention to what is *presuppositional* for Paul, to which, because it is presupposed by both himself and his readers, he can refer without the need of full explanation." Fee includes Christ's preexistence within the presuppositional. (See Gordon D. Fee, "St. Paul and the Incarnation: A Reassessment of the Data," in *The Incarnation,* ed. Stephen T. Davis et al. [Oxford: Oxford University Press, 2002], p. 65.)

earliest Christian documents show that within an astonishingly short time after his death Jesus of Nazareth was being interpreted by Jewish monotheists as well as Gentile converts as a pre-existent divine being, Son of God, not simply in the sense of Ps. 2:7 as God's agent for the establishment of his Kingdom, but in a sense approaching that of "God the Son" of later orthodoxy, to whom prayer is addressed and whom believers expect to come from heaven in divine glory.[11]

A recent collection of essays titled *Where Christology Began* was devoted to modern interpretations of the hymn in Philippians 2.[12] Because these six verses have been among the most influential in the Christian church's understanding of Jesus and are some of the earliest explicit words about the person of Jesus Christ, I begin my examination of Paul's teaching about Christ's preexistence there.

PHILIPPIANS 2:5-11

Your attitude should be the same as that of Christ Jesus:
Who being in very nature God,
    did not consider equality with God something to be grasped,
but made himself nothing,
    taking the very nature of a servant,
    being made in human likeness.
And being found in appearance as a man,
    he humbled himself
    and became obedient to death—
        even death on a cross!
Therefore God exalted him to the highest place
    and gave him the name that is above every name,
that at the name of Jesus every knee should bow,
    in heaven and on earth and under the earth,
and every tongue confess that Jesus Christ is Lord,
    to the glory of God the Father.

Lincoln Hurst calls this passage "one of the most disputed passages in the history of New Testament interpretation."[13] No less true, a person's theological pre-

---

[11]G. W. H. Lampe, "The Holy Spirit and the Person of Christ," in *Christ, Faith and History,* ed. S. W. Sykes and J. P. Clayton (Cambridge: Cambridge University Press, 1972), p. 118. This comment is all the more significant because Lampe was no supporter of traditional christology.

[12]Ralph P. Martin and Brian J. Dodd, eds., *Where Christology Began* (Louisville: Westminster John Knox, 1998).

[13]Lincoln D. Hurst, "Christ, Adam, and Preexistence Revisited," in *Where Christology Began,* ed. Ralph P. Martin and Brian J. Dodd (Louisville: Westminster John Knox, 1998), p. 84.

suppositions appear to drive his or her interpretation of the text rather than the reverse. The first thing to note about this passage, however, is that Paul intended it pastorally, not as a piece of systematic theology. This is evident from verse 5. Nevertheless, this is the key Pauline text regarding Christ's preexistence, even if its focus is on Christ's salvific work, not his preexistence. Paul was exhorting his readers to follow Christ's example of humility and self-sacrifice in their relationships with each other. Preexistence comes into play because the incarnation of the preexistent Son of God into human history in order to save sinful humanity was the greatest example of selflessness Paul could conceive. As an argument from Christ's greater act to the readers' lesser imitation, it draws its power from presenting Christ as God's preexistent Son. Fee puts the case clearly: "What is being urged upon the Philippians is not a new view of Jesus, but a reinforcement, on the basis of Paul's view of the crucifixion, that in the cross God's true character, his outlandish, lavish expression of love, was fully manifested."[14]

Because of their importance for understanding Paul's thinking about Christ's preexistence, these verses have become the subject of heated debate. That it at least appears to teach Christ's preexistence is generally accepted, even by those who deny this is the case. If, as some have suggested, the hymn predates Paul's use in this letter, belief in Christ's preexistence was widespread in the first Christian generation.[15]

Dunn, however, says the common belief that this passage is about Christ's preexistence is a presupposition brought to the text, not a conclusion derived from it.[16] He admits the passage "certainly seems on the face of it to be a straightforward statement contrasting Christ's preexistent glory and postcrucifixion exaltation with his earthly humiliation," but concludes, "It seems to me that Phil. 2.6-11 is best understood as an expression of Adam Christology."[17] In his

---

[14]Gordon D. Fee, *Paul's Letter to the Philippians,* New International Commentary on the New Testament (Grand Rapids: Eerdmans, 1995), p. 208.

[15]Hurtado says, "We would be very grateful if Paul had elaborated the idea of Christ's preexistence, but this sort of passing reference to it is in fact very important for historical purposes. It indicates that the idea had already become disseminated among his churches so early that by the time he wrote his epistles he could take it for granted as known" (*Lord Jesus Christ,* p. 124).

[16]James D. G. Dunn, *Christology in the Making* (Philadelphia: Westminster Press, 1980), p. 114.

[17]Ibid. David Brown objects that if Paul had intended a reference to Adam, he would have made it explicit (as he did elsewhere) and would have clarified the choice essential to Dunn's argument (*The Divine Trinity* [LaSalle, Ill.: Open Court, 1985], p. 156). Donald Guthrie agrees, saying the hymn makes perfectly good sense without an Adam motif, and adds, "In the absence of any specific reference to Adam, it seems best not to include it in this section of Paul's Christology" (*New Testament Theology* [Downers Grove, Ill.: InterVarsity Press, 1981], p. 338). Hurtado says Dunn's claim that Phil 2:6-8 is simply an Adam christology "greatly exceeds the warrants of the passage" and adds that he thinks Dunn sees too much Adam christology in Paul's letters in general (*Lord Jesus Christ,* p. 121).

introduction to the second edition of *Christology in the Making,* Dunn describes the presence of preexistence in the passage as an open question and a distraction from the point of the hymn.[18] The majority of Dunn's New Testament colleagues disagree. If the issue here is presuppositions, it is Dunn's presuppositions. Further, the logical conclusion of Dunn's position would appear to be some form of adoptionism (a position Dunn rejects).[19] Yet Wolfhart Pannenberg thinks the purpose of this hymn was precisely to rule out any adoptionist interpretation of Christ's exaltation.[20] Feinberg adds bluntly, *"Phil 2:6-11 precludes an adoptionist christology."*[21] If Pannenberg and Feinberg are correct, then Dunn's exegesis and theology are inconsistent.

How we interpret this hymn depends on our interpretation of two key terms: *morphē* and *harpagmos*. Deriving from this are several additional questions about the passage's structure and terminology. If, as appears to be the case, the ordering of the hymn is chronological, what is the starting point? Is it heavenly or earthly? An Adam christology would describe it as earthly. Second, does the term translated nature or form *(morphē)* mean "appearance" or "essence"? Third, what does the second line mean about not grasping at equality with God? These questions are related, and how we answer one will affect our answer to the others. What is certain, however, is how the passage ends. This Jesus who humbled himself unto death was exalted by God to the highest level and received the homage that in Isaiah 45:23 God reserves to himself alone. This too must influence our conclusion about the place preexistence holds in this passage. I am convinced the hymn's language requires acceptance of Christ's personal preexistence and that this conclusion is consistent with Paul's other christological language.

The traditional reading of this passage takes a descending-ascending form. The hymn begins with the one we know as Jesus in the heavenly realm, describes his descent to earth and his crucifixion, and concludes with his return to heaven and homage from the entire creation. Ralph Martin describes the passage as "one of the finest Christological portions of the New Testament" that

---

[18]Dunn, *Christology in the Making,* p. xix. Dunn has been sharply criticized for his exegesis of this passage. I will discuss Dunn and his critics in chap. 9.

[19]I believe this is evident from John Robinson's endorsement of Dunn's position (Robinson's was an adoptionist christology): "I have long interpreted Philippians 2 along the same lines [Dunn] does, as telling not of a divine being become man but of a man whose entire being was 'shaped' by God" (*The Priority of John,* ed. J. F. Coakley [London: SCM Press, 1985], p. 383).

[20]Wolfhart Pannenberg, *Systematic Theology,* trans. Geoffrey W. Bromiley (Grand Rapids: Eerdmans, 1994), 2:377.

[21]Paul D. Feinberg, "The Kenosis and Christology: An Exegetical-Theological Analysis of Phil. 2:6-11," *Trinity Journal,* no. 1 (1988): 45.

"powerfully portrays the drama of Christ's pre-temporal glory with the Father, His abasement and obedience upon earth . . . and his exaltation to God's presence."[22] This interpretation makes the best sense of Paul's words and underlies the church's later two-nature christology: "It looks as if Phil. ii. 6 depicts the very earliest beginnings of that Christian cosmic Christology which came to full maturity in later literature."[23] Fred Craddock describes the passage as "a rehearsal of the Christ story in three movements. . . . To say that Christ pre-existed, was with God prior to life on earth, is not uncommon in the New Testament," but moderns have trouble with these passages because the concept is alien to them.[24] The passage itself does not say this explicitly; the justification for this reading comes from how Paul described the one who experienced this descent and ascent, what Paul said about Jesus in the remainder of the letter, and Paul's general christology. Although Bultmann identified the subject of this hymn with the dying-rising savior of the mystery religions and a Gnostic heavenly redeemer, this is not supported by the evidence.[25]

The question of the starting point of this hymn is linked to the description of the hymn's subject. The hymn describes him first as being in the *morphē* of God and then says he made himself nothing (or emptied himself), and took the *morphē* of a human. It is clear that the meaning of the passage depends on the meaning of *morphē*. Although my defense of the interpretation that Paul was saying God the Son humbled himself by becoming incarnate must await further discussion of the meaning of *morphē*, whatever status the subject enjoyed before his humiliation must have been sufficiently greater than his existence in the human condition that Paul could describe the change as humbling. Some modern critics reject this idea that one individual can be both human and divine as incoherent. Philippians does not argue the matter, it simply sets out the two aspects of Jesus' career and affirms both without comment.

The term *morphē*, which appears twice in the first half of this passage, has been understood in two sharply different ways. That the word appears only twice and in different settings makes determining its meaning more complicated: the two places *morphē* appears are so close together it seems certain one meaning must apply to both. Traditionally, *morphē* has been understood to

---

[22]Ralph P. Martin, *Worship in the Early Church* (Grand Rapids: Eerdmans, 1974), p. 49.

[23]Ralph P. Martin, *Carmen Christi,* 2nd ed. (Cambridge: Cambridge University Press, 1983), pp. 106, 318. See also I. Howard Marshall, *The Origins of New Testament Christology* (Downers Grove, Ill.: InterVarsity Press, 1976), p. 107.

[24]Fred B. Craddock, *Philippians*, Interpretation (Atlanta: John Knox, 1985), p. 40.

[25]See Peter T. O'Brien, *The Epistle to the Philippians* (Grand Rapids: Eerdmans, 1991), pp. 193-94. Since Bultmann wrote, scholars have concluded Gnosticism postdates Christ's earthly life.

mean status, essence or nature. *Morphē* denotes not a superficial or illusory appearance but an essential shape or character.[26] According to O'Brien, *morphē* refers to the "form which truly and fully expresses the being which underlies it."[27] This would make the hymn first speak of its subject as possessing the divine nature and then the nature of a servant, which the hymn associates with humanity. As Witherington notes, the hymn's subject chose to take on human flesh, "a choice only a pre-existent one could make."[28] Fee points out that Paul wrote Christ came in the likeness *(homoiōma)* of humans "because on the one hand he has fully identified with us, and because on the other hand in becoming human he was not only human. He was God living out a truly human life, all of which is safeguarded by this expression."[29]

Understanding *morphē* as status makes good sense in both verses, yet biblically the only one who can enjoy the status of God is God himself. The transition from divine status to that of a servant or slave is a significant humbling. This interpretation fits neatly with the descent-ascent understanding of the passage that includes preexistence. With any other interpretation, the beginning of verse 8 merely repeats verse seven. For Wright, the passage requires we understand it to mean the one who became Jesus was from all eternity equal with God. Thus the choice of 2:6-7 was that of "the pre-existent one . . . to be obedient to the saving purpose of the Father by becoming human and dying on a cross."[30]

The second interpretation is consistent with an Adam christology and does not require preexistence.[31] Drawing on Genesis 1, it understands *morphē* to mean "image" and says that, like Adam, the subject of the hymn possessed the image of God, and thus was fully human in the way God intended humans to be. The subject accepted the image of a servant or that of fallen humanity even though there was no need for him to do so. Given Paul's teaching on the effect

[26]O. C. Quick, *Doctrines of the Church* (London: Nisbet, 1938), p. 81. He says this means Christ was from the beginning a divine person.
[27]O'Brien, *Philippians*, pp. 210-11. He adds *en morphē theou* should be understood in terms of God's glory, which means more than his external appearance.
[28]Ben Witherington III, *Jesus the Sage* (Minneapolis: Fortress, 1994), p. 263.
[29]Fee, "St. Paul and the Incarnation," p. 83.
[30]N. T. Wright, *The Climax of the Covenant* (Edinburgh: T & T Clark, 1991), pp. 94-95.
[31]Seyoon Kim offers an interpretation of Philippians 2:6-11 and Colossians 1:15-20 that includes both a preexistent Christ and a contrast with a disobedient Adam (*Origin of Paul's Gospel*, p. 265). Wright agrees Adam and incarnational christology need not be incompatible (*Climax of the Covenant*, p. 59). A. T. Hanson, however, describes Dunn's Adam christology as fundamentally flawed (*The Image of the Invisible God* [London: SCM Press, 1982], pp. 64-65). See also L. D. Hurst, "Re-enter the Preexistent Christ in Philippians 2:5-11?" *New Testament Studies* 32 (1986): 453-54. O'Neill says flatly that 2:7 rules out any attempt to read the passage as a replay of Adam's story (J. C. O'Neill, *Who Did Jesus Think He Was?* [Leiden: E. J. Brill, 1995], p. 19 n. 33).

of Adam's sin, however, the question is why he did not necessarily share the same fallen estate as every other human—why was there any choice? Dunn answers this question in terms of my third question. Jesus began in the same state and faced the same choice as did Adam, but rather than grasping for equality with God (as Adam did), he chose to empty himself of Adam's glory and accept Adam's fate, the punishment Adam had received for his disobedience.[32] Because the second Adam is merely human, this interpretation raises soteriological questions. Can he be exalted in the way the subject of this hymn is? Of what value is the crucifixion of a second Adam? How can this picture of Christ's salvific work be accommodated to Romans and Galatians? Paul is not particularly known for his references to Jesus' earthly ministry, so why would he emphasize them here?

What Paul meant by saying that Christ "did not consider equality with God something to be grasped [harpagmos]" has been as hotly debated as the meaning of morphē. Earlier, I pointed out the importance of verse five to understanding this passage. Nowhere does this seem truer than in interpreting harpagmos. The opening verses of Philippians 2 are about placing others' welfare above our own, apparently a problem in the Philippian church, and end with verse 5 offering Jesus as our model for living. Paul was saying, Don't think so much about what you want to get; think instead about what you can give—and in all this let Jesus be your example. He was giving, not grasping.

As we look to the verses preceding the hymn, we should not forget the verses that conclude the hymn. They speak of the great reward the subject of the hymn received for his actions in the opening verses of the hymn. That reward was not given because he did merely what was required of him. That too must be factored in to our interpretive conclusion.

The debate has been about whether harpagmos involves a grasping for something that does not properly belong to the individual (as in Adam's grasping after equality with God) or whether it means not holding on to something one has every right to (as in Christ's giving up the glory of deity in order to assume human existence).[33] A significant reason for the disagreement about how to interpret harpagmos is that the word appears only once in the New Testament and infrequently in extrabiblical Greek. How we understand the word will reflect our understanding of who Jesus is. If Jesus is the incarnate Son of God, then he had no need to grasp after equality with God; it was his by nature and right. If

---

[32]Dunn, *Christology in the Making*, p. 117.
[33]O'Brien says of the debate, "much has been written without any consensus being reached as to its meaning." See O'Brien, *Epistle to the Philippians*, p. 211.

Jesus was no more than a great prophet or teacher, then to have sought such equality would have been to seek what was not properly his. If the latter is correct, what is meritorious about the subject's behavior? Whatever is involved in this grasping and the alternative chosen must be sufficient to justify the conclusion of the hymn and Paul's decision to use the hymn to illustrate his point.

Roy Hoover says the translation both appropriate to Philippians and consistent with contemporary literature is, "He did not regard being equal with God as something to take advantage of." He adds that in every case he found *harpagmos* "refers to something already present and at one's disposal. The question in such instances is not whether or not one possesses something, but whether one chooses to exploit something."[34] Narrowly conceived, verses 6 and 7 can present one who existed in the divine image but did not use this as a reason for seeking to be equal with God; instead, he chose to live under the penalty imposed on his predecessor who had sought equality with God. This interpretation is consistent up to this point, but when we consider the entire hymn Dunn is right—it really does look like the author is talking about preexistence. Dunn's rejection of this conclusion remains unconvincing. Bauckham, who believes the passage clearly identifies Christ with God, says the issue is not whether Christ gains, retains or does not seek equality with God: "he has equality with God and there is no question of losing it; the issue is his attitude to it."[35]

The final criterion for any interpretation of this hymn must be Paul's words of introduction.[36] What attitude was he calling on the Philippian believers to emulate? Was he merely telling them not to reach for what was not theirs and be content with what they had? Or was he calling on them to be selflessly ready to surrender what they could properly lay claim to for the sake of others? In light of the first paragraph of Philippians 2, I see no option but to read the hymn as presenting Jesus Christ as one who acted selflessly on behalf of others when he could have used his divine status for his own benefit.[37] Fee says, "his 'equality with God' found its truest expression when 'he emptied himself.'"[38] This exhortation gets its power from speaking of the preexistent Son who became incar-

---

[34]Roy W. Hoover, "The Harpagmos Enigma: A Philological Solution," *Harvard Theological Review* 64 (1971): 118. Despite general agreement with Hoover's interpretation, O'Brien renders the phrase, "precisely *because* he was in the form of God he did not regard this equality with God as something to be used for his own advantage" (O'Brien, *Philippians,* p. 216).

[35]Richard Bauckham, *God Crucified* (Grand Rapids: Eerdmans, 1998), p. 57.

[36]After completing this chapter in draft, I found Moisés Silva makes the same argument in his commentary *Philippians* (Grand Rapids: Baker, 1992), p. 105.

[37]O'Brien notes that the latter behavior was precisely how the rulers of Paul's day and their deities acted. See his *Philippians,* p. 216.

[38]Gordon D. Fee, *Paul's Letter to the Philippians* (Grand Rapids: Eerdmans, 1995), p. 208.

nate and suffered crucifixion for our benefit at great cost to himself. Anything less strips Paul's exhortation of its power. Philippians 2:6-8 fills out John 3:16 from the perspective of God the Son.

The traditional interpretation of this hymn reads consistently whether or not we bring to it a presupposition of Christ's preexistence; it only requires we not bring a prejudice against the *possibility* of such preexistence. The hymn tells chronologically the story of one who possessed the essence of deity but did not let his divine status interfere with God's salvific plan. Instead, he entered into human existence and suffered the extreme humiliation of being rejected and killed by those he had come to save. For this great selflessness God glorified him by publicly identifying him as deity so he might receive the honor due to God alone. Such a one was necessarily a preexistent person because the Bible nowhere allows for humans to be exalted as deities in their own right, and the Jesus of Philippians 2:6-11 certainly is designated as deity. Attempts to show that the apparent meaning of the passage cannot be the real meaning have been completely unsuccessful. Silva notes that although the passage may not intend an ontological description of Christ, it nonetheless reflects an ontological interpretation of Christ.[39]

SECOND CORINTHIANS 8:9

> For you know the grace of our Lord Jesus Christ, that though he was rich, yet for your sakes he became poor, so that you through his poverty might become rich.

In a passage that looks much like the Philippians 2 hymn, Paul exhorted his readers to demonstrate the sincerity of their love by offering Christ's love as the greater example for them to emulate. To a church he was encouraging to be generous financially toward other Christians in need, Paul wrote of a Jesus who gave up riches for our sake. Yet the earthly Jesus was never rich; he had no earthly riches to give up. That being so, the question becomes when and how was Jesus rich? Further, Paul's injunction has force only if Jesus made a serious sacrifice to achieve our gain; anything less would not make a real impression on his readers. We already have seen evidence that from the earliest days of his ministry Paul believed in Christ's preexistence. For one who is preexistent deity to become human is an enormous sacrifice; identifying oneself with sinful humanity is going from being rich to being impoverished. While it is true that for a human to die for the benefit of others is sacrificial, such sacrifice pales in contrast to such a sacrifice by the Son of God.

---

[39]Silva, *Philippians,* pp. 113, 125. See also Donald Juel, "Incarnation and Redemption: A Response to Reginald H. Fuller," *Semeia* 30 (1985): 118.

Early Christian commentators understood the verse in terms of a condescension that applies only to Christ's humanity. This humiliation had the effect of restoring the true human nature without degrading the divine nature. Mackintosh concurs: "And there is general agreement that 2 Co 8[9] bears not upon the 'poverty' of Jesus' lifetime on earth, but on His sacrifice in being born; for the 'poverty' and 'riches' in question must obviously be correlative."[40] Mackintosh goes on to note that not only was Christ's incarnate state more humble than his preexistent state, but he entered into the lesser state voluntarily. Witherington agrees the verse says the preexistent Christ chose to become incarnate, and the choice involved an exchange. He also sees a close parallel with the Philippians hymn.[41] For Craddock, "becoming 'poor' refers to the essence of ultimate reality coming under the conditions of human existence, the Eternal in time, the noncontingent being made subject to all the contingencies of our common experiences."[42]

Dunn challenges these interpretations, arguing that in the other places Paul spoke of Christ's grace he meant the cross, not the incarnation.[43] Dunn's argument works only because he interprets Philippians 2:6-11 the same way. But, as we have seen, the Philippians hymn makes much better sense when understood in terms of incarnation. This verse too makes the best sense and provides the most powerful exhortation when understood of the preexistent Christ who humbled himself to become human. Marshall describes this verse as "the logical development of this [sending] formula to give the contrast between pre-existent glory and earthly humiliation."[44]

COLOSSIANS 1:15-20

> He is the image of the invisible God, the firstborn over all creation. For by him all things were created: things in heaven and on earth, visible and invisible, whether thrones or powers or rulers or authorities; all things were created by him and for him. He is before all things, and in him all things hold together. And he is the head of the body, the church; he is the beginning and the firstborn from among the dead, so that in everything he might have the supremacy. For God was pleased to have all his fullness dwell in him, and through him to reconcile to himself all things, whether things on earth or things in heaven, by making peace through his blood, shed on the cross.

---

[40]Mackintosh, *Doctrine of the Person of Christ,* p. 66.

[41]Witherington, *Jesus the Sage,* p. 263.

[42]Fred Craddock, "The Poverty of Christ: An Investigation of II Corinthians 8:9," *Interpretation* 22 (1968): 166.

[43]Dunn, *Christology in the Making,* p. 121.

[44]I. Howard Marshall, "The Christ-Hymn in Philippians 2:5-11," *Tyndale Bulletin* 19 (1968): 122.

This passage describes Christ in exalted terms. He does not exist in or after the image of God, he *is* the image of God.[45] He perfectly represents God. He created all that is and now sustains all that has been created. He has reconciled the world to God, and is supreme over the created order. For this to be true, he necessarily preexisted the created order. No other interpretation makes any sense. The antecedent to this opening "he" is found in verse 13, where Paul writes of the Son of God "in whom we have redemption, the forgiveness of sins."

Paul did not write that the Son created the rest of creation, but that he created *all* that was created. This excludes the Son from the created order, and Paul was careful enough with words for this to have been no oversight. For a Jew who would have been hesitant to use the term *theos* to describe Jesus, the language of this passage and of Colossians 2:9 ("For in Christ all the fullness of the Deity lives in bodily form") says about as clearly as can be said that Jesus is God without confusing God the Father and the Son. Fee points to the passage's theological agreement with the Johannine prologue, both asserting Christ's full deity, including his preexistence, his revelatory role and his role as the divine agent in the creation of "all things."[46]

Despite increasing agreement that this passage expresses Paul's Wisdom christology, some argue it does no more than explain Jesus' importance in Wisdom language, and thus is only a functional statement of his significance. Dunn is probably the best representative of this position, although he hedges his conclusion about whether Paul meant to teach Christ's preexistence in the passage. He says:

> What we are probably witnessing is the attempt to spell out the significance of the earthly and exalted Christ in terms which Paul's interlocutors were already using, and to do so in such a way as to give these terms exclusive bearing on Christ. In particular, Paul picked up the widespread Wisdom terminology and found it an important tool for asserting the finality of Christ's role in God's purpose.[47]

---

[45]Charles A. Gieschen, *Angelomorphic Christology* (Leiden: E. J. Brill, 1998), p. 344.

[46]Fee, "St. Paul and the Incarnation," p. 72.

[47]Dunn, *Christology in the Making,* pp. 194-95. Dunn continues, "It is at least questionable whether in doing so he intended to assert the preexistence of Christ, or to affirm that Jesus was a divine being personally active in creation. . . . To understand the Wisdom passages as ontological affirmations about 'Christ's eternal being' is most probably to misunderstand them." In the second edition of *Christology in the Making,* Dunn says he does not deny the Colossians texts speaks about Christ's preexistence, but says the meaning of this is that the preexistence of Wisdom has been attributed to Christ (p. xxxiv). Because preexistent Wisdom was a personalized hypostasis, not personal, Dunn has conceded nothing to those who believe Paul taught Christ's personal preexistence.

Bruce, however, concludes Paul was not so much implying that the personified Wisdom of Old Testament books is Christ as he was that Christ preexisted all creation.[48]

Karl-Josef Kuschel takes a far stronger position than does Dunn, but he misrepresents his opponents when he says the passage does not present Christ as an "independent creator deity."[49] Christian theology has never described Christ in this way. What Kuschel describes is bitheism, but the passage does not say that. According to Kuschel, all we find here is Christ described as mediating God's creative activity, being distinguished from the Creator on the one hand and the creatures on the other.

I believe Marshall describes the import of this passage most accurately: "Neither Colossians 1:22 nor 2:9 taken by itself necessarily points to the personal preexistence of the divine being incarnate in Jesus, but this thought is demanded by the language of the 'hymn' in 1:15-20."[50] John Balchin adds that while they may not have explained it the same way, most scholars have recognized this passage teaches plainly the existence of Christ before the creation of the world and his activity in that creation. He adds, "[Paul] had explicitly identified Christ with preexistent wisdom in a way that no ordinary Jew would ever have dared."[51]

Both Dunn and Kuschel appear to believe Paul's Jewishness seriously limited what he could and could not believe about Jesus. But Paul was a Jew who claimed he had been confronted by the risen Jesus, and that this experience fundamentally affected his Jewishness. The application of the imagery Paul used to a historical individual must surely have caused people to ask if this were more than an image and led them to think about Christ's preexistence.[52] Commenting on this passage, Wright says early Christianity burst the boundaries of history of religions analysis:

> Jewish parallels cannot by themselves explain this new departure, however much those who initiated it were claiming to remain within, and to reinterpret from within, the central Jewish tradition of creational and covenantal monotheism. It will therefore not do simply to analyze partially parallel Jewish motifs and deduce from them the shape of the new doctrine being articulated. They provide the (historically) original theme, not its new variation. In particular, to refer to the Christology

[48]F. F. Bruce, *The Epistles to the Colossians, to Philemon, and to the Ephesians,* New International Commentary on the New Testament (Grand Rapids: Eerdmans, 1984), p. 60.

[49]Karl-Josef Kuschel, *Born Before All Time?* trans. John Bowden (New York: Crossroad, 1992), p. 332.

[50]I. Howard Marshall, "Incarnational Christology in the New Testament," in *Christ the Lord,* ed. H. H. Rowdon (Downers Grove, Ill.: InterVarsity Press, 1982), p. 9.

[51]John F. Balchin, "Paul, Wisdom and Christ," in *Christ the Lord,* ed. H. H. Rowdon (Downers Grove, Ill.: InterVarsity Press, 1982), p. 215.

[52]Brown, *Divine Trinity,* p. 156.

of the poem as "wisdom-christology" cannot be taken as an indication that the problem of interpretation is in principle solved, with the details simply to be worked out in terms of Jewish wisdom-ideas.[53]

When we study the parallels closely, it is evident that Paul did not merely transfer Wisdom language to Christ but modified it as well.[54]

We can approach the question of whether the passage teaches Christ's preexistence in two ways. We can examine the language that points to Christ's deity, or we can consider the implications of the statements about Christ's role in creation. I believe a case for Christ's deity can be made from the passage (with his preexistence necessarily following), but it is easier to establish Christ's preexistence through his role in creation. If indeed everything came into being through Christ, then there is no option other than that he existed before that creation. If this is not so, then Paul was talking nonsense. Or

> we are forced to say that if the language employed here means anything, it means that Christ is *both* to be identified as the divine Wisdom, i.e. none other than the one creator God active in creation and now in redemption, and to be distinguished from the Father, not as in a dualism whereby two gods are distinguished and given different (and in principle parallel) tasks, but within the framework of Jewish creational monotheism itself.[55]

Lohse says, "he is 'before all things,' which means that as the pre-existent one he is Lord over the universe. This refers back to the designation 'firstborn before all creation' and it emphasizes once again the unique position of Christ as Lord over the cosmos."[56] Wright believes the title indicates priority in both time and rank, but temporal priority in no way implies Christ was a created being. Christ is designated firstborn because he is preexistent, *not* because he is first among the creatures.[57] O'Brien describes the passage as a statement about both Christ's preexistence and his cosmic significance. The focus is not the state of the universe but Christ's supremacy over creation.[58] He traces Paul's language to Genesis 1 and Old

[53]Wright, *Climax of the Covenant*, p. 115.
[54]Witherington, *Jesus the Sage*, p. 267.
[55]Wright, *Climax of the Covenant*, p. 117.
[56]Eduard Lohse, *Colossians and Philemon,* ed. Helmut Koester, trans. William R. Pochlmann and Robert T. Karris (Philadelphia: Fortress, 1971), p. 52. Lohse also says describing Christ as the "firstborn before all creation" does not mean he was created before the rest of creation, but instead refers to his uniqueness that distinguishes him from all creation (pp. 48-49).
[57]N. T. Wright, *The Epistles of Paul to the Colossians and to Philemon: An Introduction and Commentary*, Tyndale New Testament Commentary, ed. Leon Morris (Grand Rapids: Eerdmans, 1991), p. 71.
[58]Peter T. O'Brien, *Colossians, Philemon*, Word Bible Commentary 44 (Waco, Tex.: Word, 1982), p. 47.

Testament Wisdom literature that describes Wisdom as God's "master-workman." Paul transformed this "master-workman" from a figure of speech into a personal, heavenly being. The language of "firstborn" distinguishes Christ from the created order as the one who is both prior to and supreme over that creation.[59] O'Brien also describes image as a title of majesty emphasizing Christ as revealer of God and as preexistent. He thus considers the term both functional and ontological.[60]

W. L. Knox believes Paul used the model of divine Wisdom to teach the metaphysical truth of Christ's supremacy over all other claimants. He concludes Paul's course committed the church to what would become the theology of Nicea, even though Paul probably did not realize the full implications of his action.[61]

Hengel argues belief in Christ's preexistence led to the attribution to Christ of Wisdom's role as mediator of creation and salvation. The Pauline understanding of Christ required Wisdom be subordinated to him and that everything previously attributed to Wisdom now be attributed to Christ. "The exalted Jesus is not only pre-existent, but also shares in the *opus proprium Dei,* creation. . . . No revelation, no speech and no action of God can take place without him or beside him."[62] Hengel argues from an early belief in Christ's preexistence to consideration of the implications of this teaching. Thus he reverses the common view that attributing certain functions to Christ led to conclusions about who he was. I imagine the reality was more in the nature of a continuing interaction between functional and ontological thinking.

While Kuschel complains Paul never described what Christ's preexistence looks like,[63] Aloys Grillmeier explains Paul did not speak explicitly about this preexistence because he presupposed it.[64] In studying Paul we have seen repeatedly that preexistence appears to have been a generally accepted presupposition that Paul saw no need either to explain or defend. Gieschen suggests the answer can be found in verse 15. Christ is the *visible* image of the invisible God. It was he who appeared in the Old Testament theophanies as the angel of the Lord and all other appearances of deity because no one can see the Father.[65]

---

[59]Ibid., pp. 45-46. Even Dunn says the firstborn language indicates primacy over creation, not within creation, despite his doubt the passage teaches Christ's preexistence. His exegesis, however, would seem to imply Christ's preexistence.

[60]Ibid., p. 78.

[61]W. L. Knox, *Church of the Gentiles* (Cambridge: Cambridge University Press, 1939), p. 178.

[62]Martin Hengel, *The Son of God* (Philadelphia: Fortress, 1976), p. 72.

[63]Kuschel, *Born Before All Time?* p. 334.

[64]Aloys Grillmeier, *Christ in Christian Tradition,* vol. 1, *From the Apostolic Age to Chalcedon (451),* trans. John Bowden, 2nd ed. (Atlanta: John Knox, 1975), p. 25.

[65]Gieschen, *Angelomorphic Christology,* pp. 346-47. We will see in chap. 7 that this belief dates at least as early as the mid-second century.

This Colossians passage presents Christ as one who both was the image and fullness of God and acted in ways other biblical passages attribute only to God. As the mediator of creation, he necessarily preexisted it. Assuming the fullness of deity includes the divine attributes, Christ is eternal. The passage describes one who shares the divine nature and enjoys eternal preexistence, who is in fact God. The objections raised have not overturned this testimony of the passage.

FIRST CORINTHIANS 8:5-6

> For even if there are so-called gods, whether in heaven or on earth (as indeed there are many "gods" and many "lords"), yet for us there is but one God, the Father, from whom all things came and for whom we live; and there is but one Lord, Jesus Christ, through whom all things came and through whom we live.

Like Colossians 1:15-20 this passage presents Jesus Christ as the Mediator and Sustainer of creation.[66] The natural implication of this is that Christ preexisted all creation because a person must exist before he or she can mediate an activity. Logically, the emphasis of the passage is not Christ's preexistence but his deity. Yet deity in the Bible requires preexistence. Most of the major patristic commentators understood these verses to teach the Father, Son and Spirit are equally God.

Some today have expressed reservations about Christ's preexistence because they consider it incompatible with monotheism. Therefore, Fee's comment that Paul shows no tension here between affirming monotheism and distinguishing the two divine persons, the Father and Jesus Christ, is important. He says only the most obdurate would deny the trinitarian implications of this passage.[67] Vincent Taylor notes the affinity between this passage and the Logos doctrine. He says Paul teaches here that Christ's preexistent dignity is not even subject to argument.[68] Conzelmann reaches the same conclusion about preexistence from a linguistic analysis of the passage:

> The interpretation of *kurios*, "Lord"—despite the formal parallelism—is deliberately set in contrast to that of the concept *theos*, "God": (a) by choosing the preposition *dia*, "through"; (b) by using the same preposition twice. Jesus, as the "Lord," is the Mediator of creation. His preexistence is accordingly presupposed.[69]

---

[66]Marshall calls it significant that by 1 Corinthians Christ was seen as participating in the work of creation and says this recognition contributed to the realization of Christ's deity (I. Howard Marshall, *The Origins of New Testament Christology* [Downers Grove, Ill.: InterVarsity Press, 1976], p. 107).

[67]Gordon D. Fee, *The First Epistle to the Corinthians*, New International Commentary on the New Testament (Grand Rapids: Eerdmans, 1987), p. 375.

[68]Vincent Taylor, *The Person of Christ in New Testament Teaching* (London: Macmillan, 1958), p. 51.

[69]Hans Conzelmann, *1 Corinthians*, ed. George W. MacRae, trans. James W. Leitch (Philadelphia: Fortress, 1975), pp. 144-45.

Possibly the most powerful statement supporting Christ's personal preexistence in this passage comes from Richard Bauckham. He says Paul has clearly drawn verse 6 from the Shema of Deuteronomy 6:4 and thus includes Jesus within the identity of the one God of contemporary Judaism.[70] Paul also portrays Christ as active in the creation of all, a prerogative reserved exclusively for God. "That God is not only the agent or efficient cause of creation ('from him are all things') and the final cause or goal of all things ('to him are all things'), but also the instrumental cause ('through him are all things') well expresses the typical Jewish monotheistic concern that God used no one else to carry out his work of creation, but accomplished it alone, solely by means of his own Word and/or his own Wisdom."[71]

In this passage Paul was not arguing about Christ's preexistence; his concern was with whether Christians should eat food sacrificed to idols. In arguing idols are not God, Paul associated Jesus with the one true God as Lord and Mediator of creation. He did not need to say this to prove his case, but he did. The Jesus Paul described could be none other than preexistent deity. It is difficult to see how the words could bear any other meaning.

ROMANS 1:1-4

> Paul, a servant of Christ Jesus, called to be an apostle and set apart for the gospel of God—the gospel he promised beforehand through his prophets in the Holy Scriptures regarding his Son, who as to his human nature was a descendant of David, and who through the Spirit of holiness was declared with power to be the Son of God by his resurrection from the dead: Jesus Christ our Lord.

If there is any passage in Paul's letters that can be read as denying Christ's preexistence, this is it. Those who believe the New Testament reveals an evolution from a primitive "low" christology to a complex "high" christology offer this passage and Acts 2:36 as evidence. They understand this passage as teaching Christ became the Son of God at the time of the resurrection and his elevation as accomplished through the Spirit, possibly as a reward for Jesus' faithful ministry.[72] I will consider Acts 2:36 in the next chapter, but the first thing to notice is that if Paul did mean to be understood in this way here, his statement conflicts not only with his other letters but with other portions of this letter as well. Thus we should con-

---

[70]Richard Bauckham, *God Crucified* (Grand Rapids: Eerdmans, 1998), pp. 37ff.

[71]Ibid., p. 39.

[72]Bultmann argued that the early church believed Jesus became Son of God through the resurrection, but he said the church understood the title to mean a royal personage and not a supernatural, divine being. The difficulty occurred when Hellenistic Christians applied their understanding of Son of God to the Jewish term and made it an ontological instead of a functional title (see O'Neill, *Who Did Jesus Think He Was?* p. 10).

sider carefully other possible interpretations of this passage because if these verses can be interpreted in a way that is consistent with what Paul says elsewhere, that is the preferable interpretation. If that is possible, then these verses do not preclude Christ's preexistence and the major objection to Pauline teaching about preexistence fails.

Early Christian writers generally understood these verses to affirm both Christ's deity and his humanity. In doing so, they *assumed* his preexistence. But some interpreters spoke directly to this matter of Christ's preexistence. Origen is typical: "Without any doubt, he was made that which he had not previously been according to the flesh. But according to the Spirit he existed beforehand, and there was never a time when he did not exist." He added that "*designated* applies to someone who already exists, whereas *predestined* is only applicable to someone who does not exist."[73] Augustine, Cyril of Alexandria and Theodoret offered similar interpretations of this language. Theodoret wrote in reference to Matthew 2:5-6, "For the words 'from you shall come a leader' refer to the birth according to the flesh, which took place in the last days; but the phrase 'his goings out are from the beginning, from the days of eternity' clearly proclaims eternal existence."[74]

C. E. B. Cranfield, probably the leading modern commentator on Romans, says Paul firmly believed in Christ's preexistence in the sense that he as Son of God shared in the divine life from eternity and at a specific time assumed human nature. He also believes Paul's thinking in Romans was essentially trinitarian both in its close association of Jesus and the Spirit with God in numerous passages, and in its ascribing to Jesus and the Spirit the ability to bring about what only God can do.[75] In his Romans commentary Cranfield says the ordering of the words in Greek "would seem to imply that the One who was born of the seed of David was already Son of God before, and independently of, the action denoted by the second participle."[76] He adds that *kata sarka* here is best understood as "as a man" and thus implies Christ's human nature "is not the whole truth about him."[77]

The best route to understanding this passage is to focus on the words *de-*

---

[73]Origen, *Commentary on the Epistle to the Romans,* quoted in Gerald Bray, ed., *Romans,* Ancient Christian Commentary on Scripture, New Testament 6 (Downers Grove, Ill.: InterVarsity Press, 1998), p. 7.

[74]Theodoret of Cyrus, *Eranistes,* trans. Gerard H. Ettlinger, Fathers of the Church 106 (Washington: Catholic University of America, 2003), p. 40.

[75]C. E. B. Cranfield, "Some Comments on Professor J. D. G. Dunn's *Christology in the Making* with Special Reference to the Evidence of the Epistle to the Romans," in *The Glory of Christ in the New Testament,* ed. L. D. Hurst and N. T. Wright (Oxford: Oxford University Press, 1987), pp. 279-80.

[76]C. E. B. Cranfield, *A Critical and Exegetical Commentary on the Epistle to the Romans,* International Critical Commentary (Edinburgh: T & T Clark, 1980), 1:58.

[77]Ibid., 1:58.

clared and *with power.* Paul did not say that Jesus *became* the Son of God at the resurrection but that the resurrection was the public declaration of this already existing reality, and this declaration of his sonship revealed the truth about Jesus: divine power in contrast to the apparent weakness of his earthly life. To put it another way, Paul was saying what Christianity has said for nearly two thousand years: only after the resurrection (and because of the resurrection) did people know who Jesus really was. This is not just Paul's message; the four Gospels say the same thing. Jesus, says Paul, was a true human being, but that is only part of his story. This is O'Collins's understanding of the passage. He says, "What he had been before (Son of God) was now definitively realized, confirmed, and given clearer definition by his passage from his earthly state to his risen state."[78]

So, not only does this passage not affirm an adoptionist christology (Dunn calls such language here anachronistic), it actually supports belief in Christ's preexistence. The transition from verse 3 to verse 4 is not "from human Messiah to a divine Son of God, but from Son as Messiah to Son as Messiah and powerful, reigning Lord."[79] The structure of the Greek, says Cranfield, "would seem to imply" the one descended from David was already Son of God. He believes Paul was adapting an existing confessional formula.[80] Barrett seems to agree about the existing formula and adds that if Paul added the words "with (or in) power," there can be no denial he believed Christ already was the Son of God. Barrett believes Romans predated any exploration of the idea of preexistence but considers the adoptionist appearance of early christology superficial and the result of an initial functional approach to understanding Jesus.[81]

---

[78]Gerald O'Collins, *Christology* (New York: Oxford University Press, 1995), p. 130.

[79]Douglas Moo, *Romans 1—8,* The Wycliffe Exegetical Commentary, ed. Kenneth Barker (Chicago: Moody, 1991), pp. 39ff. Among others, Marshall, Stott, Kim and O'Collins agree the passage speaks of the resurrection confirming an already existing reality, not establishing a new one.

[80]Cranfield, *Romans,* 1:57ff. Kim adds that the Pauline version of the confession "conveys the idea of the incarnation of God's preexistent Son in the house of David just as the sending formula in Gal 4.4 does" (Kim, *Origin of Paul's Gospel,* p. 132). Marshall is skeptical of the pre-Pauline formula hypothesis but notes "all the other Pauline texts which can reasonably be claimed to reflect pre-Pauline formulas and usage have been examined by Werner Kramer who has shown that the title [Son of God] is linked with the thought of God's sending or giving up his preexistent Son for the salvation of men" (I. Howard Marshall, "The Divine Sonship of Jesus," *Interpretation* 21 [1977]: 101). Kramer concludes no passage in Paul's writings gives clear evidence of either adoption or preexistence, but he continues, "All the same, a sentence like Rom. 5:10 which speaks of the death of the *Son,* or like Rom. 8:29 which speaks of our predestination, would permit the assumption that for Paul the bearer of salvation had always been *Son of God.* This is tending towards the idea of preexistence, but we can hardly say more than this" (Werner R. Kramer, *Christ, Lord, Son of God,* trans. Brian Hardy [Naperville, Ill.: A. R. Allenson, 1966], p. 185).

[81]C. K. Barrett, *A Commentary on the Epistle to the Romans* (New York: Harper & Row, 1957), p. 20.

The issue involved in interpreting this passage is whether it can be understood in isolation or must be read as part of the entire book of Romans, or even the entire Pauline corpus. If the former, then it is possible to read the passage in terms of an evolutionary, adoptionist christology; if the latter, then the passage is about the preexistent Son who assumes humanity as a son of David. Good hermeneutical practice precludes the former option. Marshall states the difficulty with an evolutionary interpretation clearly: "Jesus did not become God's Son by being raised from the dead: it was *because* he was his Son that God raised him from the dead."[82]

FIRST CORINTHIANS 10:3-4

They [the Israelites in the wilderness] all ate the same spiritual food and drank the same spiritual drink; for they drank from the spiritual rock that accompanied them, and that rock was Christ.

In this passage Paul was pointing to the experience of Israel to warn his readers about the danger of persisting in their way of living. A key part of his argument involved explaining that the privileges the Israelites enjoyed had not protected them from God's judgment. Paul drew a parallel between the Israelite experience and the Lord's Supper. As Fee notes, the sacramental analogy is clear; what is difficult is how Paul got there.[83] (It was probably this that led most patristic commentators to spiritualize this passage, making no reference to Christ's person.)

Paul's reference to a rock that accompanied the Israelites on their wilderness journey appears to derive from a Jewish legend about Numbers 21:16-18, recounted, among other places, in the Tosefta.[84] The legend tells of a rock that provided Israel with water during its sojourn in the wilderness. Paul's interest was not the water but its source. His identification of the rock with Christ served both to indicate the typological nature of Israel's experience and to emphasize the continuity between Israel and his readers, including the possibility of divine judgment. "How much by this Paul intended to stress Christ's preexistence is moot, but it seems far more likely that he used the verb 'was' to indicate the reality of Christ's presence in the Old Testament events than that he saw him there simply in a figurative way."[85] Conzelmann

---

[82]I. Howard Marshall, *Jesus the Savior* (Downers Grove, Ill.: InterVarsity Press, 1990), p. 157.
[83]Fee, *First Epistle to the Corinthians*, pp. 446-47.
[84]Sukkah 3:11, in *The Tosefta: Second Division: Moed (The Order of Appointed Times),* ed. and trans. Jacob Neusner (New York: KTAV, 1981), p. 220.
[85]Fee, *First Epistle to the Corinthians*, p. 449.

concurs, saying, "The 'was' of the typological statement, of the interpretation of the rock being Christ, means real preexistence, not merely symbolic significance. This is plain from the dependence upon Jewish tradition, which interprets the rock as referring to preexistent Wisdom."[86] Dunn disagrees, however, considering the verb insignificant and denying Paul was talking about Christ's preexistence.

The pattern of Paul's discussion of Christ's preexistence as we have seen it and will continue to see it fits this passage well. Paul was not making a christological point to further a systematic theology; he was talking about the practical implications of the Corinthians' behavior for their spiritual well-being. In doing so, he drew a parallel with the situation of Israel in the wilderness and drew on Christ's preexistence to show the seriousness of the Israelites' behavior and its consequences in order to impress on the Corinthian Christians their need to consider seriously where they were headed.

ROMANS 9:5

Theirs are the patriarchs, and from them is traced the human ancestry of Christ, who is God over all, forever praised! Amen. (NIV)

To them belong the patriarchs, and from them, according to the flesh, comes the Messiah, who is over all, God blessed forever. Amen. (NRSV)

This is not normally considered among the Pauline passages about Christ's preexistence, but I have included it for two reasons. First, the verse presumes there is more to be said about Christ than his human existence. Second, the verse can legitimately be read to describe Christ as God. The translation disagreement results from the absence of systematic punctuation in the earliest New Testament manuscripts. The editorial committee of the United Bible Society, however, decided on grammatical grounds in favor of the Greek text reflected in the NIV translation, ascribing deity to Christ.[87] In biblical terms, if Christ can be identified as deity, he must be preexistent; the Bible has no place for any deity other than the eternal God. In any case, the New Testament evidence for Christ's deity is very strong even without this verse. To those who have argued Paul was a good Jew who would never have spoken

---

[86]Conzelmann, *1 Corinthians,* p. 167.
[87]Bruce M. Metzger, *A Textual Commentary on the Greek New Testament,* 3rd ed. (London: United Bible Societies, 1975), p. 521. In fairness, I must mention both the NIV and NRSV footnote the other reading as an alternate rendering.

in this way, two things must be said.[88] First, what Paul could or could not have done must be judged in terms of the textual evidence available to us, not our prejudgments. Second, the Paul who wrote this passage was not only the Paul who sat at the feet of Gamaliel but also the Paul who encountered the risen Jesus on the road to Damascus. Thus his Jewish background is not the whole story.

It is unusual to talk about tracing someone's *human* ancestry unless some other ancestry is also involved. But according to the Bible there is only one person of whom it can be said he has multiple ancestries. I imagine we could talk about someone in this way without intending more than a human ancestry—after all, people have been known to use rather unusual language on occasion—but such a way of speaking about someone is sufficiently unusual that unless adequate justification is offered (and none is) an alternate explanation surely must be preferred. So this verse should be seen as presuming Christ's preexistent deity.

Cranfield concludes the most likely meaning of this verse to be that Christ, who according to his human ancestry was a Jew, is Lord of all and by nature God.[89] Early Christians reached the same conclusion. Origen wrote, "It is clear from this passage that Christ is the God *who is over all*." Ambrosiaster agreed: "As there is no mention of the Father's name in this verse and Paul is talking about Christ, it cannot be disputed that he is called God here." Even Pelagius said of the verse, "Christ is of the Jews according to the flesh, and God, blessed forever."[90]

Sending Statements

The remaining Pauline passages I will consider describe Christ as having been sent or having come, language that reappears in the Gospels. Many modern commentators are skeptical that such sending language implies preexistence. Early church writers looked at the matter quite differently, however. They believed the key was not the sending but who had been sent—God's own Son. This distinguished these passages from the sending of the Old Testament prophets and John the Baptist—none of them is described in terms of divine sonship.

---

[88] A. T. Hanson says Paul, John and the author of Hebrews "make it clear that they regard Jesus Christ as having the status of God." He says they do not describe Christ as *theos* (often because this would have caused confusion. "In late Judaism the name of God was not used, for excellent theological (as well as devotional) reasons. . . . If Jesus Christ was called *theos* indiscriminately there was bound to be confusion with the proper denotation of God the Father" (Hanson, *Grace and Truth* [London: SPCK, 1975], p. 66).

[89] Cranfield, "Some Comments," p. 273.

[90] Quoted in Bray, *Romans*, pp. 246-47.

Similarly, the one who came was described in terms that imply his having existed prior to his coming. One passage that helps clarify this is John 20:21-22, although it is not itself a passage about Christ's preexistence. In this passage Jesus breathed out the Holy Spirit on his disciples that first Easter night as he commissioned them to continue the mission he had begun during his earthly ministry. He said to them, "As the Father has sent me, I am sending you." This is suggestive, rather than conclusive, but what it suggests is that just as the disciples existed prior to their sending (a sending modeled on Jesus' sending), so too did the Son of God preexist his sending.

GALATIANS 4:4-5

> But when the time had fully come, God sent his Son, born of a woman, born under law, to redeem those under law, that we might receive the full rights of sons.

This verse introduces the issue of the New Testament sending statements, but in a Pauline context rather than the more familiar Synoptic one. Paul's concern here is not christological doctrine but the status of believers as children of God. The sending language is incidental to the thrust of Paul's argument that believers are now different because of what God has done through Jesus Christ on our behalf—its emphasis is on who was sent and what he accomplished. This incidental nature is characteristic of Paul's preexistence language and is important for our understanding of Paul's thinking.

The clear implication of the passage, despite Dunn's caution about accepting surface meanings, is that the Son who was sent by God into the world already existed. This was how early Christian writers understood it. Theodoret was typical when he wrote, "It is right to point out that he has linked the sending of the eternal Son with the incarnation." Few early writers discussed the meaning of the sending language because they took for granted that the one who had been sent preexisted his earthly life.[91]

The language Paul used is common to all New Testament authors who speak of Christ having been sent, and it differs in two ways from the language describing the sending of the prophets. They were sent to one place or another, but in each case they already lived on earth. God came to them and called them from what they already were doing. Even in the case of Jeremiah, God chose Jeremiah before his conception, set him apart and appointed him to be a prophet (Jer 1:4-19). He put his words into Jeremiah's mouth, and his word "came to Jer-

---

[91]Mark J. Edwards, ed., *Galatians, Ephesians, Philippians,* Ancient Christian Commentary on Scripture, New Testament 8 (Downers Grove, Ill.: InterVarsity Press, 1999).

emiah," but Jeremiah never speaks of being sent into the world. The New Testament writers never say God put his words into Jesus' mouth or that the word of God came to Jesus. Thus Paul's sending language here differs from that used of Old Testament prophets. It presumes—there is no other word for it—the Son really existed before he was sent into the world, and not in the "ideal" way Jeremiah did. Second, as early commentators emphasized, it was the Son *of God* who had been sent, not merely some prophet.

Longenecker says that for Jews this sonship language would not have ontological significance as much as it would indicate a relationship of loving obedience.[92] The sonship of Jesus certainly exemplifies loving obedience, but this passage says more than that. Paul's call for loving obedience on the part of believers derives from the Son's prior obedience in coming into the world to make possible our new relationship with God.

In order to understand the meaning of this passage, the questions we need to answer are: Whose Son is this? Where was the Son sent from? Where was he sent to? Why was he sent? What sort of being is necessary to accomplish this purpose? Paul implies the Son was sent from heaven and says clearly he was sent into the world. He came in order to redeem fallen humanity and bring us into a relationship of sonship to God. In the context of Paul's overall theology (and the Bible as a whole), only God can redeem the world. And as early Christian commentators pointed out, it was God's *Son* whom he sent, and this presupposes the Son's preexistence.[93] In the New Testament, Christ's sonship and ours are always qualitatively different—Christ is God's Son by nature, but we become sons by adoption. I believe the evidence not only does not permit us to deny Paul teaches the preexistence of God's Son in this passage but that it is consistent with a broader Pauline affirmation of Christ's preexistence.

GALATIANS 3:19A

> What, then, was the purpose of the law? It was added because of transgressions until the Seed to whom the promise referred had come.

Paul's reference to the Seed comes from Genesis 22:18 (or "offspring," NIV),

---

[92]Richard N. Longenecker, "The Foundational Conviction of New Testament Christology: The Obedience/Faithfulness/Sonship of Christ," in *Jesus of Nazareth: Lord and Christ,* ed. Joel B. Green and Max Turner (Grand Rapids: Eerdmans, 1994), p. 478.

[93]Many commentators on Galatians understand Galatians 4:4 as presuming the Son's preexistence. Most link this verse with Romans 8:3 in offering this conclusion. Dunn and Küng reject this conclusion (although, unlike Küng, Dunn believes the New Testament teaches Christ's preexistence), and Longenecker expresses reservations about this interpretation even as he agrees Romans 8:3 does teach the Son's preexistence.

where God promised Abraham all nations would be blessed through his seed. Here Paul identifies this promised seed as Christ and engages in a rabbinic argument to prove the word *seed* is singular and so must refer to Jesus. Without Paul's commentary, modern readers would understand the promise to Abraham as referring to Isaac, Jacob and all those descended from Abraham, not as limited to one individual two millennia later. But whatever we might think of Paul's argument, he intended his readers to identify the seed of Genesis 22 with Jesus Christ.

Early Christian commentators appear to have assumed the language of coming must be interpreted in terms of preexistence. Ambrosiaster was most explicit about this, but he simply stated that it was Christ who had come, although he did so in a way that would require his preexistence. The emphasis in the patristic material, however, is on the superiority of the new covenant because of the deity of its mediator.[94]

The passage must presume no less than an ideal preexistence because according to Genesis 22 this seed must at least have been in the mind of God at the time of the promise to Abraham. The question is whether the passage intends to go beyond an ideal preexistence. I see nothing here that either requires or forbids the stronger interpretation. This is a weak argument in support of the Son's preexistence; I only mention it because it is frequently included in discussions of preexistence.

ROMANS 8:3-4

> For what the law was powerless to do in that it was weakened by the sinful nature, God did by sending his own Son in the likeness of sinful man to be a sin offering. And so he condemned sin in sinful man, in order that the righteous requirements of the law might be fully met in us, who do not live according to the sinful nature but according to the Spirit.

This passage is often considered in conjunction with Galatians 4:4 because the two passages are the key "sending" passages in Paul's letters. As in the Galatians passage, the sending language in Romans 8:3 is awkward unless the Son who was sent already existed. What else can the words "in the likeness of sinful flesh" mean except that the Son already possessed some other likeness (for lack of a better word)? That is why the early church understood this passage in incarnational terms. Theodoret and Augustine understood Paul to say Christ took to himself mortal flesh. In so interpreting, they assumed

---

[94]Edwards, *Galatians, Ephesians, Philippians,* p. 46.

Christ's personal, pre-incarnate existence. Pseudo-Constantinius and Pelagius said that the passage explicitly teaches Christ's preexistence. For early Christian writers, it was a given that the Son's having been sent required that he already exist.[95]

Stott says by itself the sending language does not necessarily imply preexistence since God sent both his Old Testament prophets and New Testament apostles, but that it was God's own Son who was sent "may well be intended to indicate that he enjoyed a prior life of intimacy with the Father."[96] Cranfield, though, warns us not to dismiss the sending language too lightly. We need to pay attention to the consequence of the sending for the one sent: he *enters into a human existence*. This makes it difficult to deny he previously enjoyed another existence.[97] Referring specifically to this passage, Kasper says, "Talk of the Son being sent by the Father clearly presupposes the pre-existence of the Son."[98] Hanson describes this verse as one of four in the undisputed Pauline letters "where Paul uses the word Son in a context which must refer to a pre-existent relationship."[99] O'Collins notes the passage focuses not on Christ's preexistence but on his being sent to effect human salvation. Nonetheless, Paul's soteriology presupposes a christology of preexistence. "It is precisely because Christ is the pre-existent Son who comes from the Father that he can turn us into God's adopted sons and daughters."[100] By itself, says Ferdinand Hahn, the idea of sending is simply about commissioning, but as soon as it becomes associated with the incarnation it moves into the realm of preexistence.[101] Ernst Käsemann considers the passage a liturgical statement describing the incarnation of the preexistent Son of God.[102] For Marinus de Jonge, the language of Romans 8:3 and Galatians 4:4 implies Christ enjoyed an earlier existence in a different form before being sent, but he argues Paul never speculated about this earlier exis-

---

[95]Bray, *Romans,* pp. 206ff.

[96]John Stott, *Romans* (Downers Grove, Ill.: InterVarsity Press, 1994), p. 219.

[97]Cranfield, "Some Comments," pp. 270-71.

[98]Walter Kasper, *The God of Jesus Christ,* trans. Matthew J. O'Connell (New York: Crossroad, 1984), p. 175.

[99]Hanson, *Grace and Truth,* p. 83. He also mentions Rom 8:32 and Gal 2:20; 4:4. Hanson's view is important because his general theological position is unsympathetic to the teaching of Christ's preexistence.

[100]O'Collins, *Christology,* p. 128.

[101]Ferdinand Hahn, *The Titles of Jesus in Christology,* trans. Harold Knight and George Ogg (London: Lutterworth, 1969), pp. 304-5.

[102]Ernst Käsemann, *Commentary on Romans,* trans. Geoffrey W. Bromiley (Grand Rapids: Eerdmans, 1980), p. 216. He reaches this conclusion based on a comparison with Gal 4:4; Jn 3:16-17.; 1 Jn 4:9; Phil 2:6ff. He says the idea is typically Johannine but rare in Paul.

tence.[103] Even Charles Talbert agrees both the Romans and Galatians passages assume Christ's preexistence in their use of sending language.[104] These citations, spanning the history of Christian interpretation and of theological beliefs, overwhelmingly support the belief that Paul's sending language presumes the preexistence of the one sent.

FIRST TIMOTHY 1:15

> Here is a trustworthy saying that deserves full acceptance: Christ Jesus came into the world to save sinners—of whom I am the worst.

This verse is similar to the Pauline sending passages we have already examined. As with those passages, the emphasis here is not on Christ's preexistence but on his work as Savior. The efficacy of this salvific work, however, depends on the truth of the preexistence Paul has presupposed: Christ is one who came from God to us, not a man who rose up from among us to represent us before God. Knight concedes "coming into the world" need not by itself indicate preexistence, but argues that when applied to Christ that is precisely what it means—as can readily be seen in John.[105] R. G. Hamerton-Kelly says the christology of the Pastorals is governed by the thought that Christ appeared in the world in the incarnation and will appear again at the end of time. He concludes, "Obviously, this type of thought presupposes the idea of the pre-existence of Christ before his epiphanies."[106]

FIRST TIMOTHY 3:16

> Beyond all question, the mystery of godliness is great:
> He appeared in a body,
>> was vindicated by the Spirit,
> was seen by angels,
>> was preached among the nations,
> was believed on in the world,
>> was taken up in glory.

---

[103]Marinus de Jonge, *Christology in Context* (Philadelphia: Westminster Press, 1988), pp. 121, 191. Jonge also identifies Romans 11:36 as implying Christ's preexistence with its mention of Christ in conjunction with God and his identification as mediator of creation and agent of redemption (p. 48).

[104]Charles H. Talbert, "The Myth of a Descending-Ascending Redeemer in Mediterranean Antiquity," *New Testament Studies* 22 (1975-1976): 435ff.

[105]George W. Knight III, *The Pastoral Epistles* (Grand Rapids: Eerdmans, 1992), p. 101.

[106]R. G. Hamerton-Kelly, *Preexistence, Wisdom, and the Son of Man* (Cambridge: Cambridge University Press, 1973), p. 187, although he interprets New Testament preexistence language as reflecting an ideal preexistence.

These verses, thought to be from an early hymn, present Christ's career in the descending-ascending pattern we have seen in such Pauline writings as Philippians 2:6-11. My focus is on the first line of the hymn because this discusses Christ's origin. Like the sending statements of Paul and other New Testament authors, the manifestation language of this hymn seems to presuppose Christ's prior existence in a nonearthly state. Schweizer says the first line "obviously presupposes existence in heaven."[107] Knight argues *ephanerōthē* shows Christ was "made known" by another, the other in this case being God the Father. Thus the line emphasizes revelation and "that he who is revealed previously existed but was unknown." The words translated "in a body" mean Christ became human, so the line is saying Christ's manifestation occurred through his incarnation.[108]

Romans 5:12-19

Blocher, in his study of original sin, says that in Romans 5 Paul presupposes Christ's preexistence in his second Adam argument. Blocher explains that Paul teaches the Redeemer had to come in Adamic flesh if he was to break the power of sin over those who were "in Adam," but if Adamic flesh completely described the person of the Redeemer, he would need salvation no less than those he came to save. But "because of his personal pre-existence, he did not depend totally on Adam. He did not owe his individual existence to Adam, and so he was not in Adam. He did not fall under Adam's headship. His birth could mark a new beginning in the life of humankind."[109]

While it would be possible to cite other Pauline passages that might be relevant to the question of Christ's preexistence, these are the most important ones. If we cannot reach a conclusion about Paul's thinking on the subject from these, additional passages will be no help. I conclude that the texts we have examined demonstrate Paul did believe in Christ's preexistence and that it was a real and personal preexistence, not merely a glimmer in God's eye. This conclusion receives support from exegetes who do not personally accept the teaching but recognize that Paul did. The claim that "it is unimaginable that Paul could have believed in the preexistence of the Son" stands in utter contradiction to the evidence.[110] Nonetheless, some leading Bible scholars have held just such a conclusion.

---

[107]Eduard Schweizer, *Jesus*, trans. David E. Green (Atlanta: John Knox, 1971), pp. 88-89.
[108]Knight, *Pastoral Epistles*, p. 184.
[109]Henri Blocher, *Original Sin* (Grand Rapids: Eerdmans, 1997), p. 132.
[110]Anthony F. Buzzard, "The Nature of Preexistence in the New Testament," *A Journal from the Radical Reformation* 6 (1996): 22.

MODERN INTERPRETATIONS

An ordinary reading of Paul's letters seems to affirm belief in Christ's personal pre-existence, as Dunn acknowledges. The exegetical tradition of the church—and even of many the church has deemed heretics—holds to the same conclusion. Nonetheless, some modern biblical scholars deny Paul taught such a doctrine and others see only an ideal preexistence in his letters.

John Knox asks what sort of preexistence Paul was talking about. He believes the early church introduced preexistence language in order to give Jesus significance beyond history:

> [Pre-existence] thus followed directly upon the postresurrection glory of him whose earthly life was still distinctly remembered. *It proved impossible to conclude that events ending in eternity had their beginning in time.* The belief in the pre-existence of Jesus was not the end result of the supernaturalizing of the earthly life . . . but the beginning of it.[111]

Knox is saying something so significant happened to Jesus—what has been called his postexistence—that his early followers decided his origin must have been pre-earthly. So they created the myth of his preexistence and used this to exalt his earthly life. Preexistence, says Knox, resulted from asking the question, "Who *was* this person whom we know as friend and teacher and whom we now know as Savior and Lord?"[112]

For Knox, preexistence explains how the early church justified its own existence. He presents the preexistence teaching of Paul and the early church as a blend of this mythological explanation, Hellenistic influences, and Jewish Logos and Wisdom speculation. He concludes it is far clearer that Paul accepted Christ's preexistence than how he understood this preexistence. Frances Young believes Paul viewed Jesus not as God incarnate but as the last Adam. For her, preexistence is eschatological, not incarnational.[113] James Dunn shares Young's opinion that Paul's was an Adam christology, but takes a more positive view of the reality of Christ's preexistence, although he denies Paul taught it. Helmut Thielicke concludes that Paul's christological statements are "merely an intellectual development of the implicit universalism which is to be found already in the synoptic Jesus."[114] A. T. Hanson, however, concludes there was no Synoptic

---

[111]Knox, *Jesus Lord and Christ,* pp. 151-52 (italics added).
[112]Ibid.
[113]Young says, "Christ is final for Paul, not as God incarnate, but as last Adam" (Frances Young, cited in James Dunn, *Christology in the Making* [Philadelphia: Westminster Press, 1980], p. 4).
[114]Helmut Thielicke, *The Evangelical Faith,* vol. 2, *The Doctrine of God and of Christ,* trans. Geoffrey W. Bromiley (Grand Rapids: Eerdmans, 1977), p. 292. Thielicke assumes here the veracity of the Synoptic picture of Jesus as well as Paul's faithfulness to that picture.

doctrine of preexistence and "no clear evidence that any of the Synoptic writers held a doctrine of pre-existence, as Paul certainly did."[115]

These examples show the lack of agreement among modern scholars about what Paul believed concerning Christ's preexistence, much less what the New Testament as a whole says. In part this is because Paul's discussion of Christ is so rich, combining several christological titles, mixing function and nature, and drawing from multiple Jewish roots in new ways. For modern scholars the difficulty arising from this richness lies in identifying which sources lie behind which doctrines. That Paul assumes preexistence and nowhere defines it does not make matters easier. So where one person sees personal preexistence in Paul, another sees ideal preexistence and a third finds no preexistence at all. This may be because Paul never offered any systematic doctrine of Christ's preexistence and used a variety of titles to refer to the preexistent Christ. Nonetheless, Fuller concludes the Pauline passages both speak about the preexistent Christ and accord him equality with God.[116]

Gerald O'Collins says the New Testament books move chronologically from speaking about Christ's "post-existence" and function to mention of his preexistence. But the transition began early and is reflected in Paul's writing, especially Galatians, Romans and Philippians.[117] Through what O'Collins calls hints, language about Christ's function and identity in his preincarnate state appear as early as Paul's first letters. Walter Kasper adds that Paul's discussion of preexistence is not speculative but soteriological, citing Philippians 2:6-11, Galatians 4:4 and Romans 8:3 as examples.[118] Hurtado calls attribution of preexistence to Christ no mere matter of intellectual adaptation or speculation; instead, early Christians were convinced by their experience of Jesus himself that he "embodied the divine salvific purpose and bore surpassing significance."[119]

Paul showed the teaching to be of value for both ethical instruction and development of Christian self-identity, but his references to Christ's preexistence also contained an ontological element. His use of Wisdom and Son of God themes in

---

[115]A. T. Hanson, "Two Consciousnesses: The Modern Version of Chalcedon," *Scottish Journal of Theology* 37 (1984): 478. I challenge Hanson's conclusion regarding the Synoptics in chap. 4.

[116]Reginald H. Fuller, *He That Cometh* (Harrisburg, Penn.: Morehouse, 1990), p. 45. Van Iersel, however, concludes exactly the opposite, saying "equality of being is incompatible with the thought that the Son of God is the image of his father" (B. Van Iersel, "'Son of God' in the New Testament," *Concilium* 153 [1982]: 45). Van Iersel's conclusion is presuppositional, not evidential. It seems necessary at this point that he explain why this equality is incompatible, because those of us who do not share his presuppositions do not reach his conclusion.

[117]O'Collins, *Interpreting Jesus*, p. 16.

[118]Walter Kasper, *Jesus the Christ*, trans. V. Green (New York: Paulist, 1976), p. 173.

[119]Larry Hurtado, "Pre-existence," in *Dictionary of Paul and His Letters*, ed. Gerald F. Hawthorne et al. (Downers Grove, Ill.: InterVarsity Press, 1993), p. 746.

his christology cannot be understood solely in functional terms. Paul's language of deity combines both functional and ontological categories.[120] And we cannot speak biblically of deity without accepting preexistence. Fortman agrees, saying, "It must be an eternal sonship that puts this son on the same divine level as the Father. The divine nature, divine origin, and divine power ascribed to Jesus cannot be the fruits of adoption. This is why Paul makes the pre-existence of Christ so explicit."[121]

That Paul considered Jesus Christ to be God incarnate seems to me indubitable, whatever one might conclude about such passages as Romans 9:5 and Titus 2:13. It is not necessary for Paul ever to have called Jesus "God" for us to conclude he believed him to be so. By applying Old Testament passages about God to Jesus, identifying Jesus with God in terms of function and similar devices, Paul placed Christ clearly on the side of Creator rather than the creature. If it is the case, as I believe it is, that Paul, raised as a devout Jew, attributed to Christ the honor, authority and deity of God, then his belief in Christ's preexistence necessarily follows.

A. T. Hanson is convinced Paul (and John and the author of Hebrews) believed the preexistent Christ had appeared at several points in Old Testament history and took an active role in Israel's destiny. Although these were theophanies, not incarnations, they required that the subject of the theophany exist. Hanson believes Paul reached this conclusion because he identified the *Kyrios* of the Septuagint with Jesus at several points.[122] Unlike Brown's belief that Paul projected preexistence back from Jesus' earthly life, Hanson thinks Paul saw Christ's incarnate life as the continuation of his divine participation in the history of God's covenant people. He considers that Paul held a doctrine of Christ's preexistence to be the simplest explanation of the evidence.[123] He also notes that Paul never emphasized Christ's preexistence. Instead, he sees Paul as emphasizing Christ's role in creation (at least in Colossians),[124] and it hardly needs men-

---

[120]Kim, *Origin of Paul's Gospel,* p. 259. David Brown also says it is impossible to avoid the ontological implications of Paul's functional language. If we take seriously what Paul says about Jesus, "the backward projection to preexistence simply cannot be resisted for otherwise the metaphor becomes an absurd projection" (David Brown, *The Divine Trinity* [LaSalle, Ill.: Open Court, 1985], p. 157).

[121]Edmund J. Fortman, *The Triune God* (Grand Rapids: Baker, 1972), p. 17.

[122]Hanson, *Grace and Truth,* p. 70, and A. T. Hanson, *Jesus Christ in the Old Testament* (London: SPCK, 1965), p. 171.

[123]Hanson, *Image of the Invisible God,* p. 62.

[124]Hanson's conclusion does not receive universal endorsement. Aloys Grillmeier believes an implicit belief in Christ's preexistence and worship of Christ as Lord are Paul's central christological ideas. Grillmeier says these ideas came from Judaism, which already had a strong preexistence tradition (although this seems to have been one of ideal preexistence), and Paul adapted them for preaching in a Hellenistic environment (Grillmeier, *Christ in Christian Tradition,* pp. 15-16).

tioning that a Christ who was not preexistent could have played no role in creation. Paul never emphasized Christ's preexistence, but neither did he ignore it. The reason for Paul's doctrine of preexistence, says Hanson, is soteriological: Paul believed that only with this doctrine could he bring out Christ's full salvific importance.[125] Among those who believe Paul taught Christ's personal preexistence there is almost complete agreement that preexistence was an essential element of Paul's soteriology.

Gerhard Schneider identifies four sources for Paul's teaching about preexistence: sending statements, Old Testament discussion of the Wisdom of God, a descending-ascending pattern, and description of Christ as the mediator of creation and salvation.[126] We have examined all four in this chapter and will look at the first again in chapter four and the second in chapter six.

Among New Testament scholars the contemporary focus in examining Christ's preexistence appears to be on Jesus as the Wisdom of God, although not all who have written on Wisdom (or Sophia) accept preexistence. Edouard Schweizer calls this strongly developed Jewish Wisdom tradition the source of Paul's ideas about preexistence and contrasts it to what he calls a nonexistent Jewish redeemer-myth tradition. This myth has often been presented as a "heavenly man" who both preexisted and was the pattern for created humanity. Even a century ago Mackintosh described the evidence for this view as the slenderest.[127] This is no less true of the Gnostic redeemer myth popularized by Bultmann.

Using the Wisdom motif enabled Paul to associate Christ with creation as well as redemption. This Wisdom was preexistent, associated with God in his actions and served as the agent of God's revelation. In Jewish thought, however, this Wisdom was a personification, not a person. Kim suggests Paul's use of Wisdom categories for Jesus resulted from his Damascus road experience and this occurred as early as the first half of the 30s. He writes:

> Since it is clear that Paul thought of Christ's pre-existence and mediatorship in creation in terms of Wisdom's, it is natural to think that he thought of God's sending his Son into the world also in terms of his sending Wisdom into the world. Once Jesus Christ, like wisdom in Jewish speculation, is conceived of as having existed in heaven from the beginning, his appearance on earth—again like Wisdom—is naturally regarded as God's sending him or his descent from heaven.[128]

---

[125]Hanson, *Image of the Invisible God*, p. 75.

[126]Gerhard Schneider, "Christologische Präexistenzaussagen im Neuen Testament," *Internationale Katholische Zeitschrift* 6 (1977): 23ff.

[127]Mackintosh, *Doctrine of the Person of Christ*, p. 68.

[128]Kim, *Origin of Paul's Gospel*, pp. 118-19.

But Paul moved beyond Old Testament personifications of Wisdom to a divine person. This is only one example of the way New Testament authors used Old Testament language and themes without thereby limiting themselves to their original intent. Although Kim focuses on the "Son of God" title, he also notes Paul used Wisdom language with the titles "Christ" and "Lord." The "Son" title, however, implies not only Christ's preexistence but also his divine origin. Caird concludes it was Paul who made the transition from a personified preexistence (as with Old Testament Wisdom) to personal preexistence. He says Jewish antecedents explain adequately *all* the New Testament language used to describe the preexistent Christ, but they cannot explain his personal preexistence. He believes it was "because in the earthly life of Jesus the eternal purpose of God appeared as a person that Paul and others after him found it impossible to imagine his precosmic existence as anything other than personal."[129]

Based on Paul's use of manifestation language (e.g., 1 Thess 4:16; 2 Thess 2:1; 1 Tim 3:16) both for Christ's earthly ministry and for his return in glory, Balchin argues for Paul's belief in Christ's preexistence. He says that as Paul presented it, Christ's final manifestation requires his existence before the event, so it is not unreasonable to conclude, given the same context, that Paul understood Christ's first manifestation to have been subsequent to his preexistence.[130] In isolation such an argument is at best suggestive, but as part of the broader pattern of Paul's christology it appears more as confirmatory.

CONCLUSION

That Paul teaches Christ's preexistence is the majority, but not the unanimous, view. James Dunn, who does find preexistence in the latest New Testament documents, says Paul works primarily from a second Adam christology that does not require preexistence (although Dunn interprets this to mean it does not include pre-existence). For Dunn preexistence is a Johannine contribution to christology. Others argue Paul's emphasis is so exclusively on the cross and resurrection that he has no time to concern himself with the other end of Christ's life. Thüsing says any preexistence in Paul's theology is that of the Spirit because Jesus' uniqueness results from his possession of the Spirit.[131] Conzelmann considers Paul's preexistence language mythological, an attempt to explain Jesus'

---

[129]G. B. Caird, "The Development of the Doctrine of Christ in the New Testament," in *Christ for Us Today,* ed. Norman Pittinger (London: SCM Press, 1968), pp. 79-80.

[130]John F. Balchin, "Paul, Wisdom and Christ," in *Christ the Lord,* ed. H. H. Rowdon (Downers Grove, Ill.: InterVarsity Press, 1982), p. 213.

[131]Wilhelm Thüsing and Karl Rahner, *A New Christology,* trans. David Smith (New York: Seabury, 1980), p. 171.

origins in light of the resurrection. For some modern critics of the doctrine, preexistence finds its source in Hellenistic thought and was imported into Christianity as it spread throughout the Mediterranean area. They continue to argue this position despite overwhelming evidence to the contrary. Others, like J. A. T. Robinson, hold to adoptionist christologies in which discussion of personal preexistence is meaningless. I will examine these objections to the doctrine in greater detail in chapter nine.

4

OTHER NEW TESTAMENT WITNESSES

Paul's letters, John's Gospel and the letter to the Hebrews have long been the most frequently cited sources in any discussion of what the New Testament has to say about Christ's preexistence. Although other New Testament books may be less explicit, many also testify to this preexistence. Despite the vigorous denials of some scholars, the Synoptic Gospels contain material relevant to our topic. There are two reasons why some deny the Synoptics teach Christ's preexistence: the implicit nature of most of the evidence, and belief that Jesus and other Gospel characters simply could not have said what they did about Jesus. Hebrews' teaching of Christ's preexistence is much more explicit. First Peter speaks about Christ in a way that appears to presume his preexistence. In this chapter we will examine passages from each of these books.

THE SYNOPTIC GOSPELS

Many New Testament scholars state unequivocally that the Synoptic Gospels do not teach Christ's preexistence. This may take the form of either denying Matthew, Mark and Luke discuss the subject at all or asserting they present Jesus in a way that precludes the possibility of his preexistence. Our examination of the Synoptics will include at least the following questions. Do they support the doctrinal claim of Jesus' deity? Do they include material that could be understood as related to Christ's preexistence and if so, how do they handle it? Who does the Synoptic Jesus understand himself to be? One important piece of evidence is the "I have come" statement and similar statements Jesus made repeatedly in the Synoptic Gospels. These are similar to the sending statements we found in Paul's letters, but do they have a similar meaning? Two of the Gospels include accounts of Christ's virginal conception and birth. Do these provide grounds for rejecting any sense of preexistence (as some theologians and biblical scholars have claimed) or do they instead require the preexistence of the virgin-born one for their significance?

The Synoptic Gospels provide accounts of Jesus' sayings and deeds with much less commentary than John. This means they are less explicitly theological than Paul's letters and John's Gospel, but it does not mean they lack theological content or interest. Like the other New Testament books, they were written from theological perspectives and for theological purposes, but their theology is for the most part implicit. Paul and John are far more explicit. As a result we need to look carefully in the text for signs of the author's belief. Such signs include the events and sayings recounted in the Gospel, the terms and titles used to describe Jesus, and Old Testament allusions.

Just as the evidence for Christ's preexistence is implicit in his words and deeds, so is the Synoptic witness to that evidence. R. G. Hamerton-Kelly suggests Wisdom and Son of Man themes express this witness. Jean Galot associates the Synoptic teaching with John by arguing the former imply what the latter declares explicitly. What John said clearly is no more than the logical consequence of the hints and allusions we find in Matthew, Mark and Luke.[1] Taylor, Marshall and a number of others conclude *all* the Gospels affirm Jesus' divine sonship. Wolfhart Pannenberg challenges this perception, however, saying neither Son of Man nor Wisdom language had anything to do with preexistence; this teaching did not appear until the Logos doctrine of John's Gospel.[2] A. T. Hanson sees no clear evidence either of a doctrine of Christ's preexistence in the Synoptics or that Jesus had any sense of personal preexistence; preexistence was a Pauline contribution.[3] Anthony F. Buzzard expresses even more complete skepticism about the doctrine of preexistence not only in the Synoptics but also in Acts and 1 Peter:

> There is complete silence about any real preexistence of Christ in Matthew, Mark, Luke, Acts and Peter. Not only do they not hint at a pre-human Son of God, they contradict the idea by talking of the origin of Jesus (Matt. 1:18) and his begetting as Son (Matt. 1:20) *in Mary's womb.*[4]

Rudolf Schnackenberg, however, warns us against attempting to understand Jesus in exclusively human terms. Instead, it is necessary to view him in terms

---

[1]Jean Galot, *Who Is Christ?* (Chicago: Franciscan Herald, 1981), pp. 122-23.

[2]Wolfhart Pannenberg, *Jesus,* trans. Lewis L. Wilkins and Duane A. Priebe, 2nd ed. (Philadelphia: Westminster Press, 1977), p. 152. We will find later that this is the conclusion James Dunn argues at length.

[3]A. T. Hanson, "Two Consciousnesses: The Modern Version of Chalcedon," *Scottish Journal of Theology* 37 (1984): 478.

[4]Anthony F. Buzzard, "The Nature of Preexistence in the New Testament," *A Journal from the Radical Reformation* 6 (1996): 20.

of his relatedness to God and his nearness to God. The mystery of who Jesus is becomes comprehensible only when we go beneath his human exterior to the heart of his being. He says, "From Gospel to Gospel the mystery of the person of Jesus is revealed, until it reaches its culmination in John through the statements about the preexistent Son of God, who was with God, was himself God, and came into the world as a human being in order to reveal God in his essence, his truth, and his glory."[5]

The Synoptic evidence about Christ's preexistence is generally indirect and implicit. These Gospels provide, with minimal commentary, an account of Jesus' earthly words and deeds. The deeds that could lead one to conclude Christ preexisted would be those that caused the first witnesses or later readers to believe in Christ's deity. The words could be teachings that led people to ask, "Who is this who speaks with such authority?" or statements by Jesus that presupposed or implied his preexistence. The latter include Jesus' enigmatic self-designation as the Son of Man and his language about having come or been sent. I intend to consider only the second group of sayings. This chapter would become intolerably long if I examined every Synoptic passage that might point to Jesus' deity. Further, those passages have been considered very competently by such scholars as Marshall, France, Morris, Moule and Taylor in my bibliography and by commentators cited in my notes. I will begin by looking first at each of the Synoptic Gospels and then at Jesus' "I have come" statements.

MATTHEW

Much of what Matthew says in regard to Christ's preexistence can be understood only in light of Easter. Contrary to Wolfhart Pannenberg, Raymond Brown and others, Matthew's account of the virgin birth is not inconsistent with the preexistence of the one so born.[6] Brown says traditional teaching was the result of harmonizing John's Gospel with Matthew's and Luke's accounts of the virgin birth, but he considers this a post-New Testament development. He says this harmonization appeared early in the second century and can be seen in Ignatius, Aristides and Melito. Both preexistence doctrine and the virgin birth teaching were intended to counteract adoptionism.[7] According to Ferdinand Hahn,

---

[5]Rudolf Schnackenberg, *Jesus in the Gospels,* trans. O. C. Dean Jr. (Louisville: Westminster/John Knox, 1995), p. 322.

[6]I will use the term *virgin birth* throughout even though the correct term is *virginal conception.* That is what both Matthew and Luke report and the church has taught—even though it has done so using the language of birth instead of conception.

[7]Raymond E. Brown, *The Birth of the Messiah* (Garden City, N.Y.: Doubleday, 1977), pp. 31, 141 n. 27.

Matthew grounded Jesus' divine sonship in his birth, not in preexistence (as did John).[8] Reginald Fuller and Pheme Perkins write that although incarnation implies the preexistence of a divine being, Matthew did not reach as far as preexistence: "The most we can say is that God's wisdom (that is, a personified aspect of his activity), which has been at work all through Israel's history, is now definitely operative in Jesus."[9]

The virgin birth account does not speak directly to the issue of Christ's preexistence, but neither does it speak against it. Matthew's report that Joseph was told the baby would be Immanuel, "God with us," can in hindsight be understood as suggestive of preexistence, although it need not be.[10] Contrary to Hahn's belief that Christ's divine sonship was based on his birth, Matthew's Jewish context would not have permitted the idea of deity arising out of a temporal birth.

Matthew did not speak explicitly about Christ's preexistence and much of his Gospel can be read to be consistent with any conclusion on the issue. This is not true for Matthew 11:27, however. The best sense of this verse not only presumes Christ's preexistence but also presumes Jesus was aware of his preexistence. Most of Jesus' "I have come" statements also appear to presume he has come from elsewhere and thus imply his preexistence.

Matthew 11:27-30

All things have been committed to me by my Father. No one knows the Son except the Father, and no one knows the Father except the Son and those to whom the Son chooses to reveal him.

Come to me, all you who are weary and burdened, and I will give you rest. Take my yoke upon you and learn from me, for I am gentle and humble in heart, and you will find rest for your souls. For my yoke is easy and my burden is light.

This is probably the most important and controversial of the Synoptics' passages relating to Christ's preexistence. (T. F. Torrance describes Matthew 11:27 as the most important verse in the New Testament for our knowledge of God.)[11] The first verse is also found in Luke 10:22. Some doubt this passage

---

[8]Ferdinand Hahn, *The Titles of Jesus in Christology,* trans. Harold Knight and George Ogg (London: Lutterworth, 1969), pp. 306-7.

[9]Reginald H. Fuller and Pheme Perkins, *Who Is This Christ? Gospel Christology and Contemporary Faith* (Philadelphia: Fortress, 1983), p. 85.

[10]Hamerton-Kelly says, "The Matthean exegetes interpreted Isaiah 7:14 to indicate that Jesus was conceived by the Holy Spirit and born of a virgin, which, while it does not say that he existed before he was conceived, does state most clearly that in Jesus 'God is with us'; his presence is a transcendental presence" (*Preexistence, Wisdom, and the Son of Man* [Cambridge: Cambridge University Press, 1973], p. 77).

[11]Thomas F. Torrance, *The Doctrine of Jesus Christ* (Eugene, Ore.: Wipf & Stock, 2002), p. 1.

even belongs in Matthew or Luke because it sounds "too Johannine," a conclusion that presumes John's theology had nothing in common with those of the Synoptic writers. It also seems to presume that associating a Synoptic text with John must necessarily discredit that text. Some think Jesus never said these words, but the early church made them up for him. Others deny Jesus was speaking about himself. Nonetheless, leading New Testament scholars consider the words to be from Jesus, the passage a part of Matthew and the subject to be Jesus' unique relationship with God. A. M. Hunter convincingly describes the Matthew passage as "perhaps the most important verses in the Synoptic Gospels."[12]

Many early Christian commentators understood Jesus to be claiming in verse 27 to be coessential with God the Father. Hilary said, "Thus in this mystery of mutual knowledge it is understood that nothing else existed in the Son than what was known to be in the Father."[13] Cyril of Alexandria says of the verse, "He said, 'Everything has been handed down to me' so that he might not seem to be a member of a different species or inferior to the Father. Jesus added this in order to show that his nature is ineffable and inconceivable, like the Father's. For only the divine nature of the Trinity comprehends itself. Only the Father knows his own Son, the fruit of his own substance."[14] Calvin interpreted the passage using Colossians 2:9, saying the intimacy of the relationship between Christ and the Father is because the fullness of the Godhead exists in bodily form.

These verses combine Jesus' sense of intimacy with God as *the* Son of God with Old Testament Wisdom thought. A. T. Wainwright understands this as Jesus contrasting himself with Jewish Wisdom and offering gifts superior to those Wisdom gives. He does not see the saying as necessarily claiming preexistence but says the implication of these verses certainly points in that direction and the functional statements require ontological conclusions.[15] Vincent Taylor notes scholars, whether they accept or reject the genuineness of this passage, agree "it implies a Sonship which ultimately is one of nature and being." He adds that while the language is Jewish, it describes a filial relation-

[12]A. M. Hunter, "Crux Criticorum—Matt. XI. 25-30—A Re-appraisal," *New Testament Studies* 8 (1962): 241.

[13]Hilary, "On Matthew" 11.2, in *Matthew 1—13*, ed. Manlio Simonetti, Ancient Christian Commentary on Scripture, New Testament 1a (Downers Grove, Ill.: InterVarsity Press, 2001), p. 231.

[14]Cyril of Alexandria, Fragment 148, *Matthew 1—13*, ed. Manlio Simonetti, Ancient Christian Commentary on Scripture, New Testament 1a (Downers Grove, Ill.: InterVarsity Press, 2001), pp. 231-32.

[15]A. T. Wainwright, *The Trinity in the New Testament* (London: SPCK, 1962), p. 141.

ship that transcends human experience.[16] Jeremias's contrary contention that
the passage reflected a generic father-son relationship has not been widely accepted. Even if the language were generic, Robert Gundry believes the best
explanation of the passage is that it reflects the exclusive and reciprocal
knowledge of Son and Father. He says the application of this passage to Jesus
and God "requires a Johannine Christology of Jesus as the Father's unique
Son."[17] Although R. T. France believes the passage does not explicitly teach a
preincarnate divine relationship, Alfred Plummer charges rejection of such a
claim by Jesus is based on prejudice, not evidence.[18] Plummer's sharp language notwithstanding, the clear import of the passage is that of one who enjoys knowledge of and a relationship with God surpassing anything humans
might properly claim. I. Howard Marshall describes the Jesus of the Lukan parallel as "[taking] up the role of the Son of God, and [claiming] to stand in an
exclusive relationship to him and be the sole mediator of the knowledge of
God to men."[19] He describes this as adequately explained by Jesus' sense of
God as Father, but adds a Christian reader would understand "an allusion to
the unique status of Jesus."

The passage, especially Matthew 11:28-30, reflects Jewish Wisdom teaching.
But whereas Wisdom was a personification closely associated with God, Jesus
is a *person* intimately related to God. This is a distinction with a significant difference. James Dunn objects to too close an association because Wisdom is feminine (in both Hebrew and Greek) as opposed to Jesus' maleness. Yet, as Dunn
notes, Jesus' claims far surpass those of Wisdom, particularly the claim to be the
exclusive mediator of the knowledge of God (and even salvation) to humanity.
John Nolland and Darrell Bock have demonstrated conclusively that although
Jesus' role is similar to that of Jewish Wisdom, it far surpasses anything claimed
for Wisdom.[20] Contrary to Daniel Harrington's statement that Matthew 11:27 presents Jesus as the incarnation of divine Wisdom, I believe Jesus is best understood as greater than Wisdom (even Harrington notes affinities in the text with

---

[16]Vincent Taylor, *The Person of Christ in New Testament Teaching* (London: Macmillan, 1958),
p. 168.

[17]Robert H. Gundry, *Matthew*, 2nd ed. (Grand Rapids: Eerdmans, 1994), p. 217.

[18]R. T. France, *The Gospel According to Matthew*, Tyndale New Testament Commentaries
(Grand Rapids: Eerdmans, 1985), pp. 199-200; Alfred Plummer, *An Exegetical Commentary
on the Gospel According to S. Matthew* (London: Robert Scott, 1909), pp. 166, 168-69.

[19]I. Howard Marshall, *The Gospel of Luke*, New International Greek Testament Commentary
(Grand Rapids: Eerdmans, 1978), pp. 437-38.

[20]John Nolland, *Luke 9:21—18:34*, Word Biblical Commentary 35B (Dallas: Word, 1993), p. 574;
Darrell L. Bock, *Luke*, vol. 2, *9:51—24:53*, Baker Exegetical Commentary on the New Testament (Grand Rapids: Baker, 1996), p. 1012.

Johannine thought),[21] although the Wisdom motif seems overemphasized with the different interpretations canceling each other out.

As we have seen, New Testament writers use Jewish themes, but they never consider themselves limited by those themes. This is no less true of Wisdom, whether the writer is Paul or Matthew or John. If Wisdom helps people understand Jesus better, they appropriate Wisdom language, but when it becomes a hindrance they drop it and continue their explanation using other terms. Dunn, however, believes the relationship is "more likely to be that of God and the one who has been specially favored with the knowledge of God and who had been specially charged with the task of making God's purpose known and of bringing God's purpose to completion among men."[22] Dunn's conclusions about the limitations of the Wisdom analogy and the unique intimacy Jesus enjoyed with God are convincing, but his view that Jesus was Wisdom's eschatological representative and the righteous man par excellence understates the evidence. I remain dubious of his conclusion that Jesus was the one who represented Israel in the last days rather than the one who represented God to Israel. (Although I do not think we need to choose one to the exclusion of the other.) Dunn seems to reject the possibility Jesus could speak about himself in language that outstrips the Jewish categories of his day.

Plummer argues from grammatical analysis that the passage teaches Christ's preexistence. He says the aorist tense used in "have been committed to me" points back to a moment in eternity and thus implies Christ's preexistence.[23] Accepting his conclusion leaves the only alternative as denying Jesus could ever have spoken such words, but this argument must be a priori.

Most modern objections have viewed Matthew 11:27 (and its Lukan parallel) as inauthentic because it was supposedly Hellenistic in origin—despite increasingly strong evidence of the entire passage's Jewish roots. Others object that Jesus never used the Son of God title of himself; it was a creation of the early church. Putting that not uncontested claim to the side, I agree with Marshall when he describes the "son of God" terminology as a nontitular self-description that paved the way for later development of the title.

To say the passage cannot be authentic because of its high christology is both circular and inconsistent with the canons of biblical criticism. On the one hand,

---

[21]Daniel J. Harrington, *The Gospel of Matthew*, Sacra Pagina 1 (Collegeville, Minn.: Liturgical Press, 1991), pp. 170, 167.

[22]James D. G. Dunn, *Christology in the Making* (Philadelphia: Westminster Press, 1980), p. 200.

[23]Plummer, *Exegetical Commentary*, p. 168. I am inclined to think Plummer places more weight on the use of the aorist than it can bear despite my agreement the passage implies Christ's knowledge of his preexistence.

it imposes an understanding of what must constitute true Synoptic christology on the text in order to judge the validity of particular Synoptic statements. This is a reversal of proper exegetical practice. On the other hand, it ignores that in passages where Jesus spoke of himself in similarly "high" terms, he also expressed his ignorance in a way the early church would never have put in Jesus' mouth. Gundry says such criticism "has the look of a Procrustean bed."[24]

The Jesus of this passage is a highly exalted being. The activity described in Matthew 11:27 and Luke 10:22 is clearly divine in character. Bock says the passage states unequivocally that Jesus knew his role in God's plan.[25] He compares Jesus' authority in terms of extent and timing with Jesus' words in Matthew 28:18. He also notes that if Jesus is the only one through whom we can understand God, then it appears Jesus plays the crucial role in mediating salvation. Hunter observes preexistence is so evident in this passage that theologians as diverse as Albert Schweitzer and P. T. Forsyth said it implied Jesus was conscious of his preexistence.[26] I conclude that not only does this passage teach Christ's preexistence, it appears to teach Christ was aware of his preexistence. The passage presents Jesus as one who possessed divine authority and an essential relationship with God the Father, and by implication preexisted the earthly life recounted in the Gospels.

MARK

Mark's Gospel opens with an implied assumption of Christ's preexistence: "The beginning of the Gospel about Jesus Christ, the Son of God." The introduction continues by quoting from Isaiah 40 the words about a messenger who would go on ahead to prepare the way for the Lord. For Mark, this preparer of the way was John, so the Lord whose way had been prepared would be Jesus. This implication of Mark's introduction is stunning in its power and simplicity. There is no argument being made here; Mark simply said, "This is what happened." According to Mark, John the Baptist was the Elijah prophesied in Malachi 4:5, so Jesus must be the Lord who would follow.

If Mark's Jesus could fulfill Old Testament passages that referred to God, then Jesus should possess the attributes that make God God. One of these is eternal existence beyond the limits of our space-time world—preexistence, if we think in human and incarnational terms. In Mark 1:8, John the Baptist said he baptizes with water but the one following him will baptize with the Holy

[24]Robert H. Gundry, *Matthew* (Grand Rapids: Eerdmans, 1982), p. 218.
[25]Bock, *Luke,* pp. 1011-12.
[26]Hunter, "Crux Criticorum," p. 247.

Spirit. Because the Holy Spirit is a divine person, baptizing with the Spirit does not appear to be a human prerogative no matter how exalted the human. John's entire attitude toward this one he is preparing the way for is inconsistent with that one being merely human, even though John was unlikely to have comprehended this. Hamerton-Kelly remarks, "The mysterious origin of Jesus is a major theme in Mark. This alone hints of his pre-existence."[27] He believes Mark's Son of Man language was derived from Daniel 7 and reveals Christ's preexistent glory.

But according to Hahn, Mark derived Jesus' divine sonship from his baptism, when he was appointed and empowered as Son of God.[28] Taylor disagrees, saying, "There is no suggestion in [Mark] that it is in consequence of the descent of the Spirit that Jesus becomes the Messiah, although this view has often been held. . . . It does not appear to be a part of St. Mark's christology to explain the supernatural element in Christ's person by the fact that he is 'filled with the Spirit.'"[29] Knox says 12:35 and following shows Mark probably interpreted Psalm 110 in terms of Jesus' supernatural preexistence.[30] Kuschel, however, concludes Mark deliberately disregarded or decided against any statement about Christ's preexistence, a decision "governed by Mark's own theological and christological interests."[31] Edouard Schweizer thinks Mark 12:1-9 may contain an unreflective preexistence christology, but adds, "Mark nowhere in his gospel hints at the teaching, and his readers could not presume such a teaching from reading the text."[32]

I agree Mark does not speak directly about Christ's preexistence, but he does introduce themes that require we assume it. This includes the sending language such as that in Mark 9:37, of which George says, "The full implications of this text can hardly be grasped in human language. In sending Jesus, God did not

---

[27]Hamerton-Kelly, *Preexistence, Wisdom, and the Son of Man,* p. 66, although Hamerton-Kelly understands this as an ideal preexistence.

[28]Hahn, *Titles of Jesus,* pp. 306-7.

[29]Taylor, *Person of Christ,* p. 7.

[30]John Knox, *Jesus* (New York: Harper & Brothers, 1958), p. 153. Knox says this could be either real or ideal preexistence.

[31]Karl-Josef Kuschel, *Born Before All Time?* trans. John Bowden (New York: Crossroad, 1992), p. 316. I disagree, believing this conclusion results from Kuschel's theological concerns, not Mark's. I will discuss Kuschel's position in chapter 9.

[32]Eduard Schweizer, "Zum religionsgeschichtlichen Hintergrund der 'Sendungsformel' Gal 4:4 f. Rm 8:3 f. Joh 3:16 f. I Joh 4:9," *Zeitschrift für die Neutestamentliche Wissenschaft und die Kunde der älteren Kirche* 57 (1966): 210. Jonge says of 12:1-9, "The sending of the son/heir is unique and final; it is clear that the parable emphasized the eschatological character of Jesus' mission and his personal relationship with his Father. However, this does not necessarily imply preexistence" (Marinus de Jonge, *Christology in Context* [Philadelphia: Westminster Press, 1988], p. 43).

send a substitute or surrogate. He came himself."[33] I do not believe it is possible
to develop a doctrine of Christ's preexistence based on Mark considered in isolation, but Mark neither exists in isolation nor may it be interpreted in isolation
from other New Testament writings. In any case, Mark seems to presume
Christ's preexistence in his presentation of Jesus as the Son of God.

LUKE

As with the other Synoptic Gospels, there is no consensus regarding Luke's christology. While some see an implicit preexistence christology, others understand
Luke's Jesus as another of the Old Testament line of miraculously conceived men
of God or as having become Son of God at his baptism. Most of the relevant Lukan passages have parallels we have already considered in Matthew or Mark.
Luke 12:8-9 (paralleled in Matthew 10:32-33), however, seems to require not only
an exalted christology but an exalted self-understanding on Jesus' part.

> I tell you, whoever acknowledges me before men, the Son of Man will also ac-
> knowledge him before the angels of God. But he who disowns me before men will
> be disowned before the angels of God. (Lk 12:8-9)

If, despite the skepticism of some modern scholars, Jesus and the Son of Man
are one and the same, then Jesus was making a very powerful claim about himself as the key to human salvation. As J. M. McDermott observes:

> Once the authenticity of Lk 12, 8-9 is granted, certain questions cannot be evaded.
> . . . It seems unlikely that the one who raised such an absolute claim for himself
> never asked himself, "Who am I?" To affirm that Jesus acted decisively and ignored
> that basic human question of self-identity would strip Jesus of a normal human
> consciousness.[34]

The parallel passage in Matthew makes the claim even stronger by saying "my
Father in heaven" instead of "the angels of God."

Hans von Campenhausen believes Luke's Jesus was not merely a man awak-
ened and filled by the Spirit; his earthly self was "ordained and begotten . . .
even in the first act of his coming into being."[35] He suggests Luke's birth narrative is in the line of Old Testament accounts of humans miraculously born in
order to serve as saviors of Israel (like Samson or Samuel?). This Jesus could not
be a preexistent being. Although Luke's birth account tells of an exceptional

[33]Timothy George, *Galatians,* New American Commentary 30 (Nashville: Broadman & Holman,
1994), pp. 301-2.
[34]J. M. McDermott, "Jesus and the Son of God Title," *Gregorianum* 62 (1981): 277-78.
[35]Hans von Campenhausen, *The Virgin Birth in the Theology of the Ancient Church,* trans.
Frank Clarke, Studies in Historical Theology (Naperville, Ill.: Alec R. Allenson, 1964), p. 27.

child miraculously conceived, there is in the text no concern about preexistence. That is not part of Luke's agenda for this passage. Luke's sending statements and reports of Jesus' authority claims are relevant to preexistence, but the
virgin birth account has other concerns.

Luke's Gospel has nothing unique either supporting or challenging belief in
Christ's preexistence. What he shares with the other Synoptic writers can be
read as consistent with the teaching, but need not be except for Matthew 11:27
and the parallel in Luke 10:22, both of which I believe require Christ's personal
preexistence. One's conclusion here depends on the interpretation of the sending language, implications of Jesus' authority claims and the authenticity and interpretation of the "Son of Man" and "Son of God" titles. I believe there is sufficient evidence to understand each of these as implying Christ's preexistence or
his deity (which requires his preexistence). I further believe such understanding
makes the best sense of Luke's and the other Synoptic accounts.

THE SON OF GOD

One reason some commentators deny the authenticity of Matthew 11:27 and
Luke 10:22 is the presence of sonship language.[36] Other commentators consider
most early sonship language to be functional rather than titular or ontological.
So what does the term "Son (or son) of God" mean? Some have claimed the Jewish sense was merely honorific; it was the Hellenistic usage that imparted some
sense of divinity (*not* deity). Would Jesus have accepted either usage? I believe
Jesus did not intend to be understood in either classic Jewish or Hellenistic
terms, but neither did his words bear the full weight of John's "God the Son."
Such a meaning would have been too exalted for his listeners to comprehend
at this point in his ministry, although Jesus' words do point toward John's later
conclusion. Jesus' Son of God language (which I consider authentic) denotes
more than an itinerant teacher and healer, but its full implications had to wait
for Easter in order to be understood. Mark 9:9-10 strikes me as Jesus' teaching
that the resurrection is the interpretive key to Son of God language and also to
his entire life and ministry.

The language, for the most part, is not titular but reflects the intimate sort of
relationship seen in Matthew 11:27. So sonship language appears to presume an
essential relationship with God that predates Jesus' earthly existence. Marshall
states the power and persuasiveness of this implicit argument well:

Despite the lack of interest in this question the Synoptic Gospels certainly present

---

[36]A fuller discussion of Son of God language appears in chapter two.

Jesus as the Son of God and they guide us to the centre of his self-consciousness
as such. It is precisely this self-consciousness which, even in the absence of any
consciousness of pre-existence, makes it unsatisfactory to think of Jesus as merely
the embodiment of God's creative and saving power and which drives us on to an
incarnational understanding of him as the personal Son of God.[37]

He adds that Jesus knew he was *the* Son, occupying a place distinct from
other humans, yet mediating to them a relationship with God. This was not a
matter of playing a role, however. "The revelatory function of Jesus was dependent upon the relationship of Sonship in which he stood toward God. The title
of 'Son' and the allied use of 'Father' express a relationship of communion in
which revelation takes place so that the Son is able to reveal the Father to
men."[38] Marshall here links the role Jesus played with who he was and the role
Jesus played required his preexistence.

Knox concludes, "There is more than sufficient reason to affirm that Mark,
Matthew, and Luke, as well as Paul, took for granted the pre-existence of
Jesus."[39] He adds that in Mark Jesus has become human without fully surrendering his divine powers, merely holding them in abeyance. Knox considers this
all myth and rejects any necessary connection between function and being, but
he still acknowledges not only Paul and John but all the Synoptic writers accepted Christ's preexistence.

"I HAVE COME"
These passages in the Synoptic Gospels complement the sending statements
found in Paul.[40] In the same way, they point to Christ's real existence in heaven
before his earthly ministry. Not everything Jesus said about coming carried this
meaning, however. There is, after all, a difference between "The Son of Man
came eating and drinking" (Mt 11:19) and "The Son of Man did not come to be
served, but to serve, and to give his life as a ransom for many" (Mt 20:28). I am
not saying Jesus' language about his having come requires it be understood as
expressing preexistence, but the words hint strongly at such preexistence and
certainly permit it. As with much of the other evidence regarding preexistence,
these statements do not stand alone but form part of a broader argument for

[37]I. Howard Marshall, "Incarnational Christology in the New Testament," in *Christ the Lord,* ed.
H. H. Rowdon (Downers Grove, Ill.: InterVarsity Press, 1982), p. 15. Marshall's language of
incarnation requires preexistence, because incarnation is a change in condition, not creation
de novo.
[38]I. Howard Marshall, *Jesus the Savior* (Downers Grove, Ill.: InterVarsity Press, 1990), p. 155.
[39]John Knox, *Jesus,* pp. 156-57.
[40]A more general survey of New Testament sending language can be found in chap. 2.

Christ's deity and eternal preexistence. Morris believes that Jesus knew himself to have existed before entering this world to be the natural (although not necessary) meaning of Matthew 20:28.[41] He writes of Matthew 9:13 that "I did not come" points to a time before Christ came to this world and serves as a summary of his mission.[42] As commonly understood, language about coming for a purpose presumes the one coming has existed before the act of coming. Another passage, Matthew 10:34, similarly implies Jesus' existence before his earthly life, speaking of "having come" and "not having come" for a purpose. Similar language can be found in Matthew 5:17 and Luke 12:49. Matthew 5:17 has an additional dimension when Jesus speaks of having come to fulfill the Law and the Prophets. That does not appear to be a human possibility. The uniform testimony of Scripture is to humanity's record of sin and failure. One who could do what Jesus claims to have come to accomplish would not seem to be merely human. In Luke 12:49, Jesus is speaking of divine judgment. Again this is not a human prerogative. Only God accomplishes God's final judgment. When the language of "having come" is linked with what Jesus came to accomplish—the salvation of the world or its judgment—something more than an earthly origin seems necessary.

The Synoptic language of coming and being sent is important because while John's Gospel speaks clearly about Jesus having come, many New Testament scholars reject it. They come to the text skeptical that John's Gospel accurately reflects Jesus' life and teaching. So it does not much matter what John said; his words carry little weight with these scholars. When that same language shows up in the Synoptics, however, it is harder for those who reject any thought of Christ's real preexistence to accept. A common response is to conclude this language has been placed in Jesus' mouth by the Gospel writer. Such a conclusion cannot easily be proven, but neither can it be readily refuted if the texts are allowed to stand in isolation. But "whoever listens without bias to the entire testimony of Scripture will discover in many utterances of the Synoptics the same background which appears so clearly in the gospel of John when he speaks of the great mystery of Christ: He has descended out of heaven."[43] Leopold Sabourin notes Jesus used the word *ēlthon* (I came) to describe his mission of salvation. He points out *ēlthon* does not necessarily refer to preexistence, but given other indicators that clearly point in that direction the term certainly can be un-

---

[41]Leon Morris, *The Gospel According to Matthew* (Grand Rapids: Eerdmans, 1992), p. 512.
[42]Ibid., p. 222.
[43]G. C. Berkouwer, *The Person of Christ,* trans. John Vriend (Grand Rapids: Eerdmans, 1954), p. 166.

derstood that way.[44] Again, the issue is not merely that Christ might have pre-existed but whether he was aware of his preexistence.

These passages read naturally in terms of a more than earthly existence, al-though it is possible to read them otherwise. When we move beyond the indi-vidual passages to place them in the context of an entire pericope or even an entire Gospel, however, the natural reading of preexistence appears consistent with the larger picture and with the testimony of such New Testament authors as Paul and John. This Synoptic evidence is neither as direct nor clear-cut as Paul, John and Hebrews, but it is fully consistent with what they say about Christ's preexistence. Addressing the purported difference between how Paul and John understood Jesus and how the Synoptic authors did, Torrance writes, "Fundamentally there is very little or no difference in the presentation of Jesus as we have it in the Synoptics from that in the Gospel of John or in the Epistles of Paul."[45]

THE ACTS OF THE APOSTLES

Because Acts reports the history and preaching of at least part of the early church, scholars look to it to learn the content of the earliest Christian message. Many who reject the doctrine of Christ's preexistence or who deny the New Tes-tament teaches the doctrine look to the Acts of the Apostles for an account of an ascending christology that predates the higher christology of Paul and John. Some have suggested the Christian understanding of Jesus evolved from the early experience of a good teacher, great prophet and miracle worker to one that came to see him in terms of the deity found in the teachings of the early ecumenical councils. I have already pointed out that Paul's letters make this position exceed-ingly difficult to defend because they predate the New Testament documents that supposedly contain this low christology, including Acts. Undeterred, a few sup-porters of this evolutionary view of christology suggest later books present the earlier low christology as historical background to the high christology that quickly developed. The book used most often for this argument is Acts because it selectively recounts the first thirty or so years of church history.

Two passages are often identified as possibly teaching an adoptionist chris-tology. Acts 2:36 and Acts 13:33 supposedly teach that in the resurrection God not only vindicated Jesus' claims and declared his atoning work sufficient, but he also raised Jesus to divine status on account of his meritorious sacrifice. To accept such an interpretation, however, requires an extensive reworking of a

[44]Leopold Sabourin, *Christology* (New York: Alba House, 1984), pp. 59-60.
[45]Torrance, *Doctrine of Jesus Christ*, p. 10.

range of Christian doctrines from the Trinity to the atonement. This, despite the fact that the orthodox understanding of these doctrines is biblically well supported. The argument loses much of its potential impact when we remember that the church of Acts 1—13 was almost exclusively Jewish in makeup. A further problem with this interpretation of Acts 2:36 is its claim that in the first public defense of Christianity, Peter had his christology all wrong, and it was not until Paul that the church began to get its picture of Jesus right (unless the argument is that the church has been wrong since Paul became influential). Such an explanation contradicts both Acts and what Paul's letters say about the subject. It is true that Peter did not preach Nicene christology in the first decades of the church's existence, but it is highly improbable he preached a christology that flatly contradicted Nicea. Taylor concludes, "In the light of all the facts it is impossible to describe the Christology of the Acts as 'Adoptionist.'"[46]

Acts 2:36 is the climax of Peter's Pentecost speech to the people of Jerusalem. As such, it was cast in terms they as Jews would understand. As Luke reports it, half the speech was quotations from the Old Testament. Peter used these Old Testament passages to explain who Jesus was and why he had come. In Acts 2:36, Peter proclaimed, "Therefore, let all Israel be assured of this: God has made this Jesus, whom you crucified, both Lord and Christ." This, it has been argued, means the decisive change in Jesus occurred at his resurrection. Some go further and say even this was only a functional designation, a change in status rather than in state. Peter would then be proclaiming that Jerusalem had killed a great prophet, but this would have been only one more in a long line of such killings.

A superficial reading of Peter's words would allow this interpretation, but is it true to the intent of the passage? It does not pass the "so what?" test: if the critics are correct, the proper response to such talk about Jesus is "so what?" Why be interested in Jesus but not in the many prophets murdered by Old Testament Israel? Prophets had been killed in Jerusalem before, but they were not made Lord or Christ, and their deaths were not the subject of biblical prophecy. As Jesus himself had pointed out, it was a very bad thing that God's prophets were killed by those who called themselves God's people in the city where God's temple stood. Nonetheless, no one was commanded to be baptized in the name of those prophets and thereby receive forgiveness of sins or the gift of the Holy Spirit. So Jesus surpassed the prophets of the Old Testament, and the citation from Psalm 110 Peter quoted indicates there was more to him than his humanity. Still, we must deal with Peter's language: Jesus was made or appointed, this is the primary meaning of *poiē*.

---

[46]Taylor, *Person of Christ*, p. 31.

Guthrie suggests Peter was saying that following Christ's death and resurrection God declared him "Messiah-Lord" in contrast to suffering Messiah. He notes other passages in Acts describing Jesus as Lord and Christ appear to support this interpretation.[47] According to Stott, Jesus was and publicly claimed to be Lord and Christ, so Peter was saying that what Jesus was by right God now made him in reality and power.[48]

J. C. O'Neill says the language is that of enthronement, not selection, election or adoption: "We should not be too hasty in drawing the conclusion that the enthronement of Jesus as Lord and Christ entailed his adoption, in the sense of his selection as the best candidate from a pool of candidates."[49] He argues the verb in Acts 2:36 cannot mean Jesus was made Lord and Christ if he was not already Lord and Christ. Logically and theologically, O'Neill makes the best sense of the passage.

F. J. Foakes-Jackson contends Peter was presenting Jesus as he had appeared to the Jews, as a man enjoying God's approval. The resurrection, by clearly proclaiming Jesus to be Lord and Christ, showed who Jesus truly was.[50] Conzelmann acknowledges the language of Acts 2:36 sounds adoptionist, but says this apparent meaning is incompatible with the christology of Luke's Gospel. He concludes, "Luke is not reflecting on the time of installation at all but simply sets forth God's action in opposition to the behavior of the Jews."[51] Conzelmann's argument becomes irrelevant if Luke was indeed simply reporting on an early sermon whose content he did not necessarily agree with. Such an approach appears to be at cross purposes with Luke's evident apologetic intent in both his Gospel and Acts, however, and that makes such an interpretation suspect.

The adoptionist tone of Acts 2:36 disappears when we consider carefully what Peter was saying in his Pentecost speech. The sense of the passage better fits proclamation than designation or transformation. The christology of Peter's first letter sounds quite similar to this speech even though it uses the language of manifestation rather than proclamation. Before discussing what Peter wrote about Jesus, however, we need to consider the second Acts text, one Dunn says

---

[47]Donald Guthrie, *New Testament Theology* (Downers Grove, Ill.: InterVarsity Press, 1981), pp. 246-47.

[48]John Stott, *The Spirit, the Church, and the World* (Downers Grove, Ill.: InterVarsity Press, 1990), p. 77. I believe Stott would be more self-consistent and in agreement with the entirety of Acts if he were to say that what Jesus was in reality God declared him to be publicly and in power.

[49]J. C. O'Neill, *Who Did Jesus Think He Was?* (Leiden: E. J. Brill, 1995), pp. 18, 16.

[50]F. J. Foakes-Jackson, *The Acts of the Apostles* (London: Hodder and Stoughton, 1931), pp. 16-17.

[51]Hans Conzelmann, *Acts of the Apostles,* trans. James Limburg, A. Thomas Kraabel and Donald H. Juel (Philadelphia: Fortress, 1987), p. 21.

shows the early church viewed Christ's divine sonship in terms of a role and status he had received at his resurrection.

ACTS 13:32-33

> We tell you the good news. What God promised our fathers, he has fulfilled for us, their children, by raising up Jesus. As it is written in the second Psalm:
> "You are my Son;
> today I have become your Father."

According to Dunn, the early Christians *"regarded Jesus' resurrection as introducing him into a relationship with God decisively new, eschatologically distinct, perhaps we should even say qualitatively different from what he had enjoyed before."*[52] The question to which Dunn presupposes an answer is whether the resurrection caused this relationship or revealed it. I believe the Spirit christology evident in Dunn's earlier work has pushed him toward the first conclusion. This leads him to interpret Psalm 2 in what can only be called an adoptionist sense (despite Dunn's argument that the term is anachronistic when considering the first century church). Conzelmann disagrees with Dunn's conclusion, saying the reference does not mean Luke thought Jesus was not the Son of God before the resurrection.[53] F. F. Bruce also denies Luke intended us to understand that Jesus entered into a new relationship of divine sonship at the resurrection.[54] Marshall says an examination of this passage and Romans 1:3 shows "the early church regarded the resurrection as the vindication of a status which Jesus had already claimed for himself."[55] Calvin wrote of this passage that it shows "Christ is the Wisdom begotten of the Eternal Father before time. But that is the secret generation and now David declareth that it was revealed to men."[56]

We need to remember this passage is an account of Paul's preaching in a synagogue. This means Paul was using Jewish terms and Scripture to evangelize a Jewish audience. Paul's christology as he expressed it in his earliest letters was in no sense adoptionist. This is the context that must govern any interpretation of Acts 13:33; it expresses human recognition, not divine designation, of Christ's lordship.

---

[52]Dunn, *Christology in the Making*, p. 36.

[53]Conzelmann, *Acts of the Apostles*, p. 105.

[54]F. F. Bruce, *Commentary on the Book of Acts: The English Text with Introduction, Exposition and Notes*, New International Commentary on the New Testament (Grand Rapids: Eerdmans, 1954), p. 276.

[55]I. Howard Marshall, "The Development of Christology in the Early Church," *Tyndale Bulletin* 18 (1967): 79.

[56]John Calvin, *Commentary on the Acts of the Apostles*, p. 440, on AGES Digital Library CD-ROM, 1996.

First Peter 1:20

> He was chosen before the creation of the world, but was revealed in these last
> times for your sake.

This comes from a passage where Peter was reminding his readers they could
have confidence in Christ's work on their behalf because of who he was and
his relationship with God. The first part of this verse, with its language of choosing, carries the sense of predestination and thus is not inconsistent with an ideal
preexistence in the mind of God. By itself it sounds no different from Paul's description of believers in Ephesians 1:11. The second half of the verse moves in
an entirely different direction, however. There, Peter wrote about what happened to the one who had been chosen and why it happened. "He was *revealed,*" wrote Peter, "for your sake." The word *revealed* strongly suggests that
who or what was revealed already existed. This means the preexistence must
have been real, not ideal. It also echoes the language of 2 Corinthians 8:9, where
Paul wrote that Christ became human for our sake.

Dunn disagrees with this conclusion, although he acknowledges the strength
of the argument. He suggests that what was revealed was not Christ but God's
plan. It was not Christ who preexisted and then was revealed, but the divine
plan that included Christ.[57] This is not what the verse says by any normal reading, however. Reginald Fuller believes Peter's language is part of the evidence
that belief in Christ's preexistence was "a common feature of the gentile mission."[58] Peter Davids notes the similarity of Peter's manifestation language to that
of 2 Timothy 3:16, Hebrews 9:26, 1 John 1:2 and 1 John 3:5, arguing Christ's
continued existence across the divide between heavenly existence and earthly
incarnation is no different from his continued existence between his first and
second coming.[59]

J. N. D. Kelly believes it is difficult to avoid concluding Peter assumed
Christ's preexistence in his letter. This preexistence could only have been personal because Kelly believes ideal preexistence says too little.[60] J. Ramsey
Michaels agrees: "*Phanerōthentos* [appeared] presupposes not only Christ's
designation in advance to be the redeemer of God's people, but his actual pre-

---

[57]Dunn, *Christology in the Making,* p. 237. Dunn is careful to say Peter "may well have meant"
to say what Dunn surmises.

[58]Reginald H. Fuller, *The Foundations of New Testament Christology* (London: Fontana, 1965),
p. 246.

[59]Peter H. Davids, *The First Epistle of Peter,* New International Commentary on the New Testament (Grand Rapids: Eerdmans, 1990), p. 74.

[60]J. N. D. Kelly, *A Commentary on the Epistles of Peter and Jude* (Grand Rapids: Baker, 1969),
p. 76.

existence."[61] Charles Laymon says Peter mentioned Christ's preexistence because he sought to understand Jesus in the context of the whole purpose of God. He also mentions the effect of Paul's thought, suggesting Peter felt no need to belabor the subject because Paul had presented it clearly already.[62] Even Adolf Harnack, whose views on the subject leave much to be desired, said:

> I Peter 1:18ff. is a classic passage. . . . Here we find a conception of the pre-existence of Christ which is not yet affected by cosmological or psychological speculation, which does not overstep the boundaries of purely religious contemplation, and which arose from the Old Testament way of thinking, and the living impression derived from the person of Jesus.[63]

E. G. Selwyn is alone in saying, "We are not entitled to say that Peter was familiar with the idea of Christ's pre-existence with the Father before the incarnation." He reaches this conclusion by focusing on the predestination language and ignoring the manifestation language. Selwyn did not reach his conclusion by denying Christ's deity or preexistence, however. He merely says Peter never moved beyond affirming Christ's deity to the point of affirming his preexistence in the way Paul and John did. I consider this conclusion untenable. I can understand affirming preexistence without deity, but not deity without preexistence. Selwyn compares Peter's christology to that of early Acts (which I have already argued allows for a high christology), although he does not present Peter as teaching a low christology.[64]

In an unobtrusive way, Peter in this passage has identified Christ as preexistent. He noted that Christ entered fully into the situation of fallen humanity in order to redeem us. Peter was not arguing preexistence in order to convince his readers of some truth about the person of Jesus Christ; he was presupposing a truth about Christ's person—his preexistence—in order to affirm the value of his salvific work in our behalf.

HEBREWS

For many, the letter to the Hebrews offers as clear a statement of Christ's personal preexistence as we will find in the entire New Testament; others, however, deny the letter says anything about Christ's deity or preexistence. Still others are

---

[61]J. Ramsey Michaels, *1 Peter*, Word Biblical Commentary 49 (Waco, Tex.: Word, 1988), p. 67.
[62]Charles M. Laymon, *Christ in the New Testament* (New York: Abingdon, 1958), pp. 211-12.
[63]Adolf von Harnack, *History of Dogma,* trans. Neil Buchanan (New York: Dover, 1961), 1:323.
[64]E. G. Selwyn, *First Epistle of St. Peter*, pp. 248, 250, quoted in Anthony F. Buzzard, "The Nature of Preexistence in the New Testament," *A Journal from the Radical Reformation* 6 (1996): 17.

convinced Hebrews teaches Christ's ideal preexistence. David Mealand explains the broad range of interpretations comes about because "on the one hand Christ is seen as pre-existent Son of God, as Lord, as divine, and as exalted at God's right hand. On the other he is seen as subordinate, and traditional language is used of the Son being appointed."[65] John Robinson points out the author combined preexistence and "designatory" language to describe Christ. The latter, he says, showed Christ to be a human approved or chosen by God and in terms of later christology appears adoptionist.[66]

The reality seems to be less simple than Mealand and Robinson portray; what they consider to be a matter of either-or is actually both-and. Christ is both the preexistent Son of God and a man approved by God. This is the heart of the mystery of Jesus Christ, and the author of Hebrews has expressed it best of all the New Testament writers. Torrance says, "Yet there in *Hebrews* where the humanity of Christ is more strongly insisted on than in any part of the Apostolic witness, the pre-existence and eternity of Christ is also more strongly insisted on than elsewhere."[67]

The language of Christ's preexistence permeates the entire letter to the Hebrews. The reality underlying this language is what underpins Jesus' full and complete humanity, and gives worth to the sacrifice he made. The author emphasizes Christ died for sinful humanity and God vindicated his sacrifice. Neither Christ's sacrifice nor the christology of Hebrews makes sense apart from belief in Christ's preexistence. Although John Knox says it is impossible to affirm both Christ's preexistence and his full humanity, that is precisely what Hebrews does. The author makes no attempt to explain how this can be; he simply pictures Jesus as deity in the strongest possible terms while at the same time presenting him as experiencing every aspect of human existence except personal sinfulness.

The author of Hebrews begins in the first paragraph to present Christ as the preexistent Son of God and continues to emphasize this aspect of his being throughout the remainder of the letter. Beginning with Christ's preexistence, the author traces his career through his earthly life, sacrificial death and glorified postexistence in heaven. The same Jesus is the subject of each of these experiences, and the later ones derive their significance from his original condition. A. T. Hanson expects that "anyone who attempts to present an adequate account

---

[65]David L. Mealand, "The Christology of the Epistle to the Hebrews," *Modern Churchman,* no. 22 (1979): 183.

[66]John A. T. Robinson, *The Priority of John* (London: SCM Press, 1985), p. 391.

[67]Torrance, *Doctrine of Jesus Christ,* p. 57.

of the doctrine of the incarnation must at some point face the question of pre-existence." This, he says, is what Hebrews does: it presents Jesus as preexistent deity and regards his existence as heavenly Son of God as continuous with his life as Jesus of Nazareth.[68] H. R. Mackintosh notes the letter says little about the details of Christ's preexistence, but "it fills a larger place than in any other New Testament epistle."[69]

The strongest modern objection to the belief Hebrews teaches Christ's personal preexistence comes from James Dunn. Dunn agrees Hebrews presents "a concept" of Christ's preexistence, but he argues this is no more than an ideal preexistence. He describes Hebrews' presentation of Christ as "in language which seems to denote pre-existence more clearly than anything we have met so far," but he adds Hebrews contains more adoptionist language than any other New Testament book. So Dunn believes the most appropriate description of Christ's preexistence is as "the existence of the platonic idea in the mind of God," charging any conclusion that Hebrews teaches Christ's personal preexistence goes beyond the evidence.

His denial that Hebrews teaches Christ's personal preexistence disregards the textual evidence (see chap. 9). It also misunderstands why Hebrews' christology pays no less attention to Christ's humanity than to his deity—this is what appears as adoptionism to Dunn. Although he says "the special contribution of Hebrews is that it seems to be the first of the NT writings to have embraced the specific thought of a pre-existent divine sonship," he concludes the author of Hebrews seems to envision this as an ideal preexistence. He surmises Hebrews' idea of preexistence derives from Philo's Logos language and Platonic idealism.[70] Dunn bases this conclusion on the supposition that Hebrews reflects a strongly Platonic Hellenistic Judaism and the interpretive key to the book's christology is to be found in Philo. The christological tensions Dunn finds in Hebrews thus are the result of his attempt to merge two worldviews.

Dunn admits the language of Hebrews sounds remarkably like that of personal preexistence, but this does not fit his interpretation of the book, so he looks elsewhere for an explanation. I believe a careful reading of the key Hebrews passages better fits the traditional interpretation than does Dunn's or those of others who reject the possibility of personal preexistence. F. F. Bruce's conclusion supports this: the language of Hebrews may reflect that of Philo and

---

[68]A. T. Hanson, *Grace and Truth* (London: SPCK, 1975), p. 64.
[69]H. R. Mackintosh, *The Doctrine of the Person of Christ,* 2nd ed. (Edinburgh: T & T Clark, 1913), p. 83.
[70]Dunn, *Christology in the Making,* pp. 52-56.

Jewish Wisdom speculation, but its meaning goes far beyond theirs. He adds, "The language is descriptive of a man who had lived and died in Palestine a few decades previously, but who nonetheless was the eternal Son and supreme revelation of God."[71]

According to Caird, preexistence in Hebrews has no ontological element. In no small measure this is because he finds here an adoptionist christology. Caird sees a high christology in Hebrews, but he believes the primary evidence for Christ's preexistence is confined to the first paragraph of the letter and the Old Testament quotations that follow. Although Caird's Hebrews does present Christ in terms of his preexistence, he finds it necessary to distinguish different kinds of preexistence. For Caird, some sort of ideal preexistence or predestination seems most congenial.

John Robinson, who generally prefers an adoptionist christology, acknowledges Hebrews teaches Christ's preexistence. He sees a conflict between incarnation and preexistence that he believes the writer was blind to, but he never justifies this claim of conflict. Robinson ends by evacuating the concept of Christ's preexistence of all significance and offense because he believes Jesus must not differ in any way from the rest of humanity.

Ernst Käsemann traces the preexistence teaching of Hebrews (as well as Paul) to a Gnostic redeemer myth and its concept of the Ürmensch.[72] Despite Käsemann's detailed argument and his claim that it fits the chronology of the New Testament, the redeemer myth is widely rejected and Gnosticism is generally seen as dependent on Christianity rather than the reverse. Current scholarship considers Gnosticism to have been a later development than Christianity, although early expressions of a Gnostic worldview appear contemporary with later New Testament writings and apparently were the target of some of their polemic.

Wilfred Knox counsels caution when suggesting Hebrews (and Paul) may have drawn their ideas about Christ's preexistence from pagan sources. He says, "At one or two points we notice a considerable similarity, but never enough to prove a direct connection."[73] Knox's caution recognizes the difficulty in attributing sources to ideas in history, especially when the purported source comes from outside the author's tradition. The only aspect of Jesus' story he thinks Hellenists would find incomprehensible was the crucifixion. He concludes, how-

---

[71]F. F. Bruce, *The Epistle to the Hebrews,* New International Commentary on the New Testament (Grand Rapids: Eerdmans, 1964), p. 5

[72]Ernst Käsemann, *The Wandering People of God,* trans. Roy A. Harrisville and Irving L. Sandberg (Minneapolis: Augsburg, 1984), pp. 101-15.

[73]Wilfred L. Knox, "The 'Divine Hero' Christology in the New Testament," *Harvard Theological Review* 41 (1948): 247.

ever, that "the Son is in 1.3 described in terms only applicable to the pre-existent Wisdom of God."

Fred Craddock says the preexistence statements of Hebrews provide a context for understanding Jesus' life. He explains, "Because the Son is pre-existent and eternal, his sharing with his flesh and blood brethren is more than a sympathetic but futile leap into our pit; he is *able* to redeem, to accomplish the work of salvation."[74] Taylor goes further, saying Hebrews shows no trace of adoptionism: Christ was not a human raised to divine dignity but a divine person who appeared in the humility of true humanity. Even the exaltation language described someone already understood as divine.[75] This is the picture of Christ I believe we will find in the preexistence passages in the letter to the Hebrews. Many of the themes we will see in Hebrews have already appeared in Paul's letters and will reappear in John.

HEBREWS 1:1-8

In the past God spoke to our forefathers through the prophets at many times and in various ways, but in these last days he has spoken to us by his Son, whom he appointed heir of all things, and through whom he made the universe. The Son is the radiance of God's glory and the exact representation of his being, sustaining all things by his powerful word. After he had provided purification for sins, he sat down at the right hand of the Majesty in heaven. So he became as much superior to the angels as the name he has inherited is superior to theirs.

For to which of the angels did God ever say,

"You are my Son;
today I have become your father"?

Or again,

"I will be his Father,
and he will be my Son"?

And again, when God brings his firstborn into the world, he says,

"Let all God's angels worship him."

In speaking of the angels he says,

---

[74]Fred B. Craddock, *The Preexistence of Christ in the New Testament* (Nashville: Abingdon, 1968), pp. 136-37. This is precisely the point Torrance considers essential to christology: unless Christ is eternal deity, his salvific claim is meaningless and the Christian doctrine of the triune God is false (Torrance, *Doctrine of Jesus Christ,* p. 107).
[75]Taylor, *The Person of Christ,* p. 233.

"He makes his angels winds,
 his servants flames of fire."

But about the Son he says,

"Your throne, O God, will last forever and ever,
 and righteousness will be the scepter of your kingdom."

This passage, which comprises most of chapter one, is the key text in Hebrews dealing with Christ's preexistence, both because it introduces the entire book and because of the clarity of its language. It associates the Son explicitly with God in language that appears ontological and connects with his preexistence his work of atonement, mediation and sustainment, and his postexistence. I believe it requires we assume the Son's preexistence based on his role in creation and the sending statement. Both the ascription to the Son of the name God and the expectation that the angels will worship the Son mean we should understand this Son in terms of his deity. The descriptions of the Son as the radiance of God's glory and the exact representation of his being also present the Son in terms of deity, although because some understand this language to mean no more than reflection and image, I will have to defend this claim.

Jesus is the Son who has spoken for God in the last days and provided purification for sins. If that identification is unclear to some here, the writer makes it plain later in the letter. Martin Hengel approaches the opening paragraph of the letter similarly, seeing it in the context of Philippians 2:6-11, and as making Christ's ontological status more precise.[76] Much of this passage parallels the language of the Johannine prologue. In fact, both passages can be understood as outlining the entire content of their respective books.

While the sonship language is straightforward, how we understand this sonship will be influenced by the way we interpret "exact representation" *(charaktēr)* of God's being and radiance *(apaugasma)* of God's glory. Our conclusions will influence whether or not we are talking about deity and whether the preexistence that appears in the passage is real or ideal. Lexical study can only influence any conclusion because we may not ignore the powerful language found in the rest of the passage. Many commentators say the two phrases in verse three are parallel and should be interpreted synonymously. Both *apaugasma* and *charaktēr* appear only here in the New Testament and are quite rare in the Greek translation of the Old Testament. This means extrabiblical sources provide most examples of usage. William Lane, however, cautions against giving these sources too much weight, because their theology (especially Philo's) con-

---

[76]Martin Hengel, *The Son of God* (Philadelphia: Fortress, 1976), p. 87.

trasts sharply with that of Hebrews.[77] Bruce explains *apaugasma* means the radiance shining from a light source and notes Philo used it of the Logos in relation to God. He points out both active and passive senses of the word appear
in later creeds and the radiant light is understood as being of the same substance
as the light source.[78] Early theologians used similar images in their effort to distinguish Christ from God the Father while maintaining their ontological equality.[79] Describing both terms as references to Christ's deity, Calvin says we "learn
that the Son is one God with the Father, and that he is yet in a sense distinct
from him, so that a substance or person belongs to them both." Calvin also says
that what the author claims here for Christ belongs to God alone.[80]

Philo used *charaktēr* to mean an imprint, as in the imprint of God on a human
soul. As Lane has noted, however, Philo's belief that nothing and no one can be
an exact representation of God denies precisely what Hebrews 1:3 affirms. So
Philo's parallels have limited value for understanding Hebrews. Lane interprets
charaktēr to mean Jesus expresses visibly and exactly the reality of God. Bruce
describes *charaktēr* as much stronger than *eikōn*, meaning not simply image but
instead precise representation and embodiment: "To see Christ is to see what the
Father is like."[81] What these New Testament scholars are suggesting is that the
author of Hebrews has transformed the traditional use of these terms in his attempt to express who Jesus Christ is. The key modification is the attribution to
Christ of providing atonement, a role far surpassing Wisdom's educational role.

God created the world and now speaks to that world through the Son of Hebrews 1. God brought this Son into the world, requires the angels worship him
and addresses him as "God" using the words of Psalm 45:6. As the mediator of
creation it is necessary that the Son existed prior to that creation. To say God
brings his firstborn into the world can only mean he existed prior to being
brought into the world. To be worthy of worship and addressed as God require
the Son's deity and thus presume his preexistence. To designate this preexistence as ideal is to ignore the clear sense of the passage. It is not a matter of
choosing a viable alternate interpretation; it requires that the language of worship and mediatorship be somehow explained away. Of this verse Calvin wrote,
"And hence is proved the eternity of Christ." He linked this sonship language

[77]William L. Lane, *Hebrews 1—8*, Word Biblical Commentary 47 (Dallas: Word, 1991), p. 13.
[78]Bruce, *Epistle to the Hebrews*, p. 48 n. 22.
[79]For example, the Nicene Creed in affirming Christ's full deity and coequality with the Father
speaks of him as "Light from Light," following up this phrase with "True God from True God"
so no one will miss the point being made.
[80]John Calvin, *The Commentaries on Epistle of Paul the Apostle to the Hebrews*, p. 33, on AGES
Digital Library CD-ROM, 1996.
[81]Bruce, *Epistle to the Hebrews*, p. 48.

with Paul's words in Romans 1:4, saying that what we have is "a sort of an external begetting" that manifests to humans the hidden and internal begetting which must remain unknown had God not provided a visible proof. Only because God has done so can humans acknowledge the eternal truth that Christ is the Son of God.[82] Nonetheless, Dunn finds here an ideal preexistence, derived from the author's "Platonic idealism," in the passage. Hurst sees a starting point for preexistence doctrine. Caird denies any divine preexistence, preferring instead to see Jesus merely as "the pioneer of man's salvation."[83] These conclusions do not appear to take seriously the language of Hebrews 1 or similar New Testament texts.

Hebrews states in several places that Jesus had to experience all the suffering and temptation that are a part of the human condition. In Hebrews 2:9, we read Jesus "was made a little lower than the angels." For Jesus to be made lower than angels, it would appear he had to have begun in a status at least equal to that of angels. If this is so, he necessarily preexisted that humbled status. Hebrews 2:14 says of Jesus that "he too shared in their humanity." This passage also seems to presume Jesus' being includes more than human existence.[84] John Chrysostom said of this verse, "Indeed, he was not 'sent': for he did not pass from place to place, but took on him flesh: whereas these change their places, and leaving those in which they were before, so come to others in which they were not."[85] Although Chrysostom did not use the term *preexistence,* he certainly used the language of preexistence. Hebrews 2:17 says Jesus "had to be made like his brothers in every way." Again this is not the way we speak of humans, because we already are like each other, so something more must be true about Jesus.

Hebrews 2:9-18 tells of a Jesus who was truly and fully human, but it implies the story of Jesus includes much more than his humanity. So as one who entered into humanity, Jesus would have had to preexist his earthly life. Origin's third-century conclusion that human souls preexist their earthly embodiment would have made Hebrews' picture of Jesus compatible with that of other humans, but

---

[82]Calvin, *Hebrews,* pp. 30, 37. Calvin's interpretation depends in no way on his belief in Pauline authorship of Hebrews.

[83]G. B. Caird, "Son by Appointment," in *The New Testament Age,* ed. William C. Weinrich (Macon, Ga.: Mercer University Press, 1984), 1:74.

[84]Chrysostom considered this to be the required interpretation. In his sermon on Hebrews 2:14, he described the Son as having taken on human flesh, adding that flesh to what he already was (John Chrysostom, *Homilies on the Epistle to the Hebrews* 3 in *Chrysostom: Homilies on the Gospel of Saint John and the Epistle to the Hebrews,* Nicene and Post-Nicene Fathers, vol. 14, ed. Philip Schaff (Grand Rapids: Eerdmans, 1978), p. 811.

[85]Ibid., 3:4.

the church quickly rejected his theorizing as Platonic rather than biblical.

A fascinating character from the book of Genesis reappeared in Psalm 110 and then again in Hebrews 7 as a type of Jesus Christ. Melchizedek, the mysterious king of Salem to whom Abraham brought the tithe, justified for the author of Hebrews Jesus' superseding the Levitical priesthood. The most direct point of comparison between Melchizedek and Jesus regards ancestry: "without father or mother, without genealogy, without beginning of days or end of life." Bruce notes this passage describes Jesus as the eternal Son of God, not in his human existence, because we can trace the beginning and end and ancestry of the earthly Jesus.[86] The Melchizedek account in Genesis made no mention of his genealogy; neither did Psalm 110. The Hebrews argument was built on the psalm's association of Melchizedek with an eternal priesthood.

The entire Melchizedek typology in Hebrews based Jesus' qualification to be the priest of God's new covenant on his eternal existence (Heb 7:24). His preexistence is even more important to the argument than his postexistence because it locates Christ prior to the Mosaic covenant and bases his mediation in his eternal being rather than his human ancestry (Heb 7:16). While the passage describes eternal postexistence as well as preexistence, it is the eternal preexistence that gives the argument its force. While some in the history of the church have identified Melchizedek with the preexistent Christ, the text offers no justification for this; Melchizedek simply offers a type who explains and justifies Christ as the mediator of the new covenant.

In Hebrews 9 the writer argues for the sufficiency of Jesus' salvific work. In Heb 9:26, he writes, "But now he has appeared once for all at the end of the ages to do away with sin by the sacrifice of himself." Hughes says this verse is about Jesus' incarnation and earthly ministry, which happened in order to achieve the salvation of sinners. He notes the verb translated "appear" is the same one found in 1 Timothy 3:16 and 1 Peter 1:20. In each case the appearance seems to be of one who existed prior to that appearance. That this appearance of Christ differs from his other appearances mentioned in Hebrews 9:24 and 9:28 is evident from the author's use of different verbs to describe those appearances.[87] Dunn cautions, however, that this may not have been the authorial intent, suggesting the passage achieved this significance "within the context of developing religious beliefs in pre-existing divine redeemers."[88] Were we dealing with only

---

[86]Bruce, *Epistle to the Hebrews*, p. 138.
[87]Philip Edgcumbe Hughes, *A Commentary on the Epistle to the Hebrews* (Grand Rapids: Eerdmans, 1977), p. 385.
[88]Dunn, *Christology in the Making*, p. 238.

one passage or one author, Dunn's skepticism might be justified, but we have
several authors—Paul, Peter, the author of Hebrews—and for most of them multiple passages with contexts that seem to require precisely what Dunn doubts.
Further, this developing belief in preexistent divine redeemers that Dunn mentions has its own set of problems. Contemporary redeemer figures appear to
have been significantly different from Jesus Christ, and those who did resemble
him were both later and dependent on Christ as their model.

In Hebrews 10 the writer contrasts the daily repetition of priestly sacrifices
under the old covenant with Christ's once-for-all sacrifice for sin. In presenting
this contrast he writes:

> Therefore, when Christ came into the world, he said,
>> "Sacrifice and offering you did not desire,
>>> but a body you prepared for me." (Heb 10:5)

This citation of Psalm 40 requires some form of preexistence. It could be an Origenist preexistence of souls, possibly an ideal preexistence (although the language would sound odd in that case), or more likely the personal preexistence
of one who was only now taking up a temporal existence. The Origenist idea,
with its Hellenistic origin, is incompatible with Jewish and Christian beliefs
about the human soul. The language of the passage appears most consistent
with that of personal preexistence, with the one receiving the body already existing in some other form. This is true not only of the natural reading of this
verse, but also of the tenor of Hebrews as a whole. We have seen already that
the author mentioned Christ's preexistence in contexts where he was stressing
the worth and superiority of Christ's salvific work. So why did he allude to
Christ's preexistence in this passage? He was arguing Christ's sacrifice was superior to those being offered daily on the temple altar because Christ was the
preexistent Son of God; in fact, because *he* was the sacrifice, it was not only
superior but all-sufficient.

The phraseology of this verse is incarnational: Christ came into the world. It
is possible this could be said of any newborn human, but the language would
sound awkward and leave hearers wondering what the speaker meant. Paul Ellingworth describes "coming into the world" as a Jewish expression for being
born,[89] but I cannot find anyone who agrees with him. If he is correct, one argument for preexistence disappears from the passage, but even this would not
remove the presumption of preexistence from the Psalm 40 quotation. The pas-

---

[89]Paul Ellingworth, *The Epistle to the Hebrews,* New International Greek Testament Commentary
(Grand Rapids: Eerdmans, 1993), p. 500.

sage in any case seems to require we understand its language in terms of Christ's personal preexistence if we are to make sense of the soteriological argument the author has been developing since the letter's opening verses.

Hebrews 13:8, the final passage I will examine, says, "Jesus Christ is the same yesterday and today and forever." What is different about this verse is that it names the preexistent one as Jesus Christ, not as the Son of God. The author made the connection between Jesus and the Son early in his letter, but technically it was not Jesus who preexisted. Jesus is the name Joseph was to give to the incarnate one who would be "God with us" (Mt 1:23). Hebrews has especially emphasized Jesus' role as the Savior introduced in the Matthew passage. Yet, as C. E. B. Cranfield points out, this is not the only New Testament passage to use the name Jesus for the Son in his pre-incarnate state; Paul did so in 2 Corinthians 8:9 and Philippians 2:5. Such usage is justified because "from all eternity the Son of God was He who in the eternal plan of the Triune God should in the fullness of time take upon Him human nature." Cranfield says specifically that the "yesterday" of this verse does not refer merely to Jesus' historical life but to his eternal preexistence.[90] We find Jesus in this passage identified with the preexistent one, thus completing the identification of the preexistent Son of God who was incarnate for the sake of our salvation with the man Jesus of Nazareth. This both identifies God as the source and initiator of human salvation and grounds that salvation in human history.

In surveying Hebrews we have found the author repeatedly alludes to Christ's preexistence in order to support his argument that Christ's sacrifice accomplished all that was necessary to atone for human sin. Thus it accomplished what the old covenant sacrifices could only point to. In presenting Christ as the preexistent Son, Hebrews sometimes sounds remarkably like John (whose argument I will take up in chap. 5). The writer draws on Jewish categories and Jewish Scripture, but goes beyond the Jewish content of the categories in order to express as fully as human language can who Jesus was and what he accomplished. While he may not have thought in such philosophical categories, the writer kept being and function tightly together. In doing so, he taught unquestionably and repeatedly Christ's personal preexistence.

CONCLUSION

In this chapter I have examined those New Testament writings not from Paul or John that I consider to offer the strongest case for Christ's preexistence. I have

---

[90]C. E. B. Cranfield, "The Witness of the New Testament to Christ," in *Essays in Christology for Karl Barth*, ed. T. H. L. Parker (London: Lutterworth, 1956), pp. 79-80.

also looked at those passages in Acts often cited against the doctrine. In Hebrews we saw not only that the author argued for Christ's preexistence and deity, but that he used these claims to justify God's new covenant with humanity and the sufficiency of Christ's salvific work that is foundational to the covenant. In Hebrews, mention of Christ's preexistence is neither speculative nor is it separated from the rest of christology. The author introduced Christ's preexistence in order to confirm our confidence in his salvific work. The conceptual framework of the Hebrews argument is often similar to that of John. Despite objections that any preexistence in Hebrews must be ideal preexistence, what the author presents can only be the personal preexistence of a divine person.

It is often claimed that the Synoptic Gospels have nothing to say about Christ's preexistence, or if they do say anything it is only to cast doubt on that preexistence. We have found that not only do they not cast doubt on the teaching, they support the teaching. This is most often by implication. At times, we find Jesus spoke in ways that should be understood to mean he knew of his own preexistence. In Acts we found what was supposed to be adoptionist language only seemed so when artificially removed from its context. Within that context these passages were consistent with the teaching of Christ's personal preexistence, even without considering Luke's authorship. When we add Luke's authorship of the book, adoptionism becomes an unrealistic interpretation. The suggestion that the early speeches are merely reports of an early Christology the author might not agree with is a dubious argument for both logical and chronological reasons. First Peter describes Christ in terms of election and revelation. The revelation aspect is similar to that found in Paul and the Synoptics. I believe it presumes the existence of the one revealed prior to that earthly revelation. Peter's subject certainly was Jesus; the context permits no other interpretation. Like all the New Testament books I have surveyed, Peter presents Christ's preexistence in the context of his soteriology and does so in a way that provides a basis for our salvation.

There are other books and other passages in those books we could investigate for what they might say about Christ's preexistence. They are, on the whole, less direct than those I have chosen. The time has now come to look at the New Testament author who discusses most clearly and boldly Christ's preexistence. In this last chapter about the New Testament evidence, we will look at the Johannine witness.

5

THE WRITINGS OF JOHN

That John in the Fourth Gospel taught Christ's preexistence is almost universally acknowledged. John offers the clearest and most powerful New Testament witness to this doctrine. But what the critics give with one hand, they take back with the other. Because John's Gospel differs in so many ways from the Synoptics, many modern scholars discount its testimony. They argue it is late and unreliable in its representation of Jesus' words and actions.[1] Some also distinguish John the Elder of the three letters from the John claimed as author of the Gospel and deny either was an eyewitness to Jesus' ministry. Recently, some scholars have challenged these views, reasserting traditional claims about Johannine authorship and reliability. Typical is Hugo Meynell, who writes, "I do not think it too much to say that *every single one* of the grounds on which historical skepticism about the Fourth Gospel was originally based, apart from its obvious *prima facie* differences from the Synoptics, has been shown to be mistaken."[2]

Despite broad agreement that John affirmed Christ' preincarnate deity, a few scholars continue to argue John said nothing of the sort. Hans Küng is an ex-

---

[1]A. T. Hanson is typical of this view: "The historical evidence that in fact Jesus of Nazareth was conscious of his divinity and remembered his pre-incarnate state is totally insufficient. Practically all the evidence for it comes from the Fourth Gospel, and critical study of that gospel makes it impossible to believe that it is retailing reliable historical information in those passages where Jesus is represented in this light" (*The Image of the Invisible God* [London: SCM Press, 1982], p. 95).

[2]Hugo Meynell, "On Believing in the Incarnation," *Clergy Review* 64 (1979): 214. See also Richard Bauckham, "The Sonship of the Historical Jesus in Christology," *Scottish Journal of Theology* 31 (1978): 254-55.: "If the Fourth Gospel preserves in particular teaching which Jesus gave privately to some of his closest disciples, this is precisely the kind of context we might expect him to have spoken of his sonship." Using a phenomenological approach to the gospels, Royce Gruenler finds all four provide "variations on a common theme," rejecting the claim that John's christology differs significantly from the Synoptics (Royce G. Gruenler, *New Approaches to Jesus and the Gospels* [Grand Rapids: Baker, 1982], pp. 97-98). A valuable new study of the historicity and reliability of John's Gospel is Craig L. Blomberg, *The Historical Reliability of John's Gospel* (Downers Grove, Ill.: InterVarsity Press, 2001).

treme representative of this view: "There is no trace of a real pre-existence christology, far less of a 'triune God' in either Paul or John."[3] Some make the astounding claim that John's christology was adoptionist.[4] Others, like James
Dunn, believe John represents the end of a long process of christological development, although Dunn concludes John does teach the personal preexistence
of the Son of God. In this chapter we will examine the Fourth Gospel and two
of the three Johannine letters, all of which I consider to have come from the
same author. Although the book of Revelation also affirms Christ's personal preexistence and deity, I will not consider it here.

In contrast to the Synoptics, John's Gospel comes across as an insider's account. It is both more reflective and more direct. From the outset it identifies
Jesus' origin as supernatural, without degrading his incarnation and full humanity. Because Koine Greek lacked quotation marks to indicate direct speech, it is
difficult, if not impossible, to always know where Jesus' words end and John's
commentary begins. The agreement of the commentary with Jesus' words is so
complete that one often shades imperceptibly into the other. I do not consider
this significant for deciding if John teaches preexistence, however.

Before looking at what John said about Christ's preexistence, I need to establish John's right to be heard on the subject and argue that the authors of the
Gospel and the Johannine letters were the same person—John the son of Zebedee. It will also be necessary to discuss John's Logos language, considering both
its source and its meaning.

JOHN'S RELIABILITY

For the first seventeen centuries of its existence, John's Gospel was considered
the primary source of information about Jesus. But in the early 1800s David
Friedrich Strauss interpreted John as myth, and almost overnight it was transformed from the most to the least reliable Gospel. During the past thirty years,
however, John's accuracy as a reporter of Palestinian geography and other factual elements has been validated.[5] Paul Barnett reminds us John contains more
historical material than does any of the Synoptics and modern research has
found this material to be accurate.[6] A standard rule for evaluating the quality

---

[3]Hans Küng, *Christianity,* trans. John Bowden (New York: Continuum, 1995), p. 93. On p. 90,
he denies John's christology included preexistence.
[4]Francis Watson, "Is John's Christology Adoptionist?" in *The Glory of Christ in the New Testament: Studies in Christology,* ed. L. D. Hurst and N. T. Wright (Oxford: Oxford University Press,
1987), pp. 112-24.
[5]D. A. Carson, *The Gospel According to John* (Grand Rapids: Eerdmans, 1991), pp. 60-61.
[6]Paul Barnett, *Is the New Testament Reliable?* (Downers Grove, Ill.: InterVarsity Press, 1986), pp.
61-62.

and accuracy of information not directly verifiable is that if information that can be checked proves accurate, information not readily open to verification should be considered reliable unless good reason can be offered to the contrary. It is true an eye for detail does not necessarily lead to accuracy in interpreting that detail, but in this Gospel most of the interpretation comes from Jesus. Thus it is the eye for detail that matters, but beyond this John's interpretation is so consistent with the teaching of Jesus he recounts that translators and interpreters find it difficult to separate the two.

For me, one of the best reasons to trust John is John Robinson's confidence in the Gospel's presentation of Jesus' life and teaching, despite his disagreement with John's christology (or with the conclusion that John taught the christology the vast majority of exegetes have concluded he did). Robinson argues convincingly for the Gospel's historical reliability from a lifetime of carefully studying John's Gospel.[7] He says that at many points "John preserves tradition with as good, and often, better claim to take us back to the source as comparable material in the other Gospels."[8] In conjunction with this, Robinson argues apostolic authorship makes the best sense of the evidence. John is increasingly accepted as a Jew nurtured in the Old Testament. Carson emphasizes the strength of John's claim to have been a witness to Jesus' life and suggests our dismissive attitude toward ancient historiography is unjustified.

Modern concerns about the reliability of John's Gospel are not unreasonable. The most important of these concerns is the sharp contrast between how the Synoptics present Jesus and how John does. There are many historical, linguistic and theological points of contact, but unlike the Synoptics there is little doubt about who John's Jesus is. The Johannine Jesus did not teach a different message, but he taught the same message differently, especially when it came to discussing himself. Because this does not appear to agree with the Synoptic portrayal of a Jesus whose real person only became evident after the resurrection, we will have to consider how a John who claimed to be an eyewitness saw a Jesus so different from the one the other Gospel writers reported. John's Jesus certainly would have been a better candidate for elimination by the Jewish leaders than the Synoptic Jesus because he more deeply offended them.

Both John and the Synoptics offer an implicit explanation for this Gospel's

---

[7]John A. T. Robinson, *The Priority of John*, ed. J. F. Coakley (London: SCM Press, 1985). Despite his defense of John's historical reliability and critique of other scholars' inconsistent interpretations, Robinson denies John taught either Christ's deity or preexistence.

[8]John A. T. Robinson, *Can We Trust the New Testament?* (Grand Rapids: Eerdmans, 1977), p. 82. He says John's doctrine and language probably predate the fall of Jerusalem even if the Gospel itself came later.

different perspective. The author of the Fourth Gospel claimed a special relationship with Jesus as the "Beloved Disciple." He saw and heard things few of the other disciples were privy to. The Synoptic Gospels repeatedly tell of occasions when Jesus took only Peter, James and John with him. So these three would have seen and heard Jesus in situations where the other nine were absent. This evidence not only helps us understand why this Gospel offers a different perspective from the Synoptics, it also provides implicit support for the author's claim to have been John, son of Zebedee.

Both external and internal evidence point to John, son of Zebedee, as the author of the Fourth Gospel. The external evidence is virtually unanimous in favor of John. But modern scholars favor internal evidence over external. Carson, therefore, offers a two-step argument in favor of Johannine authorship. First, he argues the internal evidence is overwhelming that John and the Beloved Disciple are the same person. Then, responding to claims the author must be someone else, he concludes John probably wrote the Gospel bearing his name.[9] I accept Carson's conclusion, finding neither the alternatives nor the methods used to reach them convincing. I also accept the attribution of the three Johannine letters to the author of the Gospel because of their similarities in thought and language.

If John was indeed the author of this Gospel, that removes much, but not all, of the concern about the book's reliability. The critical approach of modern biblical scholarship that requires reliability to be demonstrated instead of unreliability proven has no parallel either in modern study of the secular literature of the New Testament period or in our daily lives.

John was a theologian. This certainly influenced how he told his story, but it did not require that he create a story or manufacture events and sayings. As Carson points out, John's account did not have to be dispassionate, it merely had to be truthful. Given what John was describing, a dispassionate report would have been difficult to accept. Neither advocacy nor theological commitment necessarily makes a report untrustworthy. This was no less true two thousand years ago than it is today. We must make that decision on other grounds. It is true John wrote with a purpose—to convince readers they should recognize and accept Jesus as the Christ, the Son of God (Jn 20:31). But no evaluation of John's Gospel can be based solely on the fact that he wrote with a purpose; it can only rest on the quality of the evidence he offered in support of that purpose. If we must doubt every document whose author

---

[9]See Carson, *Gospel According to John,* pp. 68-81, for details of the argument. See also Leon Morris, *Studies in the Fourth Gospel* (Grand Rapids: Eerdmans, 1969), pp. 215-92, esp. p. 280.

is not dispassionate, we will be able to read little history and even less current news reporting. Virtually everyone who writes, including this writer and every author I have cited, has a purpose in writing. Writing is too much hard work for it to be otherwise.

What John wrote differs in no fundamental way from Paul or Hebrews; it even has parallels in the Synoptics. Some have actually sought to discredit Matthew 11:27 because it sounds too much like John! Critics still object to John's style, omissions and apparent discrepancies with the Synoptic accounts. Probably the most significant of the last are Jesus' clear statements in John about who he is. Blomberg points out, however, that these statements are much clearer in hindsight than they would have been to Jesus' contemporaries.[10] Jesus' language would have confused his hearers, which is precisely what John said happened. Blomberg evaluates each of the areas I have mentioned and finds no instance where John cannot be understood equally well in nonproblematic as in problematic terms. Both the events and discourses John omitted and the distinctiveness of his style can be explained in terms of his theological concerns, the probability that he used different sources from the Synoptics and his own personality.[11]

My study of John gives me confidence he was a reliable witness. Because those parts of his Gospel that can be verified historically or archaeologically have been found accurate, I am willing to listen to what he reported that cannot be tested. John's details are those of someone who lived in Jerusalem before the Jewish War; they bear no marks of anachronism. John claimed he was an eyewitness, and he provided information that would have been available only to an eyewitness. If this claim were untrue, his testimony would have been no more acceptable in his day than today. Mark 14:56 shows the standard for acceptable testimony was openness to confirmation by independent witnesses. John's Gospel agrees with the Synoptics, Paul and Hebrews at key points, especially those concerning Jesus' person. This agreement extends beyond facts to include interpretation. Each in his own way affirms Jesus' humanity, deity and personal preexistence. Unlike some modern scholars, none shows any discomfort in holding all three together.

---

[10]Blomberg, *Historical Reliability,* pp. 164ff.

[11]For those who might argue the use of sources contradicts claims the author was an eyewitness, I would note that should I ever decide to write down my experiences in the Vietnam War, I certainly would seek out others I had served with to fill out and correct my memories. My distance in time from that experience is probably half what John's was from the events he recounted in his Gospel.

JOHN 1:1-5, 9-18

In the beginning was the Word, and the Word was with God, and the Word was God. He was with God in the beginning.

Through him all things were made; without him nothing was made that has been made. In him was life, and that life was the light of men. The light shines in the darkness, but the darkness has not understood it. . . .

The true light that gives light to every man was coming into the world.

He was in the world, and though the world was made through him, the world did not recognize him. He came to that which was his own, but his own did not receive him. Yet to all who received him, to those who believed in his name, he gave the right to become children of God—children born not of natural descent, nor of human decision or a husband's will, but born of God.

The Word became flesh and made his dwelling among us. We have seen his glory, the glory of the One and Only, who came from the Father, full of grace and truth.

John testifies concerning him. He cries out, saying, "This was he of whom I said, 'He who comes after me has surpassed me because he was before me.' " From the fullness of his grace we have all received one blessing after another. For the law was given through Moses; grace and truth came through Jesus Christ. No one has ever seen God, but God the One and Only Son, who is at the Father's side, has made him known.

With this introduction John insisted Jesus' origin and nature are incomprehensible if seen solely in terms of this world. Only when we read it in the light of his pre-incarnate deity does Jesus' story make sense. That is why this prologue is here. It tells us who the subject really is so we can better understand his story. To show Christ's preexistence requires that it identify the Word with Jesus, which the prologue does in John 1:14-17.

Much of this passage has parallels in contemporary Jewish and Hellenistic literature, but when we get to verse 14—the Word became flesh and made his dwelling among us—we find a statement that would scandalize both Jew and Greek. The extrabiblical parallels that do exist provide little more than points of contact for John's message—none determined how John would describe Jesus. The concepts of Logos (Greek) and Word (Jewish) both pointed to something of universal significance that had its home outside the temporal world, although each affected the world and played a role in its coming into existence. So when John wrote of the Logos, people may not have understood precisely what he was saying, but they knew he was talking about something very important.[12]

---

[12]Blomberg writes, "What can be stressed from John's prologue is how at home its theology is in the world of both the Hebrew Scriptures and the Hellenistic Judaism of the first century" (*Historical Reliability,* p. 73).

John's key differences from these two traditions were to present the Logos/ Word as *someone* (not something), to affirm his complete deity and (particularly for the Greeks) to proclaim he had taken up residence in this world. The ancient world had no trouble with supernatural beings and little difficulty with the reality of this world. For the Hellenist, however, the divine could not contaminate itself by entering into the physical realm. Jews were familiar with theophanies in the Old Testament, but these were not incarnations—God was spirit and so could not become part of the physical realm. Lindars says the Hellenist could follow John until verse 14 when "he would be horrified by the thought of the Word becoming flesh. . . . Conversely a Jewish reader would object to the anthropomorphism implicit in the claim that a man known to history was himself the revelation of the invisible God, rather than an inspired messenger like the prophets."[13] Only a few verses after introducing this Logos/Word, John identified him as the man Jesus of Nazareth.

Many commentators consider the prologue an early Christian hymn that provides the key to understanding the remainder of the Gospel.[14] Witherington goes so far as to call John 1:1 that key: "The whole of this Gospel must be read in light of this very first verse, for it means that the deeds and words of Jesus are the deeds and words of a divine being, and not a created supernatural being."[15] Packed into the brief space of eighteen verses are at least six points of interest regarding Christ's preexistence. John introduced the Logos, described the Logos as God, but not God the Father, said the Logos mediated the entire creation, taught a real incarnation, presented Jesus as God the Son, and included the Baptist's testimony that Jesus' existence predated his own. Jesus' superiority to Moses may also be relevant since Moses was the one through whom God gave Torah, which some in Jesus' day considered preexistent (although in an ideal sense). As these various points come together, we are compelled to see Jesus as the preexistent Son of God who mediated creation and salvation and was incarnated in human history.

The first verse points back to Genesis 1:1. In doing so, it makes three statements about the Logos or Word. It says this Logos existed at the beginning and was with God, but it then goes on to identify the Logos as God. The Greek construction of the verse without the definite article before "God" has led some to argue that it says no more than that the Logos is a god or is godlike, but not deity. The second interpretation is easily disposed of because Greek has a dif-

---

[13]Barnabas Lindars, *The Gospel of John*, New Century Bible (Greenwood, S.C.: Attic, 1972), p. 79.
[14]Blomberg, *Historical Reliability*, pp. 71-72, 286.
[15]Ben Witherington III, *John's Wisdom* (Louisville: Westminster John Knox, 1995), p. 54.

ferent word to express divinity or godlikeness, a much weaker concept than deity. Scholars have argued convincingly that the absence of the article does not
make the word *God* adjectival. What it does is distinguish between equality with
God and identity with God. Stated another way, the absence of the article means
John was saying that what God the Father is the Logos is, but the Logos is not
God the Father.[16] At the same time, the Logos is not a second god beside God
the Father. After all, John was a Jew and the heart of biblical Judaism is the confession there is but one God.

We have not yet reached a clear binitarian (much less trinitarian) teaching
with John 1:1, but this was one of the data that convinced early Christians
there was more to God's reality than had been proclaimed previously. That
would lead the church to develop the trinitarian creeds of the fourth century.
The verse begins by describing the Logos as preexistent, but the equality of
the Logos with God shows the Logos to be a personal being, not merely an
idea. Murray Harris describes *theos ēn ho logos* ("the Word was God") as undeniably ontological, describing Jesus' nature rather than his function.[17] Reinforcing what he said about the preexistence of the Logos, John went on to identify
the Logos as the mediator of the entire creation. Emphasizing the all-encompassing nature of the Logos's creative mediation, John repeated himself in
slightly different language.

John Chrysostom argues for Christ's preexistence from the Word's role in creation: "But the Son of God is above not only times, but all ages which were before, for He is the Creator and Maker of them, as the Apostle says, 'by whom
also he made the ages.' Now the Maker necessarily is, before the thing made."[18]
In his commentary on John, Rupert of Deutz, a twelfth-century Benedictine
monk, wrote of John 1:1 that "He who out of his heart gave utterance to a good
word became in the womb of the Virgin a visible and true man although he was
the invisible God," and "Christ, who is now and forever a man, was the Word
in the beginning and even before all ages. He was not then all that he is now,
namely, flesh and the Word; he was the Word only." Attacking a range of christological heresies, he added that "the arrow of the earlier phrase which John
hurled first transfixed all those heretics who, with differing blasphemies but with

[16]A. T. Wainwright says, "*Theos* is used with or without the article indiscriminately in the New
Testament. In the Prologue to the Fourth Gospel it never has the article except in the first
verse" ("The Confession 'Jesus Is God' in the New Testament," *Scottish Journal of Theology*
10 [1957]: 288).
[17]Murray J. Harris, *Jesus as God* (Grand Rapids: Baker, 1992), pp. 284-85.
[18]John Chrysostom *Homilies on the Gospel of John* 3.2, in *Chrysostom: Homilies on the Gospel of
Saint John and the Epistle to the Hebrews,* Nicene and Post-Nicene Fathers, vol. 14, ed. Philip
Schaff (Grand Rapids: Eerdmans, 1978), p. 45.

an equal spirit of malice, denied that Christ existed before Mary."[19]

R. G. Hamerton-Kelly explains the opening verses of the prologue this way: the phrase "with God" means there have always been these two divine beings, it excludes any idea the Logos could be an emanation or other derivation from God; the phrase "was God" excludes any sense of polytheism where the Word was a second god; and the Logos and God are one God yet distinct from one another.[20] The human mind cannot understand how this can be, and our rationalism says if we cannot understand something it must be incoherent.[21] That is part of the modern objection to the trinitarian implications of this passage, although the doctrine of the Trinity has been subject to attack from the earliest decades of the church. William Thompson sees the trinitarian connection as even more direct: "The Prologue and the entire Gospel are inviting us to consider that we are moving, not simply from the man Jesus to God, but from the God-become-man Jesus to the trinitarian Word."[22] Another difficulty in this passage is the need to explain divine reality in human language, especially the language of time. Chrysostom states the problem clearly: "There is no interval therefore between the Son and the Father; and if there be none, then He is not after but Co-eternal with Him. For 'before' and 'after' are notions implying time, since without age or time, no one could possibly imagine these words, but God is above time and ages."[23]

John had one more thing to say about the Logos, and this is the distinctive truth of Christianity: this Logos took upon himself complete humanity and entered into our human history. This requires that the Logos preexisted that history and in the context of John's prologue identifies the incarnate Logos as Jesus.

Incarnation was precisely what the Hellenistic Logos could not experience. For the Greeks the Logos was associated with the divine realm where there was

---

[19]Rupert of Deutz, *Commentary on Saint John,* in *Early Medieval Theology,* ed. and trans. George E. McCracken and Allen Cabaniss, Library of Christian Classics 9 (Philadelphia: Westminster Press, 1957), pp. 260ff.

[20]R. G. Hamerton-Kelly, *Preexistence, Wisdom, and the Son of Man* (Cambridge: Cambridge University Press, 1973), pp. 202ff.

[21]H. R. Mackintosh reminds us that considering Christ's preexistence takes us to the inner life of God himself and this will inevitably exceed our capacity to understand. "We need here no hesitation in confessing that the preexistence of Christ outstrips our faculty of conception, and that no theoretical refinements alter this in the very least. Not merely are we faced here by the impossibility of beholding the life of God on its inward side . . . but in addition we encounter once more the haunting and insoluble enigma of time as ultimately related to eternity. And other not less formidable difficulties remain." And of all biblical texts, the Johannine prologue is probably the one that touches most nearly on God's inner being. (See H. R. Mackintosh, *The Doctrine of the Person of Christ,* 2nd ed. [Edinburgh: T & T Clark, 1913], p. 457.)

[22]William M. Thompson, *The Struggle for Theology's Soul* (New York: Crossroad, 1996), p. 125.

[23]Chrysostom *Homilies on the Gospel of John* 4.2.

no change or suffering; it could not enter into a history characterized by those very things. Dunn notes the incarnation of deity was no less inconceivable for Jews.[24] For the Jews, God was spirit. He could and did intervene in history, but he did not thereby become a creature. Oscar Cullmann says non-Christian thinkers may have said things about the Logos that sounded the same as John, but they certainly did not mean by them anything similar to what John did.[25] Robinson offers an interesting but unsupportable interpretation of the incarnation. He agrees the Word "was embodied totally in and as a human being," but he denies the Word was a person before the incarnation. It became both person and flesh at that point in time. Any other approach, he says, risks the charge of docetism.[26] What leads Robinson to this conclusion is the traditional insistence that the preexistent Logos was not transformed into a human person but added a complete human nature to his eternal divine person. To state it in the language of John 1:18, God the Son became Jesus of Nazareth without ceasing to be God the Son. Marshall argues that because John described the Logos as the unique Son of God, we must think of the Logos as enjoying the same personal existence we believe the Father enjoys.[27]

To understand what John was saying, we need to know what he meant when he spoke about the Logos. Both Jew and Greek would have understood John was talking about something very important, even if they did not understand the details. The prime candidates for John's sources are the Word of God of the Old Testament and the Jewish Wisdom speculation of Proverbs and intertestamental literature. Those who are more inclined to see Hellenistic influence in John attribute most of that influence to Stoic philosophy, which saw the Logos as the impersonal, universal principle of reason. Ed Miller enumerates six other possible sources, offering his conclusion that John himself originated the Logos concept as it is found in the prologue.[28] The classics scholar W. K. C. Guthrie lists eleven meanings for *Logos*, but concludes none has anything to do with John's use of the term.[29] Fred Craddock says the meaning of *Logos* must be de-

---

[24]James D. G. Dunn, *Christology in the Making* (Philadelphia: Westminster Press, 1980), p. 243.

[25]Oscar Cullmann, *The Christology of the New Testament,* rev. ed., trans. Shirlie C. Guthrie and Charles A. M. Hall (Philadelphia: Westminster Press, 1963), p. 264. He notes preexistence was especially important to John because the one who was at the center of salvation history could not simply have appeared from nowhere (p. 252).

[26]Robinson, *Priority of John,* pp. 380-81.

[27]I. Howard Marshall, *Jesus the Savior* (Downers Grove, Ill.: InterVarsity Press, 1990), pp. 166-67.

[28]Ed L. Miller, "The Johannine Origins of the Johannine Logos," *Journal of Biblical Literature* 112 (1993): 445-57.

[29]W. K. C. Guthrie, *A History of Greek Philosophy* (Cambridge: Cambridge University Press, 1967), 1:419-24.

termined by how the concept functioned for John rather than by some particular religious or philosophical source.[30]

While John may have used some of those contemporary ideas, he brought them together in a new way that transcends what those sources said. In building on these concepts, he presented Jesus to both Jew and Gentile in a way that responded to contemporary anxieties. John's Jesus was the incarnation of a loving God who intervened directly and personally in human history. In transcending them, John showed both Jew and Greek a God who was greater than the human mind could conceive. Leon Morris says, "Both Greek and Jew would be able to put meaning into what he was saying, but he was also going to surprise them."[31] The non-Christian understandings would suffice through John 1:13, but at verse 14 John said that what his readers understood as a principle or personification was really a person, and this person was God, who had entered history. The Logos has manifested himself in history and this manifestation is Jesus. This was more than their categories could handle.

Bultmann disagrees completely, saying the language of the prologue is myth and the Logos a personification of God's activity in the world. He believes this "mysterious figure" of the Logos requires such an interpretation. Bultmann's conclusion results from the unduly restrictive limits he places upon exegesis:

> And the exegesis has as its first task to discover what *possible forms of expression were open to the author; the possibilities being those he has inherited with the tradition in which he stands.* What the author intends to say here and now, is of course not simply to be deduced from those possibilities: but they have given a particular direction to what he intends to say, and have imposed particular limits.[32]

Bultmann is correct in saying one's tradition influences exegesis, but to say it limits interpretation is to deny the possibility of original thinking and the ability to go beyond one's teachers. Küng equally rejects any thought John was teaching Christ's preexistence. He says the prologue presents the Logos as preexistent but says nothing about Jesus.[33] That is an unduly narrow reading of the prologue. Küng's interpretation exemplifies what happens when we allow our presuppositions to control what the text may say.

In the Old Testament, Wisdom was with God and participated in creation

---

[30]Fred B. Craddock, *The Pre-existence of Christ in the New Testament* (Nashville: Abingdon, 1968), pp. 122-23.
[31]Leon Morris, *Expository Reflections on the Gospel of John* (Grand Rapids: Baker, 1988), p. 6.
[32]Rudolf Bultmann, *The Gospel of John,* trans. G. R. Beasley-Murray et. al. (Philadelphia: Westminster Press, 1971), pp. 19-20.
[33]Küng, *Christianity,* p. 89.

(Prov 8:22ff.). Wisdom could not mediate *all* creation because it was itself part of the created order. Wisdom was neither God nor was it a person, it was at most a personification. Although Wisdom participated in the revelation of God's word to humans and came close to being identified with that word on occasion, it never participated in human salvation. Jewish Wisdom speculation did provide a foundation for early Christian thinking about Jesus, but at key points Wisdom speculation proved insufficient. It was insubstantial, impersonal and never incarnate. For Hengel, the fusion of this Wisdom thought with the preexistent Son of God is sufficient to explain John's Logos christology, but Gnostic ideas are entirely inappropriate.[34] Rudolf Schnackenburg says not only Gnostic ideas were inappropriate, so were Jewish Wisdom speculation and Philo's Logos doctrine. None of these was adequate to explain John's presentation of the Logos as a person.[35]

Of the categories John could have chosen for the preexistent Christ, only Word was not part of the created order. Even terms like Wisdom that Jews understood as preexistent were creation, not creator. The Word, however, mediated *all* creation. This emphasis on the Word's creative role is important because the incarnate Word came to accomplish God's re-creation of the world. Of course, it is logically necessary for the Word to have existed before creation if he mediated its coming into being.

John's language in John 1:14 transcended anything Judaism would say about God's presence in the world. According to A. H. Bowman, "The personification of the Divine Word in the Old Testament is poetical, in Philo it is metaphysical, in S. John historical. The Logos of S. John is not a mere attribute of God, but the Son of God existing from all eternity, manifested, in space and time, in the Person of Christ."[36] For William Dumbrell this verse takes us almost to the two natures doctrine: "the Logos became flesh without sacrificing his essential divine nature." This verse moves from the Logos's preexistence to proximity to God and finally to full deity.[37]

Having established the identity of the Logos, John told of his "coming down" to dwell among humans. From this, he developed the theme of descent and ascent that is so prominent in this Gospel. How this incarnation happened was

---

[34]Martin Hengel, *The Son of God* (Philadelphia: Fortress, 1976), p. 73.

[35]Rudolf Schnackenburg, *The Gospel According to John,* trans. Kevin Smyth (New York; Herder & Herder, 1968), 1:233.

[36]A. H. Bowman, quoted in S. F. Davenport, *Immanence and Incarnation* (Cambridge: Cambridge University Press, 1925), p. 132.

[37]William J. Dumbrell, "Grace and Truth: The Progress of the Argument of the Prologue of John's Gospel," in *Doing Theology for the People of God,* ed. Donald Lewis and Alister McGrath (Downers Grove, Ill.: InterVarsity Press, 1996), p. 112.

not John's concern; he only wanted to assert in the strongest possible terms *that* it had happened. In the prologue it is the Logos who "came down" from God, but in the body of the Gospel it is the Son of Man who descends from and ascends back to heaven. Thus the idea of Christ's preexistence that begins in the prologue permeates the entire Gospel, and the implicit identification of the Word reappears. Michael Willett says John's Gospel "assumes the pre-existence of the Son and uses it throughout as a basis for asserting the Son's authority to speak and act in a way that confronts the world and offers life in a relationship with himself and with the Father." Preexistence serves two functions in John: it places Jesus on the divine side of reality, and it supports the exalted claims made about Jesus.[38]

In John 1:15, John the Baptist affirmed Jesus' preexistence by describing him as having been before John even though John was born several months before Jesus. What the Baptist said here was echoed in John 1:30 where he said, "This is the one I meant when I said, 'A man who comes after me has surpassed me because he was before me.' " As strange as it sounds, John appears to have been speaking about a temporal relationship: John was born before Jesus, but Jesus already existed before his birth and John's. According to Carson, Morris and Westcott, John's statement denotes not merely temporal priority but absolute priority. This is in contrast to the priority of rank others see in the passage. That interpretation reads awkwardly in verse 15, but in John 1:30 it becomes a tautology: "he has surpassed me because he was greater than I." What John said here, Jesus would say in John 8. John the Baptist claimed the source of his knowledge was supernatural. Based on this knowledge, he described Jesus as the Lamb of God, the Son of God and the one who takes away the sin of the world.

The final verse of the prologue describes Jesus as the only Son who is himself God and who has revealed God the Father. In describing both the Logos, who is the Son, and God the Father as God while maintaining their distinctness, John stretched traditional Jewish monotheism.[39] Because this one who is God the only Son is at the Father's side, it is beyond doubt that he personally preexisted his incarnation. According to Dunn it is John 1:18 that links John's claims that Christ is both the Logos incarnate and the only Son of God the Father.[40] Gieschen describes John 1:18 as "a profound interpretation of the Israelite and Jewish theophanic traditions." Because God the Father has never been seen by human

---

[38]Michael E. Willett, *Wisdom Christology in the Fourth Gospel* (San Francisco: Mellen Research University Press, 1992), pp. 50, 54.
[39]Miller, "Johannine Origins," p. 131.
[40]Dunn, *Christology in the Making,* p. 244.

eyes, it is the Son who has seen God and revealed him. "This assertion implies that the Only-Begotten was *seen* before the incarnation since he is the one who makes God known, not only *in* the incarnation, but also *before* the incarnation."[41]

JOHN 8:57-58

"You are not yet fifty years old," the Jews said to him, "and you have seen Abraham!"

"I tell you the truth," Jesus answered, "before Abraham was born, I am!"

The only way I can conceive denying that in this exchange Jesus was teaching his own personal preexistence is to deny the passage's authenticity. Jesus not only claimed he existed in Abraham's day but that he existed absolutely. Although the other Johannine passages where Jesus proclaimed "I am" do not necessarily have the divine "I am" of Exodus 3:14 in mind, this passage certainly seems to refer back to the divine name in Exodus.[42] Jesus' Jewish opponents understood he was making an exceptional claim, because they tried to stone him for blasphemy, which would have required a claim that went beyond preexistence to deity. Donald Guthrie says Jesus' words contain a deliberate personal claim to such qualities as the changelessness and preexistence that belong to God alone.[43] Chrysostom agrees that Jesus' opponents considered these words blasphemy—and, indeed, if they are not true, Jesus was no witness to God and not even a good man: "But wherefore said he not, 'Before Abraham was, I was,' instead of 'I am'? As the Father useth this expression, 'I am,' so also doth Christ; for it signifieth continuous Being, irrespective of all time. On which account the expression seemed to them to be blasphemous."[44]

John 8:58 is the climax to a debate between Jesus and a group identified as "the Jews" about Jesus' person and authority. Chapter 8 begins with a challenge to the validity of Jesus' testimony about himself. In his first defense Jesus placed himself on the side of God the Father. When his opponents failed to understand his meaning, Jesus proclaimed his authority and destiny more explicitly and accused his opponents of spiritual blindness. When some of his Jewish opponents protested their descent from Abraham and claimed God as their Father, Jesus rejected their claim

[41]Charles A. Gieschen, *Angelomorphic Christology* (Leiden: Brill, 1998), p. 273.

[42]Larry Hurtado concludes, "In light of the biblical passages to which the obvious allusions are directed, this absolute use in the gospels amounts to nothing less than designating Jesus with the same special referential formula that is used in the Greek Old Testament for God's own self-declaration" (*Lord Jesus Christ* [Grand Rapids: Eerdmans, 2003], p. 371).

[43]Donald Guthrie, *New Testament Theology* (Downers Grove, Ill.: InterVarsity Press, 1981), p. 372.

[44]Chrysostom *John* 55.2.

and called them children of Satan. When Jesus said keeping his word would preserve a person from death, his opponents responded that even Abraham had died.
"Are you greater than Abraham?" they asked. "Who do you think you are?" It was
this question that led Jesus to claim he not only was greater than Abraham but absolutely preexisted him. This was how Jesus defended his authority and responded
to his opponents' question about who he thought he was.[45]

Morris concludes that Jesus' words in John 8:58 constituted a claim to deity
and says "there is a claim to deity in the meaning we must give them."[46] He believes we must interpret Jesus' language to mean he has always existed. Jesus'
language went no further than John's words in the prologue, but it brought out
the meaning of Christ's preexistence more powerfully. Morris reminds us Jesus
said that before Abraham "I am," not "I was."[47] George Beasley-Murray agrees,
saying Jesus' words imply a personal preexistence that is possible "because the
'I' of Jesus is one with the 'I' of the divine Logos." He adds, "The revelation utterance of v 58, accordingly, is one with the Logos theology of the prologue in
declaring the Son to be the authentic revealer of the Father and his unity with
him beyond all time."[48]

Robinson agrees John 8:58 teaches Jesus' preexistence, but he denies it
teaches his deity. He says it is in no way different from the language of John
1:15 and John 1:30 in asserting Christ's preexistence, but adds that the Christ of
chapter one is clearly human. "That Jesus is arrogating to himself the divine
name is nowhere stated or implied in this Gospel."[49] Dunn agrees John's Gospel
presents Jesus as aware of his existence with God the Father before his incarnation, but wonders why language like that of John 8:58 appears nowhere in
the Synoptic Gospels.

Why should they be so completely neglected if they are part of the authentic
sayings of Jesus, and why should only John preserve them? The most obvious
explanation once again is that in a relatively insignificant element of the earlier
tradition John has found the inspiration to fashion an invaluable formula for expressing Christianity's claims about Jesus.[50]

---

[45]Calvin says Jesus first stated his heavenly origin in Jn 8:14. By v. 58, he confronted his opponents with "a remarkable testimony of his divine essence." In John Calvin, *Calvin's Commentaries: John,* on AGES Software CD-ROM, 1996.

[46]Morris, *Expository Reflections,* p. 344.

[47]Leon Morris, *The Gospel according to John,* rev. ed., New International Commentary on the
New Testament (Grand Rapids: Eerdmans, 1995), pp. 419-20.

[48]George R. Beasley-Murray, *John,* Word Biblical Commentary 36 (Waco, Tex.: Word, 1987), pp.
139-40.

[49]Robinson, *Priority of John,* p. 386.

[50]Dunn, *Christology in the Making,* p. 31.

I do not share Dunn's doubt that John 8:58 and similar language come from Jesus, and am skeptical that "a relatively insignificant element of the earlier tradition" could become so central to Christian belief about Jesus so quickly. If John's Gospel derived from an insignificant element of tradition and he wrote while any other witnesses to Jesus' life were still alive, he and his writing would have been discredited. If the author was the Beloved Disciple, what he had to say would not be insignificant. Dunn's suggestion that John created this statement and placed it in Jesus' mouth has no support beyond Dunn's skepticism that Jesus could have spoken about himself this way. I also question Robinson's method of moving from the fact that John 1:1-18 and 8:58 both teach Christ's preexistence to conclude John the Baptist's words "this was the man" must mean the Jesus of 8:58 was merely human or that it demonstrates John the Evangelist (or even John the Baptist) believed Jesus was no more than human.

The evidence that John 8:58 teaches that Jesus believed he preexisted with divine status is compelling—if the passage is authentic. Craig Blomberg, after discussing content and historicity issues, concludes, "I suggest more boldly that the tradition reflects an authentic dialogue involving the historical Jesus."[51] Both the context of John 8 and Old Testament parallels indicate Jesus was referring to himself in terms the Old Testament reserved for God alone. Objections to this interpretation are as weak as the arguments for it are strong. (Although Blomberg does note Jesus could have been understood to be making a claim to be God's agent.)[52] In fact, neither Robinson nor Dunn denies John taught Christ's preexistence; one is concerned with whether John taught Jesus' deity and the other with whether 8:58 and similar verses are authentic words of Jesus.

John 10:29-30

"My Father, who has given them to me, is greater than all; no one can snatch them out of my Father's hand. I and the Father are one."

This passage is not about Christ's preexistence, it is about his deity. But I have already said deity requires preexistence in Jesus' case because if Jesus is deity as God the Father is deity, he in his preincarnate state must have existed from all eternity just as the Father has. Thus if John 10:30 does affirm Jesus' deity, it also teaches his preexistence.[53]

---

[51]Blomberg, *Historical Reliability,* p. 150.
[52]Ibid., p. 149.
[53]Richard Bauckham points out that the eternality of God was an essential Jewish belief (see his *God Crucified* [Grand Rapids: Eerdmans, 1998], pp. 8, 12). This would require that if the Son of God is God, he must have eternally preexisted his incarnation.

The question this passage raises concerns the nature of the oneness Jesus enjoys with the Father. Is it functional or ontological, or is the reality more complex than that? Jesus was not asserting his identity with the Father—they remain distinct persons—but there is disagreement about the nature of the union he claimed. Morris and Lindars consider it essential, Borchert says it is a matter of purpose and will, and Beasley-Murray and Schnackenburg describe it as functional with a hint of the metaphysical relationship between Father and Son. Even conservative commentators recognize the functional aspect, but most do not see this as the whole story. The context for Jesus' words here is the entire Fourth Gospel, and this Gospel has already presented Jesus as God and with God. As Morris comments, "It may be true that this ought not to be understood as a metaphysical statement, but it is also true that it means more than that Jesus' will was one with that of the Father."[54] This passage does not unequivocally affirm Jesus' deity or preexistence, but it is consistent with such teachings, appears to imply the truth of those teachings, and the overall Johannine context supports such a conclusion.

JOHN 12:41

Isaiah said this because he saw Jesus' glory and spoke about him.

This fascinating statement follows a quotation from that passage in Isaiah 6 where the prophet experienced an awesome vision of God in the temple and received his prophetic call. Although the verse sounds much like what John 8:56 said about Abraham, it comes from John, not Jesus. What John wrote differed significantly from Isaiah 6. For John, Isaiah saw the glory of Christ; in Isaiah 6:1 the prophet wrote he saw "the Lord seated on a throne, high and exalted." Brown thinks John may have been using a Targum of Isaiah rather than the Masoretic or Septuagint text. He offers three possible interpretations of the passage, two of which require Christ's preexistence.[55] The third, that Isaiah looked into the future and saw Christ's glory does not sound like what Isaiah 6 says. The other alternatives are that Isaiah saw the shekinah of God, an interpretation that is consistent with the prologue's presentation of Jesus as God's shekinah, and belief that Jesus was active in the history of Israel as suggested by 1 Corinthians 10:4 and patristic interpretations of the burning bush of Exodus and the theophanies. Identifying Jesus with God's glory seems to fit best what John was saying. Calvin, in his commentary on Isaiah 6:1, supports this conclusion, "Who was that LORD? John tells us that it was Christ (John 12:41) . . . for God never

---

[54]Morris, *Gospel According to John,* pp. 464-65.
[55]Raymond E. Brown, *The Gospel According to John,* Anchor Bible (Garden City, N.Y.: Doubleday, 1966), 1:486-87.

revealed himself to the Fathers but in his eternal Word and only begotten Son."
Morris remarks that the Greek reads "*his* glory," but agrees with the NIV interpretation since Jesus is the antecedent of "his." He adds that John's idea of Jesus'
glory is not what we would expect: the Isaiah quotation includes rejection, and
John has already pointed to the cross as highest expression of Christ's glory. Carson interprets the passage explicitly in terms of Christ's preexistence. For him
the remarkable aspect of the verse is not that it ascribes preexistence and deity
to Jesus, but that it says *Isaiah* saw Christ's glory.

JOHN 17:4-5

> I have brought you glory on earth by completing the work you gave me to do. And
> now, Father, glorify me in your presence with the glory I had with you before the
> world began.

These verses appear in the first part of Jesus' high priestly prayer, the long
prayer that Jesus prayed just before his arrest, trial and crucifixion. Jesus said he
had completed the work God sent him to do. He asked now to be restored to
the glory he enjoyed with God in heaven before the world began. In John 17:24,
Jesus asked that the elect might be with him and that they too might be able to
see Jesus' glory, the glory that God gave him because he loved him before the
creation of the world.

John portrayed Jesus' prayer as asking for precisely what Paul in the Philippians hymn said God did for Jesus. Jesus' statement that he enjoyed divine glory
before the creation certainly presumes a personal preexistence; it also implies
an essential relationship with God, not merely a functional one. According to
Isaiah 42:8, God does not share his glory, so the glory Jesus claims to have enjoyed with God had to have been his by nature or not at all. Like the other passages about Christ's preexistence, there is much more to these verses than raw
material for constructing a christology. When we humans become too confident
about what God would or would not do, this passage reminds us God's glory
on earth came through what for us would be the most unlikely of instruments—
the cross. Two thousand years of history have deadened us to just how offensive
the idea of a crucified Messiah was to Jesus' Jewish contemporaries.

Calvin, commenting on this verse, said Jesus prayed simply that the majesty
he enjoyed as the Son of God might be made visible to his disciples. He was
asking for that which was properly his. Calvin adds, "This is a remarkable passage, which teaches us that Christ is not a God who has been newly contrived,
or who has existed only for a time; for if his *glory* was eternal, he himself also
has always been."

Witherington says that apart from introducing Logos language to describe Christ, John has added nothing to the thought of Paul and other early New Testament writers. This passage demonstrates that. We have the same preexistent Son who humbled himself by coming to earth only to return and be honored as Philippians 2 portrays Jesus. The same humility we find in 2 Corinthians 8:9 is evident here. The association with divine glory and completion of his assigned mission link this passage with Hebrews 1. Paul's sending language and Jesus' "I have come" statements in the Synoptics are in the background as Jesus' prayer claims a preexistent status where he participated in the divine glory. And Jesus' intimate relationship with God the Father is the consistent Johannine message as well as that of Matthew 11:27.

This is what makes Bultmann's mythological interpretation of the passage so incomprehensible. The language, he says, "accords fully with the thought-form of the gnostic myth."[56] Since Bultmann wrote this, other scholars have concluded that Gnosticism postdates Jesus and the earliest church. So if Bultmann is correct about the resemblance, the borrowing was on the part of Gnosticism, not John. Lindars notes a superficial resemblance, but concludes this results from uniting two *Jewish* concepts—the descent of Wisdom and the ascent of the Son of Man—not from Gnostic influence.[57] It should be noticed, however, that even Bultmann's conclusion presumes Christ's preexistence, although it is a lesser sort of preexistence than I believe the passage requires.

"I AM FROM ABOVE" AND SENDING STATEMENTS

Several times in this Gospel Jesus contrasted his origin with that of those he was speaking to, describing himself as being "from above" whereas they were of this world. He did this in several ways. In John 3:31, 6:33ff., 6:62 and 8:23, Jesus identified himself as having come from above; in John 8:14 he said those he was speaking to had no idea where he came from. In John 6:41-42, Jesus' listeners seem to understand his claim to heavenly origin, but disbelieve it because his earthly parents, Mary and Joseph, disproved the claim as far as they were concerned. In John 7:28-29, however, Jesus said that while his audience knew him and where he was from, they did not know the One who had sent him. *Know* in this context was a relational, not an intellectual, term. In John 3:13 and 6:62, Jesus talked about the Son of Man ascending to where he had been previously. I understand this Son of Man to be Jesus himself; the context leaves little room for Jesus' Son of Man to be anything other than self-referential. Not only do

---

[56]Bultmann, *Gospel of John,* p. 496.
[57]Lindars, *Gospel of John,* pp. 520-21.

these passages presume the Son of Man's existence prior to his earthly life, but if they were drawing on the imagery of Daniel 7:13, they disclose the Son of Man as a heavenly being, even deity. The consistent testimony of John's Gospel is that Jesus' origin was heaven, not earth.[58] His heavenly origin provided him with knowledge of heavenly realities and his divine status was the basis for his claim to authority.

The claim of Jesus' heavenly origin provides the context for interpreting the Johannine statements that Jesus was sent and had come. These statements in John differ from similar ones in the Synoptics only in being more explicit. Jesus came from heaven (Jn 3:13) and was sent into the world (Jn 3:17). At least eighteen times, Jesus describes himself as the one who was sent by the Father. The Gospel also describes John the Baptist as having been sent by God, but not from heaven. In each case, this was explained as preparing the way for Jesus.

Only Jesus is described as having come from heaven or being sent into the world. This language is never applied to John the Baptist. This suggests to me that these passages, which distinguish Jesus from both John the Baptist and the Old Testament prophets, are the interpretive key to all the sending statements (forty-one verses in the Gospel and three in 1 Jn). Furthermore, the prologue, with its statements of Christ's divine preexistence and incarnation, has established the context for interpreting the sending statements. This sending language sets Jesus apart from other religious figures, both Jewish and pagan. They may have been said to have ascended to heaven at the end of their lives, but only Jesus was declared to be *returning* to where he was before he began his earthly life.

Morris presents clearly the important role the sending language plays in regard to Christ's descent and ascent: "Christ's heavenly origin is important, otherwise he would not be our Savior. But his heavenly destination is also important, for it witnesses to the Father's seal of approval on the son's saving work."[59] The Jesus who came from the Father came for our salvation. This salvation is possible only because Christ is the preexistent Son of God, who was with God and was God from the beginning. This is the message of John's Gospel, and it permeates John's first letter as well.

---

[58]In speaking of Jesus' origin, I am not suggesting the Son of God had a beginning or that "there was a time when he was not." I am merely placing him on the side of the Creator rather than the creature.

[59]Morris, *Gospel According to John*, p. 631.

I JOHN

There is no consensus as to whether the author of the three Johannine letters was the same person as the Gospel writer or as to which came first, the Gospel or the letters. I accept common authorship for the four documents; their chronology, however important for New Testament studies, is irrelevant to our investigation. The writer claims he was an eyewitness to Jesus' ministry; had this been false, his readers would have known and rejected his claim to authority. If it is true, then John's letters have a power and urgency that can only come from one who was present for the important events of Jesus' ministry. The order in which the Gospel and letters were written has nothing to do with what John had to say about Jesus' preexistence, however.

First John opens by proclaiming the direct experience John and his associates had of Jesus. It goes on to explain what constitutes true faith in Jesus as opposed to false, and to exhort the readers to hold fast to the true. According to John, real Christian faith has a factual content, and this factual content must be demonstrated through a particular pattern of living. One part of the factual content of this faith appears to be belief in Christ's preexistence. So, for John, Christ's preexistence is an essential aspect of Christian faith in the sense that what Christians *must* believe includes doctrines that presume Christ's preexistence.

John's language can be difficult. Some of his sentences are quite complex, and it is not always clear what his pronouns refer to. As a result, some interpreters describe John's christology as ambiguous, and others disagree about specifics. This leads Judith Lieu to say that while the Jesus of 1 John could be preexistent, he might be no more than God's designated representative.[60] Although we should respect Lieu's caution, I believe her conclusions are too negative. The incarnational language is clearer than she acknowledges. First John identifies Jesus as the Son of God and says he has come in the flesh; 2 John identifies Jesus as the one who has come in the flesh. It is true 1 John 5:20, which designates Jesus as God in the NIV translation, offers a difficult teaching using difficult language, but John's presentation of Jesus as the Son of God who is preexistent deity can stand without such an explicit statement of his deity.

1 JOHN 1:1-4

> That which was from the beginning, which we have heard, which we have seen with our eyes, which we have looked at and our hands have touched—this we proclaim concerning the Word of life. The life appeared; we have seen it and testify

---

[60]Judith M. Lieu, *The Theology of the Johannine Epistles* (Cambridge: Cambridge University Press, 1991), p. 73.

to it, and we proclaim to you the eternal life, which was with the Father and has appeared to us. We proclaim to you what we have seen and heard, so that you also may have fellowship with us. And our fellowship is with the Father and with his Son, Jesus Christ. We write this to make our joy complete.

"We were not dreaming; it was not a hallucination, a vision, or a philosophical idea. This was real. We saw him, we heard him, and we touched him." This is how John began his letter. The *him* was the Word of life, who was from the beginning. We know him as Jesus Christ, but this is not the entirety of his story.

John wrote what he did because some were denying the reality of Christ's incarnation. Later in the letter he would condemn denial of the incarnation as so contrary to Christian faith that those with such beliefs have nothing at all in common with God (1 Jn 4:2). Real incarnation requires a real preexistence, so when John spoke of "that which was from the beginning," he was linking Christ's earthly life with his heavenly preexistence. Bultmann understands John's use of *Logos* to refer to the appearance of the Gospel about Jesus, not Jesus himself,[61] but this does not take full account of what John wrote. We certainly can hear the Gospel message and even see its result, but how do we touch it?

The letter begins with a clear reference to the opening verse of John's Gospel.[62] It goes on to summarize the message of the letter in a way similar to how the prologue summarizes the Fourth Gospel. John's language is perfectly understandable if he was the author of both the letter and the Gospel. If this is so, then John was emphasizing the reality of Christ's incarnation in a way that requires his preexistence. This leads Smalley to paraphrase the opening verses as, "We are proclaiming to you the life which is indeed eternal, *seeing that* this life *was* (not 'is') with the Father (pre-existingly)."[63] For Miller, the linking of the Word with life and with God means no less than that this Word is personal and preexistent. He considers the phrase "from the beginning" to be a transparent reference to preexistence.[64] Smalley writes cautiously about the relationship between Gospel and letter despite his confidence that the opening verses of the letter reflect the prologue to the Gospel. He surmises that of the four phrases in 1 John 1:1, the first was about the preexistent Word and the other three about

[61]Rudolf Bultmann, *The Johannine Epistles,* ed. Robert W. Funk, trans. R. Philip O'Hara et al. (Philadelphia: Fortress, 1973), p. 9.

[62]Because of the similarity of the opening verses of the Gospel and letter, Augustine concludes a common authorship and understands the subject of both passages to be the same—the incarnate Son of God.

[63]Stephen S. Smalley, *1, 2, 3 John,* Word Biblical Commentary 51 (Waco, Tex.: Word, 1984), p. 10.

[64]Miller, "Johannine Origins," p. 455.

the Word incarnate. John's high christology probably was intended to balance the theology of former Jews among his readers with the theology of former pagans and maintain a balanced understanding of Jesus' person. We can see this from his insistence on identifying the Logos with God while at the same time asserting the reality of his incarnation. Not only does the "from the beginning" language sound like preexistence, so does "existing with the Father."

First John opens with language distinctly similar to that of the Fourth Gospel. In the Gospel this language describes the Word as preexistent and deity, and identifies the Word with Jesus. The same can be said for this letter. It should be noted that even New Testament scholars who do not believe the letter and Gospel have the same author acknowledge their linguistic relationship. So if I am wrong in believing both documents came from the same hand, that may strengthen the New Testament evidence for Christ's preexistence by providing an additional witness who was not dependent on one of those we have already examined.

1 JOHN 2:13A

I write to you, fathers,
because you have known him who is from the beginning.

John is reminding the "fathers," the mature among his readers, that because they have known the one "who is from the beginning," they are both in a position and responsible to instruct the others among John's readers. Commentators are divided over the identity of this "who." A minority believes it to be God, but most think it is Jesus. Calvin says the subject is Christ and the verse describes Jesus as divine and coeternal with God.[65] Smalley believes the phrase applies to both God and Christ, but for first-century readers it would be a trivial reference to God—everyone knew he is eternal—and a major claim about Jesus, that he had existed from eternity. Marshall says it is clear that the "beginning" John referred to was the beginning of time, not the beginning of the Christian era or individuals' Christian experience.[66] The division over whether the eternal existence reference is to God or Jesus does not depend on the commentator's theological stance; it seems to depend much more on how each interprets the Greek text. Smalley's point is well taken: John seems more likely to have used such language to describe Jesus than God.

---

[65]This and following citations of Calvin are from John Calvin, *Calvin's Commentaries: 1 John*, on AGES Software CD-ROM, 1996.

[66]I. Howard Marshall, *The Epistles of John*, New International Commentary on the New Testament (Grand Rapids: Eerdmans, 1978), p. 139 n. 25.

1 JOHN 4:14

> And we have seen and testify that the Father has sent his Son to be the Savior of
> the world.

This verse brings together several themes we encountered in the other New
Testament writings. John presented Christ's preexistence in the context of his
having been sent by the Father for the purpose of saving humanity. In the following verses, John explained God's love was the motivation for this. This
sounds very much like John 3. We can understand that the sending statements
assume Christ's preexistence because in each case the context strongly supports
such a reading. This is no less true here—the Son who is sent already exists; he
does not come into being for the sake of the mission.

1 JOHN 5:20

> We know also that the Son of God has come and has given us understanding, so
> that we may know him who is true. And we are in him who is true—even in his
> Son Jesus Christ. He is the true God and eternal life.

This is a difficult passage, but the difficulty should not affect our conclusions
about whether the passage teaches Christ's preexistence. The difficulty involves
whether or not the passages identifies Jesus as God. The NIV translates the passage with the final phrase referring to Jesus; the NRSV is ambiguous. As commentators favoring each option point out, the grammar is not decisive; other factors
must be considered in deciding if this is one of the small number of New Testament texts that unequivocally call Jesus God.

In his commentary on 1 John the Venerable Bede wrote, "What could be
clearer than these words? . . . The eternal Son of God has come into the world
of time, and he came only in order to save us, so that we might come to know
the true God."[67] According to Calvin, Christ presents us with an understanding
of God not only because he shows us what God is like, but because he is "God
in the flesh."

Bultmann is unsure whether the concluding portion of the passage even
belongs to the original text, but if it does, he says it refers to Jesus because
describing God as the true God would be superfluous. He adds that attributing
eternal life to Jesus echoes 1 John 5:11, where John described Jesus as the
source of eternal life. Bultmann's point is well taken, but in a pagan environ-

---

[67]Venerable Bede *On 1 John*, in *James, 1-2 Peter, 1-3 John, Jude*, ed. Gerald Bray, Ancient Christian Commentary on Scripture, New Testament 11 (Downers Grove, Ill.: InterVarsity Press,
2000), p. 229.

ment I cannot help but wonder if it might not be necessary to affirm God as true against the "gods." The United Bible Society's handbook on 1 John also says the final sentence refers to Jesus. In evaluating alternative interpretations, it says taking the sentence as referring to "him who is true" (God) is tautological. Seeing *this* as referring to the general content of the letter (the gospel message) is incompatible with John's use of a masculine instead of a neuter pronoun.[68] For Smalley, regardless of how we translate the passage, it is the clearest association of God and Jesus in the entire letter. He believes the best interpretation to refer to God, not Jesus, because *this* does not need to refer to the nearest antecedent.

Marshall reminds us the purpose of the passage is soteriological, not christological. Salvation is possible only because the Son of God has entered into human history from the heavenly sphere. Because of this, we can know God not in a Gnostic but in an experiential sense. Relationship with the Son necessarily is relationship with the Father. So "it is precisely because Jesus is the true God that the person who is in him is also in the Father."[69] After carefully comparing the alternatives, Marshall concludes 1 John 5:20 portrays Jesus not only as preexistent but also as God.

2 JOHN 7-9

> Many deceivers, who do not acknowledge Jesus Christ as coming in the flesh, have gone out into the world. Any such person is the deceiver and the antichrist. Watch out that you do not lose what you have worked for, but that you may be rewarded fully. Anyone who runs ahead and does not continue in the teaching of Christ does not have God.

In this letter John was warning his readers against a false doctrine so serious that it threatened one's salvation. Marshall, noting the Greek translates best as "Jesus Christ *is* come" (not *has*), says the heresy involved denial of both a real and a continuing incarnation—that the Son of God not only took to himself human flesh, but that he never surrendered it. John's condemnation was so strong because the heresy cut to the root of Christian faith. It denied precisely what every New Testament writer said was necessary if anyone is to be saved. For C. H. Dodd, it was simply a denial of the incarnation. He thinks such a denial was a widespread early "reinterpretation" of Christianity. It was a denial of that which is distinctive about Christianity, and Dodd says

---

[68]C. Haas et al., *A Translator's Handbook on the Letters of John,* Helps for Translators 13 (London: United Bible Societies, 1972), pp. 129-30.
[69]Marshall, *Epistles of John,* p. 254 n. 47.

by rejecting Christ's real humanity it makes the Christian life one of frustration.[70] Both the Venerable Bede and Oecumenius see these verses challenging a defective understanding of the incarnation that separates Christ ontologically from the Father, either denying Christ's deity outright or making it inferior to the Father's.[71] A Christ who did not become fully human provides an unattainable model for those who would follow him. John's concern, like that of his commentators, lay in defending the reality of Christ's incarnation, and incarnation requires prior existence in a nonincarnate state. Like the rest of the New Testament witnesses to Christ's preexistence, John had a practical and salvific motive.

CONCLUSION

In his Gospel and letters, John presented Jesus as the Son of God who has been with God and is God from the beginning. Jesus' salvific mission is possible only because he has come from God and is himself God. His death has value only because of who he is and who sent him into the world. The prologue to the Gospel describes the Logos as preexistent deity, and the rest of the Gospel shows us a Jesus aware of his eternal being and divine glory. Affirmations of his deity bracket the story of Jesus' earthly life. In John 1:14, the Logos who is God became human in Jesus of Nazareth; in John 20:28, Thomas confessed that Jesus had indeed risen from death and did so using the language of deity. Despite the claims of some, it seems unlikely a devout Jew would have said something like, "Oh my God, it is true! You are alive!" That "my Lord and my God" was a confession of faith is far truer to the context. Similar affirmations of Jesus' deity may bracket the body of John's first letter.

Guthrie is convinced this means John intended his portrait of the earthly Jesus to be understood in terms of his preexistence.[72] Pollard concludes the Gospel focuses on the relationship between the eternal, preexistent Son and the Father that we see manifested in Jesus of Nazareth. John neither explained nor analyzed this reality; he simply witnessed to it.[73] This intimate relationship that so surpassed anything Abraham, Moses, David or the Old Testament prophets experienced with God can be explained only in terms of an eternal intimacy between the Father and the preexistent Son. For Jesus it validated his claim to speak and act on behalf of God. Morris draws together two aspects of John's

---

[70]C. H. Dodd, *The Johannine Epistles* (London: Hodder & Stoughton, 1946), p. 149.
[71]*James, 1-2 Peter, 1-3 John, Jude*, pp. 235-36.
[72]Guthrie, *New Testament Theology*, p. 286.
[73]T. E. Pollard, *Johannine Christology and the Early Church* (Cambridge: Cambridge University Press, 1970), pp. 18-19.

Gospel—the sending language and heaven as Christ's home—to affirm Christ was sent by the Father from heaven. This, he says, means John did not want anyone to conclude Jesus can be understood simply as one more earthly person.[74] We have seen in two of his three letters that John considered any understanding of Jesus less than his to be inadequate, even less than fully Christian, and dangerous to one's salvation.

Using statements of Jesus' deity as bookends to his Gospel, John presented Jesus as a man who knew his divine origin and purpose. The prologue in particular provides the knowledge that enables us to make sense of what was said and done in the rest of the Gospel. John's letters echo this and, like the Gospel, claim the authority of an eyewitness. John's writings present Jesus as the Son of God in an ontological sense. We can recognize who he is because of what he has done, but what he has done makes sense only because of who he is. James Denney says that acknowledging the Son's preexistence is essential to understanding Christ himself in contrast to the Old Testament preparation for him.[75]

The New Testament offers a consistent witness to Christ's deity and preexistence. This is true not only in the books generally acknowledged to contain this teaching; it is no less so, even though less explicit, in the Synoptic Gospels and Acts. I have concluded my examination of the New Testament with the Johannine materials because many believe they contain the New Testament's latest and highest christology. I hope by now that it is clear this is untrue on one count and maybe on both. John's christology is indeed high, but the earliest New Testament christology of Paul is no less high.

In every instance the New Testament authors' mention of Christ's preexistence was integral to their message that Christ came to accomplish our salvation. Preexistence was not for them an item of theological speculation. No New Testament author wrote as if this teaching were anything other than a well-established belief among his readers; instead, they used this widely held belief in order to argue for some controversial teaching. That he was the Son of God who had come from heaven provided the ontological justification for Christ's functional accomplishments. John understood this most clearly and intimately because he had been a member of Jesus' inner circle.

Some have suggested apparent parallels and causal relationships between

---

[74]Leon Morris, *Jesus Is the Christ* (Grand Rapids: Eerdmans, 1989), p. 104. Galot says, "According to Jesus' own words . . . if we acknowledge only his earthly origin we are doomed never to know him" (Jean Galot, *Who Is Christ?* [Chicago: Franciscan Herald Press, 1981], p. 396 n. 6).

[75]James Denney, *Studies in Theology,* 5th ed. (New York: A. C. Armstrong, 1897), pp. 61-62.

Jewish and Hellenistic teachings and the New Testament portrait of Jesus as the preexistent divine Son of God. Now we will take a more detailed look at these possible sources. Following that, I will begin the transition from the biblical to the theological study of Christ's preexistence by surveying how the belief developed from the New Testament era to the modern period.

6

JEWISH AND HELLENISTIC
BACKGROUND

When considering possible pre-Christian sources for belief in Christ's pre-existence, it is wise to remember Samuel Sandmel's warning against what he calls parallelomania. He reminds us it is dangerous to assume that because two different groups appear to share an idea, one must have influenced the other. Before drawing any such conclusion, we need to ask at least three questions. First, are the ideas the same, or do they merely appear to be the same? Second, if they are the same, was one really the source and the other the borrower? In the modern world, Newton and Leibniz developed differential calculus independent of one another and at virtually the same time. Darwin and Wallace arrived at theories of biological evolution independently and concurrently. So when two individuals or groups hold identical views, it is not necessarily true that one influenced the other. When the views are not identical but merely similar at points, the causal relationship becomes even murkier. Third, if there is a causal relationship, in which direction does it go? Earlier in this century some influential scholars concluded the traditional Christian understanding of Jesus had been significantly influenced by Gnosticism, particularly the Gnostic redeemer myth. More recent scholarship has determined that if a causal relationship does exist, it flows from Christianity to Gnosticism, not the reverse. Other scholars have tried to trace early Christian statements about Jesus to pre-New Testament sources, but with the same limited success.

In this chapter, I will look in greater detail at some background questions I examined briefly in earlier chapters. The topics I will examine are the role of myth, the Jewish background to the preexistence doctrine, and possible Hellenistic and other non-Jewish influences on the doctrine. As part of the last topic I will consider what does and does not constitute a legitimate parallel. Too often tenuous verbal and conceptual points of contact have been magnified into full-blown parallels that purport to explain the origin of christology. Francis Young's conclusion in *The Myth of God Incarnate* powerfully refutes arguments that christology developed in an evolutionary pattern from earlier sources: "There does not seem to be a single, exact analogy to the total Christian claim about Jesus in material which is definitely pre-Christian."[1] Other leading theologians and New Testament specialists have reached similar conclusions, specifically with regard to Christ's preexistence and incarnation. G. B. Caird acknowledges Jewish antecedents, but says the proximate source of Christian belief was Jesus himself.[2] Walter Kasper denies New Testament christology can be reduced to Jewish categories: "It is completely original and represents an unparalleled innovation. The message of the exaltation and pre-existence of the crucified Jesus was an intolerable scandal to both Jews and Greeks."[3] Gerald O'Collins concurs: "The NT doctrine of Christ's personal pre-existence and incarnation remain unique and unparalleled in religious belief up to the first century AD."[4]

MYTH

Beginning no later than David Friedrich Strauss in the early 1800s and continuing with Rudolf Bultmann, Hans Küng and John Hick, some have argued the supernatural aspects of Jesus' story include significant elements of myth. This term, *myth,* in religion is a slippery one and carries strong pejorative overtones. What these scholars mean by myth is often unclear to the reader; it may not even be clear to the writer. In the study of religion the meaning of the term *myth* can range from providing an explanation for the origin of something without regard to modern historical and scientific study to the telling of fairy tales. The first use contains no judgment about the objective truth of the subject being considered; the second certainly intends that we understand it as fiction. Between these two extremes lie several other meanings with differing truth values. Because those who talk about myth rarely define what they intend by the term, it is more confusing than helpful. Even when they do define one meaning, users are liable to slip into other meanings without warning the reader. That was one of the criticisms of *The Myth of God Incarnate* when it first appeared, that the same author used *myth* in multiple senses without distinguishing clearly among

---

[1]Francis Young, "Two Roots or a Tangled Mass?" in *The Myth of God Incarnate,* ed. John Hick (Philadelphia: Westminster Press, 1977), p. 118.

[2]G. B. Caird, "The Development of the Doctrine of Christ in the New Testament," in *Christ for Us Today,* ed. Norman Pittinger (London: SCM Press, 1968), pp. 79-80.

[3]Walter Kasper, *The God of Jesus Christ,* trans. Matthew J. O'Connell (New York: Crossroad, 1984), p. 174.

[4]Gerald O'Collins, *Christology* (New York: Oxford University Press, 1995), p. 239.

them. The problem started with the book's title, chosen apparently for its shock value. Because of its association with pagan myths of antiquity, I think the term has no place in most modern religious discussion. The potential for confusion and mischief is too great. Most people, even those trained in religious studies, tend instinctively to associate myth with fiction.

The strongest objections to the designation of biblical materials, especially those concerning Jesus, as myth comes from scholars of literature. C. S. Lewis, both student and creator of myth, has evaluated these claims about the Bible and found them wanting. Writing about the Gospel accounts of Jesus, Lewis says, "I have been reading poems, romances, vision literature, legends, myths all my life. I know what they are like. I know that none of them is like this."[5] Lewis adds that these Gospel accounts can only be reportage or "modern, novelistic, realistic narrative" some twenty centuries before its natural development. It is not that Lewis denies myth (in the technical sense) in the Bible, but he views myth in the New Testament as statements of truth about Jesus and says Jesus far exceeds anything myth could say about him. According to Lewis, biblical myth resembles other myths in neither literary style nor content. Another way of stating Lewis's sense of myth, one far different from that of most theologians, is that myth is thinking in pictures rather than abstraction. He defines myths as stories that capture universal, abstract truth in concrete form. As such, these stories satisfy a need in our scientific culture. This does not make these stories fictional or false, however. The stories of Jesus and Aslan are both stories, but Jesus is an historical figure while Aslan is one of Lewis's creations.

There are points of contact between the Christian story of Jesus and pagan stories of their gods. Whether they are parallels is an entirely different matter. C. Stephen Evans says:

> If we mean, "Are there any respects in which the story of Jesus resembles stories of Baldur and other pagan rising and dying gods?" the answer will be certainly yes, but that by itself is a trivial claim. . . . The interesting question is not whether the story of Jesus resembles the story of Baldur in some respects; rather, the question concerns how significant are the similarities as well as the dissimilarities.[6]

The point Evans is making is something like this: Human beings tell stories that try to make sense of our lives and experiences. These stories contain similar language and may even sound alike at some points, but this does not mean the

---

[5]C. S. Lewis, "Modern Theology and Biblical Criticism," in *Christian Reflections* (Grand Rapids: Eerdmans, 1967), p. 155.

[6]C. Stephen Evans, "The Incarnational Narrative as Myth and History," *Christian Scholar's Review* 23 (1994): 394.

stories are all saying the same thing. To decide whether they are, we need to consider the differences between the stories as much as the similarities, and we need to look at the details as much as at the big picture.

J. B. Phillips, the New Testament translator, shares the common understanding of and concern about the claim that the Gospel accounts are mythical. He writes, "I have read, in Greek and Latin, scores of myths, but I do not find the slightest flavor of myth here [in the Gospels]. . . . No man could have set down such artless and vulnerable accounts as these unless some real Event lay behind them."[7] Phillips is saying history and myth just do not sound the same.

The Christian doctrine of the incarnation was neither derived from myth nor itself mythological. I. Howard Marshall says James Dunn has demonstrated this conclusively. Dunn denies explicitly that there was any real precedent for the Christian doctrine of the incarnation, a teaching that necessarily includes Christ's personal preexistence. He acknowledges that some outside teachings appear similar to parts of the doctrine, but concludes they are not incarnational, citing Celsus's statement from the third century in support of his conclusion: "O Jews and Christians, no god or son of god either came or will come down (to earth)."[8] Dunn notes the "surprising absence" of writing about any son of God or divine man who descended to earth as redeemer. There are accounts of humans being exalted to divine status, gods appearing in human disguise and men who are the product of sexual relations between gods and mortal women, but all are inadequate as sources for Christian teaching about Jesus. The divine man stories are antithetical to Jewish belief about the distinction between Creator and creature, and the idea of God having sexual relations with a human would be both morally repugnant and incompatible with Jewish belief in God's incorporeality. Gerald O'Collins describes the doctrines of Christ's preexistence and incarnation as "unique and unparalleled in religious beliefs up to the first century AD."[9]

Bultmann has been the strongest and most influential advocate for the view that the New Testament picture of the world was mythical. He says "it is beyond question that the New Testament presents the event of Jesus Christ in mythical terms."[10] It is because the New Testament presents Jesus as the Son of God and

---

[7]J. B. Phillips, cited in Philip Yancey, *The Jesus I Never Knew* (Grand Rapids: Zondervan, 1995), p. 20.

[8]James D. G. Dunn, *Christology in the Making* (Philadelphia: Westminster Press, 1980), pp. 19-20.

[9]O'Collins, *Christology*, p. 239.

[10]Rudolf Bultmann, "New Testament and Mythology," in *Kerygma and Myth*, ed. Hans Werner Bartsch, trans. Reginald H. Fuller (London: SPCK, 1954), p. 34.

a preexistent divine person that Bultmann considers the portrait mythological. This is without question for Bultmann because "Son of God" and "preexistence" are mythical concepts, even when used of an historical person. He says the origin of this language can be traced easily "in the contemporary mythology of Jewish Apocalyptic and in the redemption myths of Gnosticism."[11] According to Bultmann, moderns cannot accept this worldview because they consider it obsolete, yet he seems to think it perfectly natural that people of the New Testament era believed such "myths." He argues that Jewish Wisdom speculation, Philo, Paul and "deutero-Pauline" writings all present a modified and embellished version of the basic Gnostic outlook.[12] Elsewhere, Bultmann describes Jesus' entire life in the language of myth:

> [Jesus'] person is viewed in the light of mythology when He is said to have been begotten of the Holy Spirit and born of a virgin, and this becomes clearer still in Hellenistic Christian communities where he is understood to be the Son of God in a metaphysical sense, a great, pre-existent heavenly being who became man for the sake of our redemption and took on Himself suffering, even the suffering of the cross. It is evident that such conceptions are mythological, for they were widespread in the mythologies of Jews and Gentiles and then were transferred to the historical person of Jesus. Particularly the conception of the pre-existent Son of God who descended in human guise into the world to redeem mankind is part of the Gnostic doctrine of redemption, and nobody hesitates to call this doctrine mythological.[13]

Bultmann is correct that the Gnostic perspective is myth, but not only is this myth later than the Christian story of Jesus, it differs from the Christian story at key points. One of these differences is that the Christ of Christian faith did not appear in "human guise"; he truly became human. Bultmann's assumption that people of Jesus' day accepted these teachings without question and understood them as myth is itself myth. Neither the New Testament nor extrabiblical documents report general, uncritical acceptance of the early church's teaching about Jesus, and New Testament writers offer their accounts of Jesus as anything but myth. The idea that moderns are superior to ancients because they are less credulous is a modern conceit; the skepticism of modern intellectuals may make them *less* open to truth, not more. In fact, some of Bultmann's critics have described the modern scientific outlook as mythological in the same sense Bult-

---

[11]Ibid., pp. 2-3.
[12]Rudolf Bultmann, *The Gospel of John,* trans. G. R. Beasley-Murray et al. (Philadelphia: Westminster Press, 1971), p. 27.
[13]Rudolf Bultmann, *Jesus Christ and Mythology* (New York: Charles Scribner's Sons, 1958), pp. 16-17.

mann says the Bible is.[14] The choice of the scientific "myth" must be defended no less than the rejection of the biblical "myth."

Oskar Skarsaune says that despite an active search, no myth with a structure similar to the story of Jesus has been found. "The doctrine of the incarnation arose in a religious environment which for the most part would have been thought to exclude such a possibility."[15] C. K. Barrett reports he has found no tendency during the New Testament period to create new myths. While this does not guarantee it did not happen, "it does suggest that in the New Testament event and interpretation are related to each other in a different way from that which is suggested by the language of myth."[16] Martin Hengel argues that the exaltation of Christ as Son of God and Lord restricted the possibility of mythologizing rather than encouraging it. It was Gnosticism, he says, that demoted Christ to be but one among many divine beings by its mythological speculation.[17]

Bultmann's worldview incorporates an antisupernaturalist presumption. This means that the New Testament claims about Jesus must be myth, because if they are not God *has* intervened in history to achieve human salvation and Jesus of Nazareth *has* risen from the dead and lives in heaven. For this reason Bultmann has transformed virtually every Christian belief about Jesus into myth. Bernard Ramm warns that any methodology that results in such overkill is itself suspect.[18] The greatest problem with this mythological approach, whether it comes from Bultmann or some other modern theologian, is not only that it lacks persuasive evidence, but it is inconsistent with the best evidence we have. Scholars since Bultmann have concluded that Gnosticism postdates Christianity.

J. L. Houlden goes at least as far as Bultmann when he writes that no matter how we try to explain it, we cannot call Christ the incarnate second Person of the Trinity without incorporating mythological concepts. He echoes the modern complaint that such a portrait of Jesus offends against any possibility of his real

[14]R. F. Aldwinckle writes, "If, of course, we approach our historical investigation with the assumption that 'nature' is ruled by a rigid uniformity of natural law and that we know the precise limits beyond which there can be no modification of this uniformity, then are we not again victims of myth, but this time of scientific myth?" ("Myth and Symbol in Contemporary Philosophy and Theology: The Limits of Demythologizing," *Journal of Religion* 34 [1954]: 274).

[15]Oskar Skarsaune, *Incarnation: Myth or Fact?* trans. Trygve R. Skarsten (St. Louis: Concordia, 1991), p. 131.

[16]C. K. Barrett, "Myth and the New Testament: How Far Does Myth Enter into the New Testament?" *Expository Times* 68 (1957): 361-62.

[17]Martin Hengel, *The Son of God* (Philadelphia: Fortress, 1976), p. 91.

[18]Bernard L. Ramm, *An Evangelical Christology* (Nashville: Thomas Nelson, 1985), p. 47.

humanity.[19] Unless we define *myth* as an explanation of origin with no question of truth or falsity involved, Houlden's position is no more than an attempt to have us presume his conclusion on his authority. But there are ways of discussing origins that are less ambiguous and less confusing than using the word *myth*. For Reginald Fuller and Pheme Perkins it is not a matter of myth at all: "The christology of preexistence and incarnation is not mythological, but *an interpretation of Jesus' history in terms of a poetic tradition in the Old Testament and in Judaism.*"[20] Houlden's description of basic Christian doctrine as mythical exemplifies the modern confusion of myth and worldview. Emil Brunner notes the problem is not that the doctrines depend on obsolete science, but that they offend modern people's understanding of humanity's nature and destiny.[21] He adds that the modern view is quite likely wrong.

When considering the story of Jesus, the concept of myth is more hindrance than help. It has been the source of untold mischief. In the popular mind myth carries the sense of fiction or falsehood. Even the technical sense that uses myth to express origin and significance only allows for the *possibility* of historicity. Christianity, however, requires the facticity of Jesus' incarnation. Unless we can be sure God acted in history in the man Jesus of Nazareth, we cannot be confident he acts in our history to accomplish our salvation. The first possible source for ideas about Jesus is the Jewish environment in which his disciples were raised and after Easter proclaimed their resurrected Lord.

Rejecting claims of direct dependence, H. R. Mackintosh vigorously defended the idea that God could have planted seeds in Jewish and Greek thought that readied humanity for the coming of Christ:

> That its [Christ's preexistence] similarity to a prior idea must discredit the Christian belief could only be conceded on the obviously untenable assumption that no true idea is ever providentially prepared for. It may well be that certain current Jewish theologoumena operated by suggestion, just as Greek ideas of incarnation [sic] made way for sublimer thoughts connected with Jesus. But such possibilities, which are not to be denied, no more explain St. Paul's characteristic usage of preexistence, say in Ph 2, than *In Memoriam* is explained by the fact that every word found in the poem existed previously in the dictionary. In the Jewish conceptions,

---

[19]J. L. Houlden, "The Doctrine of the Trinity and the Person of Christ," *Church Quarterly Review* 169 (1968): 15. What Houlden offers as replacement can only be described as a unitarianism where Jesus was a human especially open to God because he was created to be the vessel of God's redemptive work.

[20]Reginald H. Fuller and Pheme Perkins, *Who Is This Christ?* (Philadelphia: Fortress, 1983), p. 128.

[21]Emil Brunner, *The Christian Doctrine of Creation and Redemption,* trans. Olive Wyon (Philadelphia: Westminster Press, 1953), pp. 264ff.

be they what they may, there is nothing corresponding to the *ethical* fact of pre-temporal Divine self-sacrifice, which alone engages the apostle's attention.[22]

THE JEWISH BACKGROUND

The problem confronting the overwhelmingly Jewish early church was how to explain Jesus to their contemporaries without rejecting the contents of Jewish Scriptures, what we call the Old Testament. Those early Christians appear to have had more resources to draw from in their Jewish heritage than has often been acknowledged. Judaism had already had to wrestle with the paradoxes that people dealt face-to-face with the God who said no one could see him and live, and that God who is spirit could walk and share a meal with humans. Various Old Testament passages hinted that God is more complicated than a straightforward unitary monotheism would allow. Yet, in considering this, Jews refused to compromise the strict monotheism that distinguished them from the pagan cultures that surrounded them.

It is difficult to conceive how the first disciples could have presented Jesus to their contemporaries with no degree of continuity with his culture and environment. To have one Jew talking about another Jew in a predominately Jewish context requires that the language and concepts be Jewish. Otherwise, their message would have been incomprehensible to their audience. But at the same time we see that Paul and the other early evangelists poured a different—different as in fuller—sense into the language of their Jewish heritage, stretching it to explain the new thing they believed God was doing in their generation.[23] So Paul used the only language he knew to tell others about Jesus, but the Jesus he knew was more than Jewish thought could handle. When later Christians tried to explain Jesus solely within a Jewish framework, the result was one or another of the heretical christologies of the early church. The best known example is Ebionitism, which portrayed Jesus as a good man who taught God's word, did good works, performed some miracles and was even raised by God from death—but was not himself deity incarnate.

SECOND TEMPLE JUDAISM

There is increasing agreement that Second Temple Judaism (the Judaism that characterized Palestine during the first century B.C. through the destruction of the Jerusalem temple in A.D. 70) had a more complex understanding of God

---

[22]H. R. Mackintosh, *The Doctrine of the Person of Christ,* 2nd ed. (Edinburgh: T & T Clark, 1913), p. 449. I disagree, however, with Mackintosh's comment about Greek ideas of incarnation because Greek philosophy did not allow for anything that approached a real incarnation.
[23]See Larry W. Hurtado, *Lord Jesus Christ* (Grand Rapids: Eerdmans, 2003), p. 75.

than has the rabbinic Judaism that has dominated since.[24] This was complexity within the Godhead, not complexity surrounding God—it was as self-consciously monotheistic as Judaism has been historically.[25] While there existed a strict monotheism that rejected the thought that any but the one God could be deity and that monotheism acknowledged the existence of various heavenly beings that were creatures and not God, it also recognized that some scriptural and postscriptural texts (what are now called the Apocrypha and pseudepigrapha) spoke of "intermediary figures" that partook in some way of that which is uniquely God's. Bauckham says of this situation:

> So-called intermediary figures were not ambiguous semi-divines straddling the boundary between God and creation. Some were understood as aspects of the one God's own unique reality. Most were regarded unambiguously as creatures, exalted servants of God whom the literature often takes pains to distinguish clearly from the truly divine reality of the one and only God.[26]

He notes that two categories of intermediary figures can be distinguished in Second Temple Judaism. The first group consisted of principal angels and exalted patriarchs, all of whom play significant roles in God's governance of the world, but unequivocally are not in any way deity. The second group includes hypostatizations or personifications of aspects of God himself. These include God's Spirit, Word and Wisdom, and are unequivocally part of God's unique identity.[27] Further, as Creator, God required no helper in his work of creating or sustaining the cosmos. God does employ creatures, especially angels, in the governance of his creation, but they are clearly his creatures and in no way partake in deity. "The Jewish concern to emphasize the uniqueness of God's total sovereignty means the angels are invariably portrayed as servants whose role is simply to carry out the will of God in total obedience."[28]

Jewish monotheism clearly distinguished God from all other reality, but it did so in ways that did not prevent early Christians (themselves Jews) from including Jesus within the identity of God. This allowed a high christology to develop

---

[24]Ibid., p. 29. Richard Bauckham notes, however, that what that understanding was is the subject of significant debate among specialists in the field. See Bauckham's *God Crucified* (Grand Rapids: Eerdmans, 1998), p. 1.

[25]Hurtado writes that "the weakening or undermining of a supposedly pure Old Testament monotheism in the Judaism of the period of Christian origins alleged by some previous scholars such as Bousset is directly the opposite of the actual historical movement in Judaism of the time towards a more emphatic monotheism" (*Lord Jesus Christ*, p. 35).

[26]Bauckham, *God Crucified*, p. 3.

[27]Ibid., pp. 16-17.

[28]Ibid., p. 12.

within a Jewish environment.[29] In fact, attempts to derive christology from intermediary figures that supposedly participated somehow in deity were historically
more likely to produce an Arianlike christology, where Jesus becomes a *tertium
quid,* not quite God but not exactly human either.[30]

Bauckham also argues that the concern of Jews of Jesus' day to protect the
uniqueness of their God means no non-Jewish religious or philosophical view
could have been the source of early christology. A chain of being that stretched
from God down through various semidivine and subdivine beings to humans
was "pervasive in all non-Jewish religions and religious thought," but was not
to be found within Judaism itself. Similarly, "the God who requires what the
God of Israel requires cannot be merely the philosophical abstraction to which
the intellectual currents of contemporary Greek thought aspired."[31]

The existence of a heavenly deputy to God, responsible for helping run the
cosmos, is a fiction. Bauckham says there is no source to be found here for developing a christology.[32] One aspect of the apparent multiplicity of figures has
been the controversy about "two powers in heaven." Alan Segal says theophanies found early in the Old Testament where God is portrayed as a man or an
angel were the source of speculation about two powers. He points to Daniel 7
as the earliest biblical witness to the existence of a heavenly figure alongside
God, although most of the attributes of this figure are undefined.[33] The vision
of Daniel 7:9ff., difficult to interpret in a Jewish context, became an interpretive
key for the developing Christian understanding of Jesus.

DANIEL 7 AND "ONE LIKE A SON OF MAN"

Daniel 7 reports a mysterious vision that seems to refer to both God and a second figure in heaven who appears to have been recognized as deity. From a
Jewish perspective the vision would seem to be problematic for two reasons:
God is described in human terms and there are two enthroned powers in
heaven.

> As I looked,
> thrones were set in place,
>   and the Ancient of Days took his seat.
> His clothing was as white as snow;

---

[29]Ibid., p. 4
[30]Ibid., p. 5. Bauckham cautions that "intermediary figures who may or may not participate in
divinity are by no means characteristic of the literature of Second Temple Judaism."
[31]Ibid., pp. 15, 6-7.
[32]Ibid., p. 19.
[33]Alan F. Segal, *Two Powers in Heaven* (Leiden: E. J. Brill, 1977), p. 261.

the hair of his head was white like wool.
His throne was flaming with fire,
   and its wheels were all ablaze.
A river of fire was flowing,
   coming out from before him.
Thousands upon thousands attended him;
   ten thousand times ten thousand stood before him.
The court was seated,
   and the books were opened.

Then I continued to watch because of the boastful words the horn was speaking. I kept looking until the beast was slain and its body destroyed and thrown into the blazing fire. (The other beasts had been stripped of their authority, but were allowed to live for a period of time.)

In my vision at night I looked, and there before me was one like a son of man, coming with the clouds of heaven. He approached the Ancient of Days and was led into his presence. He was given authority, glory and sovereign power; all peoples, nations and men of every language worshiped him. His dominion is an everlasting dominion that will not pass away, and his kingdom is one that will never be destroyed. (Daniel 7:9-14)

In this vision Daniel first saw thrones (plural) being set up in heaven. Then one who would be identified as God came and sat down. This figure was described in human terms. Then comes a description of his rendering of judgment against rebellious creatures described as various beasts. The vision concludes with the enigmatic account of "one like a son of man" coming into the divine presence and receiving what can only be described as the prerogatives of deity (worship, sovereign power, eternal dominion) with the apparent approval of God. The description of the "one like a son of man" does not require that he have been human, only that he identified in some way with humanity. Indeed, all the symbolism of the passage points to the figure's deity. That was the problem recognized by early Jewish interpreters of the passage.

Segal describes this passage as dangerous because of how it portrays God.[34] The rabbinic interpretation (which would have postdated the inception of Christianity) used the idea of multiple manifestations of God to explain it. The rabbis also pointed to the singular pronoun *him* in verse 10, where the river of fire comes out from before "him," as indicating the presence of only one person.[35] As Segal acknowledges, the weakness of this argument is that the verse could

---

[34]Ibid., p. 39 n. 7. He also mentions Ex 15:3, Is 42:13 and Ezra 1:26 as dangerous.
[35]Ibid., p. 40.

be referring only to one of the figures—after all, the second figure does not appear in the vision until three verses later. Early rabbinic interpretation saw God and his nondivine messiah in these verses, but apparently soon changed to seeing God in two hypostases.[36] Despite the rabbis' best efforts, Segal sees the passage at least as much the source of their problem with two powers in heaven as its solution:

> When the whole biblical passage is seen, the passage seems to describe more a danger than a solution. . . . Not only does the passage allow the interpretation that God changes aspect, it may easily be describing two separate, divine figures. More than one throne is revealed and scripture describes two divine figures to fill them. One sits and the other seems to be invested with power, possibly enthroned. The Ancient of Days may be responsible for judgment, but delegates the operation to a "son of man." . . . All of this makes it more likely that Daniel 7:9f. is seen as central to the heresy as it is to the defense against it. . . . The midrash immediately follows the exegesis with a warning that no doctrine of "two powers in heaven" should be derived from the passage.[37]

Segal also notes that the apparent dating of the rabbinic commentary implies that the Christian community identified Jesus with the "one like a son of man" before A.D. 70.[38]

Son of Man

"Son of Man" was Jesus' favorite self-designation, but where the term comes from remains a subject of debate. Many Old Testament uses of the term clearly show the subject to have been human—for example, God's frequent address of Ezekiel as "son of man"—but some Old Testament uses and many intertestamental uses seem to portray the "son of man" as far more than simply human. Daniel 7:13 is only one of these passages; Hurtado considers Psalms 8 to have been more influential in developing an understanding of the term.[39] Segal points to Daniel 7 and 1 Enoch 37—71 as sources. He notes there is little agreement about the Danielic figure, who could be understood as an angel, but the Enoch son of man "is a salvific figure of some prominence, having many divine perquisites." This son of man is likely a preexistent being, but some details of the

---

[36]Ibid., p. 48. Segal is describing that alteration in Rabbi Akiba's view during the early second century A.D.

[37]Ibid., pp. 35-36.

[38]Ibid., p. 95.

[39]Hurtado, *Lord Jesus Christ*, p. 298. He believes several psalms were more influential in developing the Son of Man theme than was Daniel 7 (although not all those psalms use son of man language).

text are the subject of serious disagreement among scholars.[40]

Despite earlier doubts, 1 Enoch has been increasingly accepted as "Jewish, Palestinian, and probably pre-70."[41] In 1 Enoch 48, the Son of Man received a name in the presence of God "before the creation of the stars." Those on earth who glorify God will worship this Son of Man. Fred Craddock distinguishes this preexistence from predestination, saying it is personal preexistence that we find in Enoch. This is different from the preexistence of rabbinic thought. That was an ideal preexistence and thus virtually equivalent to predestination.[42] Reginald Fuller considers 1 Enoch the most complete picture of the Son of Man in the entire Jewish apocalyptic tradition. In it the Son of Man is a preexistent divine being, hidden in God's presence from the beginning, revealed at the end times and the deliverer of the elect from persecution.[43] Fuller sums up the evidence regarding the Son of Man as indicating the Jewish apocalyptic tradition had a Son of Man who was a preexistent divine agent of salvation and judgment. There does appear to be agreement that "Son of Man" was not a title in Jewish thought.

Pre-Christian Jewish writings show a variety of interpretations regarding the Son of Man and appear to include "two powers in heaven" interpretations at least a century before Jesus. Some of these may have been heretical, associating angels and exalted humans with the Godhead. The Septuagint may have been translated so as to counter such heresies—Segal notes that one version has the one like a son of man approaching *as* the Ancient of Days, thus conflating the two figures described in the Hebrew text.[44]

MESSIAH

A second term in Jewish thought was messiah (Gk *Christos*). There was no single, clear understanding of the messiah among Jews of Jesus' day; some may even have held mutually contradictory ideas about the messiah. The basic meaning of the word is that of an eschatological figure who has been anointed by God. The term *messiah* appears to have associated with both Son of God and Son of Man language. Some Jews joined the Son of Man language from Daniel 7 with messianic expectations.

---

[40]Segal, *Two Powers in Heaven,* pp. 200ff.

[41]James H. Charlesworth, "From Jewish Messianology to Christian Christology: Some Caveats and Perspectives," in *Judaisms and Their Messiahs at the Turn of the Christian Era,* ed. Jacob Neusner (Cambridge: Cambridge University Press, 1987), p. 31.

[42]Fred Craddock, *The Pre-existence of Christ in the New Testament* (Nashville: Abingdon, 1968), p. 46.

[43]Reginald H. Fuller, *The Foundations of New Testament Christology* (London: Fontana, 1965), pp. 39-40. See also R. G. Hamerton-Kelly, *Preexistence, Wisdom, and the Son of Man* (Cambridge: Cambridge University Press, 1973), pp. 17-18, 41ff.

[44]Segal, *Two Powers in Heaven,* p. 202.

For first-century Jews the messiah appears to have been human and no more, although he may have been preexistent. In that case the messiah would have been hidden with God and only appeared when the time was right. This hidden existence with God, says Geza Vermes, need not have in any way affected his humanity. Qumran documents point to the messiah as one whom God would raise up from among the people, but the exact role of the messiah is unclear (1QSa 2:11-12). Other Qumran documents seem to expect at least two messiahs, one priestly and one royal. According to some New Testament passages there were Jews who looked to the messiah as a political or military liberator from Roman rule. This appears to have been a sufficiently widespread expectation that accepting acclamation as messiah could be a personally hazardous decision.

WISDOM

In chapter two we examined Wisdom in its New Testament context. Wisdom is important to any consideration of christology, especially of Christ's preexistence. Many modern scholars consider it the key to interpreting what the New Testament says about Jesus. Because it is a part of the Jewish background, I will examine the Wisdom theme in its pre-Christian context to see where it is similar and dissimilar to the story of Jesus of Nazareth. There appears to be a sharp division between those who believe Jewish Wisdom speculation provides sufficient background for understanding Jesus and those who argue it can take us only part way. On the periphery of this debate are some who think Wisdom speculation derived from extra-Jewish sources.

In the Old Testament, Wisdom appears in Job and Proverbs; in both settings it was preexistent. The question is about the nature of that preexistence. Jewish thinking about Wisdom underwent further development in apocryphal and intertestamental literature. As it moved from the Old Testament through the intertestamental period, the Wisdom tradition became more sophisticated, even suggestive of something beyond poetic personification, but it never attained real personhood.[45]

The most significant Wisdom passage relating to preexistence in the Jewish Scriptures is Proverbs 8:22-32:

The LORD brought me forth as the first of his works,

---

[45]Harmut Gese, however, argues that to call Wisdom in Job 28 and Proverbs 8 no more than a personification is to ignore the role Wisdom plays in each instance. He says not only do these passages present Wisdom in terms similar to those of the Old Testament prophets but they speak of Wisdom's preexistence and intimate relationship to both Creator and creation ("Wisdom, Son of Man, and the Origins of Christology: The Consistent Development of Biblical Theology," *Horizons in Biblical Theology* 3 [1981]: 29-30).

before his deeds of old;
I was appointed from eternity,
  from the beginning, before the world began.
When there were no oceans, I was given birth,
  when there were no springs abounding with water;
before the mountains were settled in place,
  before the hills, I was given birth,
before he made the earth or its fields
  or any of the dust of the world.
I was there when he set the heavens in place,
  when he marked out the horizon on the face of the deep,
when he established the clouds above
  and fixed securely the fountains of the deep,
when he gave the sea its boundary
  so the waters would not overstep his command,
and when he marked out the foundations of the earth.
  Then I was the craftsman at his side.
I was filled with delight day after day,
  rejoicing always in his presence,
rejoicing in his whole world
  and delighting in mankind.
Now then, my sons, listen to me;
  blessed are those who keep my ways.

In this passage Wisdom is undoubtedly part of creation, even if it is the earliest part of creation. Wisdom speaks to whomever will listen in the much longer Wisdom passage of Proverbs 1:4—9:18, warning them not to ignore her counsel. This Wisdom is not yet a hypostatization, but it is personified, being spoken of as "she" and speaking, calling out, dwelling, loving, walking, bestowing, possessing and taking her stand. One of the difficulties in associating Wisdom with the preexistent Christ is that Wisdom is feminine in both Hebrew and Greek, whereas the incarnate Christ was male.

Wisdom has a mouth. But it was

By wisdom the Lord laid the earth's foundations,
  by understanding he set the heavens in place;
by his knowledge the deeps were divided,
  and the clouds let drop the dew. (Proverbs 3:19-20)

Here Wisdom is not a person, but an attribute of God, who creates unassisted. Segal reports the existence of various heretical understandings of God centered on the participation by Wisdom, a principal angel, or some other being in the creation of Genesis 1.[46] Proverbs 8 would become part of early Christianity's debate about the person of Jesus. The best known users of the passage were the followers of Arius, who used the passage to argue, despite the Son's preexistence, that he was inferior to God because he was the first among creatures, not fully deity. Thus the Wisdom tradition by itself is insufficient to justify belief in Christ's personal preexistence. Jewish Wisdom never went beyond personification to become a personal being.

Oskar Skarsaune, however, argues Old Testament Wisdom thought goes beyond poetic personification to at least the appearance of autonomous personhood, but he says that when Wisdom language was applied to Jesus, "the discussion of Wisdom as a person took on a totally new shape."[47] The Wisdom tradition provided a providential tool for Jesus and the early church to express something about who Jesus was to their contemporaries, but it could provide only part of the picture. Without the use of the Wisdom tradition, however, Jesus would not have been comprehensible. Fuller says the tradition made an important contribution to understanding Christ in terms of creation, revelation and incarnation. But Wisdom is only part of the story: "Even if it could be established that the cult of Wisdom already existed, it would still be a new thing that a man of recent history, who had been crucified the other day, should come to occupy the position of this divine Wisdom."[48]

Despite suggestions that "the Wisdom myth does not have its origin in the O.T. or in Israel at all—it can only spring from pagan mythology"[49]—there is no evidence the Wisdom tradition was ever anything but Jewish. Kuschel describes the history-of-religions approach to Wisdom as "largely regarded as being itself an academic myth, without adequate support in the sources."[50]

THE WORD OF GOD

The current fascination with Wisdom has distracted attention from the role the Word of God plays in christology and in Second Temple Jewish thought. As an expression of God's activity in the material world culminating in the incarnation, the biblical concept of the Word of God stands in sharp contrast to Hellenism. But while Judaism understood the Word of God as preexistent, it lacked any

---

[46]Segal, *Two Powers in Heaven*, p. 114.

[47]Skarsaune, *Incarnation*, p. 27.

[48]C. F. D. Moule, *The Origin of Christology* (Cambridge: Cambridge University Press, 1977), p. 154.

[49]Rudolf Bultmann, *The Gospel of John*, trans. George R. Beasley-Murray et al. (Philadelphia: Westminster Press, 1971), p. 23.

[50]Karl-Josef Kuschel, *Born Before All Time?* trans. John Bowden (New York: Crossroad, 1992), p. 192.

sense of the Word as personal. Like Wisdom, God's Word was a personification of an aspect of God's own identity.

> In general, the personifications of God's Word and God's Wisdom in the litera-
> ture are not parallel to the depictions of exalted angels as God's servants. The
> personifications have been developed precisely out of the ideas of God's own
> Wisdom and God's own word, that is, aspects of God's own identity. . . . They
> are not created beings, but nor are they semi-divine entities occupying some am-
> biguous status between the one God and the rest of reality. They belong to the
> unique divine identity.[51]

Because God's Word and Wisdom were seen as aspects of God himself, and not as part of his creation, Second Temple Judaism could speculate on their status without compromising its monotheism. Lacking independent existence, they were personifications, not hypostases. But because of their identification with God, they provided some of the raw material early Christianity would use to describe Christ (or the Logos/Word) as God and with God (Jn 1:1).

Schmidt believes the hypostatization of the *dābhar YHWH* began in the Old Testament and is visible especially in Psalms and several of the prophets. Although neither personal nor independent of God, the Word was associated with both the creation and the preservation of the world. By the time of Isaiah the Word appears as a real power sent by God to accomplish a mission, even like a person acting by God's authority.[52] Charlesworth considers the Jewish idea of the Word of God to have been the linguistic, even the theological, background to the Logos of John's prologue. He says the Word is personified in passages like Isaiah 55:11[53] and appears hypostatized in the Wisdom of Solomon 18:15-16.[54] Even Philo, who joined Hellenistic influence to his Jewish background, remained a monotheist while affirming the divinity of God's Word.[55] For Schnack-

---

[51]Bauckham, *God Crucified,* p. 21.

[52]W. H. Schmidt, *"dābhar," Theological Dictionary of the Old Testament,* ed. G. Johannes Bot-
terweck and Helmer Ringgren, trans. John T. Willis et al. (Grand Rapids: Eerdmans, 1978),
3:120ff.

[53]"So is my word that goes out of my mouth: it will not return to me empty, but will accomplish
what I desire, and achieve the purpose for which I sent it." Here the word of God becomes
the agent that (who?) accomplishes the work of God. There is thus a hint of the personhood
required of an agent and an echo of God's word as the agent of creation in Genesis 1. In the
New Testament this personification becomes the person of God the Son incarnated in Jesus.

[54]"Your all-powerful word leaped from heaven, from the royal throne, into the midst of the land
that was doomed, a stern warrior carrying the sharp sword of your authentic command, and
stood and filled all things with death, and touched heaven while standing on the earth." Here
the word of God, which exists in heaven, leaps to earth in the form of a warrior, taking the
personification found in Isaiah further in the direction of personhood.

[55]Philo *On Dreams* 1.229.

enburg, Jewish thinking about the Word of God was the product of reflection on God's wisdom and word as well as Torah. It did not come from Hellenism or mystery religions.[56] He finds in Philo merely a Logos that is the "firstborn" son in contrast to the world that is the younger son. Thomas Oden adds, "The main stream of New Testament usage of Logos is not Greek but the ancient Hebrew *dābhar YHWH* ('Word of God') by which the world was made and the prophets inspired. . . . It is this eternal Word *(logos)* that becomes flesh *(sarx)*, contrary to all Hellenistic assumptions and expectations. Were one seeking to accommodate a Hellenistic audience, one would certainly not say: Logos becomes flesh."[57] Each of these interpretations carries a presumption of the Word's preexistence.

ANGELS AND THE ANGEL OF THE LORD

Second Temple Judaism included speculation on the place of angels in the divine order. Jewish Scripture names only two angels, Gabriel and Michael. Extrabiblical writings name other angelic beings such as Melchizedek, Metatron, Uriel and even the Patriarch Jacob. Angels were considered possibly to have been involved in creation and were mediators of divine revelation. "Many early Jews *tended* to conceive of God as distant, visiting humanity only through intermediaries such as angels."[58] The humanlike figure in Daniel 7:13 was sometimes understood as an angel, and the intertestamental writers tended to interpret any theophany in human form as the appearance of an angel.[59] The Qumran community had a highly developed angelology as part of its eschatology.

Some of the most fascinating passages in Jewish Scripture are the appearances of the angel of the Lord. When this mysterious figure appeared to Israelites, they worshiped him without reservation or rebuke—other angelic beings refused to accept worship because they were creatures, not God. When Jews realized whom they had seen, they feared the direst consequences for having been in God's immediate presence (Judg 13:22). The angel of the Lord came and went as he pleased, always in a supernatural manner. In several passages, references to the angel of the Lord and God himself blend into one. This happens most clearly in the stories of the burning bush in Exodus 3,[60] Balaam and

---

[56]Rudolf Schnackenburg, *Jesus in the Gospels,* trans. O. C. Dean Jr. (Louisville: Westminster/John Knox, 1995), p. 284.

[57]Thomas C. Oden, *The Word of Life: Systematic Theology* 2 (San Francisco: Harper & Row, 1989), pp. 69-70.

[58]James H. Charlesworth, *Jesus Within Judaism* (New York: Doubleday, 1988), p. 134.

[59]Segal, *Two Powers in Heaven,* p. 190.

[60]Segal says of this passage, "References to the angel of YHWH and Elohim are confused in the text" (ibid., p. 149).

his donkey in Numbers 22, the calling of Gideon in Judges 6 and the announcement to Samson's mother in Judges 13. Segal describes the angel of the Lord passages as among the dangerous passages, which also include Daniel 7 with its "son of man" figure, the Exodus 24 theophany and verses describing God as plural (e.g., Gen 1:27).[61]

This angel appeared repeatedly to Old Testament people but is never mentioned in the New Testament. This is consistent with the angel being the preexistent Christ, although it is not conclusive. In both testaments angels, not the angel of the Lord, emphatically declared their creatureliness when people sought to worship them. This is precisely what the angel of the Lord did not do. Often linked to these appearances of the angel of the Lord are God's appearance to Abraham in Genesis 18 and the man who wrestled with Jacob in Genesis 32.

PREEXISTENCE IN JEWISH THOUGHT

Pre-Christian Judaism had a concept of preexistence, but the precise nature of this preexistence is a matter of much debate. In part, the debate has occurred because Jewish thinking about preexistent beings developed during the intertestamental period from a clearly "ideal" preexistence toward personification and, in some eyes, personal preexistence. As this relates to Christ and his preexistence, it also involves a dispute about the dates of some extracanonical Jewish writings. Fundamental to this discussion is disagreement about the extent of continuity between Jewish and Christian thinking.

Hengel believes the preexistence of the redeemer is evident as early as Psalm 110, although the nature of the preexistence is unclear. Messianic preexistence was affirmed by the rabbinic concept of the preexistence of the name of the messiah. This, however, was an ideal preexistence. Enoch's Son of Man was preexistent. God's Wisdom of Proverbs 8 certainly preexisted, and Hengel says, "At least Wisdom or the Logos must have been associated with God. Indeed one could not conceive of God without his Wisdom."[62] Hengel warns, however, that the concept of preexistence remained fluid during this period.

Second Temple Judaism viewed a variety of beings and things as preexistent in some sense. These included the Messiah, possibly Moses, repentance, Torah, probably the Son of Man, the Logos or Word of God, and Wisdom.[63] Some of

---

[61]Ibid., pp. 183-84. He identifies the following passages as ones where God (YHWH) and an angel are confused: Gen 16:7ff.; 21:17ff.; 22:11ff.; 31:11ff.; Ex 3:2ff.; 23:21ff.; and Judg 2:1ff., but says the rabbis did not discuss most of the passages.

[62]Hengel, *Son of God,* pp. 69-70.

[63]Dunn says rabbinic speculation about what preexisted creation seems to have begun in the late first century to early second century A.D. (Dunn, *Christology in the Making,* p. 260).

these would have had ideal preexistence in the mind of God, others as personifications or attributes of God.

But is any of this relevant? Some think not. F. F. Bruce describes the preexistent beings of pre-Christian Judaism as "largely ideal."[64] Dunn denies Second
Temple Judaism had arrived at any concept of personal preexistence, although
Wisdom came close.[65] Schnackenburg emphasizes that these preexistent beings
were at most personifications, not hypostatizations. He says Wisdom offers no
clue of the Logos's personal character.[66] Craddock reminds us to be careful in
how we speak about preexistence: "Ideas and principles do not pre-exist; they
lack independence, individuality, the clear imagery that gives focus and identity."[67] Morris, however, says that during the first century A.D., Old Testament
concepts like "Word" and "Wisdom" were receiving special attention. "While
nothing was said to compromise the basic monotheism of Judaism, attention
was increasingly directed to passages where such entities are given an almost
independent existence."[68] Mackintosh is not impressed by discussions of Jewish
speculation about preexistence because he considers them to be beside the
point. "It is one thing to speculate freely on pre-existence in the abstract and
quite another to believe in the eternal reality of a specific person, with whom
the speaker has lived in the most intimate association."[69]

HELLENISTIC JUDAISM

In Jesus' day there existed a variety of Jewish factions and sects. They disagreed
about many things, and most had come to terms in some way with the prevail-
ing Hellenistic culture, but none had removed the distinction between Creator
and creature (although several appear to have blurred it somewhat). From this
we see two things. The Jews remained Jews in their fundamental beliefs, yet all
had been sufficiently affected by Hellenism that the distinction between Palestinian and Hellenistic Jew can only be understood in relative terms. One implication of this is that the claim that Judaism, especially Palestinian Judaism, was
interested in function in contrast to a Hellenistic concern about nature must be
recognized as a caricature. Hamerton-Kelly says the Jewish interest in preexistent figures in the intertestamental apocalyptic texts and the prominence of pre-

---

[64]F. F. Bruce, *The Epistles to the Colossians, to Philemon, and to the Ephesians,* New International
Commentary on the New Testament (Grand Rapids, Mich.: Eerdmans, 1984), pp. 60-61.
[65]A. T. Hanson, *The Image of the Invisible God* (London: SCM Press, 1982), p. 75.
[66]R. Schnackenberg, "The Origin and Nature of the Johannine Concept of the Logos," in *The
Gospel of John,* vol. 1, trans. Kevin Smyth (New York: Harder & Harder, 1968), p. 485.
[67]Craddock, *Pre-existence of Christ,* p. 80.
[68]Leon Morris, *The Gospel According to John,* rev. ed. (Grand Rapids: Eerdmans, 1995), p. 104.
[69]Mackintosh, *Doctrine of the Person of Christ,* pp. 449-50.

existent Wisdom indicate interest in what can only be called metaphysical entities.[70] This makes sense: function and nature are inextricably interconnected,
even if one does not engage in pure philosophical speculation about them.
Thus Jews had to think about what kind of God it was they worshiped who
acted as he did, and Greeks thought about what substances of particular natures
were able or expected to do. Nature and function are inextricably linked. That
is not Hellenistic philosophy, it is how the universe works.

Lest we think the impact of Hellenism on pre-Christian Jewish culture necessarily transformed its religious consciousness in a direction more amenable to
Hellenistic syncretism and paganism, Walter Moberly offers a forceful reminder
about the nature of Jewish culture:

> A vital religious tradition and culture, such as that of Israel, is not some diffuse re-
> pository for miscellaneous beliefs and practices of other religions and cultures.
> Rather, because it has a coherence and identity of its own, it will only embrace
> those elements from outside which it perceives as congenial and able to help de-
> velop that which is already inherent within itself. And in so doing it will to a greater
> or lesser extent transform those elements it adopts.[71]

PHILO OF ALEXANDRIA

Philo, a contemporary of Jesus and Paul, was a Jew living in Alexandria, Egypt.
He is the primary resource for understanding Hellenistic Judaism at the time of
Jesus. While he sought to remain faithful to Jewish teaching, he also attempted
to explain Judaism to his non-Jewish contemporaries using Greek, especially
Platonic, thought. Segal suggests Philo provides us an insight into the traditions
of first century A.D. Hellenistic Jewish communities. Because it was against these
traditions that the rabbis directed some of their arguments, it is possible that second-century rabbinic arguments against "two powers in heaven" may actually
be a century older.

Philo offers up a teaching about a "second God" *(deuteros theos)*, but also
affirms that there is only one true God. This "second God" is no more than the
visible emanation of the one true God. Philo uses this concept to help explain
the anthropomorphisms of Jewish Scripture, both the terms used to describe

---

[70]Hamerton-Kelly, *Preexistence, Wisdom, and the Son of Man*, p. 273.
[71]Walter Moberly, "God Incarnate: Some Reflections from an Old Testament Perspective,"
Churchman 98 (1983): 53. Segal, Hurtado and Bauckham have shown the truth of this statement in an earlier section of this chapter. Francis Young says, "Judaism was therefore the context of early Christian origins, and Judaism in this period was resistant to pagan influences"
("Two Roots or a Twisted Mass?" in *The Myth of God Incarnate*, ed. John Hick [Philadelphia:
Westminster Press, 1977], p. 103).

God physically and emotionally, and the theophanic appearances to the patriarchs and others. Thus, for Philo, the Logos is the explanation for all manifestations of deity, angelic and human, found in Jewish Scripture.[72]

The Logos becomes for Philo a divine hypostasis separate from God. The
Logos is not properly a second god, but the means by which God has chosen
to reveal himself to humans. Thus Philo's carefully defined use of the term "second God" poses no threat to monotheism, although it can be confusing and may
encourage others who are less careful to understand a multiplicity of gods in
heaven. Thus it has been said that a Hellenistic Jew like Philo could accept the
language of the prologue to John's Gospel up to, but not including, verse 14.
This would include some sort of preexistence for the Logos, but at the point of
incarnation and personal preexistence Philo would object. The embodiment (incarnation) of God, as opposed to a theophany, would offend both his Jewish
heritage and his Greek philosophy.

Philo's Logos is an emanation from God. As such, it was God's partner in creation. He also describes the Logos as God's offspring or firstborn son. Because
the Logos is of (not from) God, monotheistic concerns are respected.

At least part of Philo's rationale for this language is his reluctance to believe
the eternal God can become directly involved in the corruption of this transitory
world. In positing the Logos as the mediator between God and creation, Philo
is following the lead of Greek philosophy. Yet Philo reserves the role of God's
mediator to the Logos alone. He does allow for exemplary humans to participate
in a journey to God, in the process becoming divinized, but not deified, again
maintaining the qualitative distinction between Creator and creature at the heart
of monotheism.[73]

Philo's thought is complex and draws heavily on allegorical interpretation.
Yet we can see here both the concern to affirm monotheism and a recognition
that Jewish Scripture's representation of God is difficult to integrate into a simple
monotheism. Philo wrestles with this problem, reaching conclusions that have
points of contact with Christian thought about Jesus, but not going so far as to
serve as a source or inspiration for that thought.

EVALUATION

"Jewish antecedents adequately explain all the terminology used in the New
Testament to describe the pre-existent Christ, but they cannot explain how
Christians came to believe in his pre-existence as a person; for the Jews believed

---

[72]Segal, *Two Powers in Heaven,* pp. 159ff., 169.
[73]Ibid., p. 173.

only in the pre-existence of a personification."[74] What these antecedents are unable to explain is precisely that which, less than two decades after his crucifixion, Paul claimed was true about Jesus, namely, that he personally preexisted. A. T. Wainwright calls Jewish categories insufficient for the task of describing Jesus because they were unable to accommodate his claim to divine functions. He suggests this need was why the church had to draw on Hellenistic thought, but emphasizes the early church's accomplishment in expressing Jesus' deity was neither Jewish nor Hellenistic, but Christian.[75]

Fuller believes many of his fellow scholars understand Jewish monotheism too narrowly. Agreeing with Fuller, Donald Juel points to lively Jewish speculation during the intertestamental period about heavenly intermediaries. He says that while we lack evidence of Jewish discussion of the possibility of an incarnation, "the resources for fashioning such a conception were available within the tradition."[76] N. T. Wright argues that for Jews of this period monotheism was not concerned with analyzing the inner essence of God. "It was always a polemical statement directed outwards against the pagan nations. . . . When Jews said they believed in one true God, this was what they meant: that their own God was not merely a local or tribal deity, but was the God of the whole earth."[77]

Jewish literature shows Jews speaking about God in ways that show them to have been far less concerned about numerical analysis of God's essence than are rabbis of the Christian era.[78] This literature, all from the late intertestamental or early Christian period, draws from a variety of Old Testament passages in an attempt to understand the meaning of biblical monotheism because their experience was more complex than most modern understandings of monotheism acknowledge. Nonetheless, these same Jews did not hesitate to recite the Shema. Bauckham says, "Jewish monotheism clearly distinguished the one God and all other reality, but the way in which it distinguished the one God from all else did not prevent the early Christians [from] including Jesus in this unique divine reality." He adds that those who assume no Jewish monotheism could have accepted a christology that includes Jesus in the divine identity without abandon-

---

[74]Caird, "Development of the Doctrine of Christ," pp. 79-80.

[75]A. T. Wainwright, *The Trinity in the New Testament* (London: SPCK, 1962), pp. 39-40.

[76]Donald Juel, "Incarnation and Redemption: A Response to Reginald H. Fuller," *Semeia* 30 (1985): 118.

[77]N. T. Wright, *Who Was Jesus?* (Grand Rapids: Eerdmans, 1992), pp. 48-49. See also N. T. Wright, *Jesus and the Victory of God* (Minneapolis: Fortress, 1996), 2:625ff.

[78]Both Segal and Hurtado show a narrowing during rabbinic Judaism in the understanding of God that had been acceptable during Second Temple Judaism. The "two powers in heaven" debate was part of this and evidenced the Jewish response to the challenge seen on the part of Christian and other groups.

ing Jewish monotheism "have not understood Jewish monotheism."[79] Jewish thinking about monotheism since the destruction of the Jerusalem temple appears to have developed in response to Christian trinitarian doctrine, especially to what Christians affirmed about Jesus of Nazareth.

Jewish thinking during the Second Temple period did not provide a basis for the christology that would emerge out of the early Christian church, yet it did provide some linguistic and conceptual resources that could be adapted to express that christology. Segal makes a good case that Jewish consideration of their Scripture as early as the first century A.D. was faced with the need to explain passages where God was said to have appeared to humans, was described anthropomorphically and possibly appeared in multiple forms. Often these were the same passages the early church used to develop its christological and trinitarian theology.

Segal concludes that "before Christianity there is evidence of many different exegetical traditions but no central, single redemption myth. It looks as if the unity was reached by applying all the traditions to Jesus."[80] He says that while the church's understanding of Jesus developed out of its Jewish setting, early Christians did not simply take an existing title and job description and apply them to Jesus. "Rather, it appears that the debate between Christianity and Judaism proceeded partially on midrashic or exegetical lines."[81] This means early Christians entered into the Jewish debate regarding the meaning of monotheism, interpretation of specific scriptural passages, and the relationship between God and creation, including the "two powers in heaven" debate, but became a source of contention because they claimed a recently executed Jewish male was the incarnation of God. That claim included such implications as his preexistent deity.

HELLENISTIC BACKGROUND

The role of Judaism as background for the doctrine of Christ's preexistence is evident. The earliest Christians were Jews raised on Jewish Scripture and enculturated with Jewish ways of thinking. But even Palestinian Judaism existed in an environment affected to some degree by Hellenistic thought, and the early church quickly spread beyond Palestine to Hellenistic Jewish and Gentile populations. What influence did these audiences and converts from these audiences have on the development of early christology, particularly the doctrine of Christ's preexistence?

---

[79]Richard Bauckham, *God Crucified* (Grand Rapids: Eerdmans, 1998), pp. 4, 72.
[80]Segal, *Two Powers in Heaven,* p. 208.
[81]Ibid., p. x.

While the way one thinks about a subject and the language used in that thinking are related, there are also distinctions between them. These distinctions only become greater when one communicates those thoughts to people of another culture (or worldview). Because the original language may not be understandable, it has to be translated into concepts comprehensible to the target audience. Thus one recent scholar wrote:

> In making use of the Hellenistic language and traditions as *means,* the Christian Church does not derive the essence of her teaching from them, but tries through them to explicate the far-reaching implications of the Christian revelation. . . . Language and *paradeigmata* do not constitute the Faith, but serve it. They are means, not the end.[82]

T. F. Torrance makes a similar argument:

> It is certainly true that the Gospel was translated into Greek from the very start and it was largely in Greek thought-forms that the early Church gave public expression to its preaching and teaching. However, far from a radical Hellenization having taken place something very different happened, for in making use of Greek thought-forms Christian theology radically transformed them in making them vehicles of fundamental doctrines and ideas quite alien to Hellenism. In fact, the mission of the church had the effect of altering the basic ideas of classical Hellenism. . . . This was one of the most significant features of Nicene theology: not the Hellenizing of Christianity but the Christianizing of Hellenism.[83]

Where Hellenism did significantly influence Christian theology, that theology was soon deemed heretical because it was unable to fully bridge the gap between matter and spirit. With regard to christology, this can be seen most readily in the teachings of Arius condemned at the Council of Nicea in A.D. 325.

Leading Hellenistic candidates to have influenced the doctrine of Christ's preexistence are the Gnostic redeemer myth popularized by Bultmann and the concept of the Logos as universal reason. From a history of religions perspective, others have sought to explain away the doctrine in terms of a supposed *theios anēr* or *theios anthropos* (divine man) figure or some form of adoptionism or apotheosis. These interpretations remove the possibility of preexistence because the divine man was exalted to the gods from an essential humanity; he did not come down from heaven to live among humans. One danger in all these cases lies in assuming that because different religious traditions use the same

---

[82]Archbishop Methodios, "The Homoousion," in *The Incarnation: Ecumenical Studies in the Nicene-Constantinopolitan Creed, A.D. 381,* ed. Thomas F. Torrance (Edinburgh: Handsel, 1981), p. 7.

[83]Thomas F. Torrance, *Trinitarian Faith* (Edinburgh: T & T Clark, 1995), p. 68.

language, they are talking about the same thing. Moreover, Kasper warns that our earliest sources for the mystery religions and Gnosticism come from the second and third centuries A.D., so we have no justification for projecting them back to the first century and claiming them as sources for Christian doctrine.[84]

The early Gentile mission was entirely the work of Christian Jews, so that during this early period in the church's history any significant direct pagan influence seems extremely unlikely. This means the idea of the Son of God being sent is far more likely to have drawn from Jewish Wisdom speculation than any pre-Christian Gnostic myth (assuming there was such a myth).[85] Hengel adds that the confession "Jesus is Lord" was not borrowed from the cult of Attis, Serapis or Isis, but was primarily influenced by Psalm 110:1.[86]

That Christianity appropriated a full-grown incarnational idea from one of the cults has never been particularly believable.[87] O. C. Quick says that if Hellenistic thought is to remain consistent, it can affirm no more than that "the historical life of Jesus symbolizes the perfect goodness of the Godhead more truly than any other human and passable life." He bases this on the Hellenistic idea of divine impassibility, which denies God can either change or enter into relationships outside himself.[88] Dunn rejects any thought that in the pre-Christian Near East there was a serious belief in any god or son of a god who descended from heaven in order to effect human salvation, unless it was in the realm of popular superstition.[89] What this means is that neither Hellenistic thought nor the pagan religions of the Mediterranean basin understood deity or the material world in a way that could have served as a source for the Christian doctrine of the incarnation.

Some of the debate surrounding the source of "Word of God" language for christology seems to result from a confusion between the source and the application of an idea. The Hellenistic environment was familiar with Logos language from Greek philosophy. For New Testament writers to draw on this familiarity to explain their thinking about Jesus was good crosscultural communication. But this does not require that the Christian idea of Logos, or Word of God, had its origin in Hellenistic thinking. The clear difference be-

---

[84]Kasper, *God of Jesus Christ*, p. 173.

[85]Stephen Neill writes, "We can now be almost certain that there never was a pre-Christian Gnostic redeemer; when a redeemer appears in Gnostic sources, this is almost certainly a borrowing from Christian doctrines rather than the other way around" ("Jesus and Myth," in *The Truth of God Incarnate*, ed. Michael Green [Grand Rapids: Eerdmans, 1977], pp. 61-62).

[86]Martin Hengel, *Between Jesus and Paul* (Philadelphia: Fortress, 1983), p. 41.

[87]Dunn, *Christology in the Making*, p. 251.

[88]O. C. Quick, *Doctrines of the Church* (London: Nisbet, 1938), pp. 122-23, 125. This was why Philo used the Logos as God's mediator with the created order.

[89]Dunn, *Christology in the Making*, p. 22.

tween Christian and Hellenistic understandings of the Logos shows that while Christianity used the idea to explain itself to its world, the context for the Logos language came from its Jewish heritage. Using Logos language enabled early Christians to speak to the Hellenistic world in a way it could understand (but not on its terms). Greek thought had no close parallels to the language we find, especially in the Fourth Gospel. Morris notes that although Jews and Greeks would have understood Logos differently, both would have understood John was talking about something important that had to do with the beginning of all. He could have expected his readers to grasp his essential meaning, even if not all the details.[90]

OTHER POSSIBLE INFLUENCES

Apart from ancient Judaism and Platonism, three influences have been claimed for early christology: the deification or apotheosis of prominent individuals, the Gnostic redeemer myth and the oriental mystery religions. These three overlap at many points and display many common features. All have implications for the doctrine of Christ's preexistence. The Greek idea of apotheosis involved the honoring of heroes as divine figures at their death. Such people may have been military heroes, political leaders, philosophers, sages or miracle workers. Deification has been differentiated from this to mean the restoring of the individual soul to its true status as an immortal god. So apotheosis saw people as simply human and honored the great among them by ascribing to them the language of divinity. In Greek the linguistic distinction between divinity and deity, while small, is significant. God, or deity, is *theos;* divinity (an honorific) is *theios*. As would be seen in the debate at Nicea, one iota makes all the difference. Deification made people *theios,* not *theos*. Frequently, apotheosized individuals were mythical heroes from antiquity. This changed when the Romans began to treat their emperors this way, and at least one claimed the status prior to his death. One may wonder how seriously this was to be taken in light of Vespasian's deathbed lament that he was about to become a god.

In contrast to apotheosis, which was an honorific, deification understood the essence of each person to be an immortal divine soul, so deification was the return of that soul (without the body) to its original habitation. This was in many ways similar to Gnosticism's explanation of the human condition and salvation, but it is in utter contrast to the Bible's portrayal of humans as creations of God and not as little pieces of God. It is also inconsistent with the biblical understanding of humans as embodied souls, with the body a necessary and good

---

[90]Morris, *Gospel According to John,* pp. 103, 108.

part of creation.[91] The immortality of the soul is a Greek idea; it has no biblical warrant. Deification presupposed the preexistence of the soul of the one deified, whereas apotheosis was more akin to promotion to a divine status based on one's accomplishments or office.

A similar group, the so-called divine men, had no preincarnate existence.[92] There is some question, however, whether these individuals are more than figments of the scholarly imagination. Assuming they are, A. D. Nock says the concept may have made it easier to understand the idea of a more-than-human teacher who lived in this world before leaving to receive divine status. It does not, however, explain how the Jerusalem church could consider Jesus to be Son of God and Lord. Nock believes the most satisfactory explanation for the early church's christology is the belief of Jesus and his disciples that he was more than human—the divine man idea played no part.[93] Carl Holliday argues that rather than blurring the distinction between God and humans, the divine man concept actually widened it.[94]

GNOSTICISM

Gnosticism was a religious understanding that emphasized knowledge or *gnosis* as the way of salvation. The saved constituted an "in" group possessing secret knowledge, and the possession of this knowledge was itself salvific. The basic beliefs of Gnosticism were that this material world is evil, the immaterial soul is good, and salvation consists in freeing this soul from its material prison to return to its heavenly home. In every case, Gnosticism made the concrete abstract in its teaching. Depending on the Gnostic group, ethics could be either ascetic or libertine, since in either case the body was devalued. However many deities there might be, each only imperfectly manifests the one, unknowable God.

There is still no consensus as to whether Gnosticism was a pre-Christian phenomenon or developed as a blending of Christian teaching with ideas taken from surrounding cultures. Given the sharp contradiction between Christian and Gnostic understandings of the world, the chronology may not be as important as often thought. Bultmann's claim that New Testament christology derived from an Iranian Gnostic redeemer myth has been disproved. It

---

[91]In Christian thought the goal for humanity is not liberation of the soul from the confines of the body, but the ultimate reunion of redeemed soul and body in the eschaton.
[92]Young writes, "*Theios anēr* is by no means a fixed expression and there is no such thing as a specific and defined class of people commonly called 'divine men.' The adjective *theios* by itself conveys little more than the sense 'inspired' " ("Two Roots or a Tangled Mass?" p. 100).
[93]A. D. Nock, *Early Gentile Christianity and Its Hellenistic Background* (New York: Harper & Row, 1964), p. 46.
[94]Carl R. Holliday, cited in James R. Brady, *Jesus Christ: Divine Man or Son of God?* (Lanham, Md.: University Press of America, 1991), pp. 114-15.

appears instead that to the extent Christ was incorporated into Gnostic systems, his life was allegorically interpreted or details were modified to make them consistent with the Gnostic worldview.

The stark division between an evil material world and a good spiritual realm made difficult any communication between them—and communication was necessary if people were to receive saving *gnosis*. In Christianized Gnostic systems this world was created by an inferior god, the god of the Old Testament. The higher New Testament God cannot contaminate himself through direct communication with this world so he created a chain of intermediaries to perform the task. Humans wrongly concluded one or another of these intermediaries was God. Unable to affirm both his full deity and full humanity, post-Christian Gnostics located Jesus at some point along this chain. Fuller believes there was a pre-Christian Gnostic myth about a human fall and an offer of redemption through a series of representatives from the heavenly realm, but he says there is no evidence of a preexistent redeemer *who became human.* This only appeared in the second-century Christian Gnostic heresies. Even then it retained a strong docetic flavor.[95] Schnackenburg describes the Gnostic redeemer as no more than a mythical figure whose lack of personhood was consistent with Gnosticism's ahistorical nature.[96]

Gnostic dualism was fundamentally incompatible with Christianity, and this incompatibility had profound consequences for its understanding of Jesus. This was true not only for beliefs about who Jesus is but equally for the consequences of his coming. Gnostic "knowledge" taught that because this world is evil we may force our unspiritual behavior into submission or freely indulge it. Both ways express the worthlessness of the material world. In Christianity, however, Paul and John taught that Christ's coming redeemed this world and transformed those whose lives Jesus touched. Consequently, Christianity had individual ethical consequences unacceptable to Gnostics.

Schnackenburg says the Gnostic idea of preexistence differs fundamentally from that of Judaism. Its "mythical language, origin, and home in eternal, highest, purely spiritual beings are ascribed to the human pneumatic core of being. All souls have this preexistence." This is utterly different from John's concept of preexistence because he has no place for the preexistence of all souls or finding one's way back into the heavenly mode of being through self-knowledge, where salvation consists in returning to the place where the soul originally existed. Heaven

---

[95]Reginald H. Fuller, *The Foundations of New Testament Christology* (London: Fontana, 1965), p. 97.

[96]Rudolf Schnackenburg, "The Origin and Nature of the Johannine Concept of the Logos," in *The Gospel of John,* trans. Kevin Smyth (New York: Herder & Herder, 1968), 1:493.

is not humanity's natural home and knowledge alone cannot bring salvation. So the origin of John's idea of preexistence is far more likely to be found in Judaism.[97] Although Christianity and Gnosticism look as if they are talking about the same thing, this is only superficial—they really have nothing in common. The Christian commonality is with Jewish thought, and that is similarity, not identity. Even if Gnosticism were a pre-Christian system, its basic worldview is so inconsistent with that of Christianity that it is inconceivable it could have served as the source for any element of orthodox christology. In fact, the early church developed elements of its christology *against* the claims of Gnosticism.[98]

MYSTERY RELIGIONS

The mystery religions were direct competitors of Christianity during the first Christian centuries. Superficially, they resembled Christianity because some rituals and teachings appeared similar. The meanings were quite dissimilar, however. There is no convincing evidence the gods of the mystery religions were truly "dying and rising" gods, especially with regard to their "rising." Much more, the lives of these gods reflected the annual cycle of natural fertility, with a fall death and a spring return to life. These "dying gods" were also believed to have been born on earth without any descent from heaven. Nock denies any ancient deity was believed to have descended to earth and assumed complete humanity. He quotes Celsus to support his claim: "No god, O Jews and Christians, and no child of a god has come down or could come down."[99] Initiates to these religions participated in rebirth rituals, but the rituals contained no element of forgiveness. Thus they were not true counterparts to Christianity's teaching that Jesus died to achieve forgiveness for our sin. Further, in their explanation of dying and rising and its application to initiates, the mystery religions blurred the distinction between mortal and immortal. By contrast, Christianity emphasized this distinction. So, although they appeared superficially similar, Christianity and the mystery religions disagreed sharply on each of the key doctrines of Christian faith.

PARALLELS WITH PRE-CHRISTIAN RELIGIONS AND PHILOSOPHIES

The attempt to explain the career of Jesus of Nazareth is but one aspect of the

---

[97]Schnackenburg, *Jesus in the Gospels,* pp. 287-88.
[98]See, e.g., Irenaeus *Against Heresies.*
[99]A. D. Nock, review of *Paulus: Die Theologie des Apostels im Lichte der jüdischen Religionsgeschichte* by Hans-Joachim Schoeps, *Gnomon* 33 (1961): 585-86.

effort to find parallels in the Jewish background or Hellenistic environment to key elements of Christian belief and practice. The goal of this effort is to determine whether there might be some causal relationship—whether the Christian understanding of Jesus depends on one or more images or characters or concepts from another tradition. Hurtado correctly notes that "much history of religions work can be characterized as zealous but misguided in its use of alleged parallels and sources involving the 'etymological fallacy'—religious terms and symbols are assumed to carry the same meaning and function anywhere they appear."[100] It is not enough, however, to identify points of similarity to establish parallels and causation. No less important are the differences. We have seen this already in considering claims that the Jesus story is myth. Even were we to grant points of similarity between Jesus and Jewish or pagan figures, at the key points there are clear differences. This is nowhere more evident than in the Christian doctrine of the incarnation, a teaching without parallel in Judaism or pre-Christian Hellenism.

Pannenberg is skeptical that concepts can be readily explained in terms of influence. He writes, "The history of ideas is not a chemistry of concepts that have been arbitrarily stirred together and are then neatly separated again by the modern historian. In order for an 'influence' of alien concepts to be absorbed, a situation must have previously emerged within which these concepts could be greeted as an aid for the expression of a problem already present."[101] Pannenberg is saying similar language is not enough; the context also must be similar *at the relevant points*. If this is not so, then we are not talking about the same concept, even when we use the same words. That is the case with the New Testament writers' discussions of Jesus. The incarnation and personal preexistence they are talking about is something neither Judaism nor Hellenism could accept.

Early Christians drew on existing categories in order to communicate their experience of Jesus to their contemporaries—this is the only way they could hope to be understood—but they always qualified in some way the language they borrowed because it only approximated what they sought to express.[102]

---

[100]Larry T. Hurtado, *One God, One Lord* (Philadelphia: Fortress, 1988), p. 48.

[101]Wolfhart Pannenberg, *Jesus,* trans. Lewis L. Wilkins and Duane A. Priebe, 2nd ed. (Philadelphia: Westminster Press, 1977), p. 153.

[102]Hurtado says, "Virtually all the Christological rhetoric of early Christians was appropriated from their environment, although in a great many cases the meanings were significantly altered." He adds, "Healthy religious movements use and redefine terms and categories they inherit from their parent traditions, as any scholarly observer of new religious movements can attest. But this appropriation is for the purpose of expressing and commending the *convictions of the new movement.* The impetus comes from these convictions, and these convictions are prompted and shaped primarily by the religious experiences and ethos of the movement" (Hurtado, *Lord Jesus Christ,* pp. 75, 367).

Had the first Christians not used contemporary language and concepts, they would have been incomprehensible to those around them, and thus failed in their intention to communicate the gospel. Paul certainly did this on Mars Hill, and preachers, teachers, missionaries and evangelists do it every day. As Dunn says, "If the contemporary cosmologies of Hellenism, Judaism and Stoicism determined what *words* should be used in describing the cosmic significance of the Christ-event, the *meaning* of these words is determined by the Christ-event itself."[103] In saying this, Dunn is expressing a widely held opinion that there is nothing in pre-Christian Judaism or Hellenistic thought that can explain the Christian doctrine of the incarnation. Where there are similarities, he believes the probability is that Christian claims about Jesus were the source or inspiration for the other groups.[104] Because Christ's preexistence and incarnation are so intimately related, what appear as similarities regarding his preexistence are no more real than those linked to the incarnation.

Morris goes further. He says it is fallacious to claim we should be able to explain the New Testament in terms of its background. He points out that no other writer can be explained completely in terms of context, so we should not expect it of the biblical writers.[105] This is true even if we know the writer drew on sources: discovering the writer's sources is not the same as knowing the meaning of a document. A familiar example of this is William Shakespeare. His plays drew on historical and fictional accounts, but they certainly are not reducible to those accounts. If they were, few of us would ever have heard of Shakespeare, much less read him. The genius of Shakespeare was that he transcended his sources. He used those sources to fashion plays that were artistically far superior to the sources themselves.

Alan Segal, examining Jewish belief in God during the early rabbinic period, concludes, "According to rabbinic description it does not seem necessary to believe that early Christians merely associated Jesus with some pre-existent savior model who came equipped with a fixed title and job description. Rather, it appears that the debate between Christianity and Judaism proceeded partially on midrashic or exegetical lines."[106] Segal's point is that Christian belief in Jesus did not simply derive from Jewish thought but arose out of a dynamic interchange with Jewish opponents of the early church that extended over decades. Segal's emphasis on the Jewish-Christian interaction is noteworthy in light of claims for non-Jewish Hellenistic influence.

---

[103]Dunn, *Christology in the Making,* p. 211.
[104]Ibid., p. 253.
[105]Leon Morris, "The Emergence of the Doctrine of the Incarnation," *Themelios* 8 (1982): 16.
[106]Segal, *Two Powers in Heaven,* p. x.

Oden speaks of providential preparation. This is what Christians since the earliest days have said about the Old Testament and occasionally about extra-biblical concepts. The Old Testament itself even suggests this when it talks about a new covenant. This means something new has happened in Jesus of Nazareth so that whatever apparent parallels or preparations we discern do no more than point toward Jesus—they do not explain him, and when people try to explain Jesus on these terms they inevitably fall short of what the New Testament says—but they do point to him. Caird concludes that even where parallels do exist, they prove nothing. Parallels do not necessarily mean dependence and "even where dependence can be proved, the fact remains that to trace a word, an idea, or a practice to its origin helps us very little to explain what it means in its new setting."[107]

Just as the Gilgamesh Epic appears at first sight to have much in common with the Genesis creation account, so too do the mystery religions, the Roman emperor cult and some of the Greek myths appear at points to be something like parts of the story of Jesus. But the worldview of Gilgamesh is essentially opposed to that of the Bible. Likewise, the biblical story of Jesus is unique because it claims deity, incarnation and resurrection are aspects of the life of an historical person. C. S. Lewis suggests that the degree to which these other stories connect with Jesus' story is the degree to which they partake of reality. But the primary focus of these other stories is at best a distortion of the reality found in Jesus' story, a distortion that leads away from God, not toward him.

Chronologically, the Christian teachings of preexistence and incarnation predate other ancient incarnational and savior accounts. Holliday says, "The Christian doctrine of the incarnation is unique, without precedent in the Near Eastern world or in the Greco-Roman world, is inextricably tied up with the person of Jesus of Nazareth, and is catalytic." He says not only apocalyptic and redeemer myths and accounts of heavenly figures drawn from Old Testament history, but even pagan incarnational ideas are responses to Christian claims about Jesus of Nazareth. "It is within Christianity, then, that the notion of 'incarnation' actually enters the history of ideas, and the figure of Jesus of Nazareth, though not making the claim about himself, may be said to have been the 'efficient cause' of the doctrine."[108] Holliday's conclusion that Jesus made no such claim about himself is inconsistent with the Gospel evidence, but otherwise the available evi-

---

[107]G. B. Caird, "The Development of the Doctrine of Christ in the New Testament," in *Christ for Us Today,* ed. Norman Pittinger (London: SCM Press, 1968), p. 69.

[108]Carl R. Holliday, "New Testament Christology: A Consideration of Dunn's *Christology in the Making,*" *Semeia* 30 (1985): 71.

dence best fits his conclusion that contemporary "parallels" are drawn from the Christian story of Jesus and not the reverse.

To the extent Hellenistic thought derived from Plato, it pictured a material realm utterly distinct from the realm of forms or ideals. Christianity and Platonism could agree the fullness of reality is to be found in the transcendent realm, but they would not agree precisely on why this is true and what the nature of that realm is. For Christians, God is living, active and personal. He can act directly in the material world he created, even to the extent of incarnating himself. For Plato the realm of forms is perfect, unchanging and impersonal. The platonic form of Good is not the biblical God. Because the material realm is less than fully real, it is a prison to the immaterial soul that seeks release to the immaterial realm. This understanding of the physical world has infected Christian teaching at different times over history, but it stands in sharp contradiction to the biblical view that God created the world good and is redeeming it from the results of humanity's rebellion. For platonic thought, the idea of an incarnation was not false, it was incomprehensible. Too often, the result of the contact of biblical teaching with Greek philosophy was either the Greek conclusion that incarnational teaching was foolishness (1 Cor 1:23) or a compromised Christianity like Arianism or docetism.

In *The Myth of God Incarnate,* Young finds preexistent beings in all traditions, but she concludes neither paganism nor Judaism was able to move from this preexistence to a real incarnation. Paganism could conceive only of a docetic incarnation, and Judaism could not transcend the appearance of an angel in disguise. She concludes that it was true "the association of historical or contemporary personages with the appearances of the gods was occasionally made, but hardly seems to have been taken seriously. . . . The distinctive characteristic of mainstream Christian belief is its inability to stray too far from the historical reality of Jesus of Nazareth, a man crucified under Pontius Pilate."[109] According to Robert Crawford, Gnosticism was the form mythology took when it entered into Christian thought.[110] Wright traces the claim that incarnational teaching must have come from Hellenism to an attempt to dissociate Christianity from its Jewish roots.[111] He is not saying Christian incarnational teaching derived directly from Jewish belief, but that the Jewish understanding of God and creation provided the basis for later development of incarnational teaching (which Hellenism could not).

---

[109]Young, "Two Roots or a Tangled Mass?" p. 119.

[110]Robert G. Crawford, *The Saga of God Incarnate* (Pretoria: University of South Africa Press, 1985), p. 86.

[111]N. T. Wright, "'Constraints' and the Jesus of History," *Scottish Journal of Theology* 39 (1986): 207.

Despite the many arguments against and the lack of compelling evidence for extra-Christian parallels that stand behind christology, some continue to claim such parallels exist. Why? I think Davis is right when he says the reason is presuppositional. Some continue to believe Jesus was a purely human figure and ideas about his preexistence and divine sonship "were arrived at years later through a long and complicated quasi-evolutionary process primarily involving embellishments in the tradition due to the influence of other cultures and religions."[112] Davis says no definite parallels or influences have yet been discovered. He considers the possibility of extensive pagan syncretistic influence on pre-Pauline christology to be "extremely implausible." Davis's most emphatic conclusion is that no one has discovered the purely human Jesus who is necessary to justify the alleged parallels and influences he denies exist. Davis is saying, then, that belief in Christ's preexistence and deity are Christian in origin, not the result of external influences. The preexistence he is defending is a *personal* preexistence in contrast to the ideal preexistence Judaism affirmed of Torah or the preexisting ideas of Platonism and neo-Platonism.

Are there parallels in pre-Christian Judaism and Hellenism to the teachings of the New Testament and early Christianity about Jesus? With significant qualifications, I believe the answer is yes. These parallels are not the cause of Christian belief, however. They might better be called anticipations than parallels. They do little more than provide terminology to explain Jesus to humans of several societies and to make possible conceptual points of contact so members of these cultures can understand the challenge and opportunity Jesus poses for them.[113]

CONCLUSION

Our survey of the Jewish and Hellenistic backgrounds to Christianity has shown far more discontinuity and innovation than continuity. There are clear points of contact with the Jewish teaching of the Old Testament and intertestamental periods, and these teachings formed much of the worldview of Jesus and his earliest followers. These points of contact enabled his followers to explain who Jesus was and what he had come to accomplish in language their audience could understand. But in every case Jesus was and did more than the original meaning of the language conveyed. So while the New Testament authors em-

---

[112]Stephen T. Davis, "Jesus Christ: Savior or Guru?" in *Encountering Jesus*, ed. Stephen T. Davis (Atlanta: John Knox, 1988), pp. 45-46.

[113]Hurtado says of parallels, "Although at a certain high level of generalization one can draw some comparisons with other Roman-era groups and movements, we have no full analogue in the Roman world, which makes the task of historical explanation particularly difficult" (*Lord Jesus Christ*, p. 7).

ployed Jewish concepts, they did so with the caution that they had enhanced their meaning. Whatever the similarities between Judaism and Christianity, their irreducible difference lies in Christianity's insistence on applying the language of personal preexistence, incarnation and deity to a historical person, one who had lived during the lifetime of the New Testament writers.

The language the New Testament authors used was sometimes meaningful to Hellenist as well as Jew. Often the Hellenistic meaning differed significantly from the Jewish, and in any case the terms had been filled with new content by Paul, John and the other New Testament writers. Yet despite the differences, using these terms enabled the New Testament writers to communicate to their non-Jewish audiences as well as to fellow Jews. But there was a limit to this communication. In Athens, Paul was able to begin telling his Greek audience about Jesus in language they could hear and accept, but when he began to speak in a distinctively Christian way, many of his listeners found what he was saying offensive or meaningless. Mühlenberg notes those who assert significant outside influence on New Testament christology must explain why that christology remained so offensive to an audience whose views supposedly had been appropriated.[114]

Some of the parallels with New Testament christology that may have substance are actually the result of Christian influence on the other religion. Some of the commonalities may be the result of God's providential preparation for Christ's coming—a possibility any theist should acknowledge—but in Christ God really was doing something new. Who Jesus was and what he accomplished transcended what Jewish and Hellenistic categories could conceive or express. Judaism in particular held to some sense of preexistence, but neither Judaism nor Hellenism could tolerate a preexistence that would allow for an incarnation of God. This, however, is precisely what New Testament christology says is true of Jesus. Succeeding generations of Christians would defend this teaching against all challenges.

Writing in a different context, Wright has expressed well the doubt that New Testament christology was determined in any significant way by Jewish or Hellenistic thought. He says recent scholarship has benefited from its recognition that the New Testament writers were theologians who thought deeply about Scripture, God and Jesus. They were not mere copyists or editors. But that same scholarship has been reluctant to admit the same about Jesus. "Precisely because Matthew, Mark, Luke and John appear to be creative and intelligent writ-

---

[114]E. Mühlenberg, "The Divinity of Jesus in Early Christian Faith," in *Studia Patristica* 17, pt. 1, ed. Elizabeth A. Livingstone (Oxford: Pergamon, 1982), pp. 137-38.

ers and theologians, we must hypothesize, as the common element standing behind all four (not to mention the sources they may or may not have used), some greater, more original, more subtle mind."[115] It was the mind of Jesus that transformed his Jewish heritage and opened the way for the development of christology that included preexistence and incarnation.

---

[115]Wright, *Jesus and the Victory of God,* pp. 478-79.

7

POSTAPOSTOLIC DEVELOPMENT OF THE DOCTRINE

W hen the earliest Christians thought about Jesus, they did so in the light of Easter. This made all the difference in how they saw him. These early Christians believed the resurrection was God's vindication of Jesus' claims and deeds. In all four Gospels we have seen that Jesus made powerful claims about himself: among these were that his origin was from heaven, that he enjoyed a unique relationship of sonship with God and that his existence had not begun with his birth on earth. Over the following centuries Christians fashioned from this an explicit doctrine of Christ's personal preexistence. The New Testament evidence has shown conclusively that this doctrine was not something designed simply to honor Jesus in the eyes of his contemporaries. Instead, it was the natural result of Jesus' claims about himself and of his followers' experience of him. Although the church did not formulate a doctrine of Christ's incarnation, and thus his preexistence, until the fourth and fifth centuries, the religious fact of Christ's deity and all it entailed was generally accepted from the earliest days of Christianity. Both Christians and their opponents testified to this.[1] For most Christians in the early church, the pressing question was not "How could Jesus be God?" but "How could Jesus be really human?"[2]

WORSHIP AND CHRISTOLOGICAL HYMNS

One of the most significant aspects in considering how Christians saw Jesus dur-

---

[1]H. E. W. Turner, cited in H. P. Owen, "The New Testament and the Incarnation: A Study in Doctrinal Development," *Religious Studies* 8 (1972): 230.

[2]"Amid the diversity of earliest Christianity, belief in Jesus' divine status was amazingly common. The 'heresies' of earliest Christianity largely presuppose the view that Jesus is divine. That is not the issue. The problematic issue, in fact, was whether a genuinely *human* Jesus could be accommodated" (Larry W. Hurtado, *Lord Jesus Christ* [Grand Rapids: Eerdmans, 2003], p. 650).

ing the first centuries of the church is their worship, especially their hymns. We looked at some of these hymns when we explored what the New Testament authors said about Jesus. Their early hymns expressed belief in Christ's preexistence, and hymns have continued to do so up to the present. While this hymnic language seems to have been generally accepted, other practices like worship of and prayer to Jesus became matters of controversy during the early centuries. Yet these practices did not appear from nowhere; they were the response of early Christians to the events of Jesus' life and death as seen through his resurrection. Neither did the practices exist in isolation. They developed in tandem with theological doctrines, each serving to balance the other, protecting the other from excesses while forcing it to consider the implications of what it said. As R. T. France has written, "The basic fact which lies behind all the theological terms and titles is the worship of the carpenter. This is a phenomenon sufficiently arresting to require explanation, even if they had never progressed to the stage of openly calling him 'God.' This worship was not an easy option for pious Jews."[3] Jesus' earliest followers were Jews, and as such they considered worship of humans unacceptable. The refusal of these early Christians to perform such worship is documented in extrabiblical records and occasionally resulted in their martyrdom. Nevertheless, worship of Jesus had become a Christian distinctive by the time Paul wrote. Such worship inevitably involved acknowledging Christ's preexistence as an aspect of his deity.

Although the church took over four hundred years to formulate its essential understanding of Jesus, the key ingredients of its christology were in place within the first Christian generation. This is Martin Hengel's conclusion: "One is tempted to say *that more happened in this period of less than two decades than in the whole of the next seven centuries, up to the time when the doctrine of the early church was completed.*"[4] This means, among other things, that the claim of a major modification of beliefs about Jesus during a purported transition from an early Palestinian Jewish to a Hellenistic Jewish Christianity is simply untrue. Hengel denies two such distinct versions of either Judaism or Christianity can even be identified. I. Howard Marshall notes the evidence shows that from the first these views existed in close proximity and were even intermingled.[5] He writes:

---

[3]R. T. France, "The Worship of Jesus," in *Christ the Lord,* ed. H. H. Rowdon (Downers Grove, Ill.: InterVarsity Press, 1982), p. 35.
[4]Martin Hengel, *The Son of God* (Philadelphia: Fortress, 1976), p. 2.
[5]I. Howard Marshall, *The Origins of New Testament Christology* (Downers Grove, Ill.: InterVarsity Press, 1976), p. 38.

Within this period a distinction between Palestinian and Hellenistic Jewish Christianity is an unreal one, and there is no evidence for a period in the early church in which Jesus was not regarded as being the Son of God, not merely in function but in person. It is clear that during this stage of development the ontological aspects of the Son of God Christology were not developed for their own sake, but that such implications were none the less present.[6]

Larry Hurtado concludes that "although the doctrinal reflection on Christ continued and developed over several centuries, the essential steps in treating the exalted Christ as divine were taken while Christianity was still almost entirely made up of Jews dominated by Jewish theological categories."[7] This means the crucial steps taken in what has become christological orthodoxy occurred early in the first generation of Christians and everything since has been a matter of filling in details, drawing logical connections, and attempting to understand implications. Marshall says much the same. He concludes an essential part of Jewish Christian christology was the belief that during his early life Jesus enjoyed a special relationship with God that had existed prior to his birth and was confirmed by his resurrection and exaltation.[8] This is precisely what we have seen such New Testament writers as Paul and the author of Hebrews, neither of whom appears to have experienced the earthly Jesus, were doing in their writing.

This means christology did not evolve from an early low to a later high, *low* being a christology that emphasized Jesus' humanity at the expense of his deity. There simply was not enough time for such a development, and the earliest New Testament books contain christologies no less high than the latest—that is, assuming there are any as low as some claim. Hengel, who believes the key christological development occurred very early, says "it is extremely improbable that to begin with there was a multiplicity of mutually exclusive, rival 'christologies.' " He argues that the earliest Christian communities might be said to have experimented with various language about Jesus, but they did not intend this to be exclusive. These ideas, far from being mutually exclusive, were mutually reinforcing in the effort to come to grips with the fullness of who Jesus was.[9] This early theology was not simply reproducing Jewish speculation about heavenly intermediaries but bore clear marks of originality. It can only have been rooted in the historical events of Jesus' life, death and resurrection.[10] Ben Witherington

[6]I. Howard Marshall, "The Development of Christology in the Early Church," *Tyndale Bulletin* 18 (1967): 93.
[7]Larry W. Hurtado, "The Origins of the Worship of Christ," *Themelios* 19, no. 2 (1994): 5.
[8]Marshall, "Development of Christology," p. 93.
[9]Martin Hengel, *Between Jesus and Paul* (Philadelphia: Fortress, 1983). p. 41,
[10]Hengel, *Son of God,* pp. 58-59.

has reached a conclusion similar to Hengel's, but he has followed a different path. He concludes the christology of the New Testament is very high in the following way:

> Wisdom Christology, as it is expressed in these hymns, is a very high Christology indeed. When the sapiential hymn material was applied to the historical person Jesus, this led to the predicating of pre-existence, incarnation, and even divinity to this same historical person. The existence of these hymns in so many different sorts of sources . . . suggests that this Wisdom Christology was both widespread and popular with a variety of Christian writers and their audiences. The fact that one finds such Christology nearly in full flower used by Paul in Philippians 2, suggests that this Christology had already developed within the first two or three decades of early Christianity. That is, this Christology had developed *before* the writing of any of the canonical Gospels.[11]

C. F. D. Moule argues so convincingly against the "evolutionary" model for christology that someone has remarked that had the authors of *The Myth of God Incarnate* bothered to read Moule's book (published a few months before *Myth*), they would not have wasted their time writing it. Moule considers a developmental understanding of christology much more consistent with the history of the early church than any evolutionary alternative. It was a drawing out and articulating of the implications of what already was present.[12]

Responding to the arguments of *The Myth of God Incarnate*, Stephen Neill says the pre-Pauline Hellenistic Christian congregations that joined Hellenistic ideas to the story of Jesus never existed. They were created by German scholars early in this century.[13] Neill points out that the Septuagint had already provided a link between Jewish and Hellenistic thought for well over a century, so the idea of conflicting sources or alien input to the earliest christological thinking has no basis in reality. It means too that early worship of Jesus was not "the result of some Gentile neglect of Jewish monotheism, but originated within and had to be accommodated within a Jewish monotheistic faith," and only then passed into Gentile Christianity.[14]

The Jesus of early Christianity was the product of the apostles' reflection about the earthly and resurrected Jesus as the Spirit enabled them. Jesus said in

---

[11]Ben Witherington III, *Jesus the Sage: The Pilgrimage of Wisdom* (Minneapolis: Fortress, 1994), p. 290.

[12]C. F. D. Moule, *The Origin of Christology* (Cambridge: Cambridge University Press, 1977).

[13]Stephen Neill, "Jesus and Myth," in *The Truth of God Incarnate*, ed. Michael Green (Grand Rapids: Eerdmans, 1977), p. 61.

[14]Richard Bauckham, "The Worship of Jesus," in *Anchor Bible Dictionary*, ed. David Noel Freedman (New York: Doubleday, 1992), 3:813.

John 16—17 that the Spirit would guide his followers and glorify him by enabling them to understand him. This was what happened, because the Christ of the early church was not some alien figure forced on later believers but the necessary result of the first disciples' reflection on their experience of Jesus through the lens of the resurrection. One implication of this early thinking was the confession of Christ's preexistence that appeared in writing as early as the mid-50s and continued to be affirmed during the following centuries in the face of challenges by dissident individuals and groups.

Some have argued the early church was the scene of multiple conflicting understandings of Jesus, that this tension is evident in the New Testament, and only in succeeding centuries did one interpretation come to the fore as the others fell by the wayside or were suppressed. I believe it is more accurate to see a multiplicity of complementary understandings of Jesus that resulted from the richness of his disciples' experience of him and their drawing from portions of the Old Testament to explain who Jesus was, why he had come and what he accomplished. Marinus de Jonge describes early christology as both inclusive and complementary: "In speaking about Jesus, there was little room for either/ or. There was so much to be expressed, because so much had been discovered."[15] The New Testament documents exemplify the variety of ways early Christians tried to explain Jesus. For the most part these had their roots in the Old Testament and later Judaism. These various approaches were complementary, however; they did not contradict one another but instead portrayed Jesus from multiple perspectives. Such a diversity of approaches and conclusions should not surprise us. A quick visit to the local library is sure to produce biographies of major modern figures that approach their subject from an even wider range of perspectives, many of which are not complementary but obviously contradictory. Complete unity of approach and conclusion in matters of history and current events is usually reason for suspicion rather than confidence. It makes us suspect collusion among the various witnesses.

One result of the early Christian consideration of Jesus was that he quickly became the subject of worship. Less than a hundred years after Jesus' death, a Roman official sought guidance from the emperor in dealing with a group of individuals whose only fault appears to have been that "they worship Christ as a god." The worship, prayers and hymns exalting Jesus Christ are important evidence for his deity and preexistence. This evidence is early and widespread. It is important because it is not the product of theological speculation but the result of meditating on the implications of what the earliest Christians personally

---

[15]Marinus de Jonge, *Christology in Context* (Philadelphia: Westminster Press, 1988), p. 28.

saw and heard. Hurtado dates the earliest expressions of worship of Jesus as occurring within the first decade of the church.[16]

The early church worshiped Jesus, and the New Testament tells us Jesus worshiped God. Because the early church was overwhelmingly Jewish, we are faced with the question of how Jews who recited the Shema daily could readily worship Jesus in conjunction with God without some sense of inconsistency or abandonment of Judaism. Yet we read in Acts that Paul visited the temple in Jerusalem and participated in its rituals at the encouragement of local Christian leaders, so early Christians do not seem to have considered such behavior as inconsistent or an abandonment of their religious tradition.

As we look more closely at the early hymns, we find a scholarly disagreement about whether they contain any ontological implications. There is general agreement that the hymns contain functional descriptions of Jesus, but while some conclude that is all they contain, others argue the functional statements have ontological implications and that in some cases the hymns go beyond this to make ontological claims. We saw this when we looked at the New Testament hymns earlier. Postbiblical hymns are far more explicit in their ontological claims, one of which is affirmation of Christ's preexistence. Jonge's conclusion that close examination of the language used in the hymns "does not allow for metaphysical or systematic theological conclusions"[17] is borne out neither by the practice of the early church nor by careful study of the hymns themselves. In fact, Jonge's claim is inconsistent with what he himself says about the necessary relationship between function and being.

As Hurtado considers the various aspects of early Christian worship of Jesus, he reminds us these first worshipers were monotheistic Jews. As such, they would never have applied any sort of apotheosis to Jesus. If Jesus could not have become deity after his death, the necessary implication is that he must have been such before his birth (or never was deity, a conclusion most early Christians rejected on other grounds). This line of thinking leads necessarily to a doctrine of preexistence.[18] Hurtado is saying early Christian worship of Jesus was inextricably linked with belief in his divine preexistence. Elsewhere, he writes that belief in Christ's preexistence was not a matter of intellectual adaptation or speculation. "Fundamental was the conviction, born of Jesus' career and the subsequent powerful religious life of the earliest Christian groups, that

---

[16]Larry W. Hurtado, *One God, One Lord* (Philadelphia: Fortress, 1988), p. 5. If Hurtado is correct, this means there is no room for extra-Jewish influences on crucial christological conclusions and practices.

[17]Jonge, *Christology in Context,* p. 197.

[18]Hurtado, "Origins of the Worship," p. 5.

Christ personally and uniquely embodied the divine salvific purpose and bore surpassing significance. And the Pauline writings show that the pre-existence of Christ was meaningful in the practical purpose of ethical exhortation."[19] The earliest Christians quickly concluded that Jesus was more than a great teacher, ethical example or tragic martyr. They quickly associated Jesus with God both functionally and ontologically, only later refining their language and concepts in response to challenges to their christology. The impetus for this development included their conviction that Christ had preexisted his earthly life.

The earliest Christians concluded from their experience of the earthly Jesus and his resurrection that there was more to Jesus than his humanity. This conclusion drew on the words Jesus said and the acts he performed in presenting himself as God's agent of human salvation. As we have seen from the documents of the New Testament church, it understood Jesus as one who was preexistent deity. Succeeding centuries of Christian theology would wrestle with what this language means and what it implies. With few exceptions, however, neither orthodox nor heretic denied Christ's preexistence. Their disagreement concerned the precise nature of the one who was preexistent. One consequence of this disagreement, however, was that while there was agreement that Christ had preexisted his earthly life, the implications of this preexistence remained a matter of debate.

A. T. Wainwright believes it was in worship that Jesus first was treated as deity and only later did this become doctrine.[20] I think he is right. Worship was an immediate response to the risen Jesus, seen even in the Gospel accounts, whereas the doctrinal justification for the practice came later. That has been the pattern of doctrinal development throughout the history of Christianity. Bauckham says much the same: "It is likely that it was the attribution of explicitly divine worship to Jesus which promoted the development of more explicit statements about his divine being."[21] He says the prevalence and centrality of this worship has often been underestimated by scholars, as has its role in explaining christological development. I think it remarkable that Jesus' first Jewish followers considered worship to be the natural and appropriate response to their experience of Jesus. The hymnic expression of this worship focused on three themes: who Jesus was, what he had accomplished and his preexistent glory.[22]

---

[19]Larry W. Hurtado, "Preexistence," in *Dictionary of Paul and His Letters,* ed. Gerald F. Hawthorne et al. (Downers Grove, Ill.: InterVarsity Press, 1993), p. 746.

[20]A. T. Wainwright, "The Confession 'Jesus Is God' in the New Testament," *Scottish Journal of Theology* 10 (1957): 296-97.

[21]Bauckham, "The Worship of Jesus," p. 815.

[22]Ralph P. Martin, *Worship in the Early Church* (Grand Rapids: Eerdmans, 1974), pp. 51-52.

Geoffrey Wainwright concludes that the New Testament church saw Jesus not simply as the mediator between God and humans but also as one who was himself worthy of "cultic honor." He adds that "we have also seen enough pre-existence language to be sure that the apostolic Church could not remain satisfied—if ever it was satisfied—with an account that made of Christ a man 'adopted' by God."[23] The early transition to unambiguously divine worship of Jesus offers no evidence of resistance or opposition, although the implications of such worship for monotheistic religion still would need to be faced since this all occurred in a Jewish setting.

The hymnic declaration of Christ's preexistent deity that began in the first decades after Jesus' death has continued to this day. Many of these hymns are, as we might expect, Christmas carols, but other hymns, both well known and unfamiliar, clearly affirm Christ's preexistence. My survey of one hymnal turned up some thirty hymns that spoke of Christ's preexistence—this does not include those hymns that merely allude to or presuppose his preexistence.[24] The dates of these hymns range from the 300s to the early 1900s. They include such authors as Prudentius, Martin Luther, Isaac Watts, Charles Wesley and James Montgomery. In no case was Christ's preexistence the focus of the hymns; instead, it served to emphasize the magnitude of Christ's condescension or the certainty of his accomplished work. They include such obvious hymns as Wesley's "Hark, the Herald Angels Sing" (1739) with its words, "Veiled in flesh the Godhead see; / Hail th' Incarnate Deity / Pleased as man with men to dwell, / Jesus, our Emmanuel. . . . / Mild he lays his glory by, / Born that man no more may die"; "Behold, a Branch Is Growing" (1500s) with its words, "How Christ, the Lord of Glory, / Was born on earth this night," and "O Come, All Ye Faithful," (1700s) with two stanzas that echo the language of the Nicene Creed. But they also include Luther's "A Mighty Fortress Is Our God" (1529), which says, "Christ Jesus, it is he, / Lord Sabaoth his Name, / From age to age the same," and Prudentius' "Of the Father's Love Begotten" (300s),with the words, "Of the Father's love begotten, Ere the worlds began to be / He is the Alpha and Omega, He the source, the ending he / Of the things that are, that have been, And that future years shall see." In what they say, these hymns differ little from the New Testament hymns except that they tend to present Christ's deity and preexistence more explicitly. To a great extent, they use New Testament language, rearranging the phrases and amplifying them. These hymns span the history of the church.

[23]Geoffrey Wainwright, "'Son of God' in Liturgical Doxologies," in *Jesus, Son of God?* ed. Edward Schillebeeckx and Johannes-Baptist Metz (New York, Seabury, 1982), p. 50.
[24]See *The Trinity Hymnal* (Philadelphia: Great Commission Publications, 1961).

The easy path for early Christians, one taken by some of their number and by many of later generations, would have been to accommodate themselves to their environment. This was the route that has led to many of the christological heresies during Christianity's history. Instead, the early church wrestled with the mystery of the one they knew as Jesus of Nazareth. They refused to relax the tension between evidence for his deity and that for his humanity, recognizing they must follow where the evidence led. They also understood that a Christ who was less than fully divine (and thus not preexistent) and at the same time fully human could not be their Savior. Recognizing this, they celebrated it in their worship and in their hymns.

THE PATRISTIC WITNESS

The earliest noncanonical church documents we have date from about the time of the last New Testament books.[25] They show the postapostolic church no less accepting of Christ's preexistence than its predecessors. According to J. N. D. Kelly, the apostolic fathers generally took for granted Christ's preexistence and his role in creation and redemption.[26]

These writings of early church pastors and theologians are an important link between the New Testament documents and twenty-first-century Christians. The authors are overwhelmingly Gentile, whereas probably all but one of the New Testament authors (Luke) were Jews. These postapostolic writings document the movement of Christian faith into the Hellenistic Gentile environment of the Mediterranean basin. Some of the documents are difficult because of the language and philosophy involved, but they show early Christians attempting to communicate to their contemporaries using concepts the audience can understand. At the same time, many of these concepts underwent a significant transformation at their hands to make them more adequate vehicles of communication. Today, we call this contextualization. It was during this period that the writings of the Bible began to be organized into Christian doctrine. This was a necessary process that drew connections between subjects, probed implications and established boundaries for what constituted legitimate interpretation. During this time, Christians debated a number of subjects whose conclusions many now take for granted. The first series of these debates dealt with who Jesus Christ is.

---

[25]Unless otherwise specified, all quotations of the church fathers come from *Ante-Nicene Fathers,* ed. Alexander Roberts and James Donaldson (Grand Rapids, Mich.: Eerdmans, 1988); or *Nicene and Post-Nicene Fathers,* ed. Philip Schaff (Grand Rapids, Mich.: Eerdmans, 1979).

[26]J. N. D. Kelly, *Early Christian Doctrines,* 2nd ed. (New York: Harper & Row, 1960), p. 95.

CLEMENT OF ROME AND BARNABAS

Writing just before the end of the first century in the document known as *1 Clement,* Clement of Rome appears to have assumed Christ's personal preexistence. Twice he said Christ spoke through a psalm (*1 Clem.* 16:15; 22:1); he also described Christ as "sent from God" (*1 Clem.* 42:2). Because Clement's letter deals primarily with authority relationships in the church of his day, not with doctrine, this christological content is significant. At approximately the same time, the letter of Barnabas presented Christ as preexistent because he spoke with Moses, received his commission from the Father before his birth, and prior to that birth was part of the Trinity—God the Father, Christ the Son of God and the Spirit of God. Barnabas interpreted the "we" of Genesis 1:26 in a trinitarian sense, writing, "For the Scripture says concerning us, while he speaks to the Son, 'Let us make man after our image, and after our likeness. . . .' These things were spoken to the Son" (*Barn.* 6). Both J. N. D. Kelly and Edmund Fortman consider the chief theological interest of this letter to be "the prominence it gives to Christ's pre-existence."[27]

THE SHEPHERD OF HERMAS

Another early document, *The Shepherd* of Hermas, identified the preexistent Christ with the Holy Spirit, whom the author called the Son of God. He also referred to him as "far older than all [God's] creation" and "the Father's counselor in his creation." The particular route Hermas followed would be rejected by succeeding generations of Christians, however, as they wrested with the data that ultimately would lead to an explicit doctrine of the Trinity. By the opening of the second century, Jesus was called God in extrabiblical sources. Wainwright remarks, "This form of address, this manner of description, did not suddenly spring into being at the beginning of the second century."[28]

In the second century the designations of Jesus found in the New Testament came to be interpreted differently than they had been previously. "Son of Man" no longer identified Jesus as preexistent deity but instead emphasized his real humanity. In succeeding centuries "Son of God" would express Christ's deity. As Christians sought ever more clearly to state their trinitarian belief, "Son" would replace the less-obviously personal "Logos," although this Logos language proclaimed Christ's preexistence, and through Justin and the Alexandrians influenced the development of trinitarian thought. In part this shift away from Logos language occurred because of a patristic shift toward understanding

---

[27]Ibid., pp. 91-92; Edmund J. Fortman, *The Triune God* (Grand Rapids: Baker, 1972), p. 42.
[28]Wainwright, "Confession 'Jesus Is God,' " p. 294.

Logos more in a Stoic "world-reason" sense and less in the Johannine sense of
the Word as the personal expression of God the Father.

IGNATIUS OF ANTIOCH

Early in the second century (approximately A.D. 107), Ignatius, bishop of Antioch, wrote to several churches while en route to his martyrdom. Of the fifteen letters attributed to him, seven appear authentic. Of these seven, five
clearly describe Christ as preexistent deity. Four call Jesus God. In his *Letter
to the Ephesians,* Ignatius said "God was revealing himself as a man" (Ign. *Eph.*
19:3). He also described him as "born yet unbegotten, God incarnate" (Ign.
Eph. 7:2). In chapter eighteen, Ignatius described Jesus as "the Son of God,
who was begotten before time began" and afterward conceived in the womb
of Mary. In his *Letter to the Smyrneans* he wrote of Christ "that on the human
side he was actually sprung from David's line, Son of God according to God's
will and power" (Ign. *Smyrn.* 1:1). In that same passage Ignatius also described Jesus Christ as "the son of God, 'the firstborn of every creature,' God
the Word, the only-begotten Son." In his *Letter to the Romans,* Ignatius said,
"Our God Jesus Christ, indeed, has revealed himself more clearly by returning
to the Father" (Ign. *Rom.* 3:3) and in chapter seven, "The Son of God who became afterwards of the seed of David and Abraham." Ignatius's language to
the Magnesians was similar: "to one Jesus Christ, who came forth from one
Father, while still remaining one with him, and returned to him" (Ign. *Magn.*
7:2). In chapter six, he described Jesus Christ as having been with the Father
before the beginning of time, and he repeated this in chapter eleven, where
Ignatius linked Christ's preexistence and subsequent virgin birth.

In his *Letter to Polycarp,* Ignatius wrote, "Look for Christ, the Son of God;
who was before all time, yet appeared in time; who was invisible by nature, yet
visible in the flesh; who was impalpable and could not be touched, as being
without a body, but for our sakes became such, might be touched and handled
in the body; who was impassable as God, but became passable for our sakes as
man; and who in every way suffered for our sakes."

Because Ignatius's concern in his letters was the churches' responsibility to
respect and obey their leaders, his repeated affirmation of Christ's preexistence
and deity and his incarnation for the sake of our salvation stands out. In his *Letter to the Trallians,* Ignatius described Christ as "truly begotten of God and the
Virgin, but not after the same manner. . . . He truly assumed a body; for 'the
Word was made flesh.' " He added, "And God the Word was truly born of the
Virgin, having clothed himself with a body of like passions with our own."

THE LETTER TO DIOGNETUS

In the decades following Ignatius, the meaning of Jesus' divine sonship became the subject of much discussion. This led to increased confession of Jesus as God's unique Son, with sonship language predominating in the discussion. This sonship language required Christ's preexistent deity because if the Father was always the Father, so too must the Son always have been the Son. In the *Letter to Diognetus* (c. A.D. 130), Christ was described as the one who is from the beginning yet who has appeared as if new, "he who being from everlasting, is today called the Son" (*Diogn.* 11). The writer added that when God sent his representative to be among humans, he did not send a servant or angel but "the very Creator and Fashioner of all things" (*Diogn.* 7).

JUSTIN MARTYR

Justin Martyr was an apologist during the middle of the second century. Demetrius Trakatellis has examined in detail his views on Christ's preexistence.[29] In receiving such attention, Justin is unique among patristic authors, although what he has to say about the preexistent Christ is far from unique. Trakatellis concludes Justin believed in Christ's preexistence and considered it a personal preexistence. Justin understood preexistence in terms of a divine status, not merely temporal priority, and he understood every visible manifestation of God to humans to have been the preexistent Christ. Adolf Harnack offers an even stronger conclusion: "Justin shows that he cannot conceive of a Christianity without the belief in a real pre-existence of Christ."[30] Based on his careful study, Trakatellis reaches a conclusion different from Harnack regarding the source of Justin's view, however. He says Justin's doctrine of Christ's preexistence was always linked to Scripture and based on exegesis; it was not the product of philosophical speculation as Harnack believed. Justin did not simply repeat the creedal formulas of the New Testament, as had his predecessors, although his thinking did follow the same preexistence, incarnation and exaltation structure found in Paul, Hebrews and John.

Justin's adherence, nonetheless, to a traditional christological pattern does not mean that he simply repeated the early creedal formulations. What he did was to interpret them, and, while keeping the basic scheme of preexistence, humiliation and exaltation, to bring these concepts into a discussion of current

[29]Demetrius Christ Trakatellis, *The Pre-existence of Christ in the Writings of Justin Martyr* (Missoula, Mont.: Scholars Press, 1976).

[30]Adolf von Harnack, *History of Dogma,* trans. Neil Buchanan (New York: Dover, 1961), 1:198 n. 1, 199.

theological problems. In this respect he transformed the creedal-hymnic language of the early traditions such as the one preserved in Philippians 2:6-11, for instance, into a language of theological explicitness.[31]

Justin's confession of Christ's divine preexistence appears grounded in the worship of the early church, but it was not limited by this worship. Justin demonstrated a flexibility and freedom absent from New Testament christological texts and used liturgical sources for clearly theological and apologetic purposes. Hurtado says Justin exemplified early Christian belief that Jesus was "the incarnate form of the preexistent and divine Son," and with such a belief, it was not unusual for Justin and others to looks for references to him in his preincarnate state in Scripture. Hurtado adds that belief in a personal preexistence was not a matter of academic debate about Scripture but a confirmation and celebration of Jesus' divine status to encourage believers and convert nonbelievers.[32]

Justin also has a lesson in christology for some modern theologians. He taught both Christ's virgin birth and his preexistence, doctrines theologians like Pannenberg consider incompatible and believe were originally alternative explanations of Christ's origin. In fact, most of Justin's mentions of the virgin birth are accompanied by preexistence language.[33] Justin was the first Christian writer to discuss Isaiah 7:14 extensively and to see it as clear and decisive testimony to the virgin birth and Christ's divine preexistence. In thus emphasizing the reality of Christ's humanity as well as the identity between the preexistent divine Christ and Jesus the human, Justin was rejecting the conclusions of both docetism and Gnosticism. Like his predecessors, Justin linked Christ's preexistence with his work of salvation:

> And his son, who alone is properly called Son, the Word, who also was with him and was begotten before the works, when at first he created and arranged all things by him, is called Christ, in reference to his being anointed and God's ordering all things through him. . . . But "Jesus," his name as man and Savior, has also significance, for he was made man also, as we said before, having been conceived according to the will of God the Father, for the sake of believing men, and for the destruction of the demons. (*Apol. II* 6)[34]

---

[31]Trakatellis, *Pre-existence of Christ,* p. 174.

[32]Hurtado, *Lord Jesus Christ,* p. 576.

[33]Trakatellis, *Pre-existence of Christ,* p. 157. He quotes nine passages from the *Apology I* and the *Dialogue with Trypho* where this occurs. A representative passage is in *Dialogue* 48, where Justin said he believed Christ "existed formerly as Son of the Maker of all things, being God, and was born a man by the Virgin," although he could not prove it. In chap. 105, however, Justin said he had already proved this to Trypho.

[34]Justin's first and second *Apology* will be abbreviated as *Apol. I* and *Apol. II.* His *Dialogue with Trypho* is abbreviated as *Dial. Tryph.*

Justin went beyond his predecessors by saying Christ's preexistence can be understood in terms of the manifestations of God to the people of Old Testament Israel (*Apol. I* 62-63; *Dial. Tryph.* 75; 113; 126; 128). Trakatellis groups Justin's preexistence language into four categories: Christ's existence before creation, Old Testament theophanies and other manifestations of God, the relationship between the preexistent Logos and pagan groups or individuals, and preexistence and incarnation.[35] In the first category Justin concluded that the "we" language of Genesis 1 requires a plurality within the Godhead. Justin was the first to emphasize Old Testament theophanies as manifestations of the preexistent Christ. He saw Christ in Genesis 18—19; 28:10-19; 32:22-32; 35:6-15; Exodus 3; 23:20-21; Joshua 5:13-6:5; and Psalm 98:6-8 (by implication).[36] Theologians would echo Justin on this point until Augustine. As might be expected of an apologist, Justin referred to these theophanies often in his *Dialogue with Trypho,* but they also appear in his *Apology I.*

For Justin the preexistent Christ acted in pagan antiquity as the light that helped some to realize the truth about God and live a virtuous life. Christ was also active in opposing demonic activity in every place it was directed against God or *aretē*. He drew on the Hellenistic *logos spermatikos* concept to explain this influence, but he first tried to purge it of its more obvious Platonic and Stoic aspects. Nevertheless, this move by Justin was a shift away from John's Old Testament-based Logos thinking. Trakatellis notes while these roles of the preexistent Christ in pagan society are the product of Justin's philosophical speculation, they are his attempt to deal with specific concerns of his day. These include persecution of Christians promoted by demonic forces, human moral responsibility before as well as after the incarnation, and the possibility of and desire for knowledge of God.[37]

Justin clearly identified the Word with Jesus. He said the Word "himself, who took shape, and became man . . . was called Jesus Christ" (*Apol. I* 5). Chapter thirty-two, despite its subordinationist tone, says, "And the first power after God the Father and Lord of all is the Son; and of him we will, in what follows, relate how he took flesh and became man." In the *Dialogue with Trypho* 100, Justin, after discussing the virgin birth, said, "And since we call Him the Son, we have understood that he proceeded before all creatures from the Father by his power and will . . . and that He became man by the Virgin." In *On the Resurrection,* he

---

[35]Trakatellis, *Pre-existence of Christ,* p. 7.

[36]Although John 12:41's interpretation of Isaiah's vision of God as a vision of the preexistent Son predates Justin, I mean by theophany the appearances to men and women in space and time, not dreams and visions.

[37]Trakatellis, *Pre-existence of Christ,* pp. 93ff., 133.

wrote, "And the Word, being [God's] Son, came to us, having put on flesh, revealing both himself and the Father, giving to us in Himself resurrection from the dead, and eternal life afterward. And this is Jesus Christ, our Savior and Lord."

Justin's strong emphasis on Christ's preexistence caused him to describe the incarnation in terms of humiliation. Because Christ was preexistent deity, his appearance on earth as a human was a major step down in the order of being. This was precisely what Paul had written in Philippians 2:6-11. Justin, however, used the language of humiliation to emphasize the reality of the incarnation against docetic opponents because had it been merely appearance, there would have been no humiliation.

Little more than a century after Christ's death, Justin made a major contribution to the already widespread Christian belief in Christ's divine preexistence with his interpretation of the Old Testament theophanies. By finding Christ in them, he linked the old and new covenants in terms of continuity as well as discontinuity. Despite the dangers involved in his use of the *logos spermatikos* concept, Justin argued Christ's providential role was much broader than Old Testament Israel and the New Testament church. In presenting preexistence and the virgin birth as two aspects of the larger career of Christ, he showed they were complementary rather than alternative explanations of Jesus.

THEOPHILUS OF ANTIOCH

Theophilus of Antioch, probably writing in the A.D. 170s, emphasized, as had Justin, that all contact between humans and God was with the Word, who was the preincarnate Son of God (*To Autolycus* 2.22). He supported this understanding of the eternal preexistence of the Word from John 1:1-3. "The Word, then, being God, and being naturally produced from God, whenever the Father of the universe wills, he sends him to any place; and he, coming, is both heard and seen, being sent by him, and is found in a place." Theophilus added that "The God and Father, indeed, cannot be contained, and is not found in a place . . . but his Word, through whom He made all things, being His Power and His Wisdom, assuming the role of the Father and Lord of all, went to the garden and conversed with Adam."

The Apologists attempted to present an intellectually satisfying explanation of how Christ related to the Father. In doing this they drew more on Hellenistic than biblical categories, although they did not intend to leave the biblical behind. They simply sought to explain Jesus to a Gentile audience in terms it could understand. As Kelly explains it:

> The solution they proposed . . . was that, as pre-existent, Christ was the Father's

thought or mind, and that, as manifested in creation and revelation, He was its extrapolation or expression. . . . [T]he Apologists' originality . . . lay in drawing out the further implications of the Logos idea in order to make plausible the twofold fact of Christ's pre-temporal oneness with the Father and His manifestation in space and time.[38]

The Logos concept used by the Apologists more nearly resembled that of Greek philosophy than that of John's prologue, however.

IRENAEUS OF LYONS

Although intervening Christian writers assumed Christ's preexistence in their work, Irenaeus, writing between A.D. 177 and 203, was the next major figure to make a sustained argument for Christ's preexistent deity. In *Against Heresies,*[39] written at the end of the second century, Irenaeus attacked in detail the theology of his Gnostic opponents and defended Christian orthodoxy. He argued that the teachings of the church had been handed down from the apostles whereas the Gnostic doctrines were innovations: "The Church . . . has received from the apostles and their disciples this faith: [The Church believes] in one God, the Father almighty, the Maker of heaven, the earth, and the sea, and all things that are in them; and in one Christ Jesus, the Son of God, who became incarnate for our salvation" (*Haer.* 1.10.1). For Irenaeus, Christ's personal preexistence and incarnation are essential elements of the apostolic tradition dating back to the earliest days of the church.

Irenaeus's opponents did not disagree with him regarding Christ's preexistence; their objection was to the claim that he possessed the fullness of deity. Thus preexistence, while understood differently by each side, was a common premise in the debate. Irenaeus argued for the equality of Christ with God, the identity of the Word with Christ, and the reality of the incarnation. The second point was necessary because Gnosticism saw spirit and matter as antithetical, and denied the possibility of direct contact between the two. Although he argued for Christ's deity and incarnation, Irenaeus never tried to explain how both could be. Irenaeus repeatedly insisted that our knowledge of God and our salvation depend on the truth of the claim that the preexistent Christ became a real human at a point in time: "For in no other way could we have learned the things of God, unless our Master, existing as the Word, had become man" (*Haer.* 5.1.1). Because Christ is the Son who has always existed with the Father, we can be confident he truly reveals the Father: "The Son, eternally co-existing with the

---

[38]Kelly, *Early Christian Doctrines,* pp. 95-96.
[39]*Against Heresies* is abbreviated as *Haer.*

Father from old, yea, from the beginning, always reveals the Father to Angels, Powers, Virtues, and all to whom He wills that God should be revealed" (*Haer.* 2.30.9).

Irenaeus contended the preexistent Christ had appeared to Adam, Noah, Abraham, Jacob and Moses (*Haer.* 4.10.1) and was with Daniel's friends in the fiery furnace (*Haer.* 4.20.11). Even in his preincarnate existence, Christ guided and sustained the people of God. Irenaeus also agreed with Justin's view that all human contact with God occurred through the preincarnate Son, including the occasions where he appeared as an angel. Christ was the one "like a son of man" described in Daniel 7:13 (*Haer.* 4.20.11). And like several of his theological predecessors, Irenaeus understood the "us" in Genesis 1:26 in a trinitarian sense (*Haer.* 4.20.1).

Irenaeus's argument was not speculative but soteriological.[40] Christ's work has salvific value because he is the preexistent Son of God. His incarnation was for the purpose of our salvation: "Christ, who was called the Son of God before all ages, was manifested in the fullness of time, in order that he might cleanse us through his blood, who were under the power of sin, presenting us as pure sons to his Father" (Fragment 39). Because he was the preexistent Son of God, Christ, by becoming human, could make humans precious to God due to their resemblance to his Son (*Haer.* 5.16.2). If these things are untrue, then we have no hope of salvation. Irenaeus said that that which the Son saved, he first called into existence (*Haer.* 3.22.3; 5.18.3).

According to Irenaeus, it is only through Christ that any creature can know God: "Through [Christ] He is revealed and manifested to all to whom He is revealed; for those [only] know Him to whom the Son has revealed Him. But the Son, eternally co-existing with the Father, from old, yea, from the beginning, always reveals the Father to Angels, Archangels, Powers, Virtues, and all to whom He wills that God should be revealed" (*Haer.* 3.30.9). The only way we could learn the things of God was because the Word became incarnate (*Haer.* 5.1.1). In saying this Irenaeus linked revelation with the possibility of salvation since Christian salvation requires a relationship with God.

CLEMENT OF ALEXANDRIA

Contemporary with Irenaeus, Clement of Alexandria described Jesus as "the holy God Jesus, the Word, who is the guide of all humanity."[41] In the same section

---

[40]Examples of Irenaeus's arguments can be found in *Haer.* 1.10.1; 3.4.2; 3.11.3; 3.18.3; 3.19.2; 5.1.1.

[41]Clement of Alexandria, *Christ the Educator,* Fathers of the Church: A New Translation 23 (Washington, D.C.: Catholic University of America, 1954), p. 51.

Clement also used angelomorphic language to describe the preincarnate Christ:

> For it is really the Lord [the Son] that was the Instructor of the new people by Him-
> self, face to face. . . . Formerly the older people had an old covenant, and the law
> disciplined the people with fear, and the Word was an angel; but to the fresh and
> new people has also been given a new covenant, and the Word has appeared, and
> fear is turned to love, and that mystic angel is born—Jesus.

He says it was Christ who led the Israelites through the wilderness, appeared
to Abraham and Moses, saved the Israelites out of Egypt, wrestled with Jacob
and spoke with Jeremiah. In his *Exhortation to the Heathen,* Clement explained
Christ's incarnation was for our salvation: "Yea, I say, the Word of God became
man, that thou mayest learn from man how man may become God" (chap. 1).
He described Christ as "the cause of both our being at first (for he was in God)
and of our well-being, this very Word has now appeared as a man." In chapter
twelve, he wrote, "This Jesus, who is eternal, the one great High Priest of the
one God, and of his Father, prays for and exhorts men" and "a spectacle most
beautiful to the Father is the eternal Son crowned with victory."

TERTULLIAN

Not long after Irenaeus and Clement, Tertullian would derive new theological
conclusions from Christ's preexistent deity. He used the belief that Christ had
existed eternally as the Son of God and was himself deity to coin the language
of the Trinity. It was not that this was a completely new idea, but Tertullian gave
a name to the idea and began thinking about it systematically.

> Now the Word of life became flesh, and was heard, and was seen, and was han-
> dled, because he was flesh who, before he came in the flesh, was the "Word in the
> beginning with God" the Father, and not the Father with the Word. For although
> the Word was God, yet he was with God, because he is God of God; and being
> joined to the Father, is with the Father. "And we have seen his glory, the glory as
> of the only begotten of the Father"; that is, of course, (the glory) of the Son, even
> his who was visible, and was glorified by the invisible Father. . . . He shows us also
> that the Son of God, which is the Word of God, is visible, because he who became
> flesh was called Christ. . . . "For no man shall see God, and live." This being the
> case, it is evident that he was always seen from the beginning, who became visible
> in the end. . . . It was the Son, therefore, who was always seen, and the Son who
> always conversed with men, and the Son who has always worked by the authority
> and will of the Father. (*Prax.* 15)[42]

---

[42]*Prax.* is the abbreviation for Tertullian's *Against Praxeas; Marc.* is the abbreviation of *Against
Marcion.*

Tertullian said that when God appeared to humans, he always did so in the person of the preexistent Son. It was God the Son who walked with Adam in the garden, closed the ark after Noah, dispersed humanity at Babel, visited Abraham before destroying Sodom and Gomorrah, spoke to Moses from the burning bush and stood with Daniel's friends in the fiery furnace. Of the persons of the Godhead, only the Son has been made flesh. Like theologians of the Eastern church, Tertullian believed that all divine communication with humanity happened through "the Word which was to be made flesh" (*Prax.* 16). In *Against Marcion,* Tertullian said, "God held converse with man, that man might learn to act as God. God dealt on equal terms with man, that man might be able to deal on equal terms with God. God was found little, that man might become very great." All this happened through the incarnation of the preexistent Son of God who united in himself God and man (*Marc.* 2.27).

In *The Prescription Against Heretics,* Tertullian set forth what the early third century North African church considered normative about Christ:

> You must know that which prescribes the belief that there is one only God, and that he is none other than the Creator of the world, who produced all things out of nothing through his own word, first of all things sent forth; that this Word is called his son, and under the name of God, was seen variously by the patriarchs, heard always in the prophets, at last brought down by the Spirit and Power of the Father into the virgin Mary, was made flesh in her womb, and, being born of her, went forth as Jesus Christ; thenceforth he preached the new law and the new promise of the kingdom of heaven, worked miracles; having been crucified, he rose again on the third day; having ascended into heaven, he sat at the right hand of the Father; sent the vicarious power of the Holy Spirit who leads the faithful; will come with glory to take the saints to the enjoyment of everlasting life and the celestial promises, and to condemn the wicked to everlasting fire, after a resurrection of both classes has been effected, together with the restoration of the flesh. This rule, as it will be proved, was taught by Christ.[43]

NOVATIAN

Shortly after Tertullian introduced the language of Trinity to Christian theology, Novatian (c. A.D. 250) probed the meaning of the doctrine in his *On the Trinity.* In chapter eighteen, he discussed the books of Moses which said both that "no man can see God and live" and that Abraham had seen God. Novatian concluded that no one had ever seen God the Father, but the Son or Word of God, who is Christ, appeared to numerous Old Testament figures before he became

---

[43]Tertullian "The Prescription against Heretics" 13.

incarnate and dwelt on earth. In offering this conclusion, Novatian emphasized that the Son of God, who appeared on occasion as an angel and other times as a man, is God but is other than the Father.[44] "For he is the image of the invisible God, being so in order that weak and frail human nature might in time become accustomed to see, in Him, who is the Image of God, that is, in the Son of God, God the Father." For Novatian, as for some of his patristic predecessors, the angel of the Lord who appeared various times in the Old Testament was none other than the preincarnate Christ. He thus distinguished within the Godhead between One who is called God and One who is variously called God, Son, and Angel. In chapter twenty-one, interpreting *firstborn* chronologically, Novatian argued Christ must have preexisted his incarnation because if he did not it would be impossible for him to be the firstborn of every creature.

> And how is he the first-born of every creature, except by being that Word which is before every creature; and therefore, the first-born of every creature, he becomes flesh and dwells in us, that is, assuming that man's nature which is after every creature, and so dwells with him and in him, that neither is humanity taken away from Christ, nor his divinity denied? For if he is only before every creature, humanity is taken away from him; but if he is only man, the divinity which is before every creature is interfered with. Both of these, therefore, are leagued together in Christ, and both are conjoined, and both are linked with one another. (*On the Trinity* 21)

In the next chapter Novatian examined Philippians 2:6-11, arguing that because Christ was described as being in the form of God, he must possess the very nature of God, otherwise he would have been described as being in the image of God as are God's human creations. Working from Philippians 2, he said that by possessing the form of God, the Son is no less God than the Father although he willingly subordinated himself to the Father and in time took upon himself the form of a human. Thus from several perspectives Novatian concluded Christ preexisted his earthly life as the divine Son of God who was by his very nature deity.

ORIGEN

The first Christian theologian to write a systematic theology was Origen, who lived during the first half of the third century. A biblical commentator and author of works on practical theology as well as a systematic theology, Origen held some views the church would soon decide were unacceptable. Among these

---

[44]Novatian *On the Trinity* 18:1-3, in *Colossians, 1-2 Thessalonians, 1-2 Timothy, Titus, Philemon*, ed. Peter Gorday, Ancient Christian Commentary on Scripture, New Testament 9 (Downers Grove, Ill.: InterVarsity Press, 2000), p. 12.

was the preexistence of human souls. That belief was not the product of biblical but platonic thinking—but Origin's belief in Christ's preexistent deity was biblical. His commentary on John's Gospel makes this clear, although Origen's Neo-Platonism is evident in his interpretation. On John 1:1-3, Origen wrote, "Neither did he come to be in the beginning after he had not been in it, nor did he come to be with God after not having been with him. For before all time and the remotest age the Word was in the beginning, and the word was with God" (*Commentary on the Gospel According to John* 2.1). As to beginning, Origen wrote, "The term beginning may be taken of the beginning of the world, so we may learn from what is said that the Word was older than the things which were made from the beginning" (*Commentary on the Gospel According to John* 2.4). For Origen, not only was Christ preexistent deity, but all human souls preexisted their appearance on earth. This does not mean, however, that Origen placed the preexistent Christ and human souls in the same class. Origen believed "Christ took flesh, that he was born, that he went up to heaven in the flesh in which he rose again, that he is sitting at the right hand of the Father, and that thence he shall come and judge the living and the dead, being God and man."[45] In his *On First Principles,* Origen assumed Christ's eternal preexistence and creation of the world. He also described Christ as consubstantial with the Father. Origen's christology finely balanced the Son's eternal generation by the Father and his subordination to the Father. Any easing of the tension must lead either to the merging of Father and Son or to the loss of the Son's deity if the subordination is pressed too far.[46] Despite the awkwardness of Origen's language at some points, which would no longer be acceptable a century later, he offered a fundamentally sound christology.

ATHANASIUS

A pillar of the early church, Athanasius was a staunch defender of Christ's personal preexistence. What is probably his best-known work, *On the Incarnation of the Word,* presupposes Christ's preexistence in its argument that the Word of God had become incarnate for the sake of human salvation. As with Irenaeus, Athanasius was engaged in a conflict not about Christ's preexistence but about his deity. This affected how he would understand preexistence, but it did not affect his belief that Christ had preexisted his earthly life. Athanasius was con-

[45]Origen *Dialogues of Origen: With Heraclides and the Bishops with Him* 120, in *Alexandrian Christianity,* ed. John Ernest, Leonard Oulten and Henry Chadwick, Library of Christian Classics, vol. 2 (Philadelphia: Westminster Press, 1954), p. 437.
[46]Hans Schwarz, *Responsible Faith* (Minneapolis: Augsburg, 1986), pp. 223-24.

cerned to defend the reality of salvation as offered in Jesus Christ, but he realized he could do so only by first arguing the Savior's preexistent deity and full humanity.

Athanasius's Arian opponents also acknowledged Christ preexisted his earthly appearance, but they argued he was neither God nor human but rather some form of intermediate being. He was a creature, not the Creator ("There was [a time] when he was not"). They might agree to describe Christ as divine, but not as deity; Jesus was the highest of creatures. Thus they asserted Christ's preexistence was not eternal but temporal. The Arians' failure to accept Christ's preexistent deity resulted from their overdependence on Hellenistic categories and concepts, which limited their horizon and made them unable to understand God was doing something new in Jesus, something not contrary to reason but beyond the capacity of human reason to comprehend it. Arians used Hellenistic language and concepts in a way that denied what the New Testament affirmed about Jesus. Robert Jenson describes Arianism as "the theology of those controlled more by culture's intellectual fashion than by the gospel."[47]

Athanasius and his allies used Hellenistic language to express the implications of biblical thought in a non-Jewish environment. Their conclusions, however, were emphatically not Hellenistic. The Arian challenge to early orthodoxy placed church practice in clear perspective, probably clearer than intended. Arianism forced Christianity to decide between acknowledging that Christians worship a creature in addition to the Creator or recognizing that Christ is fully God and thus deserves our worship. The Arian controversy led Emperor Constantine to call the first ecumenical council of the Christian church at Nicea in A.D. 325. The council produced a creed that emphasized Christ's preexistent deity, equality with God the Father and incarnation. The more familiar creed of A.D. 381 came from the first council of Constantinople and fleshed out the earlier creed with a clear statement of the deity of the Holy Spirit. So by the early fourth century, Christ's preexistent deity had become a dogma of the church, although full acceptance of this conciliar teaching would require another six decades.

Torrance has described the practical effect of Arianism, which he calls paganism in Christian garb, as diminishing the significance of Christ by removing him as the focus of faith, which "inevitably leads to the detaching of 'Christianity' from Christ, and the grounding of the Christian religion once more in the self-understanding of man and human culture."[48] Although Torrance does not say

---

[47]Robert Jenson, *Systematic Theology,* vol. 1, *The Triune God* (Oxford: Oxford University Press, 1997), p. 104.
[48]Thomas F. Torrance, ed., *The Incarnation* (Edinburgh: Handel, 1981), p. xix.

so, this Arian error was possible only because of a fundamental misunderstanding of the preexistence of Christ, because the biblical concept of preexistence requires Christ's deity and thus his unity and essential equality with God.

Arguing soteriologically, Athanasius said the Word of God was naturally incorporeal and eternal, but out of mercy he was "manifested to us in a human body for our salvation" (*De Incarn.* 1.3).[49] "For he was made man that we might be made God; and he manifested Himself by a body that we might receive the idea of the unseen Father; and He endured the insolence of men that we might inherit immortality" (*De Incarn.* 54.3). The preexistent Son of God became human without surrendering his divine functions or nature. The humanity he assumed was no less real than his deity. Were this not the case, he could not be our Savior. In making his argument Athanasius did not emphasize Christ's preexistence, but he everywhere considered it essential to his argument. Like his predecessor Justin, Athanasius regularly linked Christ's preexistence with his virgin birth. Athanasius described Christ as both preexistent and personal: "Whence, lest this should be so, being good, he gives them a share in his own image, our Lord Jesus Christ, and makes them after his own image and after his likeness; so that by such grace perceiving the image, that is, the Word of the Father, they may be able through him to get an idea of the Father, and knowing their Maker, live the happy and truly blessed life" (*De Incarn.* 11.3). Repeatedly in *On the Incarnation of the Word,* Athanasius wrote of the Word of God, who was God and would be known to humans as Jesus Christ, as making everything from nothing, as taking to himself a body and as coming down from heaven.

J. M. McDermott considers the consequence of the Arian challenge to Christ's preexistent deity to be that it forced Athanasius and his allies back to the Father-Son relationship found throughout the New Testament and to conclude Fatherhood requires sonship, and on this basis to assert Christ's deity. He concludes, "In this they performed a double service. First, they justified speculatively the early faith of Paul and the evangelists in the divinity of Christ, the Church's faith from at least 49 AD (*Phil.* 2, 6-11), which interpreted Jesus as the pre-existent one, the son sent by the Father for the salvation of the world."[50] Athanasius saw the Arians' basic error as attempting to understand God in terms of humanity. This meant they believed that if God had a Son, the Son had to come after the Father, just as happens with human fathers and sons. What is theologically analogous, the Arians insisted must be identical.

---

[49] *De Incarn.* is the abbreviation for *On the Incarnation of the Word.* See also *De Incarn.* 4.3; 9.1, 3; 10.3.

[50] J. M. McDermott, "Jesus and the Son of God Title," *Gregorianum* 62 (1981): 316.

T. E. Pollard's assessment of the enduring value of Athanasius's work does not use the term *preexistence,* but the concept permeates what he has to say:

Athanasius accomplished the task bequeathed by Origen. He asserted the identity of the Logos and the Son, while at the same time making the Son-concept regulative. He transposed the doctrine of eternal generation into the theological key by asserting the co-eternity and co-essentiality of the son with the Father as the Only-begotten Son of the Unbegotten God, interpreting *monogenēs* in the sense of "unique," "only one of its kind." . . . In doing so, Athanasius is brought very close to the position taken up by Irenaeus and the Western Church which had never made the Logos-concept regulative, which had always identified the Logos and the Son, and had assumed the co-eternity, or consubstantiality, of the Logos-son with the Father. . . . Whereas for Origen eternal Generation and Subordination were cosmological postulates, for Athanasius they were soteriological postulates. Only one who is eternally God and yet at the same time really Incarnate as man can save mankind.[51]

Athanasius has long been recognized as a crucial figure in the history of Christianity because of his successful defense of orthodoxy against the superficially attractive view of Arius. What is less frequently remembered is that his belief in Christ's preexistence was the presuppositional basis for his argument.

Challenges to christological orthodoxy during the first Christian centuries arose from Ebionitism, forms of modalism, Gnosticism and Arianism. Only the first denied outright Christ's preexistence; the others altered the idea of preexistence in ways that denied what the church was affirming because they rejected the orthodox claim that Jesus is fully God. Ebionites viewed Jesus as a good man whom God exalted. They accepted Christ's virgin birth but denied his preexistence just as they denied his deity. Ebionitism was a form of Jewish Christianity that was unwilling to accept that God was doing something new in Jesus. It was the earliest form of adoptionism. Gnosticism rejected the material order as evil. Thus, while it could believe in a preexistent divine Word, it denied the possibility that the Word could in any way be identified with human flesh. Depending on the form it took, modalism either subordinated the Son of God ontologically to the Father or understood the Son's preexistence in an ideal or potential sense. Arianism accepted Christ's preexistence, but it was the preexistence of the greatest among the creatures. In each case, affirming the reality of Christ's incarnation was crucial. Against the Ebionites and Arians, orthodoxy affirmed Christ's deity; against the Gnostics and Arians, it affirmed Christ's real humanity. Although

---

[51]T. E. Pollard, "Logos and Son in Origen, Arius, and Athanasius," in *Studia Patristica,* ed. Kurt Aland and F. L. Cross (Berlin: Akademie-Verlag, 1957), 2:287.

each of these views was condemned and went into decline, all have continued to reappear in one form or another in later centuries.

GENESIS 1 AND THE TRINITY

A key text for many elements of theology is the account of the creation of the human species in Genesis 1:26-27. It may have received more attention from early Christian writers than any other part of the Old Testament, and that attention has not diminished in later centuries. Andrew Louth says, "Most of the early Fathers and later Greek Fathers take the image according to which man is created to be Christ himself," a conclusion that requires Christ's personal preexistence. He also notes that many of these early commentators believed the plural "we" to refer to the Trinity.[52] Prudentius, the early Christian poet and hymn writer, said of this text:

> The inspired historian makes it very clear
> That at earth's dawn the Father not alone
> Nor without Christ his new creation formed.[53]

Marius Victorinus, writing against Arianism, said of the passage, "Moses says what was said by God, 'Let us make man according to our image and likeness.' God says that. He says, 'Let us make' to a co-operator, necessarily to Christ."[54] Those who considered the preexistent Christ to be the one in whose image humanity was created include Irenaeus, Marius Victorinus and Augustine.

JOHN CHRYSOSTOM

Following Athanasius in eastern Christianity, John Chrysostom, bishop of Constantinople, offered a high christology that included Christ's preexistent deity. In his commentary on John's Gospel, Chrysostom made clear that Christ had always existed as the Son of God. In his second homily on the Gospel, he wrote that "the expression 'in the beginning was' means nothing else than, and must signify, everlasting existence and existence without end."[55] In his fourth homily, Chrysostom said:

---

[52]Andrew Louth, ed., *Genesis 1—11,* Ancient Christian Commentary on Scripture, Old Testament 1 (Downers Grove, Ill.: InterVarsity Press, 2001), p. 27.

[53]Prudentius *Poems,* Fathers of the Church: A New Translation 52 (Washington, D.C.: Catholic University of America Press, 1965), p. 15.

[54]Marius Victorinus *Against Arius,* Fathers of the Church: A New Translation 69 (Washington, D.C.: Catholic University of America Press, 1981), p. 117.

[55]John Chrysostom *Commentary on Saint John the Apostle and Evangelist: Homilies 1-47,* trans. Thomas Aquinas Goggin, The Fathers of the Church: A New Translation (Washington, D.C.: Catholic University of America Press, 1957), p. 22. All quotations from John Chrysostom are from this volume or its companion covering homilies 48-88, published in 1959.

The Word, however, is a Being, a distinct Person, proceeding from the Father himself without alteration. . . . Therefore, just as the expression "In the beginning was the Word" reveals his eternity, so "He was in the beginning with God" has revealed his co-eternity. . . . He was as eternal as the Father himself, for the Father was never without the Word but always God was with God, though each in his own Person." (1:46)

On John 8:58, Chrysostom wrote, "But why did He not say: 'Before Abraham came into being, I was' but 'I am'? He did so in the way in which His Father used the expression: 'I am.' For it meant that He has always existed, since it is free from all limitations of time" (Homily 55, 2.82). Carefully distinguishing the phrases of John 1:1-3, Chrysostom argued that John intended to say the Word was no less eternal than the Father. In Homily 3, Chrysostom described the eternal existence of the Word as a personal existence; the Word was not merely an intention in the Father's mind (1.33).

Even before the first ecumenical council made the doctrine of Christ's eternal, divine preexistence dogma, the theologians of the early church were consistently teaching it. Their arguments were not speculative but soteriological, and they enabled these early Christians to explain how God could be invisible yet appear to people. Whatever they owed to Hellenistic thought, these writers sought to interpret faithfully the words of both the Old and New Testaments. Little more than a century after Jesus' death, several show the presence of widely held normative formulas that affirmed Christ's preexistent deity and his incarnation in time. In the next stage, that of the ecumenical councils, these formulas would become church dogma, and the argument would be about how to interpret them, not whether they were true.

THE CHRISTOLOGICAL COUNCILS

Athanasius is widely remembered for his key role at the Council of Nicea in A.D. 325 and his later defense of its conclusions. This first ecumenical council was called by the emperor to settle the Arian dispute. The creed it produced and all subsequent ecumenical council statements about Christ affirm not only his preexistence but his *eternal* preexistence. The creed of 325 says in part:

And in one Lord Jesus Christ, the Son of God, begotten of the Father, only-begotten, *that is, of the substance of the Father,* God of God, Light of Light, *true God of true God, begotten not made, of one substance with the Father,* through whom all things were made, *things in heaven and things on the earth;* who for us men and our salvation came down and was made flesh, *and became man.* . . .

And those who say "There was when he was not,"
and, "Before he was begotten he was not,"

and that, "He came into being from what-is-not,"
or those who allege, that the son of God is
   "Of another substance or essence"
or "created,"
or "changeable"
or "alterable,"
these the Catholic and Apostolic Church anathematizes.[56]

The creed affirms Christ's preexistence unequivocally and does so because human salvation depends on it, not because it fits neatly into some philosophical system. The Nicene-Constantinopolitan Creed of A.D. 381 reaffirms the earlier creed, adding language about the Holy Spirit and specifying that it was *from the heavens* that Christ came down. Unlike the version of the Nicene Creed recited weekly in many Christian churches, the original versions contain sharp anathemas against those who deny Christ's preexistent deity.

In the controversies that followed the council of 381, Christ's preexistence was a matter of common agreement. The disagreements dealt with the extent of the incarnation—how much of Jesus was the preincarnate Son and how much was creature. The Council of Chalcedon in A.D. 451 reaffirmed the creed of 381 and established boundaries for any future discussion of Christ's person. It described Christ "as in regards his Godhead, begotten of the Father before all ages, but yet as regards his manhood begotten, for us men and for our salvation, of Mary the Virgin." The Chalcedonian Definition juxtaposed "God the Word" and "Lord Jesus Christ" in such a way that it was undeniable it was talking about the same person. During the following centuries, Christ's preexistence remained a matter of common agreement as theological disputes moved in other directions.

Modern critics of the conciliar statements are correct when they charge these statements are not written in biblical language and do not discuss in any detail Jesus' earthly ministry. What they fail to notice, however, is that the parties to the debate were not Jewish but Gentile, and the issue was not the details of Jesus' earthly ministry but rather who it was who had engaged in that ministry. What did it mean to talk of a man who had preexisted his earthly life, was incarnated and resurrected from death? As Raymond Brown has written, "Today, in some circles, it has become fashionable to deprecate as hopelessly abstruse the strenuous debates of the early Christian centuries about the person and nature of Jesus Christ. But these debates show that instinctively Christians realized

---

[56]Henry Bettenson, ed., *Documents of the Christian Church,* 2nd ed. (London: Oxford University Press, 1963), p. 25.

how important it was that nothing be allowed to obscure the true divinity and true humanity of Jesus."[57]

AUGUSTINE, ANSELM, AQUINAS AND MEDIEVAL CHRISTOLOGY

Among succeeding generations of Christians in the Western church, Augustine has exerted a powerful influence. But different Christian traditions tend to draw from different aspects of Augustine. Thus he is a major figure for both Roman Catholics and Calvinistic Protestants, but for different reasons. All agree, however, with what Augustine had to say about Jesus Christ. He presented the incarnation as an instance of divine condescension carried out for the sake of human salvation. Christ, for Augustine, was preexistent deity who was born of the Virgin Mary and assumed a complete human nature. As the author of a treatise on the Trinity, Augustine believed firmly in Christ's preexistent deity and ontological equality with the Father. This was no less evident in his sermons than in his theological works,[58] reaffirming the intimate connection that has existed between worship and christology from the beginning. Echoing Athanasius, he argued Christ's preexistence from the nature of the divine Father-Son relationship: "So then if it is in God's very nature to be the eternal Father, and if there was never a time when he was not the Father, then he never existed without the Son."[59]

Anselm of Canterbury is probably best known for his ontological argument for God's existence. Late in the eleventh century, however, he wrote a long discourse on the Atonement titled *Why God Became Man*. He argued that humanity had incurred an infinite debt before God that had to be paid in order to get right with God. Although humanity owed it, it could not pay it; God could pay it, but he did not owe it. In the incarnation God bridged the chasm between God and humans by entering fully into humanity. By becoming human, the God-man Jesus Christ was able to assume the debt; because he was God, he was able to pay it. The premise underlying the entire argument was that of Christ's preexistent deity. As with the other discussions of Christ's preexistence we have examined, Anselm's argument is based not on speculation but on soteriology. The incarnation happened so humans could be saved from the consequences of our sins, and the incarnation was possible only because Christ existed eternally as

---

[57]Raymond E. Brown, *New Testament Essays* (Milwaukee: Bruce, 1965), p. 98.
[58]See, for example, Augustine's sermons on 1 Jn 1:1—2:11; 2:27—3:8; 3:19—4:3, where he affirms Christ's preexistence, deity and incarnation for the sake of human salvation.
[59]Augustine *Eighty-three Different Questions,* trans. David L. Mosher, The Fathers of the Church: A New Translation 70 (Washington, D.C.: Catholic University of America Press, 1982), p. 45.

the Son of God. In the discussion Anselm manufactured with his character Boso, the latter's objections to Anselm, while derived from a misunderstanding of the relationship between natures and person in Christ and between the Father and the Son, nonetheless include agreement on Christ's preexistent deity.[60]

The best-known Christian thinker of the Middle Ages is remembered more for his philosophy than his theology or biblical studies. But according to one recent study, Thomas Aquinas's entire program was christologically based.[61] Eugene Rogers shows that Thomas considered Christ to be God's self-revelation through his incarnation. This, as well as such language as the Word becoming flesh, presumes Christ's real preexistence if Thomas's arguments are to have any meaning. According to Rogers, the christological language in Thomas is what makes the rest of his thought, including his Aristotelian philosophy, coherent. Brian Davies describes Thomas as "uncompromisingly orthodox in his teaching about Christ."[62]

Thomas's discussion of Jesus was "an attempt to explore the sense and significance of what he takes to be the meaning of Chalcedon." Further, he believed Jesus himself taught his deity; it was not a conclusion reached after the resurrection by his followers. Thomas tackled the issue of Christ's preexistence head-on in part 3, question 16 of his *Summa Theologiae*. He wrote, "I answer that, We must not say that 'this Man'—pointing to Christ—'began to be,' unless we add something. . . . The words quoted must be qualified, i.e. we must say that the Man Jesus Christ was not, before the world was, 'in his humanity.' . . . Therefore this is false: 'The Man Christ began to be': but this is true: 'Christ began to be Man.' " The following passage from the *Summa Theologiae* expresses clearly Christ's preexistence:

> The Word of God . . . from all eternity had complete being in hypostasis or person, but human nature came to be his in time, not as assumed into a single esse as this pertains to nature (as a body is assumed to be the esse of the soul), but to the single esse as this pertains to hypostasis or person. And thus the joining of human nature to the Son of God is not in the manner of an accident.[63]

For Thomas, Christ, or the Word, is the second person of the Trinity, and thus preexistent deity.

---

[60]See, e.g., Anselm of Canterbury *Why God Became Man* 1.8; 2.6-9.
[61]Eugene F. Rogers Jr., *Thomas Aquinas and Karl Barth* (Notre Dame, Ind.: University of Notre Dame Press, 1995).
[62]Brian Davies, *The Thought of Thomas Aquinas* (Oxford: Oxford University Press, 1992), p. 297.
[63]Thomas Aquinas *Summa Theologiae* 3.2.6 ad. 2.

For him, of course, the second person of the Trinity, the Word, is eternal. So it would have been true to say "The Word exists" before the birth of Christ. . . . Aquinas concludes that we may speak of the Incarnation as a matter of it coming about in time that a human nature, involving the existence of a human being, came to be assumed by a divine person. The term "assumed" is required, he thinks, in order not to deny the eternal being of God the Son. As we may put it, "since the person of the Word pre-exists, Christ's created human nature does not constitute his person but rather joins it."[64]

In part 1 of the *Summa,* Thomas insisted the Son existed prior to being sent into the world and that the "sending" the New Testament describes was a visible sending because even before the incarnation the Son was in the world: "For the divine person sent neither begins to exist where he did not previously exist, nor ceases to exist where he was."[65]

For Thomas, Christ's preexistence was a necessary truth given his belief in the Trinity and the incarnation. It included a soteriological element, although not as prominently as had previous thinkers. His language is entirely in line with that of the New Testament, church councils and the orthodox theologians who preceded him.

FROM THE REFORMATION TO THE ENLIGHTENMENT

The christological statements of the magisterial Reformation were in deliberate agreement with those of the earlier church. The Reformers disagreed with the Roman Catholic Church on a wide range of matters, but not on the person of Jesus Christ. The magisterial Reformers and the Catholic Church were agreed in their acceptance of the substance of the teachings of the early christological councils. Their disagreement lay in a different understanding of the authority of the conciliar decisions. The Reformers contended the conciliar statements must remain subordinate to and reformable by Scripture; they are not intrinsically infallible. The Catholic Church considered them to be infallible statements of the church. The same acceptance of Christ's preexistent deity was not to be found among some elements of what is called the Radical Reformation, however. Among the extreme—and only the extreme—Anabaptists, Jesus was seen as a great man, but neither deity nor preexistent.[66]

---

[64]Davies, *Thought of Thomas Aquinas,* pp. 304-5. He discusses Thomas's views in greater detail on pp. 305-7.

[65]Thomas Aquinas *Summa Theologiae* 1.43.1.3.

[66]This can still be seen in such sources as *The Journal from the Radical Reformation,* which recently ran a series of articles challenging the orthodoxy of the doctrine of Christ's preexistent deity.

Of the Reformers, John Calvin was the most comprehensive and systematic. He was also a biblical scholar who wrote commentaries on almost every book of the Bible and a preacher who preached almost daily in Geneva. His *Institutes of the Christian Religion,* commentaries, sermons and occasional writings provide a comprehensive statement of Christian belief from the Reformed perspective. He affirmed a high christology that includes Christ's preexistence as the Son of God. Calvin organized the *Institutes* using the trinitarian structure of the Apostles' Creed, and the content reflects his familiarity with and appreciation of the thinking of early church writers. Book one of the *Institutes* considers Christ's deity and preexistence in the context of the Trinity; book two includes a discussion of Christ's deity, humanity and incarnation in terms of his salvific mission. Calvin's belief in Christ's preexistence was evident when he wrote, "Here is something marvelous: the Son of God descended from heaven in such a way that, without leaving heaven, he willed to be borne in the virgin's womb, to go about the earth, and to hang upon the cross; yet he continuously filled the world even as he had done from the beginning!"[67]

Calvin's strong affirmation of Christ's preexistent deity derived first from his biblical studies and second from his reading of the church fathers—before he was a systematic theologian, Calvin was an Old Testament scholar, and despite authoring the *Institutes* he always considered himself primarily a biblical scholar. He quoted freely from the Old and New Testaments and the Apocrypha[68] to show Christ was from all eternity God. Of all Scripture, Calvin considered the prologue to John's Gospel the clearest statement that Christ has always been with God and is God.[69] In his commentary on the opening verses of the prologue, Calvin wrote, "In this introduction [John] asserts the eternal divinity of Christ, in order to inform us that he is the eternal God, w*ho was manifested in the flesh.* . . . He was always united to God, before the world existed." Calvin forcefully defended Christ's deity when he commented on Philippians 2:

> Christ's humility consisted in his abasing himself from the highest pinnacle of glory to the lowest ignominy. . . . The *form of God* means here his majesty. . . . Christ, then, before the creation of the world, was in the form of God, because from the beginning he had his glory with the Father, as he says in John 17:5. . . . Farther, that man is utterly blind who does not perceive that his eternal divinity is clearly set forth in these words. . . . For where can there be *equality with* God without

---

[67]John Calvin, *Institutes of the Christian Religion,* ed. John T. McNeill, trans. Ford Lewis Battles (Philadelphia: Westminster Press, 1960), 2.13.4.

[68]Calvin considered the Apocrypha as exemplary rather than normative. It was a source similar in value to patristic writings, not Scripture.

[69]Calvin *Institutes* 1.13.7.

robbery, excepting only where there is the essence of God; for God always remains the same.[70]

Calvin defended the position argued by Justin but rejected by Augustine that the angel of the Lord was the preexistent Christ acting as God's mediator with humans even prior to the incarnation. This appears in the section of the *Institutes* intended to demonstrate Christ's deity. In his commentary on Isaiah, Calvin identified the Lord of Isaiah 6:1 as Christ, "for God never revealed himself to the Fathers but in his eternal word and only begotten Son." Likewise, the one like a son of man in Daniel 7:13, "without a doubt, this is to be understood of Christ. . . . For the prophet says, *he appeared* to him as the *Son of Man,* as Christ had not yet taken upon him our flesh." In explaining this appearance in Daniel 7:13, Calvin continued:

> For if we hold this principle that Christ is described to us, not as either the word of God, or the seed of Abraham, but as Mediator, that is, eternal God who was willing to become man, to become subject to God the Father, to be made like us, and to be our advocate, then no difficulty will remain. Thus he appeared to Daniel, like the Son of man, who became afterwards truly and really so.

As he argued for Christ's full deity, so too did Calvin argue for his full humanity. For Calvin the deity was first and basic, and to this deity Christ added a full and real humanity. It could not be otherwise, Calvin concluded, if humans were to be saved. Having outlined the argument that Christ was fully deity and fully human, Calvin turned to critique erroneous understandings of Christ's person. In doing so, he once again argued for Christ's eternal preexistence. In arguing against his contemporary Michael Servetus, Calvin wrote, "The church's definition stands firm: he is believed to be the Son of God because the Word begotten of the Father before all ages took human nature in a hypostatic union."[71] Calvin argued from the language of Father and Son, terms that refer to a relation that existed before the incarnation, for Christ's preexistent deity.

Many of the passages modern biblical scholars have denied teach Christ's preexistence Calvin took for granted as teaching the doctrine. This includes the "sending" statements found in the Gospels and Paul's letters, Jesus' words about having come (from heaven), and Paul's language in Acts 13:33 and Romans 1:3. Of the last he wrote, "[Paul] adds, *according to the flesh,* and he adds this, that we may understand that he had something more excellent than flesh, which he brought from heaven, and did not take from David, even that which he after-

---

[70]John Calvin, *Philippians,* Calvin's Commentaries, AGES Software CD-ROM, 1996, pp. 45ff.
[71]Calvin *Institutes* 2.14.5.

wards mentions, the glory of the divine nature."

Martin Luther held the same high christology as the historic creeds and his contemporary Calvin. Luther believed the preincarnate Son had appeared to Old Testament people in various forms. He wrote:

> The patriarch Jacob distinguishes the persons in the Holy Trinity. . . . [H]e calls the Lord Christ an 'Angel,' not as if He were an angel according to His essence and nature. . . . By his prayer Jacob, then, confesses this angel to be the true, essential God. But he is not forever to conduct Himself as the invisible God; for He is to be sent to earth, to be clothed in our flesh, and to be sacrificed for our sin.[72]

Luther linked preexistence and incarnation, not for speculative but for soteriological reasons. The Son of God "descended from heaven into this lowliness, came to us in our flesh, laid Himself into the womb of His mother and into the manger and went to the cross."[73] The same belief with the same rationale was echoed by the other leaders of the magisterial Reformation.

The Radical Reformation included an antitrinitarian element. Influential among these were Simon Budny, Faustus Socinus and Laelius Socinus. They denied Christ's preexistent deity and rejected his receiving of worship. These early unitarians argued variously that Christ was a good man exalted by God because of his faithful witness, or that Christ was some sort of mixture of divine and human elements, constituting a great creation of God, but no more than that. Socinianism taught among other beliefs that Jesus was God's revelation, but not God. He offered a moral example to his followers, not an atoning sacrifice. No more than a good man, Jesus did not enjoy a personal preexistence, especially as the second person of the Trinity. Christ's deity was not essential but resulted from his adoption by God at his ascension. Although the Counter Reformation suppressed Socinianism, its influence continued to be felt among those who sought a rationalistic religion.

About a century after Calvin, writers claiming to endorse true Christianity began to interpret it rationalistically. This theology, which came to be called deism, rejected not only Christ's preexistent deity but any appeal to the supernatural. It considered the Creator of the world a remote being who, having created, had no further involvement with the world. As expressed by such writers as John Toland, this view believed the Bible in its entirety must be understood in a way consistent with human reason. Traditional Christianity, with its high christology, was dismissed as superstition. Although the first advocates of these views ap-

---

[72]Martin Luther, *What Luther Says,* comp. Ewald M. Plass (St. Louis: Concordia, 1959), 1:147.
[73]Ibid., 1:155.

peared in England, deistic thought became most influential in France and Germany (and was prevalent among the founders of the United States). It might well be said that the Hellenism some writers claim infected the church during the first century, leading to belief in Christ as preexistent deity, actually became influential at the time of the Enlightenment and resulted in the rejection of this high christology as contrary to human reason. This line of reasoning has continued to the present with theologians arguing for a nonsupernaturalist conclusion because they fear the language and thought forms of classical Christian theology are intellectually unacceptable to modern people.

CONCLUSION

From its earliest days Christianity has understood Jesus Christ as deity and as preexistent. It took centuries for the church to formulate the implications of this belief. These formulations were invariably responses to competing interpretations of Jesus that most Christians considered insufficient to accomplish human salvation. Belief in Christ's preexistent deity appeared very early in hymns and public worship. Because the earliest Christians were Jews, this behavior is particularly noteworthy. A high christology, consistent with that of the creeds, developed early and widely in the church. Postapostolic writers defended Christ's preexistent deity and succeeding generations of theologians expanded on their statements. In virtually every case the discussion of Christ's preexistence occurred not in the context of speculative thought but out of a concern to guard the reality of human salvation. Early theologians presented Christ's preexistence as an expression of God's loving concern for his fallen creatures and of his condescension in reaching out to save them. Only later did other writers specifically address the implications of this soteriological concern.

Through the Reformation era, Christian confessions and theology affirmed Christ's preexistent deity. They too did so out of concern for human salvation and on the basis of Scripture and earlier Christian teaching. Only with the rationalistic thought characteristic of the Enlightenment did Christ's preexistent deity come under sustained attack. Hellenistic philosophy sought to make inroads into Christian theology in the early church, and in every case it pulled those it influenced toward heresy. Since the Enlightenment, and, as many have noted, particularly since Descartes, this Hellenistic rationalism has played a significant role in Western thought—including theology—and has led some theologians to conclude that the historic christological doctrines are in error, or, as Wiles has suggested, rest on a mistake. These modern objections will be the subject of chapter nine, but first we will consider the role Christ's preexistence plays within the structure of Christian theology.

8

THEOLOGICAL ISSUES

Many today question even the possibility of systematic theology. They see theology as a collection of conclusions about disparate religious topics, the various parts of which share no necessary relationship. Despite this modern opinion, Christianity retains a systematic theology where our conclusions about each part necessarily affect what we can say about every other part. To state this in the context of my study, removing the doctrine of Christ's preexistence would leave us with different concepts of God, Christ, humanity, salvation and creation, to name only the most prominent areas affected. Moreover, the Christianity of those who deny Christ's preexistence is not the Christianity affirmed in the church's historic creeds and confessions or in the New Testament.

When I refer to the "preexistence of Christ" or "Christ's preexistence," I am speaking about God the Son in distinction from Jesus of Nazareth.[1] I am also speaking of a real or personal preexistence, as opposed to an ideal, eschatological or some other kind of preexistence. The terminology is traditional, even if not precisely accurate. What I am asserting is that the one we know as the man Jesus of Nazareth preexisted his earthly life and did so eternally as deity; what I am denying is that the *man* Jesus of Nazareth preexisted his earthly life. The deity of Jesus Christ is eternal, his humanity began at a point in time about two thousand years ago.

PREEXISTENCE AND THE TRINITY

At the heart of Christian faith lies the doctrine of the Trinity, the conviction that the one God exists in three persons. The church arrived at this conclusion from

---

[1]This is not to say they are different persons. What I intend by this distinction is that God the Son has existed from all eternity whereas Jesus of Nazareth is the name of the incarnated God the Son who in his incarnation took to his divine person a human nature which did not preexist this incarnation. According to Matthew 1:21, it was the son born to Mary who received the name Jesus.

its consideration of what the New Testament says about God and especially what it says about Jesus. What primarily distinguishes Christianity from Judaism is the conviction that God has revealed himself absolutely and acted in an unsurpassable way in Jesus Christ, a way that requires he be no less than God. This is more than a matter of intellectual curiosity. P. T. Forsyth reminds us, "Faith in Christ involves the Godhead of Christ. . . . It means that the deity of Christ is at the centre of Christian truth for us because . . . it alone makes the classic Christian experience possible for thought."[2] The church finalized the doctrine as the result of a series of disputes about who Jesus was, what he had accomplished and how the two are related. Consideration of Jesus' earthly life and resurrection forced his disciples early and inexorably to the conclusion that what God was Jesus was. Geoffrey Lampe, whose christology is a sophisticated form of adoptionism, acknowledges, "If these traditional pictures, or any others which depict salvation as a decisive act of God performed at a definite point in history, represent that which God has done for us in Jesus, then no doubt the best model for Christology is the divine person of the pre-existent Son who comes down into the world of human sin."[3] This preexistence is no theological construct but an essential and original element of historic Christianity's understanding of God's salvific plan.

From this consideration, having deepened their understanding of God, early Christians then recognized the New Testament evidence required they acknowledge the deity of the Holy Spirit as well. This oversimplifies the long and difficult route the church followed in understanding God, but it leads me to point out that once Christians accepted the preexistent deity of Christ, they were able to recognize the Spirit is equally deity and personal. When we surrender Christ's preexistent deity, we risk losing the Spirit's personhood and deity as well. This has occurred with the Jehovah's Witnesses and some versions of Spirit christology.

Discussion of the Trinity in Christian theology must start from the person of Jesus Christ because he has become part of human experience. In Jesus, God has entered personally into human history. This means two things. First, Jesus is the epitome of God's self-revelation. If we want to know what God is like, we need to look at and listen to Jesus. As Jesus said to Philip, "Anyone who has seen me has seen the Father. How can you say, 'Show us the Father'?" (Jn 14:9).

---

[2]P. T. Forsyth, quoted in A. W. Argyle, "The Evidence for the Belief That Our Lord Himself Claimed to be Divine," *Expository Times* 61 (1950): 232.
[3]Geoffrey Lampe, quoted in Walter Moberly, "God Incarnate: Some Reflections from an Old Testament Perspective," *Churchman* 98 (1983): 48.

Earlier in the same Gospel, John wrote, "No one has ever seen God, but God the One and Only, who is at the Father's side, has made him known" (Jn 1:18). So God has revealed himself in Jesus Christ. It is not an exhaustive revelation— it does not answer every question we have about God—but it is a sufficient revelation. It tells us everything we *need* to know about God. Second, but related to the first, is that the questions we ask and answer about Jesus force us to see God as more than the Old Testament, and certainly more than philosophy of religion, seems to show God to be. Or to understand God we must let the reality of Jesus Christ change our preconceived notions about God.

What I am saying is a lesson learned very early in the study of theology, one equally true of any systematic study. This truth is that all the facets of Christian belief are interrelated. They are so closely connected that any noticeable change in one teaching must ripple through the rest, modifying each in such a way that the teachings can once again fit together, although the picture they now form is somehow different from the old. In studying the doctrine of Christ's preexistence, this truth once again was brought home to me forcefully. My initial purpose in writing was that I believed (and still believe) modern attempts to explain away or reformulate the doctrine must have serious and detrimental effects on our understanding of God and Jesus Christ, and humanity's relationship with them. It is true: changes in Christian belief in these two areas will certainly affect everything else about Christianity. But as I have written, I have been reminded that the whole Christian understanding of salvation stands or falls on what at first seems a minor teaching of the Christian church. Depending on our conclusions about Christ's preexistence, we will see Jesus either as one among many world religious leaders or as God incarnate who has intervened in our history to effect our salvation.

Although Christian theology in its classic form has tended to work from God and the Trinity to Christ, passing through the doctrines of creation, anthropology and sin, I am going to start from Christ and work out to the other doctrines. These doctrines are intimately interlinked and the path the earliest Christians moved along is the direction I will follow. The earliest Christians had experienced the Jesus who had lived among them and then risen from death, and they used this as their key to achieve a fuller understanding of their world and their Scripture.

Whether Christ preexisted his earthly life makes all the difference in what we can say about him. As a result, our conclusion about who Jesus was (and is) will lead us in different and even incompatible directions in our understanding of God and of God's relation to and concern for us and our world. To state it negatively, everything Christianity has affirmed about Jesus (except his full humanity) would have to be denied if the doctrine of Christ's preexistence were false. This is true not only of Christ's person but also of his work. If Christ had been merely human and not preexistent deity, he could no more be the Savior of humanity than you or I. Although, by itself, Christ's preexistence is not sufficient ground for affirming his deity, it remains a necessary prerequisite. A Christ who was not preexistent could not be deity in any biblical sense of the term; if Christ is deity, then he necessarily preexisted his earthly life and did so from all eternity.[4]

The leading alternative to traditional christology is some form of adoptionism. Despite the claims of its advocates, adoptionism raises far more problems than it purports to solve. Adoptionism portrays Jesus as a human specially chosen by God to act as Savior. It often describes Jesus as unusually open to God and thus as living an exemplary life. But this raises three questions adoptionism fails to deal with satisfactorily. First, why Jesus and not some other individual? For the adoptionist the answer must be some sort of arbitrary choice. Only for the traditional Christian is there a logical explanation for Jesus' election—Jesus is the incarnate Son of God and his election occurred not at or after his incarnation but in the eternal counsel of God. Second, if Jesus was a human like us and no more, then of all humans how was he alone able to overcome our propensity to sin and live a life pleasing to God? None of the rest of us does this. If Jesus could live that way and I cannot, should that not discourage me rather than being a comfort and encouragement? Third, if some other human at some point in time should live a life as exemplary as Jesus' (given the adoptionist assumptions, not mine), then what is God supposed to do? Is Jesus still Savior? What would be the status of this figment of my imagination, a second Savior? So, adoptionism is not a solution; it merely creates more problems.

INCARNATION AND RESURRECTION

The two foci around which our entire understanding of Jesus Christ revolve are the incarnation and the resurrection. God could have raised a merely human Jesus from death, but I doubt God would have raised such a Jesus if he claimed divine authority and associated himself with God in a way that his disciples' conclusion about him required ontological equality with God. Such a Jesus God could neither vindicate nor describe as his beloved Son with whom he was well pleased. But it is at least possible God could have resurrected, not resuscitated, a merely human Jesus.

---

[4]Gerald O'Collins says, "Belief in Jesus' divinity stands or falls with accepting his *personal* preexistence within the eternal life of the Trinity. This belief is not to be confused with false ideas about some preexistence of his created humanity" ("The Critical Issues," in *The Incarnation*, ed. Stephen T. Davis et al. [Oxford: Oxford University Press, 2002], p. 3).

I believe Jacques Dupuis is correct when he says the resurrection in isolation would not have convinced the disciples about Jesus. Only because the resurrection was the clarification and confirmation of how Jesus had lived and what he had taught did it ground the church's faith in Jesus. "Jesus . . . had lived his divine Sonship in all his attitudes and actions, above all in his prayer to God whom he called Abba. . . . The elaborate New Testament Christology of Jesus' ontological Sonship of God gives objective expression to the filial consciousness that had been at the centre of Jesus' subjective experience of God during his earthly life."[5] Yet the resurrection provoked questions about who it was who had been resurrected.

> Initially no doubt the precise definition of who or what pre-existed was not directly raised, and further explorations both within the New Testament and later would be necessary before its full implications could be grasped. It occurs at first in quite untheological contexts which do not give the impression that a new and highly controversial point is being made.[6]

Those who have argued that Christ's postexistence required consideration of a preexistence are correct—unless the preexistence is merely created to balance the postexistence, instead of providing a recognition of who it was who had risen from the dead.

The incarnation is another matter altogether. Unless Christ preexisted his earthly life, the language of incarnation is nonsense. For Christ to have *become* flesh, he first must have existed as other than flesh. A nonincarnational christology (in the next chapter we will see there are such) must be either utterly different from traditional christology or it must be internally inconsistent. Brian Hebblethwaite writes, "If we were forced to reject the doctrine of the incarnation, there would certainly have to be a complete re-fashioning of the Christian framework of interpretation; for . . . the specifically Christian understanding of revelation and reconciliation—i.e., the Christian gospel—depends for its distinctive contribution wholly on the incarnation."[7]

THE VIRGIN BIRTH

As early as the beginning of the third century, creedal statements identified Christ both as the Son of God and as virgin-born (not to mention that two Gospels did so in the first century). In our century some consider the affir-

---

[5]Jacques Dupuis, *Who Do You Say I Am?* (Maryknoll, N.Y.: Orbis, 1994), p. 70.
[6]H. E. W. Turner, *Jesus the Christ* (London: Mowbrays, 1976), p. 15.
[7]Brian Hebblethwaite, "The Appeal to Experience in Christology," in *Christ, Faith and History*, ed. S. W. Sykes and J. P. Clayton (Cambridge: Cambridge University Press, 1972), p. 270.

mations of Christ's preexistence and virgin birth to be competing rather than complementary explanations of Jesus' origin. I. Howard Marshall acknowledges preexistence is not an explicit element of Matthew and Luke's birth narratives, but describes the claim of incompatibility as faulty. Both types of language appear together in the New Testament without any author betraying the thought they might be incompatible. "The stories of the birth of Jesus relate his divine Sonship to his conception by the Spirit and show that he was to be regarded as the Son of God during his earthly life. Here divine Sonship is clearly characteristic of his nature and not simply an expression of function or status."[8]

There is no convincing theological reason to set Christ's preexistence and the virgin birth against each other. If Christ is indeed the preexistent Son, it would seem strange for his incarnation to have been in no way different from our births. The virgin birth both protects the reality of his humanity and says there is more to his story than this humanity alone. Christ's preexistence can stand without reference to the virgin birth, but the virgin birth "strongly suggests" preexistence.[9]

Wolfhart Pannenberg, however, finds linking preexistence and the virgin birth problematic, but not because he denies either the incarnation or the preexistence of the Son of God. He says, "We also must view the earthly existence of Jesus as the event of the incarnation of the preexistent Son."[10] There seem to be four reasons for his concern. First, he considers the virgin birth to be legend. Second, Pannenberg argues that everything we can say about Jesus is possible only in the light of the resurrection, so both preexistence and incarnation must be understood retrospectively from the resurrection, not directly in relation to each other.[11] Third, Pannenberg refuses to identify the incarnation with the event of Jesus' birth. He says that apart from Luke the New Testament links incarnation with sending, not birth. Jesus' birth only gains significance from the course of his life that reveals him to be Messiah and Son of God. The key here, of course, is Easter.[12] Fourth, preexistence does not require deity, so even if it could be linked with Jesus' birth it would not show him to be the incarnate Son of God. For Pannenberg the early church's equation of the incarnation of the

---

[8]I. Howard Marshall, *The Origins of New Testament Christology* (Downers Grove, Ill.: InterVarsity Press, 1976), pp. 122-23.
[9]Turner, *Jesus the Christ,* p. 17.
[10]Wolfhart Pannenberg, *Systematic Theology,* trans. Geoffrey W. Bromiley (Grand Rapids: Eerdmans, 1991), 2:368.
[11]Ibid., 368ff.
[12]Ibid., pp. 302-3.

preexistent Logos with Jesus' birth was a wrong turn that blocked the possibility of "any evaluating of the human uniqueness of Jesus of Nazareth as a medium of the revelation of the divine Logos" as had already begun in Paul's second Adam christology.[13]

SIN AND SALVATION

Christ's preexistence places him on the side of God before he is on our side. Because the Bible insists we cannot get to God in our own strength or on our own merit, that Christ was with God and came from God is good news. This is precisely what the doctrine of preexistence claims. The doctrine of the incarnation says the preexistent Son took upon himself humanity in order to bridge the chasm between God and humans, not that we might cross over to God but that God himself might come among us to save us from ourselves and our sinful behavior. To take the step of incarnation says not only that Christ came from God and represents God to us, but he is himself God. This means that in representing God he does so perfectly; his actions will not later be repudiated as exceeding his authority or being inconsistent with God's wishes. Possibly the greatest meaning of the incarnation is as a statement of God's direct, personal concern with the well being of his disobedient creatures. Incarnation says God himself came among us by entering into our condition—this is the first scandal of Christianity that sets it at odds with every other religious tradition. But incarnation only carries this message if Christ really preexisted his earthly life and did so as God the Son. This moves us naturally in the directions both of God's nature and of our need. Following the New Testament pattern of explaining Jesus Christ as the one who has dealt conclusively with our sin problem, I turn to briefly consider what it means that we are sinners.

Saying that humans are sinful and denying that we are masters of our situation is considered impolite in our modern world. But human sinfulness is one Christian doctrine that can be verified empirically, and the sense we are accountable for our actions lies deep within each of us. We dispense with belief in our sinfulness at peril to our psychological no less than our spiritual well being. Christianity describes sin as the rebellious response of the human will to God's authority. It declares our desire to be our own god. The consequence of our sin is that having made ourselves enemies of God, we stand under his judgment. This is a universal condition—Paul declared all have sinned, each of us has turned to his or her own way. The desperation of our condition is not only that we cannot resolve this problem we have made for ourselves, but that we

---

[13]Ibid., p. 301.

will not. Left to ourselves, we refuse to admit we have done anything seriously wrong. It is here that God the Holy Spirit steps in to show us the enormity of our wrongdoing and to instill within us the faith we need in order to accept what Christ has done for us. But this is to get ahead of myself; we need to deal with who this Jesus is and what he has done before we are ready to look at how the Spirit applies his work. This is just one more reminder of how intricately the different aspects of Christian belief interlock.

Christian theology has come to understand Jesus' person and salvific role in a way that requires his preexistence. This was the result of three converging lines of evidence. From the first, Christians have had to explain what sort of person Jesus had to be in order to speak and act as he did and for these words and deeds to be vindicated by God. They also had to decide what sort of person was commensurate with their experience. Finally, they had to answer what sort of person Jesus would have to be in order to be their Savior. Increasingly, their answers to these questions emphasized his preexistence and deity. If we separate Christ's person and work, the inevitable result is theological error. "That is why Athanasius and those who stood with him in the fourth century so clearly perceived that a false doctrine of the person of Christ must inevitably result in a false doctrine of the work of Christ and consequently undermine the whole system of the gospel."[14]

A PREEXISTENT HUMANITY?

It is God the Son, or the Word, who became incarnate as Jesus Christ and who preexisted, not the God-man Jesus. Jesus is the name we normally associate with the *incarnate* One, and it is incorrect to refer to Jesus' existence at any time before the annunciation to Mary. The preexistence of the human Jesus is taught nowhere in Christian doctrine (although some heretical groups have taught Christ's "celestial flesh"). Sixteen hundred years ago Gregory Nazianzen wrote, "If anyone assert that his flesh came down from heaven, and is not from hence, nor of us though above us, let him be anathema."[15] "The Incarnation was not the manifestation of a humanity ever in the heart of God—such an idea has only been promulgated in line with some kind of Platonic or Neo-Platonic idealism."[16] H. R. Mackintosh writes that "the Church has never affirmed that the

---

[14]Philip Edgcumbe Hughes, *A Commentary on the Epistle to the Hebrews* (Grand Rapids: Eerdmans, 1977), p. 43.
[15]Gregory Nazianzen, "To Cledonius the Priest against Apollinarius," in A Select Library of Nicene and Post-Nicene Fathers of the Christian Church, 2nd ser., ed. Philip Schaff and Henry Wace (Grand Rapids: Eerdmans, 1978), 7:440.
[16]Thomas F. Torrance, *The Doctrine of Jesus Christ* (Eugene, Ore.: Wipf & Stock, 2002), p. 58.

humanity of Christ was real prior to the birth in Bethlehem."[17]

Teaching Jesus' preexistent humanity would also violate one of the major concerns of modern theologians, making his humanity radically different from everyone else's even as it sought to make that humanity a common denominator. Such teaching would be a soteriological as well as a christological concern. Macquarrie warns that to claim preexistence for the human Jesus would be to deny his real humanity.[18] It follows that a Jesus whose humanity differed from ours (apart from its sinlessness) could not be our Savior. This has been an essential Christian teaching since the condemnation of Apollinarius.

Some have said it is superfluous to argue against attaching the language of preexistence to Jesus of Nazareth because no one has claimed preexistence for Jesus. Several recent systematic theologians, however, seem to make precisely that claim. Stanley Grenz writes:

> Whatever it may mean, according to the New Testament, preexistence is an attribute describing Jesus of Nazareth. We are concerned, therefore, to understand the preexistence of *Jesus,* and not that of some purported eternal being—whether Logos or the Son—viewed apart from him. . . . We must never use preexistence as a means of separating the Son from Jesus of Nazareth, in order to speculate about the activities of the Logos apart from the historical person.[19]

The language of this passage seems to be attacking a Nestorian interpretation of Jesus, but in rejecting something that must be rejected—Nestorianism—it appears to affirm something that must also be rejected, namely, the preexistence of Christ's human nature. Such an affirmation would remove the power of what Paul wrote about the incarnation, especially in Philippians 2:6-11 and 2 Corinthians 8:9. It would appear to make humanity an eternal part of the Godhead, thereby reducing the significance of the incarnation with its claim that "God became man" in Jesus Christ. When someone speaks of the preexistence of Jesus, that person needs to specify what he or she means by *Jesus.* Is it the God-man, the one who would come to be known as Jesus after the incarnation, or is it someone else?

The language of a preexistent Jesus also detracts from the power of the incarnation's message that "God became man." Christian tradition has taught that

---

[17]H. R. Mackintosh, *The Doctrine of the Person of Christ,* 2nd ed. (Edinburgh: T & T Clark, 1913), p. 457. Mackintosh adds that we cannot simply equate the preexistent Son of God with the risen Lord Jesus because the two are separated by "a vast redemptive net of self-humiliation, initiated on the Divine side of reality."

[18]John Macquarrie, *Jesus Christ in Modern Thought* (London: SCM Press, 1990), pp. 389-90.

[19]Stanley J. Grenz, *Theology for the Community of God* (Nashville: Broadman & Holman, 1994), pp. 406-7.

there is something different about the Godhead after Easter. We must consider the incarnation as "something 'new' even for God, for the Son was not eternally man any more than the Father was eternally Creator."[20] C. E. B. Cranfield says, "It is precisely this, that He is now at God's right hand not only as God but also as Man, that is the new thing about the exaltation of Christ over against the glory possessed by the Son of God from eternity."[21]

On Christmas as well as on Good Friday, God in the person of the Son humbled himself. He first condescended to take to himself human nature and then to die for the salvation of fallen humanity. In exploring the preexistence of Christ we are probing the mystery of the Godhead, and we must do so humbly. The witness of Scripture requires that we affirm certain things about this mystery, it permits us to suggest certain other things, but it also requires we deny some things. I believe the preexistence of the man Jesus falls into the third category. Gerald O'Collins says that to believe the human consciousness of Jesus preexisted in heaven "would be to threaten the genuineness of his humanity" and "any notion of the preexistence of Jesus' humanity or human nature would be incompatible with Chalcedon." But the preexistence of the person we know historically as Jesus is another matter altogether.[22] This is because the preexistent person is God the Son, who would assume human nature only at the incarnation.

BARTH ON CHRIST'S PREEXISTENCE

Karl Barth pointed in the direction of the preexistent God-man with his virtual identification of ideal and real preexistence.[23] Barth's discussion occurs within his consideration of Christ's election and, while seemingly essential to his argument, is not its focus. He argues that Christ has been foreordained as the elected man, and this elected man is distinct from God from the beginning of creation, not only from the incarnation. This elect man is part of creation, but a part of creation inseparably linked with the eternal Son of God. Barth's language, and he is struggling to express the inexpressible, seems to identify foreordination with existence: when God decrees something, it is, not it will be. This conflation

---

[20]T. F. Torrance, *The Trinitarian Faith* (Edinburgh: T & T Clark, 1995), p. 155. Torrance writes, "God was always Father, not always Creator, but now he is Creator as well as Father. It is in similar terms that we may speak of the eternal Son who *became* Man. The Son was always Son of God, but now he is Man as well as God" (ibid., p. 88).

[21]C. E. B. Cranfield, *A Critical and Exegetical Commentary on the Epistle to the Romans,* International Critical Commentary (Edinburgh: T & T Clark, 1980), 1:60 n. 3.

[22]Gerald O'Collins, *Christology* (New York: Oxford University Press, 1995), p. 243.

[23]Karl Barth, *Church Dogmatics* 2/2, trans. Geoffrey Bromiley et al. (Edinburgh: T & T Clark, 1975), pp. 107ff.

of real and ideal preexistence, if taken to its logical conclusion, has the potential of raising a separate set of problems.

Recognizing the difficulty of affirming the preexistence of Christ's humanity, Donald Bloesch poses the key question regarding Barth's approach: "If there is no Logos apart from the flesh *(logos asarkos)*, as Karl Barth maintains, then Jesus too and not just the Word preexisted with God in eternity. But if this is so, can we then speak of a real 'incarnation'?"[24] Bloesch answers affirmatively. He believes several New Testament authors teach Christ's preexistent humanity.[25] But Bloesch then says affirming the preexistent humanity of Jesus is a way of saying the incarnation was not an absolute beginning, that "there is a continuity between the historical Jesus and the eternal Christ."[26] He adds that Barth did not believe Jesus existed in the flesh from eternity, but "that the man Jesus was prefigured in the eternal Word of God." Thus the Word identified himself with Jesus prior to the incarnation but only assumed human flesh after his conception.[27] This is unexceptionable; the question becomes why use what is clearly misleading language to say the Son of God was not acting contrary to his nature by becoming incarnate? But then Bloesch explains Barth in this way:

> Barth argues that the incarnation happened in eternity before all time, and its occurrence in time is a transition from concealment to publicity. He does not mean that the male Jesus preexisted as a pretemporal spirit but that the Son of God chose to become Jesus before the actual incarnation in history.[28]

This is speculation rather than biblical exegesis and involves the question of the nature of time, which is what the relationship between personal preexistence and foreordination is all about. As the passage I quote has presented the position, it seems to understate the significance of human history in the divine revelation and plan. In doing so, it adds nothing to the traditional language of incarnation, except the possibility of confusion. But that the Son of God chose to become incarnate prior to the event seems commonsensical.

Paul Molnar has examined Barth's view of the *logos asarkos* and has come to

---

[24]Donald G. Bloesch, *Jesus Christ* (Downers Grove, Ill.: InterVarsity Press, 1997), pp. 132-33.

[25]Ibid., pp. 134-35. He cites the following verses as teaching Christ's preexistent humanity: Jn 1:15; 6:62; 8:58; 17:5; 1 Cor 8:6; Col 1:15; 2 Tim 1:9; Heb 13:8; 1 Pet 1:20; Rev 13:8; and other verses he does not list. One needs to bring a belief in Christ's preexistent humanity to these verses to find it there—they do not deny the teaching, but neither do they require it. Many are passages I cited in earlier chapters as teaching the preexistence of the Son of God.

[26]Ibid., pp. 141-42.

[27]Ibid., p. 138. To use the language of earlier chapters, we could say Bloesch is talking about the *ideal* preexistence of the man Jesus.

[28]Ibid., p. 138.

a somewhat different conclusion from Bloesch. He says Barth was concerned about the teaching because he feared it might be used to get around God's self-revelation in Christ, but he also recognized the teaching is an essential part of the doctrine of the Trinity. At the same time, Jesus' human nature came into existence at a particular point in space and time; the preexistent Son of God did not bring it with him to the incarnation.[29]

While the language of a preexistent Jesus might be theologically acceptable if it is made clear that the only thing being done is to use the name of the incarnate God-man for the preincarnate Son of God, this is at best theological shorthand. Its use in technical theology is confusing and misleading. If the intent, however, is to say God the Son has always been the God-man, this has no biblical warrant. It is simply wrong. The best path, because it is the clearest and most accurate, is not to speak of a preexistent Jesus.

PREEXISTENCE AND INCARNATION

In making possible the incarnation—because incarnation is impossible unless a person exists to become incarnate—the doctrine of Christ's preexistence says the Son personally existed at the side of God before he existed at our side. That is an essential truth for the biblical idea of salvation, but it also tells us a very important truth about God. It says God loves us so much that he came in person to save us; he did not send a representative or agent. John Wright states my concern in the negative: "As I contemplate a purely human Jesus, though one in whom the Spirit is fully operative, I experience an immense sadness and sense of loss: for this would mean that God after all did not love us enough to become one of us and die for us."[30] O. C. Quick adds, "Such love as the New Testament attributes to God can only be revealed to man in person and in act. No mere message or oracle on the lips of a semi-divine mediator, or of a man, however divinely inspired, could ever have conveyed it."[31]

The preexistence the church attributes to Christ is a real or personal preexistence. Without that there could be no true deity. Some form of ideal preexistence may be consistent with Christ's humanity, but never with his deity. Yet it is his deity that guarantees the efficacy of Christ's salvific work. Because the human race is under God's judgment as a result of its rebellion, it cannot offer God satisfaction for its sin. That must come from outside. In both Testaments, the Bi-

[29]Paul D. Molnar, *Divine Freedom and the Doctrine of the Immanent Trinity* (New York: Continuum, 2002), pp. 61ff.
[30]John H. Wright, "Roger Haight's Spirit Christology," *Theological Studies* 53 (1992): 734.
[31]O. C. Quick, *Doctrines of the Church* (London: Nisbet, 1938), p. 142.

ble tells us God himself provides satisfaction for us. Paul did not lay out systematically the details of Christ's person and work as we might find it in a systematic
theology. He did, however, describe as God's Son the one who offered the sacrifice (Rom 5:10), presenting Christ's sacrificial death as God's gift to humanity
(Rom 5:16) and the demonstration of God's love (Rom 5:8). This sonship language certainly implies Jesus was more than human, and the language of love
and gift reinforces the impression of Christ's essential relationship with God.
Otherwise, the love is rather paltry and the gift something given at little or no
cost to God. Yet Paul described this as a grand and gracious action on God's
part. The writer of Hebrews described the one who "provided purification for
sins" (Heb 1:3) in terms of deity. The reality of Christ's preexistence was further
affirmed when the New Testament writers described Christ as having made decisions to humble himself to assume human existence and even to suffer death.
If those early theologians who linked the preexistent Christ with the angel of
the Lord and other Old Testament theophanies were correct, the preexistent
Christ not only made decisions, he acted.

The incarnation links who Christ is with what he has accomplished. Christ's
ministry, death and resurrection were possible only because he lived within human history. They had value only because he was more than simply another
member of fallen humanity. The doctrine of Christ's preexistence underpins the
claim to Christ's deity that is so necessary for his work to be efficacious. A human born under Adam and sharing the common human condition would have
been just one more part of the problem, not the solution. This is not to deny
Jesus of Nazareth shared fully in human existence, possessing a complete human nature. It is simply to say Christ's human nature was as God intended ours
to be; it was untainted by either original or performed sin.[32]

FUNCTION VERSUS BEING?

This century has witnessed an argument between those who advocate an ontological christology and those who favor a functional christology. The latter has
frequently been associated with an emphasis on Christ's humanity at the expense of his deity. The response of many theologians to this argument (echoing
the thinking of the church over the centuries) has been that if we are to understand Jesus Christ at all, we must see him in terms of both function and being,

---

[32]In saying this I part company with those who assert that the Son took to himself a fallen human nature, although a fallen human nature that itself remained unsullied by performance of
sinful acts. I base my position on the belief that a fallen human nature bears with it the guilt
of original sin. Even this would have left Jesus in need of a savior himself. And as Adam and
Eve showed, an unfallen human nature is no guarantee against succumbing to temptation.

of humanity and deity. Dupuis says, "Implied in *what* he is *for us* is *who* he is *in himself*. Functional Christology naturally ends with questions concerning the person of Jesus Christ, and the answer to these necessarily marks the advent of a Christology which rises from the functional to the ontological level. The inner dynamic of the Easter faith leads from one to the other."[33] The early church's (and the biblical) recognition that function makes sense only in the context of prior being has been accepted by many recent theologians. Those who have rejected the need to include ontology in any discussion of function have yet to justify their decision. If Jesus Christ is at the heart of our faith, we must be able to say who he is if we hope to justify any claim about what he has done.[34]

The first generation of Christians reached its understanding of Jesus generally in terms of what is called a christology from below—although the resurrection, the definitive revelation of Jesus' person, hardly seems to qualify as christology from below—and some modern scholars advocate that we too pursue our christology from below rather than from above. But the disciples' christology from below was a failure without the resurrection. This is evident from any reading of the Gospels. It is true the Synoptic Gospels approach Jesus "from below," but the authors who did so already knew who Jesus was; they wanted to provoke or confirm their readers in this belief as they led them along the path the first disciples trod.

The New Testament also contains what has been called christology from above—in John's Gospel—and this approach was characteristic of the early church. I am skeptical of the possibility of a pure christology from below today because it seems to require that we somehow go back before Easter as if it hadn't happened, and that is impossible. Klaas Runia expresses his skepticism this way:

> The fundamental question, of course, is whether the model used by John (and also by Paul and the writer of Hebrews . . .) is just "a" model that can be discarded and replaced at will. Or does it represent the most comprehensive and inclusive model, which is able to incorporate all the valuable elements of other models, while the latter models are too limited to include the fundamental concern of the incarnational model? Or, to put it another way, once Jesus' coming has been revealed in terms of incarnation, can one still go back to earlier levels of understanding and deal with "incarnation" as just one of the many models which are at our disposal?[35]

---

[33]Dupuis, *Who Do You Say I Am?* p. 69.

[34]See Peter Hinchliff, "Christology and Tradition," in *God Incarnate,* ed. A. E. Harvey (London: SPCK, 1981), p. 95.

[35]Klaas Runia, *The Present-Day Christological Debate* (Downers Grove: InterVarsity, 1984), p. 77.

While biblical scholars and theologians since World War II have corrected a docetic tendency evident among conservatives by reminding Christians that Jesus was fully human, some have gone beyond this to ignore or downplay his deity. In terms of the soteriological interest we have seen as early as Paul's first letters, this is a no less fatal flaw than the docetic. Roger Haight says this modern historical consciousness begins by stressing Jesus' humanity in contrast to what he calls "an overly abstract portrayal of the identity and status of Jesus."[36] He denies the approach he advocates has a negative effect on our appreciation of Christ's deity (which he calls divinity), but he does say how that deity should be expressed is "an open question." John Knox, however, says, "There is no way of distinguishing Jesus' humanity from ours which does not deny the reality of his manhood in every sense which makes the affirmation of it significant." For Knox, the content of the term *preexistence* would distinguish Christ from us in an unacceptable way. "We can have the humanity without the pre-existence and we can have the pre-existence without the humanity. *There is absolutely no way of having both.*"[37] I see no justification for this blanket claim. Colin Gunton agrees: "What is required is the possibility of the consistency of divine pre-existence and full humanity. In that case, we are back to the same problem, which seems to be an assumption that the ascription of divinity, whether pre-existent or otherwise, is inconsistent with a doctrine of the humanity of Christ that is to be saved from docetism."[38] When the renewed appreciation of Christ's humanity has been balanced with his preincarnate deity, the result is an increased appreciation of the incarnation and of God's graciousness and love in effecting our salvation.

Classic christology affirms the incarnate Christ was one divine person existing in two complete and distinct natures, divine and human. The definition of Chalcedon stated it this way in A.D. 451:

> Following the holy Fathers we teach with one voice that the Son [of God] and our Lord Jesus Christ is to be confessed as one and the same [Person], that he is perfect in Godhead and perfect in manhood, very God and very man, of a reasonable soul and [human] body consisting, consubstantial with the Father as touching his Godhead, and consubstantial with us as touching his manhood; made in all things like unto us, sin only excepted; begotten of his Father before the worlds according to

---

[36]Roger Haight, "The Case for Spirit Christology," *Theological Studies* 53 (1992): 257.

[37]John Knox, *The Humanity and Divinity of Christ* (Cambridge: Cambridge University Press, 1967), p. 106 (emphasis added).

[38]Colin Gunton, *Yesterday & Today* (Grand Rapids: Eerdmans, 1983), p. 68. What we will find with Knox and theologians sharing his view is that having rejected the doctrine of Christ's preexistence they are unable consistently and coherently to hold on to his deity.

his Godhead; but in these last days for us men and for our salvation born [into the world] of the Virgin Mary, the Mother of God according to his manhood.[39]

The passage goes on to detail the distinctiveness of Christ's divine and human natures and the unity of the person possessing the two natures. It claims the testimony of the Old Testament prophets, Jesus himself and the creed of Nicea as its support.

The council taught the unity of Christ's person and the duality of his natures because it was convinced anything else would endanger the possibility of human salvation. The deity has priority, and preexistence is presumed. Given the presumption of Christ's preexistence, his person could only be deity. The modern attempt to interpret Chalcedon as affirming a human person to which a divine nature has been somehow attached is nonsensical. This would require that divine nature came into being, a concept utterly at odds with the meaning of deity, at least with the biblical meaning of deity, and that the nature of deity be able to exist separate from the person of deity. Belief in Christ's preexistence, which we have seen predates Chalcedon by over four centuries, requires what in broad outline the council taught. The details are the necessary consequence of this, formulated in order to preserve the possibility of Christ's salvific work. Hebblethwaite draws, as did the bishops at Chalcedon, on the church's belief that at the heart of Jesus' life lies the reality of God, and concludes, "If indeed the human life of Jesus Christ is lived out from a centre in God, then we shall need to speak of his pre-existence. For that centre in God must be thought of as ontologically and temporally . . . prior to his incarnate life. The 'pre-existence' of Christ is therefore the 'pre-existence' of God the Son."[40]

Christology leads naturally to the doctrine of the Trinity. This was true in the patristic age and it remains true today. J. L. Houlden says, "The lynch-pin [of the doctrine of the Trinity] was the assertion of the pre-existence of Christ." He draws together evidence from Paul, Hebrews and John that identifies Christ with God, presents him as God's mediator, and describes his role in creation to conclude, "All these disparate ideas come together in the key concept of the pre-existence of Christ."[41] The doctrine of the Trinity is an admittedly difficult concept and attempts to explain it often err on one side or the other, but it does not seem possible to understand either Jesus of Nazareth or God's dealings with the

---

[39]Philip Schaff and Henry Wace, eds., *A Select Library of Nicene and Post-Nicene Fathers of the Christian Church,* The Seven Ecumenical Councils, vol. 14 (Grand Rapids: Eerdmans, 1979), p. 264.
[40]Brian Hebblethwaite, *The Incarnation* (Cambridge: Cambridge University Press, 1987), p. 71.
[41]J. L. Houlden, "The Doctrine of the Trinity and the Person of Christ," *Church Quarterly Review* 169 (1968): 10.

human race apart from this doctrine. That is to say, the Trinity was not some marvelous idea early Christians thought up as a result of their philosophical training and speculative interests, but was instead the only conclusion they could draw from their reading of the Old Testament and their experience of Jesus' words, deeds, and resurrection. Augustine summed up the thinking of the early church about trinitarian doctrine when he said "So we say three persons, not in order to say that precisely, but in order not to be reduced to silence."[42] Helmut Thielicke also considers Christ's preexistence essential to any serious trinitarian theology:

> Christ's pre-existence is in fact an inalienable element in any theology with a Trinitarian orientation. The problem is not whether pre-existence has to be accepted but how it is to be expressed. Its denial is always connected to an Antiochene Christology which finally leads to an understanding of Christ merely as the most human of men. . . . No matter how we may speak of Christ's pre-existence, and no matter how dubious many of our reflections on it may be, the thesis at issue, namely, that Christ's reality is not restricted to his historical existence, but includes the "yesterday, today, and forever," is still an essential element in Christian theology.[43]

CHRIST, THE SELF-REVELATION OF GOD

In John's Gospel we read that on the eve of Calvary the disciples asked Jesus to show them God the Father. Jesus responded bluntly, "If you've seen me, you've seen the Father." The New Testament presents Jesus as the self-revelation of God. God certainly revealed himself in creation and the Old Testament, but neither of these was complete. Both were external to God himself. Both looked forward to a fuller, final revelation. This occurred with the incarnation of the Son. In Paul, Hebrews, John and even Matthew we see Jesus as the one who makes God known. Each writer described Jesus in language that either explicitly or implicitly included his deity. For John the completeness of this revelation is possible because the Son existed with God before coming to earth to reveal him to humanity. This is important. Were the incarnate Christ not the preexistent Son, we would merely have one more holy man telling us what he thinks God is like and what he thinks God expects of us. As Lesslie Newbigen reminds us,

---

[42]Augustine *De Trinitate* 5.9.10, in Augustine, *The Trinity*, ed. John E. Rotelle, trans. Edmund Hill (Brooklyn: New City Press, 1991), p. 196.

[43]Helmut Thielicke, *The Evangelical Faith*, trans. Geoffrey W. Bromiley (Grand Rapids: Eerdmans, 1977), 2:264. I disagree with Thielicke's blanket conclusion about Antiochene christology, but not his basic point that christology without preexistence becomes merely Jesusology. Wright's complaint about the disappointment that results when Jesus is no more than God's human agent seems to be Thielicke's objection in different words.

the gospel is a story. While there are many different stories in human history, the gospel is the true story, and all others must be evaluated in reference to it.[44] Because Jesus is who he is, we see God in action. There is no opportunity for mistranslation, no occasion to suggest God might see things differently if only he could see them from our perspective. Least of all is it possible to suggest that for some reason God does not care. The incarnation of the preexistent Son demonstrates the real measure of caring is not us but God. Do we care as much as God does? Will we go as far for others (or God) as God has gone for us?

T. F. Torrance, writing about the Trinity, says the Christian understanding of God is not something abstract and metaphysical.

> The self-revelation of God in the Gospel amounts to the greatest *revolution in our knowledge of God*. It is precisely when we grasp its truth that we discern the enormous significance of the doctrine of the Holy Trinity. For Judaism or for Greek philosophy, or indeed for every religion apart from Christianity, God remains ultimately incomprehensible to men and women in the bare and unfigured simplicity of his being. . . . The Word of God and the Spirit of God are not just ephemeral modes of God's presence to us in history; nor are they transient media external to himself through which God has revealed to us something about himself; they belong to what God ever is in his communion with us. They are objective ontological forms of his self-giving and self-imparting in the dynamic outgoing of the holy love which God himself is.[45]

What we find Jesus revealing about God is not only his perfection, constancy and holiness—although we do see him revealing these—but his unsurpassable and gracious love. In Jesus we see this love in the condescension of the preexistent Son, in his becoming human and, because of his incarnation, in his words and deeds, including his death on the cross. Because Christ is the preexistent Son, "he is not some created intermediary between God and the world but the very word and Son of God who eternally inheres in the Being of God so that for us to know God in Jesus Christ, and to know him as the God and Father of the Lord Jesus Christ, is really to know God as he is in himself in his eternal Being as God and in the transcendent Love that God is."[46]

One great concern of our age is freedom, but this freedom is often understood merely as the absence of limits. Christianity has never understood freedom in this way, and neither did pre-Enlightenment societies. According to Walter Kasper, our assertion of Christ's preexistence constitutes an affirmation

[44]Lesslie Newbigen, *Proper Confidence* (Grand Rapids: Eerdmans, 1995), p. 76.
[45]Thomas F. Torrance, *The Christian Doctrine of God* (Edinburgh: T & T Clark, 1996), p. 3.
[46]Ibid., p. 18.

that "God's self-giving love has entered once and for all into history in order that this self-disclosure of God's freedom in love may ground the freedom of the children of God."[47] I believe Kasper is saying that through his incarnation and historical existence, Jesus has revealed to us the true nature of freedom. Elsewhere, Kasper says because in Christ God has "definitively, unreservedly, and unsurpassedly" revealed himself, Christ is part of the definition of God's essential nature. "Thus the New Testament pre-existence statements lead to a new, comprehensive interpretation of the term God."[48]

In revealing God to us, the preexistent Son took to himself a full human nature, becoming the God-man. In doing so, he demonstrated something about both God and humanity. Some theologians object that the term God-man is a logical contradiction, but this is a philosophical claim with no evidential basis. C. Stephen Evans finds no good reason to conclude on metaphysical grounds that God cannot become a human.[49] Dupuis writes, "Humans cannot become God, but God can become human, and did in Jesus Christ. This is the unheard-of affirmation to which the faith reflection of the early Christians was inescapably leading, if only the implications of the Christology of the early kerygma were fully developed."[50] Those who say that for God to have become human or exist in three persons is incomprehensible forget they are talking about the nature of God, and it never has been a requirement that the creature comprehend fully the Creator. Turner challenges those who complain christological doctrine is incomprehensible and thus argue in favor of something easier to understand:

> Adherents of a Christology from the side of God would claim that the uniqueness of the Incarnation must ultimately transcend human efforts to grasp it completely. . . . The fact [of what God has done] itself is too big for human comprehension and does not admit of a neat and tidy solution which answers all the questions and solves all the problems. . . . This is why words like mystery and paradox, however unfashionable they may be in the present thought-climate, are important for Christology. . . . It is not a direct appeal to the irrational, otherwise Christianity could not have gotten started at all, but a realistic assessment that there are limits beyond which human thought cannot carry us, while its subject-matter goes on. It is not the "murder of logic" but an admission that human logic is not omnicompetent in the expression of divine truth.[51]

[47]Walter Kasper, *The God of Jesus Christ,* trans. Matthew J. O'Connell (New York: Crossroad, 1984), pp. 176-77.
[48]Walter Kasper, *Jesus the Christ,* trans. V. Green (New York: Paulist, 1976), p. 175.
[49]C. Stephen Evans, *The Historical Jesus and the Christ of Faith* (Oxford: Oxford University Press, 1996), p. 170.
[50]Dupuis, *Who Do You Say I Am?* p. 67.
[51]Turner, *Jesus the Christ,* pp. 130-31.

The role of the preexistent Christ in relation to the creation speaks clearly about God's valuation of the created order. In Colossians, Paul described Christ as Creator, Sustainer and Redeemer of the creation. Only as the preexistent One could Christ have played any role in the creation of the world, yet Paul described him as the key actor. Paul described the sustaining of the world as an ongoing process that began at creation, so it seems equally necessary that this was part of Christ's preexistent role. Christ's redemptive work occurred at the end of his incarnate life, but, as we have seen, it derived its worth from Christ's essential deity, something that also requires his preexistence. Jean Galot denies preexistence is "a luxury of theological speculation." On the contrary, it is important because it is about Christ's relation to humanity:

> He who possesses eternity in its fulness in common with the Father has the power to make men share in it by communicating eternal life to them. Furthermore, it is in the pre-existence that there is situated the decision of the redeeming incarnation, the act of love which has brought about the coming of the Son among men. The mystery is governed by a divine attitude; it is the expression of a divine dynamism which dominates all the earthly life of Jesus by being anterior to it.[52]

Paul's description of the preexistent Christ's involvement with creation has several important consequences. First, it says the existence and order of the creation are part of God's plan, not an accident. The world and we who live in it are not the product of mindless mutations over unnumbered years. Second, and implied in the existence of any divine plan, the creation and its creatures had worth to God. Humanity, as the species created in the divine image and into which the Son of God was incarnated, had special worth. Third, despite the reality of human sin and rebellion, the creation and we human creatures continue to have worth in God's eyes. This is why the preexistent Son has sustained the created order rather than destroying it or allowing it to disintegrate. No less, it is the reason why he became incarnate and died to save fallen humanity and set the creation aright, as Paul wrote in Romans 8.

Christians, like most other people, live by the principle that effects must have adequate causes, or that the effect cannot be greater than its cause. As Quick points out, this means our judgment about the adequacy of an ostensible cause necessarily depends on our conclusion about the worth of its effect. He reminds us this means what we think about the worth of Christian faith necessarily affects our valuation of "the historical causes which are adequate to account for

[52]Jean Galot, *Vers une Nouvelle Christologie,* pp. 62ff., quoted in E. L. Mascall, *Theology and the Gospel of Christ* (London: SPCK, 1977), p. 175.

it."[53] This is not a comprehensive defense of Christ's preexistence, but it reminds us that if Christianity provides peace with God and meaning to life, there must be more to Jesus' story than that of a great moral teacher or an exemplary life.

CHRISTIAN SPIRITUALITY AND THE PREEXISTENT CHRIST

Essential to our Christian faith but often ignored in the arguments between various interpretations of Jesus Christ's person and work is what Tim Dearborn calls incarnational spirituality. Just as I have challenged people when considering different worldviews to ask whether they can live their life consistently with this outlook on the world, so too I would frame this spirituality as a question: Can I worship God consistently if this is my theology? Those of us trained in theology rarely encountered this approach in the classroom; we were too busy learning the views of many different theologians and why they were right or wrong. Some of us learned to organize our thinking in terms of one of the great traditions, in my case the Reformed tradition. This is necessary, but it is not enough, certainly not if Barth is correct that theology is properly done only within the context of faith. Dearborn presents the need in this way:

> Our spirituality does not require us to strive to escape into some ideal realm uncontaminated by evil and sin. Christian spirituality is historical—within time—and mundane—within the world; for it is rooted in the Incarnation of the Son of God in the man Jesus of Nazareth. . . . As a result, we find God within our broken, fallen lives and world. *In Christ we find meaning and hope in the mundane moments of our lives.*[54]

The sentence I have emphasized says we need to be able to explain why we can say of an obscure carpenter executed at a young age in Roman-occupied Palestine two thousand years that he provides meaning and hope for our lives today.

The traditional alternatives to acknowledging his preexistent deity do not satisfy. Like Wright, I find it depressing to think of Jesus simply as my example, because I cannot come close to emulating his quality of living. I might be tempted, like Muslims, to wonder, if Jesus lived so faithfully for God, why God would abandon him to ignominious death. But unlike Muslims I cannot deny it happened. Why would a mere human be able to bridge the chasm between sinful humanity and the holy God? Is supreme God consciousness, whatever that might mean, enough to lift him above the morass where the rest of us live our

---

[53]Quick, *Doctrines of the Church,* p. 155.
[54]Tim Dearborn, *Taste & See* (Downers Grove, Ill.: InterVarsity Press, 1996), pp. 50-51 (emphasis added).

lives day in and day out? For me and the entire historic tradition of Christianity, this is not good enough. We need more. The first disciples needed more to make sense of their experience of Jesus. As Karl-Josef Kuschel writes, "Statements about the origin of Jesus from God remain indissolubly bound up with human spiritual experiences of the Christ who is exalted to God. This is the legitimate biblical foundation for reflection on the Father, Son, and Spirit, the differentiation between them and their unity."[55]

As the New Testament writers, especially the author of Hebrews, make clear, recognition that Jesus has made us right with God is central to Christian faith. Moberly, writing about a contemporary advocate of Spirit christology, says:

> Yet the fact that it is those who have laid greater stress on the radical nature of sin and salvation—over against a stance which is prone to succumb to moralism—who have generally been recognized as somehow the more central and authentically Christian voices, should at least make one hesitant in espousing the sort of view of salvation that Lampe proposes. And doubts about his soteriology will also become doubts about his Christology.[56]

The Jesus we worship must be great enough to make us recognize the enormity of our sin and the greatness of God's grace in saving us. Yet he must also fit the Gospel picture of him as one who was immersed in our world and whom sinners could approach. Neither Jesus the god nor Jesus the human suffices; we need both aspects of Jesus and this requires his preexistence and incarnation.

Our modern age emphasizes pluralism in all things, including religion. Christianity has existed in a world characterized by plurality from its beginning, but today advocates of pluralism can be found within the church as well as outside. They portray Christianity as one among many ways to God and Jesus as one of the great religious leaders of world history. This is an option only if everything I have said so far about Christ's preexistence is untrue.

> The vitally significant fact of Christ's preexistence with God differentiates Him from all the prophets, teachers, and revealers of God that have appeared during the long course of religious history. "In the beginning was the Word" is the transcendent note which exalts Him above all temporal and finite evolution by assigning Him a place in ultimate reality.[57]

If Jesus Christ is indeed God among us in a unique, unsurpassable and es-

---

[55]Karl-Josef Kuschel, *Born Before All Time?* trans. John Bowden (New York: Crossroad, 1992), p. 494.
[56]Moberly, "God Incarnate," p. 49.
[57]S. F. Davenport, *Immanence and Incarnation* (Cambridge: Cambridge University Press, 1925), p. 268.

sential way, then the faith that worships Jesus is the truth, and to the extent they are not in agreement with that faith all other religions are false. This is not to deny other religions might contain elements of truth, but it does mean these elements lack salvific value.[58]

CONCLUSION

How we understand one part of Christian faith influences how we see every other part. Whether or not we accept the doctrine of Christ's preexistence, and how we interpret that doctrine if we do, determines what we understand Christianity to be. It is obvious the doctrine governs our understanding of Jesus, but it equally governs what we believe about God and salvation. Every essential Christian belief rides on our acceptance or rejection of Christ's preexistent deity.

Rejecting Christ's personal preexistence means denying his incarnation and deity. This means the historic Christian belief in Jesus' saving work must be modified or rejected. Christians confess God as Father, Son and Holy Spirit. We can only know that if Christ was indeed the preexistent Son who came from the Father to reveal God.

Adoptionism in some form has always been a tempting alternative to incarnational christology. Instead of solving the problems preexistence and incarnation are accused of causing, however, adoptionism merely substitutes a different set. Offering a salvation based on revelation and example, it can only be a cause of despair for those who recognize the awfulness of human sin and the holiness of God. Adoptionism does preserve Christ's humanity—a key modern concern—but it does so at the cost of denying his deity. Rightly understood, the doctrines of preexistence and incarnation affirm both Christ's deity and humanity.

One question we need to ask of any broad outlook on the world is whether we can live with its implications. The historic Christian faith, with Christ's preexistence as one of its essential beliefs, makes the best sense of our world and ourselves. We can live and believe it consistently, and that some have not done so does not make it untrue. In our generation, however, the doctrine of Christ's preexistence has come under increasing attack for a variety of reasons. The time has come to turn to these objections to examine their strengths and weaknesses and to consider the dynamic that has motivated them.

---

[58]In chap. 9, some of the most vigorous opponents of the traditional doctrine of Christ's preexistence argue their case precisely because the doctrine relativizes all other religious claims, and, considering this conclusion unacceptable in the modern world, they have chosen to reject the doctrine that leads inescapably to the conclusion. It is necessary to realize the objection is a priori, it is not the result of a careful sifting of the evidence.

9

THE PREEXISTENCE OF CHRIST
AND MODERN THEOLOGY

The natural place to begin considering how Christ's preexistence fits into modern theology is with the father of modern theology, Friedrich Schleiermacher. Because he was unsure where it belonged in his theology yet did not want to discard it, Schleiermacher put the doctrine of the Trinity at the end of his *Glaubenslehre*. His description of Jesus as a man with perfect God consciousness is a classic expression of the desire to honor Jesus without affirming his deity. This left Schleiermacher room for no more than an ideal preexistence. Schleiermacher aimed to present Christianity to its "cultured despisers" in a way that removed unnecessary barriers to their acceptance and overcame their disdain. Much modern theology has followed this path in seeking to win over its culture; therefore, it shared Schleiermacher's discomfort with the doctrines of Christ's personal preexistence and deity. Both liberalism and Schleiermacher, one of its leading lights, exemplify one of several understandings of how Christians should relate to the broader culture. They believe culture's concerns and claims must be taken seriously to the point of accommodating them, even allowing them to determine the terms of the discussion.

For Schleiermacher what distinguished Jesus from other humans was "the constant potency of his God-consciousness, which was a veritable existence of God in Him."[1] Jesus was fully and fundamentally human; God's presence in him was an indwelling, not an incarnation. "To ascribe to Christ an absolutely powerful God-consciousness, and to attribute to Him an existence of God in Him, are exactly the same thing."[2] What traditional christology has seen as a difference in kind between Jesus and the rest of humanity, Schleiermacher saw as

---

[1] Friedrich Schleiermacher, *The Christian Faith*, trans. H. R. Mackintosh and J. S. Stewart (Philadelphia: Fortress, 1976), p. 385.
[2] Ibid., p. 387.

one of degree: what each of us possesses in a limited and imperfect way, Jesus possessed fully and perfectly. This emphasis on Jesus' humanity resulted from the fear that traditional christology had succumbed to docetism. Jesus' person originated at his conception and his God consciousness developed over his lifetime. Even to portray Jesus as enjoying perfect God consciousness or complete indwelling by God risked docetism, Schleiermacher believed. On the popular level, his fear of docetism certainly was justified. Too many conservative Christians, even today, describe Jesus simply (and incorrectly) as God, and in doing so they fail to realize the early defenders of orthodoxy fought as hard to defend Christ's humanity as they did his deity.

Seeking to defend Christ's real humanity against its absorption into an utterly divine Christ, Schleiermacher for all intents and purposes gave up Christ's deity. He described the divine in Christ as "the divine love in Christ which, once for all or in every moment—whichever expression be chosen—gave direction to His feelings for the spiritual conditions of men."[3] Christ's deity is functional rather than ontological. It consists in God inspiring and indwelling the man Jesus; it has no room for an incarnation in any meaningful sense of the term. The result of God's action is one who is fully human but only human.

> It is not a special nature which comes into being in this way, one which could and must be distinguished from other human existence; what comes into existence through the being of God in Christ is all perfectly human, and in its totality constitutes a unity, the unity of a natural life-story, in which everything that emerges is purely human, and one thing can be deduced from another, since every moment presupposes those which have gone before, yet in which everything can be completely understood only upon the presupposition of that union through which alone this Person could come into being, so that every moment also reveals the divine in Christ as that which conditions it.[4]

Schleiermacher explicitly denied any preexistent divine person was incarnated in Jesus of Nazareth. Christ's person came into being at his conception.[5]

The fundamental flaw in Schleiermacher's attempt to make Jesus fully human by emphasizing his humanity and denigrating his deity lies in its consequences for salvation. In order for the humanity to accomplish everything required of the Redeemer, the humanity must be transformed out of all similarity to our own. Thomas Weinandy rightly complains:

---

[3]Ibid., p. 407.
[4]Ibid., p. 409.
[5]George H. Tavard, *Images of the Christ* (Washington, D.C.: University Press of America, 1982), p. 75.

Schleiermacher substituted a Christology of God-consciousness. Jesus' divinity consisted in his human consciousness being thoroughly centered upon and absorbed by the divine. Paradoxically, what happens in such a Christology is that, while it is proffered in order to make Jesus more like us, in actual fact, it makes him less like us for it makes his humanity so radically different from our own. There could have been no inner conflict, no true agony or struggle.[6]

By ignoring Christ's deity, Schleiermacher sought to make Christ different from other humans only in degree, but the result was to create a humanity so radically different from ours that Christ again differs from the rest of us in kind. Furthermore, Schleiermacher's attempt separates Christ from us in a way orthodoxy never could. The biblical God-man Jesus is united to us in his humanity; Schleiermacher's Jesus differs from us precisely at the point of his humanity.

Schleiermacher's intent of removing unessential barriers to his contemporaries' belief and making Christianity understandable to early nineteenth century European culture can only be commended. It is an attempt to carry out the church's mandate since Pentecost to proclaim the good news to all peoples and cultures. But by accommodating the rationalism and skepticism of his day, Schleiermacher surrendered an essential Christian belief that the early church had labored long and hard to explain and defend. Schleiermacher's pietistic moderation of the cold rationalism of the Enlightenment puts a human face to God's relationship with the world but offers no satisfying solution to the problem of human sin, which must instead be made less serious.

The weakness of Schleiermacher's approach is evident in the work of many who have followed him. Where it least is evident is in those cases where a concern to make Jesus just like the rest of humanity is joined with a belief in humanity's basic goodness. In that case, we do not need a savior but merely a guide, and a human Jesus who understands perfectly the will of God is an unsurpassable guide.

Schleiermacher's understanding of Jesus necessarily affected other areas of his theology. I have already noted he relocated his discussion of the Trinity to a brief section at the conclusion of his theology.[7] Schleiermacher was clearly uncomfortable with the doctrine in its traditional form because it required Christ's personal preexistence, something he was convinced was incompatible with Jesus' real humanity. He argued in deliberate contrast to traditional theology that "the main points of the ecclesiastical doctrine—the being of God in Christ and in the Christian Church—are independent of the doctrine of the

---

[6]Thomas G. Weinandy, *In the Likeness of Sinful Flesh* (Edinburgh: T & T Clark, 1993), p. 55 n. 2.
[7]In *The Christian Faith,* Schleiermacher devoted less than 20 pages to his discussion of the Trinity out of a total of 751 pages (in the English translation).

Trinity."[8] He was troubled by the language of personhood, fearing that attributing personhood to the preexistent Christ would rob the human Jesus of his independence and thus result in docetism.

Soteriology was equally affected by this christology of indwelling. Belief that Christ died for our sins was replaced by the statement, "The Redeemer assumes believers into the power of His God-consciousness and this is His redemptive activity."[9] Jesus does indeed transform believers to be like him, but for Schleiermacher this could be done without cost. He offers transformation and relationship without the need for redemption. In the New Testament, Jesus distinguished clearly between the relationship he enjoyed with God and the relationship his disciples would enjoy. He invariably spoke of "my Father and your Father," never of "our Father." In Matthew 6 when he taught his disciples to pray "our Father," that was their prayer, not his. Schleiermacher, at least potentially, erased this distinction because his Jesus differed from other humans only in degree, not in kind.

Schleiermacher's Jesus epitomizes human existence. There is no need for a personal preexistence because of what he believed the consequences would be for Christ's humanity and his relationship to and example for humanity. Schleiermacher was correct that a Jesus who is simply God offers us neither an example nor encouragement. For the most part modern objections to the doctrine of Christ's personal preexistence are merely adaptations of Schleiermacher's themes. The points where today's objections move beyond Schleiermacher result from modern critical study of the Bible and concern for a pluralism that validates other world religions.

OBJECTIONS TO CHRIST'S PREEXISTENCE

There are four basic responses to the traditional Christian teaching regarding Christ's personal preexistence. These responses do not stand in isolation. The advocates of each draw from the others to make their arguments and occasionally add additional concerns. Probably the most common objection is that the doctrine of Christ's personal preexistence denigrates or denies his true humanity. An objection gaining increasing currency among one group of scholars is that the doctrine is either inconsistent with or not taught in the Bible. Those interested in interreligious dialogue charge the doctrine is the cause of Christian exclusivism. A fourth position recommends a Spirit christology that portrays Jesus as a man indwelt by the Spirit with no need for his deity, personal pre-

---

[8]Ibid., p. 741.
[9]Ibid., p. 425.

existence or the doctrines affirmed by the early church councils. Despite its ancient pedigree, this approach invariably ends up as adoptionism in some form.
There can be no getting around the truth that the man Jesus of Nazareth was
empowered by the same Spirit as the Old Testament prophets and New Testament apostles, but this is only half of the reality of Jesus. To mistake it for the
whole is as devastating to salvation as an exclusive emphasis on Christ's deity.
We also find in some writers the charge that the mentality underlying such doctrines as Christ's preexistence is out of step with the modern world. I do not
intend to deal with this final claim at length because it misunderstands the nature of Christianity, its relation to the surrounding culture, and the relationship
between God and his creation. It is less an argument than a complaint.

To bring some order to the variety of modern objections to preexistence doctrine, I have organized these four basic responses in terms of their leading representatives. Because most of these representatives argue in terms of more than
one objection, I have tried to order them according to what I consider their primary christological concern to be. Thus I hope to show the unity and structure
of their thinking by incorporating each person's other objections to the doctrine
of Christ's personal preexistence under what I consider to be the key objection
to the doctrine.

Despite their good intentions, I consider each of these objections to the traditional doctrine to be misguided, inconsistent with the biblical evidence and its
classic development, and dangerous to Christian faith and the salvation it offers.
Lesslie Newbigin's comment on all efforts to contextualize Christianity speaks to
my concern:

> Christianity, as it presents itself at any time or place in history for inspection as an
> empirical reality, is always subject to judgment and correction in the light of that
> which it seeks to express and to embody, namely, God's actions for the creation
> and redemption of the world.[10]

Newbigin has identified the standard and what the standard measures. It is significant that he does not mention the cultural norms of the society we live and
work in. This is not because this experienced missionary considers them unim-
portant, but because the focus is on God's activity. Until we are clear about that,
it is useless to consider how we will explain it to our culture. It is dangerous to
Christian faith and practice to make the norms and presuppositions of contemporary culture the driving force of our theology, although some have tried to do so
in every generation and geographic locale since the birth of the church.

---

[10]Lesslie Newbigin, *Proper Confidence* (Grand Rapids: Eerdmans, 1995), p. 52.

A Man Inspired by God

The most common modern objection to the doctrine of Christ's personal preexistence has been that such preexistence is incompatible with the affirmation of Christ's full humanity. He could be preexistent or he could be human, but not both. When forced to choose between the two, the anthropological turn in modern theology has always favored the humanity (although not all those who have taken this turn see a need to choose). Those who follow this path argue a Jesus who differs from other humans in kind rather than in degree cannot be fully human. They see such a Jesus as either swallowing up his humanity in his deity or becoming some third sort of being, part deity and part human, because they consider it nonsense to think one person can be both fully human and fully God at the same time. Actually, this view of Jesus is very old, dating back to Jewish Christians of the first centuries of Christianity. The first position has come down to us under the name Ebionitism and portrays Jesus as a great man of God but no more than that; the second position is Arianism, the christological opinion that almost overwhelmed the church in the fourth century.

Three vocal, modern advocates for the position that Jesus of Nazareth was a human and simply or predominately a human are John Knox, John Macquarrie and Piet Schoonenberg.

John Knox was a New Testament scholar, while the other two were theologians. They are willing to admit the New Testament teaches Christ's preexistence, but they conclude it can be no more than an ideal preexistence. Only an ideal preexistence, they believe, allows the necessary affirmation of Christ's full humanity. This conclusion is presuppositional on their part, thus they offer no argument to justify it. Knox states the position clearly and succinctly:

> There is no way of distinguishing Jesus' humanity from ours which does not deny the reality of his manhood in every sense which makes the affirmation of it significant. But the idea that Jesus' existence as a man was in some self-conscious way continuous with his earlier existence as a heavenly being—and this is surely what has usually been meant by the "pre-existence"—this idea does distinguish his humanity from ours; and there is no way, however circuitous or ingenious, of escaping that fact or its consequences. . . . *We can have the humanity without the pre-existence and we can have the pre-existence without the humanity. There is absolutely no way of having both.*[11]

This reflects the legitimate concern that many Christians in practice have acted as if Jesus is simply God and not the God-man. But the desire to correct an error

---

[11]John Knox, *The Humanity and Divinity of Christ* (Cambridge: Cambridge University Press, 1967), p. 106 (italics added).

in one direction cannot justify an equal error in the opposite direction.

John Knox. At the heart of Knox's argument lies the premise that humanity and deity are not only different, but incompatible. If he is correct, the church took a terribly wrong turn when it began to teach Christ's preexistence. If he is wrong, preexistent deity is a viable doctrine, although the case for it must be made on grounds other than its possibility. There are two questions we need to consider in regard to Knox's position. Where did this idea of the fundamental inconsistency of deity and humanity come from? And is it valid? That is, is it biblical? It will not do, as representatives of this position usually seem to think, simply to state this presupposition as a generally accepted conclusion. We also need to consider the implications of Knox's claim for soteriology, the doctrine of God and other aspects of Christian theology.

Although Knox's conclusion results from his premise that humanity and deity are incompatible, he tries to demonstrate from the New Testament, particularly Paul, that Christ's personal preexistence is not a legitimate biblical teaching. Knox admits belief in Christ's preexistence arose early in the church as a result of reflection on Christ's resurrection and postresurrection status.[12] This means, he says, that belief in Christ's preexistence was not the product of evolutionary thinking where Christ was progressively exalted beyond his earthly existence (as some other New Testament scholars have argued). In fact, "the doctrine of pre-existence was the first, not the last, consequence of reflection upon the question: 'Who *was* this person whom we knew as friend and teacher and whom we now know as Savior and Lord?' "[13] According to Knox, belief in Christ's preexistence preceded "the gradual exaltation of his earthly life," by which he means the increasingly supernatural interpretation of Jesus' earthly life that he sees as more and more evident as we move from the Synoptic Gospels into John. "Reflection upon the resurrection led to the idea of pre-existence, and reflection upon the pre-existence led to the gradual supernaturalizing of Jesus' whole career."[14] The option of a gradual evolutionary development—still proposed by some even today—simply cannot be fit within the time available: "Such a process would have required time and hardly could have been completed early enough to account for the general acceptance of the idea in the period of Paul's letters."[15] In fact, he describes the development of belief in Christ's

---

[12]Knox, *Humanity and Divinity*, pp. 10-11. "Reflection on the resurrection and on the postresurrection status of Christ led directly and immediately to the affirmation of his preexistence" (ibid.).

[13]John Knox, *Jesus Lord and Christ* (New York: Harper & Brothers, 1958), p. 150.

[14]Ibid., p. 147.

[15]Knox, *Humanity and Divinity*, p. 11.

preexistence as the direct result of reflection on the resurrection as "inherently probable." Despite this, Knox says in the same passage that Paul both took Christ's preexistence for granted and evidently shares an "adoptionist" view of the significance of the resurrection.

As early as Paul, belief in Christ's preexistence was widespread. Knox acknowledges there is evidence in Paul's letters that "he identified the Pre-existent Christ with the hypostatized Logos or Wisdom of God, who according to certain Hellenistic Jewish leaders, functioned as God's agent and mediator in creating and sustaining the world."[16] In Philippians 2:6-11 Knox recognizes that Paul combined Christ's preexistent Godhood, historical manhood and final exaltation to form a complete picture. "This passage makes quite clear that Paul was able to hold closely together a belief in the divine pre-existence of Jesus [sic] and a recognition of the lowly and unqualified humanity of the earthly life."[17]

What is surprising about Knox's position is that having offered the evidence he does, Knox proceeds to deny the possibility of Christ's personal preexistence and incarnation. "Not only is it impossible, by definition, that God should become a man, it is impossible, by definition, that he should 'make' one. A true human being could not be freshly created. Such a creation might look like a man and even speak like a man. He might be given flesh like a man's and a man's facilities, but he would not *be* a man."[18] This statement explains the distance between the New Testament evidence and Knox's conclusion. He has defined humanity in terms of our fallenness. William Temple has identified the problem and offered a response: "We must not form a conception of Humanity and either ask if Christ is Human or insist on reducing Him to the limits of our conception; we must ask, 'What is Humanity?' and look at Christ to find the answer."[19] Jesus Christ is our only measure of humanity as well as of deity. If we look elsewhere, we are certain to get it wrong.

Knox finds it incredible that "a divine person should have become a fully and normally human person—that is, if he was also to continue to be, in his essential identity, the same person."[20] It is incredible, but the insistent message of the New Testament is that the incredible happened. No one is claiming that what happened is God's standard practice or that it will ever be repeated, quite the contrary. Like everything else in the gospel, the incarnation of the preexistent

---

[16]Knox, *Jesus Lord and Christ,* p. 233.
[17]Ibid., pp. 148-49.
[18]Knox, *Humanity and Divinity,* pp. 67-68.
[19]William Temple, "The Divinity of Christ," pp. 258-59, in B. H. Streeter, *Foundations* (London: Macmillan, 1920), p. 77.
[20]Knox, *Humanity and Divinity,* p. 98.

Son is incredible, but that does not mean it did not happen. According to Knox, three courses of action were open to the early church when it had to deal with the story of Jesus:

> Either one rejects the story as false, or, recognizing the nature of the story as story and acknowledging its truth as such, one seeks to interpret its intention and meaning, as best we can, in empirical and rational terms, or one changes the story in hope of making it more credible. The first of these alternatives was out of the question for the early church; the second was hardly possible for it; only the third was really open and available.[21]

If these were the only three options, I would have to agree with Knox. But he has unnecessarily limited his options. Why could the early church not have decided, as I believe it did, to accept at face value the story of Jesus and try to explain that as best it could (with the promised guidance of the Holy Spirit)?

Because Christ's preexistence is part of the New Testament witness and the church's confession, Knox is unwilling to jettison it. He has decided instead to reinterpret it in functional terms.

> When we join the congregation in confessing the pre-existence, we are asserting, as we are bound by our own existence as Christians to do, that God, the Father Almighty, Maker of the heavens and earth, was back of, present in, and acting through the whole event of which the human life of Jesus was the centre. We are saying that *God* was in Christ—not in the resurrection only, but in the whole of the human career from conception through death. . . . If we suppose that such an *understanding* of the pre-existence involves denying, or disregarding, some essential truth expressed in the church's *confession* of it, then, I venture to say, either we do not truly grasp the intention of the confession or else we do not see the full implications of the understanding.[22]

Knox says any understanding of Christ's preexistence different from this is docetic. It is not enough to assert such a point against one's opponents—especially when they include the leading theologians and biblical scholars of pre-Enlightenment Christianity—one must also defend it. Knox appears convinced what he is saying is so obvious that it needs no defense, merely to say it is to demonstrate its truth.

Unwilling to admit the possibility of Christ's personal preexistence, yet constrained by the New Testament evidence to acknowledge some sort of preexistence, Knox opts for an ideal preexistence. In doing so, he recognizes how close

---

[21]Ibid.
[22]Ibid, pp. 107-8.

these two can be as we attempt to understand God's work. He rejects adoptionism of the sort Schleiermacher proposed because "it would have been quite impossible for any primitive Jewish Christian to entertain even for a little while the notion that God had merely happened to find a man worthy of becoming the Messiah."[23] He does this despite the possibility ideal preexistence and adoptionism can coexist. He says there exists a logical connection between Christ's preexistence in the mind of God and the idea of a preexisting hypostasis, which he describes as "more personal and objective" than ideal preexistence. "The affirmation of Jesus' pre-existence was all but implicit in the affirmation of God's foreknowledge of him and was bound to have become explicit eventually, whether in a Jewish or a Greek environment."[24]

I disagree with Knox on several counts. As we have seen, ideal preexistence can be posited of everything that will ever come into existence. That is what divine foreknowledge means. This need not result in transforming the ideally preexisting "thing" into a preexisting hypostasis. It is possible but neither necessary nor, in a Jewish environment, likely. Thus the preexistence of Jesus that would be affirmed on the basis of God's foreknowledge need be no more than ideal. Unless there is very good reason to conclude otherwise, it could be no more than ideal. Knox affirms Christ's ideal preexistence, but he seems to want to include in that term more than it is meant to contain without going so far as to affirm a personal preexistence because that is inconsistent with his understanding of God, humanity and their interrelationship. It is probably better to describe Knox's attitude toward Christ's preexistence as intending to tell us a story. We are not supposed to take the concept literally. It intends for us to recognize "God was in Christ—not in the resurrection only, but in the whole of the human career from conception through death."[25] He sees no consequence of his view for the doctrine of the Trinity because he denies any ontological connection exists between Jesus of Nazareth and the Son of God.

Knox offers an excellent example of the role our presuppositions play in our thinking. His facts differ only slightly from those of such New Testament scholars as Marshall, Moule and France, but his conclusions are utterly different. The only apparent reason for this difference is that Knox rejects the possibility of any common ground between deity and humanity, while the other three see no necessary incompatibility, at least within carefully defined bounds. The result of this, as I see it, is that, conclusions apart, Knox offers some of the best reasons

---

[23]Ibid., pp. 9-10.
[24]Ibid.
[25]Ibid., pp. 107-8.

why we should accept Christ's personal preexistence.

John Macquarrie. A fascinating theologian, John Macquarrie labors mightily to be both modern and orthodox, but in the end he is unsuccessful at holding the two together. Macquarrie believes attributing deity to Jesus necessarily means denying his real humanity. Unlike many who advocate renewed emphasis on Christ's real humanity, Macquarrie rejects modern adoptionist tendencies. Christians must continue to affirm the paradox of Christ's real humanity and real deity because "this alone is able to express the full significance of Christ and his continuing inexhaustible interest."[26] Language about preexistence and incarnation is unintelligible to modern people even though it says something very important about Jesus. Macquarrie aims to strip away the mythological associations of the language to expose the religious truths that underlie that language.[27] The true meaning of the mythological language is something like:

> If anyone believes that in some sense Jesus reveals God, or that God was in Christ, then he certainly seems to be claiming that Jesus Christ was not just the product of blind chance, but he may believe that in all the ages before Christ, a process was going on that had been initiated in the beginning by God and which culminated in the Christ-event.[28]

He adds that "God's metaphorical 'sending' of his metaphorical 'son' can be understood in ways that do not imply pre-existence, once we accept that the language is metaphorical and not literal."[29]

In the New Testament, John, Paul and Hebrews assume Christ's preexistence, yet both incarnationism and adoptionism have a proper place in the New Testament. Macquarrie believes adoptionism was the christology of the emerging church, but this developed rapidly in the direction of incarnational theology. Accordingly the church needs to retain a balance between the two approaches because each contains an element of truth.

My impression of Macquarrie is of a person whose spirituality exceeds what his theology permits, a condition common among modern theologians.[30] He of-

---

[26]John Macquarrie, "The Humanity of Christ," *Theology* 74 (1971): 243.

[27]John Macquarrie, "The Preexistence of Jesus Christ," *Expository Times* 77 (1966): 200.

[28]John Macquarrie, *Jesus Christ in Modern Thought* (London: SCM Press, 1990), p. 116.

[29]Ibid., p. 56.

[30]In "The Humanity of Christ" he criticizes other modern theologians as inconsistent, saying, "For in acknowledging the ultimacy of Christ, they are according to him a place and an allegiance which may not properly be ascribed to any finite entity. They are putting Jesus in place of God, and this is either an act of idolatry or a tacit admission that Jesus is God in the flesh" (p. 249). Some who have challenged preexistence doctrine have avoided Macquarrie's criticism by denying Christ this ultimacy, in the process creating for themselves a whole new set of criticisms.

fers a sharp critique of the substance and methods of *The Myth of God Incarnate*, but his own theology is not fully incarnational in the traditional sense. What he says is true, but it is also incomplete. For Macquarrie, incarnation implies three things: the initiative comes from God, not humans; God is deeply involved in his creation; and the focus of God's initiative and involvement is Jesus Christ.[31] Macquarrie is much clearer in explaining the first two than he is the third, even though the first two must be seen through the third. He appears to believe the preexistent Logos or Wisdom of God indwelt the man Jesus, but this resulted in neither incarnation nor hypostatic union. Preexistence is one of the ways the New Testament writers sought to express their belief God had taken the initiative in the story of Jesus Christ and the term (when cleansed of its mythological associations) may be an indispensable symbol for understanding Christ's deepest significance.[32]

> While some of the New Testament writers do believe in a pre-existent Logos or Wisdom which could not be anything but pre-existent, since it is a mode of the divine Being, and while they also believed that this pre-existent hypostasis dwelt in the human Jesus, they did not teach that Jesus himself was pre-existent. If they had, that would have been a denial of his true humanity and a lapse into mythology.[33]

In the formal sense Macquarrie is correct that New Testament writers believe in a preexistent Logos or Wisdom and none teaches the preexistence of the man Jesus, but the thrust of his argument is toward an indwelling christology that is inconsistent with what we have seen the New Testament authors did say about Jesus.[34]

Macquarrie clearly intends the term *mythology* in a pejorative, nontruthful sense. But the New Testament presentation of Jesus in terms both divine and human bears none of the marks of myth in that sense. Unlike Knox, Macquarrie does not wrestle with the New Testament evidence in detail. He opts for a concept of preexistence in which Christ is "the signal manifestation of the presence and action of God in the world" and in which Jesus "brings to actualization the potentialities for being that belong to the creation."[35] Here he uses the language

---

[31]John Macquarrie, "Christianity Without Incarnation? Some Critical Comments," in *The Truth of God Incarnate*, ed. Michael Green (Grand Rapids: Eerdmans, 1977), p. 143.

[32]Macquarrie, "Preexistence of Jesus Christ," p. 202.

[33]Macquarrie, *Jesus Christ in Modern Thought*, p. 390.

[34]My objection is to the belief that Jesus Christ can be explained wholly or even primarily by referring to his indwelling by the Spirit of God. The Spirit in indwelling plays an essential role in the life of the man Jesus of Nazareth, but this cannot serve as the integrating center for a viable christology. I will explain this more fully during my evaluation of modern Spirit christologies.

[35]Macquarrie, "Preexistence of Jesus Christ," pp. 201-2.

of prefigurement, suggesting what he says explicitly in other places: when we talk about the preexistence of Christ, we should think of ideal preexistence. Despite the orthodox tone of some of his other language, ideal preexistence creates no conflict within Macquarrie's theology because his soteriology is existentialist and deals in terms of commitment and fulfillment rather than forgiveness and redemption. He even says, "I myself am inclined to think that we may equate pre-existence in the mind of God with *real* pre-existence."[36] A problematic but necessary implication of this can be seen in his comment that preexistence "does mean that from the beginning Christ the incarnate Word was there in the counsels of God, and even his humanity, like the humanity of us all, was taking shape in the long ages of cosmic evolution."[37] Although Macquarrie attempts to offer a consistent and orthodox christology, his existentialist commitment prevents him from doing so.

Piet Schoonenberg. Schoonenberg is known as the man who turned Chalcedon on its head. In the days following Vatican II, this Dutch Catholic theologian proposed that the language of Chalcedon should be understood to say Jesus was a human person with a human nature to which a divine nature was added. This divine nature did not exist before Jesus' birth. For Schoonenberg the Son's personal preexistence is not essential to the New Testament message and is absent from the Synoptics. Although he recognizes his christology has implications across the field of theology, he seeks to preserve other elements of Christian theology, especially the Trinity, by arguing speculatively and appealing to silence, and thus human ignorance. Tavard summarizes Schoonenberg's christology while highlighting its devastating effect on other essential elements of Christian faith.

> Schoonenberg proposes a new model, which should finally restore the humanity of Jesus to its integrity. But he does so at the expense of Trinitarian doctrine. It is not, for him, the Word, the Second Person, who becomes flesh as Jesus. Rather, Jesus is a man—and this means a human person—filled with God. What is without personality *(an-hypostatos)* is not the humanity of Jesus; it is the divinity. . . . In this sense, God becomes man, and Jesus is the Son of God. But there is no pre-existing Son or divine person. Jesus relates to God as his Father; but God is not Father before the birth of Jesus of Nazareth. There is no pre-existent or immanent Trinity. Rather God becomes Trinity in the process of personalizing himself as Jesus.[38]

---

[36]John Macquarrie, *Christology Revisited* (Harrisburg, Penn.: Trinity Press, 1998), p. 64. I think it better to equate ideal preexistence with election, not personal preexistence. Macquarrie's statement commits him to too much. It requires the preexistence of the entire created order.
[37]Ibid., p. 114.
[38]George H. Tavard, *Images of the Christ* (Washington, D.C.: University Press of America, 1982), p. 87.

Schoonenberg attempts to forestall objections by what I can only describe as obfuscation. He says:

> It is pointless to ask whether the Word in God existed before the incarnation: in God there is no time. But we can speak of "before" and "after" insofar as God is concerned in our history, or rather: insofar as he refers himself to our history. We can then say that for us God's Word or God's only-begotten Son exists not only in Jesus Christ but also originates in the latter's pre-history.[39]

Schoonenberg seems to be saying here that the language of preexistence is meaningless because the concept of time does not apply to God. Yet if we want to talk about the Son's preexistence, he is willing to humor us and provide us with a way talking like that as long as we realize what we're saying is meaningless. That Schoonenberg is concerned solely with Christ's real humanity is evident when he writes:

> Just as there is certainly no pre-existent person of the Word *insofar* as this would nullify or lessen the natural human personhood of Jesus, so is there likewise no pre-existent choice of his own circumstances of life *insofar as* this would nullify or lessen a genuine human fate of Jesus.[40]

Schoonenberg is telling us it is permissible to use preexistence language only as long as it is superfluous. As soon as it begins to affect Jesus' humanity in any way, it becomes illegitimate. The problem with this is that if preexistence is something superfluous to Jesus' history, why bother mentioning it at all? Is not the point of the classic teaching that his preexistence is the determinative and explanatory heart of Jesus' story?

Precisely what we need to hear from God is the very thing Schoonenberg is determined to take away from us. "Whoever assumes a pre-existent divine person in Jesus places this person outside his history, and to the degree that one sacrifices the human personhood of Jesus to his divine person, Jesus' history is robbed of its actual source, the personal decisions of the man."[41] Schoonenberg is wrong because he has everything backward. When we focus on Jesus' humanity, even to the extreme of making that humanity the center of his existence, we lose sight of the actual source of Jesus' history and ignore the essential truth that his origin was in God, not in Mary. Because he cannot reduce the tension inherent in Chalcedon's statement about Jesus to simple, rational terms, Schoonenberg chooses to reformulate Chalcedon on his terms. He suggests what he

---

[39]Piet Schoonenberg, *The Christ,* trans. Della Couling (New York: Herder & Herder, 1971), p. 86.
[40]Ibid., p. 107.
[41]Ibid., p. 117.

describes as the impasse of Chalcedon's two-nature christology enables us to "conceive of the incarnation christology without starting from the personal pre-existence."[42] Unless we redefine the meaning of *incarnation* in a way that removes everything it intends to say, Schoonenberg's suggestion is impossible. You can only enflesh that which already exists outside human flesh, but that is precisely what Schoonenberg denies about Jesus.

Schoonenberg seeks to buttress his argument by appealing to the claim the early church was unduly influenced by Hellenistic philosophy in a way that perverted the original Christian message. Thus he attributes the argument from the deity of Christ to a preexistent Trinity to conscious or unconscious use of "a concept of God's immutability that is open to criticism."[43] But he tries to have it both ways in his conclusion: "Thus we do not consider it justified, from this viewpoint to say that God is 'already' threefold in his pre-existence. But it is just as unjustified to deny the pre-existent Trinity for this too is not contained in God's revelation in his salvific economy." Schoonenberg's solution draws from Hegel and modern process thought to posit a becoming in God that results from God's communicating himself in and through the man Jesus.[44] There are many problems with Schoonenberg's approach, but possibly the most basic is that whereas the early church may have sought to present trinitarian doctrine using language drawn from Greek philosophy, the impetus for its move lay in the New Testament documents themselves, documents written for the most part by Jews who had come to believe in Jesus.

The concern to protect Christ's real humanity is a legitimate one, especially in light of the popular tendency to transform the God-man into God. But the cost when this is achieved through denying Christ's preexistent deity is simply too high. No one has demonstrated satisfactorily that humanity and deity are so utterly incompatible that God is unable to take to himself true humanity. We should remember that this is the same humanity God created in the divine image—that certainly indicates some measure of commonality. An unsubstantiated assertion cannot substitute for an argument, but all we have seen regarding the impossibility of God adding humanity to himself are assertions. Schoonenberg's suggestion that a divine nature can simply pop into existence contradicts the whole meaning of deity, and I do not intend a meaning derived from Hellenistic philosophy. No Jew would ever have entertained such a thought.

While each of these writers offers us someone who might be an example,

---

[42]Ibid., pp. 115-16.
[43]Ibid., pp. 82-83, 85n.
[44]Ibid.

none offers us one who can be our Savior, and none seems to take human sin seriously enough to recognize that what we need is not an example but a Savior.

Those who focus on Jesus' humanity frequently object that Jesus had to be like other humans in every respect. Unless this is the case, they argue, Jesus must have been less than fully human. Marshall describes this presupposition as absurd. The question, he says, "is whether the evidence that he was the Logos constituted a denial of the real humanity of Jesus."[45] Marshall suggests we have the New Testament emphasis backward: "Our modern tendency is to insist that Jesus was every bit a man, just the same as one of us. This may perhaps cause us to do less than justice to the New Testament representation of him as primarily the Son of God who took on the form of a man. Where modern discussion emphasizes the fullness of his humanity, the New Testament emphasizes the fullness of his divinity."[46]

BIBLICAL OBJECTIONS TO CHRIST'S PREEXISTENCE

By biblical objections to the doctrine of Christ's preexistence, I mean claims that the New Testament passages presumed to teach Christ's preexistence do no such thing. Those who make such arguments may take the Bible seriously as a source for Christian doctrine, but they find in the Bible very different content than do advocates of preexistence doctrine. One great weakness on the part of these biblical objections, however, is that no two exegetes seem able to agree on the details. Most admit at least some parts of the New Testament teach Christ's preexistence, but they cannot reach consensus on which parts do. I will look at the objections of James D. G. Dunn, whose expertise is on Paul's writings, and John A. T. Robinson, a Johannine scholar. Dunn accepts the doctrine of Christ's personal preexistence whereas Robinson does not.[47]

James D. G. Dunn. Responding to the claims made in *The Myth of God Incarnate,* Dunn investigated the background for and New Testament claims about the incarnation. The result, *Christology in the Making,* created quite a stir among New Testament scholars. Although he concludes that the New Testament does teach Christ's personal preexistence and incarnation, Dunn finds such teaching only in John's Gospel. He interprets many of the other New Testament passages

---

[45]I. Howard Marshall, "Incarnational Christology in the New Testament," in *Christ the Lord,* ed. H. H. Rowdon (Downers Grove, Ill.: InterVarsity Press, 1982), p. 5.
[46]Ibid., p. 7.
[47]These two New Testament scholars may seem more appropriately discussed in the New Testament chapters, but I have chosen to discuss them here both because their arguments cover the entire New Testament witness and because their conclusions have significantly influenced the theological discussion of preexistence.

historically believed to teach preexistence and incarnation in ways that have shocked his peers and led to sharp critiques of his work.[48] According to Dunn, the Synoptics contain no hint of the teachings, and Paul and Hebrews affirm no more than an ideal preexistence. Dunn bases his firm conclusions on preliminary findings that can best be described as equivocal. Dunn sees the doctrine of Christ's personal preexistence as the natural consequence and the unfolding of the earliest disciples' teaching, not as its content.

Acceptance of this teaching in one of the latest New Testament writings combined with a denial of its presence in earlier strands drives a wedge into the unity of New Testament christology and constitutes a radical, even if unintended, challenge to traditional beliefs with serious consequences ensuing. If Dunn is correct, then Jesus probably did not speak of himself as preexistent, and his followers did not recognize and formulate the truth of his preexistence into doctrine until at least a generation after Pentecost.

By denying that Paul, the earliest New Testament writer, taught the doctrine and reserving this for the Johannine prologue, Dunn has made it easier for those who reject the doctrine entirely to maintain their position. This is because they already reject the Fourth Gospel as a source for Christian belief, preferring instead the Synoptics. As a consequence they feel freer to deny Christ's personal preexistence on the supposed ground that it is not found in the earlier New Testament documents (which they consider more historically reliable), but only in John's "theological meditation." Dunn's belief that John's explicit teaching is but the unfolding of that which was implicit (or preconscious) in the earliest New Testament writings is ignored.

Dunn denies the earliest New Testament authors even considered the possibility of Christ's preexistence. So it is not that they rejected such an idea; they had not even thought of it![49] Crucial to Dunn's conclusion is his premise that New Testament writers before John described Jesus in exclusively functional language.

> What we are probably witnessing is the attempt to spell out the significance of the earthly and exalted Christ in terms which Paul's interlocutors were already using, and to do so in such a way as to give these terms exclusive bearing on Christ. In particular, Paul picked up the widespread Wisdom terminology and found it an important tool for asserting the finality of Christ's role in God's purpose for man and creation.[50]

---

[48]Dunn has found much more sympathy for his conclusions among theologians than among New Testament scholars, which is why I am considering him here.

[49]James D. G. Dunn, *Christology in the Making* (Philadelphia: Westminster Press, 1980), pp. 62, 263.

[50]Ibid., pp. 194-95.

The use of Wisdom language would ultimately lead to development of the concepts of incarnation and preexistence, but this, Dunn believes, was certainly a post-Pauline phenomenon. Only with John's Gospel did the conceptions become actual doctrine.

> When such [Wisdom] language is used of Christ then, what does it mean? Does it mean any more than when the Torah was identified as the Wisdom of God? That is to say, is it simply a way of asserting that Christ in his life, death, and resurrection so embodied and expressed God's wisdom that we need look no further for our definition of God and our understanding of his purposes? . . . Such an argument is certainly arguable. Even the language of pre-existence can then be simply conceived as a way of expressing continuity between God's creative power and his saving purpose in Christ: it is the same God, the same power, the same wisdom that created all things and was active in and through Christ.[51]

Only when we reach John's Gospel does the possibility of an adoptionist interpretation become impossible. Only now do we find language with clearly ontological intention.

> The Fourth Evangelist clarified the tension that had always been present in the Jewish conception of God—between God transcendent and God immanent, between the experience of the divine both as personal address and impersonal numinous power. . . . Now in John the word of God is identified with a particular historical person, whose pre-existence as a person with God is asserted throughout. Now the Christian conception of God must make room for the person who was Christ, the Logos incarnate.[52]

When he writes, "Without the Fourth Gospel all the other assertions we have been looking at would have been resolvable into more modest assertions," Dunn opens the door to understanding the remainder of the New Testament in the light of John's language, but he never takes this any further. He continues to argue that those other writings cannot be understood as teaching Christ's preexistence and incarnation. Having clearly acknowledged John believed and taught such doctrines,[53] Dunn pulls back by citing Philo's use of the anarthrous *theos* to argue that describing Christ this way may intend to present Christ as a lesser being than God.

---

[51]James D. G. Dunn, "Was Christianity a Monotheistic Faith from the Beginning?" *Scottish Journal of Theology* 35 (1982): 329.

[52]Dunn, *Christology in the Making,* pp. 249-50.

[53]Writing about Jn 1:1-18, Dunn says, "Here, beyond dispute, the Word is preexistent, and Christ is the preexistent Word incarnate," and "In the Logos poem we are confronted with the *preexistent* Logos; the Logos *was* (not 'came to be') in the beginning. . . . The Logos *became* flesh—not merely entered into, clothed himself with, not merely appeared as, but became flesh. Here we have an explicit statement of *incarnation*" (ibid., pp. 239, 240-41).

Dunn categorizes christological texts according to types he finds in Jewish and pagan literature. He identifies much of the Pauline corpus as having an Adam christology and sees Wisdom christology as influential elsewhere. The background material he presents is helpful in understanding the New Testament environment, but I cannot help wondering if the New Testament writers were as completely controlled by their background as Dunn presumes. Dunn's citation of Goodenough—"The religious point of view of the author of each document which survives from the period must be reconstructed out of the document itself, and its relation to any other document or tradition is the end, not the beginning of our search,"[54]—only increases my concern about his conclusions because Dunn does not seem to heed what he quotes. The result is exegesis of many passages that is superficially convincing but leaves the reader with the nagging sense something has been left out. Philippians 2:6-11 is the clearest example of this. Elsewhere, Dunn writes, "If the contemporary cosmologies of Hellenistic Judaism and Stoicism determined what *words* should be used in describing the cosmic significance of the Christ-event, the *meaning* of these words is determined by the Christ-event itself."[55] Dunn, however, focuses on the setting to determine the meaning of the terms, not on the event the words describe.

It is true we need to use words in a reasonable relationship to their usual setting if we hope to communicate. But this raises a serious problem when we consider the matter of preexistence. Dunn believes there is no true parallel to the preexistence and incarnation pattern found in John (the only place where he acknowledges personal preexistence in the New Testament). If this is so, we cannot rely on an extra-Christian context to understand the New Testament at this point—that environment would have had no philosophical or religious basis for believing in preexistence in an incarnational context.

Dunn's extended treatment of the Philippians passage is representative of his approach to the biblical texts and his predisposition to understand them in a nonincarnational way, and thus has no need for a personal preexistence. Because the passage is almost universally understood to teach Christ's personal preexistence, even by those who reject the doctrine, it illustrates clearly the differences between Dunn's exegesis and that of his critics. Dunn begins his discussion of the passage by admitting, "Phil. 2.6-11 certainly seems on the face of it to be a straightforward statement contrasting Christ's pre-existent glory and post-crucifixion exaltation with his earthly humiliation."[56] But he argues that

---

[54]Ibid., p. 341.
[55]Ibid., p. 211.
[56]Ibid., p. 114.

this appearance results from presuppositions brought to the text, not conclusions drawn from the text. The presupposition of preexistence then determines how the disputed terms in the passage are to be understood (i.e., the argument is circular).

Without this presupposition Dunn seems to think those terms will be understood quite differently. He suggests the passage is best understood as an expression of Adam christology.[57] This becomes Dunn's controlling presupposition and determines how *he* will interpret the passage. I see little if any difference here between Dunn's method and the method he criticizes. It is merely a matter of which presuppositions one chooses to begin with; we cannot begin with none. The key is being able to justify the presuppositions we choose.

From his suggestion that Adam christology provides the key to understanding Philippians 2:6-11, Dunn constructs a hypothetical interpretation of the text in terms of the second Adam. A second Adam interpretation does not require preexistence; preexistence actually gets in the way of such an interpretation for Dunn. Five pages later, however, the suggested Adam christology has become the certain Adam christology.[58] Not only has Dunn done what he accuses others of, namely, interpreting the text on the basis of a presupposition about the text, but he has offered a sure conclusion built on successive possibilities and probabilities. Where he does not do this, he offers unsubstantiated assertions to make his point.

In exegeting the passage Dunn focuses on the double contrast of *form of God/form of a slave* and *equality with God/in likeness of men*. As exegetes have long recognized, the interpretation of the text hangs on the meaning of *form (morphē)*. Using Genesis 1—3 as his interpretive key, Dunn concludes *morphē* means "image." Thus, "form of God" denotes Adam as he was created—in the image of God—and "form of a slave" was Adam's status after the Fall. Neither use of *form* implies deity or preexistence. According to Dunn the second contrast refers to the temptation Adam failed but Jesus passed. Dunn concludes that the passage deals with what Irenaeus called recapitulation: the path Adam unsuccessfully trod, Christ walked successfully.

---

[57]Hurtado believes Dunn overstates this Adam christology: "But Dunn's claim that Philippians 2:6-11 is a clear and direct allusion to the Genesis account and is thus intended to be read simply as 'Adam Christology' greatly exceeds the warrants of the passage" (Larry W. Hurtado, *Lord Jesus Christ* [Grand Rapids: Eerdmans, 2003], p. 121).

[58]Dunn says, "The point to be grasped is that the question [of whether the passage speaks of Christ's preexistence] cannot be answered without reference to the Adam christology which forms the backbone of the hymn. Since the thought is dominated by the Adam/Christ parallel and contrast, the individual expressions must be understood within the context" (Dunn, *Christology in the Making*, p. 119).

If Dunn is correct, the passage deals with Christ only in his humanity; it says nothing about his deity. Dunn's argument has some conviction when considered in isolation, but to make his interpretation work Dunn has to reinterpret the rest of the Pauline corpus along the same line. Even then, as Dunn said at the outset, the passage does seem to be a straightforward statement of Christ's preexistence, incarnation and return to pre-incarnate glory. Dunn handles the other New Testament passages dealing with Christ's preexistence and incarnation similarly. He fails to see preexistence in these passages, not because it is not there but because he does not want it to be there. The presence of explicit teaching about Christ's preexistence at this early stage of the New Testament would mean Dunn's functional interpretation of these documents is wrong.

Dunn's book and its skepticism about New Testament teaching of Christ's preexistence and incarnation aroused such sharp criticism that in the introduction to the second edition, Dunn expressed shock and dismay that those he considered friends would attack him so fiercely in public.[59] Such a comment shows a great deal of naiveté about the implications of his conclusions for Christian faith. It was precisely this concern, as well as objections to Dunn's methodology, that prompted his New Testament peers to react so vehemently to his hypotheses. From my perspective, Dunn has misinterpreted so many New Testament passages because he attempted to force the passages into his predetermined mold without sufficient regard for whether or not the passages fit.[60]

Even those who deny Christ's preexistence do not necessarily agree with Dunn's exegetical conclusions. Robinson believes both Hebrews and John are "much closer than [Dunn] allows" in presenting a personal preexistence and genuine incarnation, although Robinson's adoptionism gets in the way of his appreciating the implications of what he says. A. T. Hanson believes Paul had a doctrine of preexistence although he does not hold to the doctrine himself. He justifies his position by saying the New Testament teaching on Christ's preexistence is untenable today. Nonetheless, he describes Dunn as "too sweeping in his elimination of a doctrine of pre-existence from Paul's writings." He says Dunn fails to see preexistence in Paul because he does not want to see it.[61] In support of his conclusion Hanson cites Paul's sending language, description of

---

[59]The only difference between the first and second editions of *Christology in the Making* is that the latter contains a long introduction defending the original against its many critics. The body of the text remained unchanged.

[60]Donald MacKinnon offers a similar complaint in a narrower context. See Donald M. MacKinnon, review of *Christology in the Making* by James D. G. Dunn, *Scottish Journal of Theology* 35 (1982): 364.

[61]A. T. Hanson, *The Image of the Invisible God* (London: SCM Press, 1982), pp. 59-60, 75.

Christ as being in the form of God and references to Christ's pre-incarnate role in Israel's history. Hanson complains, "Dunn's arguments grow more and more improbable as he works his way through the Pauline corpus," and describes Dunn's exegesis of Romans 8:3 as special pleading.[62] Dunn's greatest fault is that on the foundation of these increasingly improbable arguments he erects what he considers a sure conclusion.

Exegetical objections to Dunn have emphasized his treatment of Philippians 2:6-11, although his work on the rest of Paul and Hebrews is equally flawed with regard to preexistence. Dunn's conclusion depends the same sort of evolutionary scheme that Moule has shown to be of dubious merit. Leon Morris highlights Dunn's admission that some Pauline texts "could be readily interpreted of pre-existence."[63] He concludes Dunn has not shown the idea of Christ's preexistence cannot be found in Paul. A key aspect of Dunn's argument that Paul did not teach Christ's personal preexistence comes from his discussion of Adam's place in the Jewish thought of Jesus' day. Morris charges Dunn has erred by moving from the reality of Adamic thought to the conclusion that "the sense of Paul's words *is determined by their role within the Adam christology,* by their function in describing Adam or more generally God's purpose for man."[64] Marshall offers a commendation, but does so in a highly critical context. He notes Dunn has shown Christian incarnational thought was neither derived from myth nor was it mythological in character. This was the stated intent of Dunn's work in responding to *The Myth of God Incarnate.* Marshall goes on to say, however, that in achieving this end Dunn has reduced the biblical language of incarnation "to such propositions as that Jesus fully embodies the creative power and purpose of God." As a result, he has virtually denied divine sonship is a personal category.[65]

In Paul, the Philippians hymn has been considered the most powerful statement of Christ's preexistence. Dunn, therefore, concentrates his energies in explaining why this passage is not about preexistence at all. His argument is simply unconvincing. Morris objects to Dunn's treatment of the language of the passage. He says it is one thing to say the text can be interpreted without reference to preexistence, but it quite another to say this is what Paul meant. Gordon Fee cuts to the heart of the matter in his commentary on Philippians when he says Dunn's exegesis "requires a considerable accumulation of merely possible,

---

[62]Ibid., pp. 61, 73-74.
[63]Dunn, *Christology in the Making,* p. 255, cited by Leon Morris, "The Emergence of the Doctrine of the Incarnation," *Themelios* 8 (1982): 19.
[64]Morris, "Emergence of the Doctrine," p. 16.
[65]I. Howard Marshall, *Jesus the Savior* (Downers Grove, Ill.: InterVarsity Press, 1990), p. 180.

but highly improbable, meanings, *all of which are necessary to make it work.*"[66] Marshall contrasts Dunn's exegesis unfavorably with Kim's traditional argument. He notes Dunn is "especially weak" in his effort to explain "and being found in form as a man" (Phil 2:8). Had Christ only ever been in the form of a human, the contrast Paul is seeking to draw is nonsensical.[67] Ralph Martin concurs in his discussion of 2 Corinthians 8:9, where he describes Dunn's attempt to deny the passage speaks of Christ's preexistence as "no more successful here than in Phil. 2:6, for identical reasons, namely, only one who shared the divine existence in eternity may be said to exercise a choice to abandon it in a lowly Incarnation."[68]

C. E. B. Cranfield offers a detailed critique of Dunn's exegesis, looking primarily at passages in Romans and Galatians. He is dissatisfied with the way Dunn treats Paul's sending statements, saying Dunn dismisses too readily the possibility they refer to Christ's preexistence. This is especially true, he says, regarding Galatians 4:4, where the sending has the consequence of entering into human existence. Cranfield also complains that in Romans 1:3-4, Dunn understands "after the flesh" to be descriptive of Christ's entire person and not only of his descent from David. The structure of the Greek text makes Dunn's interpretation improbable. That Christ was the legal descendent of David in terms of his humanity is quite important, says Cranfield, but it is only part of the story.[69]

Like many modern scholars writing about Jesus, Dunn emphasizes function at the expense of being. While objecting to Dunn's treatment of various Pauline passages, David Brown says accepting Dunn's reading of Colossians 1:15-20 still requires obvious ontological conclusions. He says Dunn suggests Paul claims to be declaring Jesus is the embodiment of divine wisdom and that Paul wants us to consider Christ "as embodying and expressing (and defining) that power of God which is the manifestation of God in and to his creation." If we take this language seriously, thinks Brown, "the backward projection to preexistence simply cannot be resisted for otherwise the metaphor becomes an absurd exaggeration."[70]

Dunn's argument comes to us as a package. If he can convince us to accept all the pieces of the package, then his argument against pre-Johannine state-

---

[66]Gordon D. Fee, *Paul's Letter to the Philippians*, New International Commentary on the New Testament (Grand Rapids: Eerdmans, 1995), p. 203 n. 41.

[67]Marshall, *Jesus the Savior*, p. 170.

[68]Ralph P. Martin, *2 Corinthians*, Word Bible Commentary 40 (Dallas: Word, 1986), p. 263.

[69]C. E. B. Cranfield, "Some Comments on Professor J. D. G. Dunn's *Christology in the Making* with Special Reference to the Evidence of the Epistle to the Romans," in *The Glory of Christ in the New TestamentL Studies in Christology*, ed. L. D. Hurst and N. T. Wright (Oxford: Oxford University Press, 1987), p. 270.

[70]David Brown, *The Divine Trinity* (LaSalle, Ill.: Open Court, 1985), p. 157.

ments of Christ's preexistence and incarnation is compelling. But if any of his pieces is flawed, the entire argument falls apart. The flaw, however, is not limited to one verse or passage. Dunn frequently offers conclusions that go beyond the evidence in the passage or, alternatively, that fail to consider the full content of the passage. In each case, he supports his action on the basis of probabilities or possibilities. But having presented these intermediate steps as merely possible, the conclusions that follow are transformed into assured results of biblical criticism.

John A. T. Robinson. John Robinson made his reputation as a maverick in the 1960s with *Honest to God,* a book that angered theological conservatives. By the early 1980s he was equally upsetting many New Testament scholars with his books redating John's Gospel. Robinson takes a close look at Jesus in his *The Human Face of God,* but the quality of his interpretive work is marred by his avowed adoptionist tendencies. Robinson's theological understanding is also heavily determined by a late modern worldview. This leads him to say of our subject, "So far from making things more real, pre-existence is a most unnatural way of stating our conviction about the cosmic significance of Christ in an evolutionary universe."[71]

Part of the current debate about Jesus—actually the recurrence of an ancient debate—is about whether Jesus differs from the rest of humanity in degree or kind. Traditional christology has affirmed he differs in kind: Jesus at least at one point differs fundamentally from all other humans who have lived—he is free of personal sin. Robinson, however, opts for a difference in degree: at most Jesus has in fuller measure (or to a lesser extent) some quality or attribute that all humans possess. "If one had to choose, I should side with those who opt for a 'degree Christology'—however enormous the degree. For to speak of Jesus as different in kind from all other [humans] is to threaten, if not destroy, his total solidarity with all other [humans] which we have regarded as unexpendable."[72] It is this prejudgment that determines how Robinson will read the New Testament texts he examines concerning Christ's preexistence. He brings to the texts an understanding of the meanings of deity and humanity that precludes even the possibility of there being a God-man.

Robinson concentrated his work on the Gospel of John, a difficult document in which to deny any teaching of Christ's deity, preexistence and incarnation. He opts for a process understanding of Christ, not unlike that of Schoonenberg. Thus he concludes:

---

[71]John A. T. Robinson, *The Human Face of God* (London: SCM Press, 1973), p. 22.
[72]Ibid., pp. 209-10.

What I believe John is saying is that the Word, which was *theos* (1:1), God in his self-revelation and expression, *sarksegento* (1:14), was embodied totally in and as a human being, became a person, was personalized, not just personified. But that the Logos came into existence or expression as a person does not mean that it was a person before.[73]

Robinson appears willing to grant that the Logos preexisted the earthly life of Jesus, but he says this was an impersonal (anhypostatic?) existence (this sounds something like Schoonenberg's inversion of Chalcedon). Only when the human person Jesus came into existence did the Logos attach itself to this person, and only then was the Logos associated with personhood, although that personhood was not its own. This is difficult to conceive. If the preexisting Logos was not personal, was it a self-existing nature? The question is what is it that can exist by itself yet attach itself to a human person that comes into existence at some later time?

Following Rudolf Bultmann, Robinson describes the language of Christ's preexistence as myth. It is the picturing of "the other side" in terms of "this side." "It is pushing the truth of the sonship that Jesus embodied back to the very beginning of God's purpose—as well as, with the Synoptists, forward to its end."[74] Robinson is willing to say "what [Jesus] was the Logos was and what the Logos was God was, so that in his 'I' God is speaking and acting."[75] Yet in the same context he says Jesus' "I am" statements are mystical statements where Jesus can claim an astounding oneness with God without claiming an identity with him.[76] The question we need to ask Robinson at this point is what sort of identity with God is he thinking of. There are different senses of identity between God and Christ, and orthodox Christianity does not admit all of these senses; in fact, it strongly repudiates any claim of a simple identity between God and Christ. This is precisely what John rejected in his prologue and the doctrine of the Trinity continues to deny.

Jesus' language in John where he claimed his teaching was not his own but, like his being, had a heavenly origin is the author's attempt to express Jesus' special position in spatial and temporal terms. Again, Robinson sounds like Bultmann. It is the language of Hellenistic-Jewish myth, but, if taken literally, it destroys the possibility of his genuine humanity.[77] The fault, says Robinson, is that

---

[73]John A. T. Robinson, *The Priority of John,* ed. J. F. Coakley (London: SCM Press, 1985), pp. 380-81.
[74]Ibid., p. 389.
[75]Ibid., p. 388.
[76]Ibid., p. 387. Robinson cites Carl Jung in support of his interpretation.
[77]John A. T. Robinson, *Twelve More New Testament Studies* (London: SCM Press, 1984), p. 15.

patristic commentators took John's words out of context, transforming the functional language of relationships into ontological language. Thus there is no reason to think of John as suggesting more than one divine person preexisted hypostatically who entered into history by assuming or indwelling a human nature. "His human personality was then retrojected on to the pre-existent Logos—rather than a pre-existent diving Being taking on an 'impersonal' humanity."[78] So only if we read back the personhood of the man Jesus on to the Logos is it possible to make him into a divine being prior to the incarnation. But, says Robinson, we cannot find any such concept in John.

Robinson takes issue with Dunn, saying John presents "the richest and most mature interpretation of this 'initial' doctrine of the incarnation," and rejects Dunn's view that he transforms it into something else. Robinson also portrays his orthodox opponents as understanding Jesus as God *simpliciter,* in his incarnation as "a divine being who came to earth, in the manner of Ovid's *Metamorphoses,*" deity but presenting himself in the form of a human—God dressed up as a human.[79] This is a false portrait of Jesus, but it is not a portrait believed or taught by orthodox Christians; it is no more than a caricature of their belief.

Robinson argues primarily from John that Jesus was fully human, and this humanity means he could not be deity. The two states are necessarily incompatible. Robinson's source for his view appears to be the modern outlook, not the evidence of the Bible. Robinson's Jesus was a man adopted by God, differing from the rest of us only in the degree of his intimacy with God. Like Dunn, he denies Paul or Hebrews taught Christ's preexistent deity, but he steps beyond Dunn by denying even John taught such a doctrine. (Dunn concludes John is the one New Testament book where we find Jesus as the preexistent Son of God who became human.) Statements about Christ's preexistence are not to be taken literally because they are expressions of his significance cast in the terminology of antiquity. Neither Dunn nor Robinson is comfortable with thinking the New Testament authors present Jesus in both divine and human terms because that is what they experienced and what the Holy Spirit led them to recognize. So, unable to hold the two truths together, they have chosen to emphasize the New Testament witness to Jesus' humanity. But their option is just as wrong as the one they attack, that of acknowledging only Christ's deity.

JESUS CHRIST AND WORLD RELIGIONS

John Hick has stated clearly the crisis the doctrines of Christ's preexistence and

---

[78]Ibid., p. 174.
[79]Robinson, *Priority of John,* pp. 393-94. This is a description of docetism.

incarnation create for those who see all religions as ways to God. "If [Jesus] was indeed God incarnate, Christianity is the only religion founded by God in person, and must as such be uniquely superior to all other religions."[80] Hick disbelieves this, seeing Jesus as simply one religious teacher among many. He wishes to reconceive Christianity as a religion that is "centered upon the universally relevant religious experience and ethical insights of Jesus when these are freed from the mass of ecclesiastical dogmas and practices that have developed over the centuries."[81] This requires, says Hick, breaking free of the network of theories about the Trinity, incarnation and atonement that he says once helped focus Christian thinking.

The doctrine of Christ's preexistence makes meaningful each of these beliefs Hick wants to jettison; this explains why the doctrine has become so problematic to theologians like Hick. The facticity of the incarnation, says Hick, only became a problem when he was confronted by the claims and practices of other world religions after his return to Britain in the mid-1960s.[82] Christ's preexistence, virgin birth and ascension had already become mythological, even excess baggage to his theology by this time.[83]

For Hick the doctrine is also morally objectionable. If preexistence is true, then Christianity's claim that there is no salvation apart from Christ is also true. Hick considers this unacceptable because the vast majority of humanity has existed and continues to exist outside that salvation. Hick thinks this is wrong. For him, religious pluralism is a value, not simply an observed fact, so God *must* work in a pluralistic way.

> The great world religions are fundamentally alike in exhibiting a soteriological structure. . . . Each begins by declaring that our ordinary human life is profoundly lacking and distorted. . . . Thus they are all concerned to bring about the transformation of human existence from self-centeredness to Reality-centeredness.[84]

Hick understands salvation as an extended process requiring more than an earthly lifetime in which people fulfill the God-given potentialities of their nature.

Hick considers the church's claims about Jesus to be untrue. Thus Christian beliefs about human salvation are without foundation. Hick's Jesus differs from other religious teachers only in degree, not in kind. This means those teachers'

---

[80]John Hick, *The Metaphor of God Incarnate* (Louisville: Westminster/John Knox, 1993), p. ix.
[81]Ibid., p. 13.
[82]John Hick, *Problems of Religious Pluralism* (New York: St. Martin's, 1985), p. 11.
[83]John Hick, "Christology at the Cross Roads," in *Prospects for Theology,* ed. F. G. Healey (Digswell Place, U.K.: Nisbit, 1966), p. 141.
[84]John Hick, *The Second Christianity* (London: SCM Press, 1983), p. 86.

religions can be equally salvific. Thus Christianity is but one way—the Christian way—through which people are able to experience salvation. Hick surmises that if Christianity had moved eastward toward India and China instead of westward into Europe and North Africa, Jesus probably would have been seen as a bodhisattva rather than the divine Logos or Son of God. Hick considers all religions to be the human perceptions of what he calls "Reality." Using Kantian philosophical categories, he argues the Reality behind the universe transcends all categories that divide the world religions. Thus none of these religions is final or absolutely true. Each expresses the truth as one group of humans experience it.[85] The obvious question at this point is, if we cannot know the Real but only its phenomenal appearances, how can Hick know such a Real exists?

Early in his academic career Hick wrote a scathing review of Donald M. Baillie's *God Was in Christ,* attacking its adoptionist tone. By the 1960s Hick had come to hold a view of Jesus little different from Baillie's. This is a "degree christology" where Jesus is by nature like the rest of the human race. This Jesus was a man remarkably open to God, with an intense God consciousness, who was able to declare God's word and serve as a channel for the divine power. "He was so powerfully God-conscious that his life vibrated, as it were, to the divine life."[86] Any resemblance to the famous statement of Schleiermacher is not accidental; Hick sees himself in the tradition of Schleiermacher, Strauss and Harnack.[87]

Jesus has made God real to us and opened our hearts to God's claim on us, but saying this requires no ontological claims about Jesus. If incarnation means the coexistence of divine and human natures in one person (assuming this is even possible), then to the extent anyone is Christlike God is incarnate in that person. So incarnation is not a unique event. Thinking that it is unique leads inevitably to Christian exclusivism regarding other religions. The language of preexistence must be recognized as mythical or, if we prefer, metaphorical, but it cannot denote an ontological reality. Emphasizing the value of his degree christology in a pluralistic setting, Hick notes it makes Jesus more like the founders of other major religions. Hick, a philosopher by training, seems to believe the issue of religious pluralism has only recently surfaced in Christian theology.

In all this, Hick sees himself as affirming the real importance of Jesus, not denying it. Christology, he claims, went wrong very early when it mistook the devotional language of worship for literal description. It is impossible to make

---

[85]For a more complete presentation of Hick's christology, see my "The Disintegration of John Hick's Christology," *Journal of the Evangelical Theological Society* 39 (1996): 257-70.
[86]John Hick, *The Myth of God Incarnate* (Philadelphia: Westminster Press, 1977), p. 172.
[87]Hick, *Metaphor of God Incarnate,* p. 18.

sense of the language of preexistence and incarnation.

> It seems impossible to take the thought of God-Man beyond the phrase "God-Man"
> and to find any definitive meaning or content in it. . . . The lesson of those early
> attempts to understand the Incarnation, each of which misrepresented it by trying
> to spell it out in an intelligible hypothesis, is surely that the Incarnation is not a
> theological theory but a religious myth.[88]

This means that incarnational language is about Jesus' significance as a vehicle
for God's actions in the world, not an ontological claim about his person. The
language of preexistence and incarnation is no more than the honorific expression of the believer's attitude toward Jesus. It expresses what Jesus has done,
not who he is. Such language, says Hick, is similar to that of other religions that
have exalted their founding figure, and it was a common way to honor a person
in Jesus' day.

Jesus never saw himself as God the Son nor taught the doctrine of the Trinity.
Hick's Jesus did good and pointed people to the coming kingdom of God. The
heart of his teaching was the Lord's prayer, the parables and his moral guidance.
Not even Jesus' first disciples ever thought of him as God incarnate.[89]

The christological development that led to the statements of Nicea and Chalcedon was the result of a linguistic misunderstanding. Hick believes that as
Christianity spread through the Roman Empire, what had been myth, poetry and
metaphor came to be (mis)understood literally. This included such christological titles as "Son of God" and ideas like preexistence, virgin birth and bodily
resurrection. Gillis notes, however, that Hick's argument is insufficient to exclude an ontological interpretation of the language used to describe Jesus. While
Son of God language can be properly understood as metaphor, the use of metaphor in no way tells against an ontological interpretation when that is the sense
of the passage. Gillis reminds us that ontological language found its way into
New Testament descriptions of Jesus early and "unless one dismisses the relevance of scripture as in any way authoritative, one cannot ignore the interpretation of Jesus as God that is developed in the canon."[90]

Hick rejects the doctrines of Christ's preexistence and incarnation because he
dislikes their implications. He claims these doctrines are illogical and lack any

---

[88]John Hick, *God and the Universe of Faiths* (Houndmills, U.K.: Macmillan, 1988), p. 170.

[89]See ibid., pp. 145, 114; John Hick, "The Non-Absoluteness of Christianity," in *The Myth of
Christian Uniqueness,* ed. John Hick and Paul F. Knitter (Maryknoll, N.Y.: Orbis, 1987), p. 31;
and John Hick, *Disputed Questions in Theology and the Philosophy of Religion* (New Haven,
Conn.: Yale University Press, 1993), p. 49.

[90]Chester Gillis, "John Hick's Christology," *Tijdschrift voor Filosofie en Theologie* 49 (1988): 54-
55. See also his *A Question of Final Belief* (New York: St. Martin's, 1989), p. 95.

factual basis, but his arguments result from his a priori rejection of the doctrines. They are not the reason for that rejection. When examined apart from his presuppositions, Hick's arguments are demonstrably lacking in historical, linguistic and philosophical foundation. Hick has concluded it cannot be true that the religions of a majority of the world's population are false, so he has decided those Christian doctrines—doctrines that distinguish Christianity from other religions—cannot be true. Writing in another context, Leon Morris offers counsel that responds to the heart of Hick's error: "We have a firm idea of how God should act, and we persist in seeing his actions the way we imagine them instead of listening to what in fact he has chosen to do."[91]

TÜBINGEN CHRISTOLOGY AND WORLD RELIGIONS

At the University of Tübingen, Hans Küng and Karl-Josef Kuschel were for many years colleagues in the Institute for Ecumenical Studies. A key aspect of their developing theology has been an appreciation for the role of world religions. Building on the new attitude toward non-Roman Catholic faiths that came out of Vatican II, Küng and Kuschel are trying to reformulate Christian doctrine, not least christology, to make room for other religions as valid paths for human salvation. For Küng, a priest, this was part of the reason for his discipline by Rome in 1979, but Kuschel, a layman, has enjoyed greater freedom in developing Küng's ideas.

Küng's two massive volumes *On Being a Christian* and *Does God Exist?* laid out the preliminary statements of Küng's developing christology, but particularly with regard to the doctrine of preexistence Kuschel's *Born Before All Time?*[92] and Küng's *Christianity* have challenged traditional christological belief. Kuschel bases his case primarily on exegesis and history of doctrine, and Küng on history of doctrine, but the driving impulse for both is their belief preexistence and incarnational doctrine as traditionally understood are inimical to the modern, pluralistic understanding of world religions. Both incorporate all of the objections we have examined so far in support of their more basic objection that Christ's personal preexistence is inconsistent with religious pluralism.

Karl-Josef Kuschel. Kuschel says the theme of preexistence comes to the fore in Christian thought during times of danger or distress for the believing community. He does not appear to believe the New Testament treats Christ's preexistence speculatively and does believe it can be understood only in light of

---

[91]Leon Morris, *Reflections on the Gospel of John* (Grand Rapids: Baker, 1986), p. 244.
[92]Kuschel's argument has received a German response in *Gottes ewiger Sohn,* ed. R. Laufen (Paderborn: Schöningh, 1997).

Christ's resurrection and exaltation. None of these is a controversial position, yet Kuschel is obviously dissatisfied with the traditional understanding of the doctrine. His alternative, however, remains less clear than his dissatisfaction.

Kuschel offers a threefold starting point for understanding Christ's preexistence: Jesus himself, the early church's experience of the exalted Christ and a genuinely biblical understanding of God.[93] He says it is only Jesus whom we may describe as the "eternal son." This is because in him "the eternal God and Father has revealed himself" and "the person, cause and fate of Jesus Christ belong definitively to the determination of the eternal being of God."[94] Nonetheless, preexistence remains an "unfortunate theological coinage" because it encourages us to believe the person of Jesus Christ can be split into the two phases of "eternal Son" and "temporal Son."

Kuschel believes preexistence language is not primarily about the historical Jesus but is drawn from existing Jewish tradition and reinterpreted in the light of Jesus' specific conduct and fate and his new life with God. "Their function is not to deify Jesus of Nazareth, to turn him into a mythical or semi-mythical being, but to make comprehensible the historical depth and universal significance of the 'event of Jesus.' "[95]

"Eschatological preexistence" is the term Kuschel prefers to use. He says the end of Jesus' life (the "Easter experience") requires a justification the language of preexistence can provide. Eschatological preexistence is statements "about the risen and exalted Christ, who is, however, identical with the earthly crucified Jesus of Nazareth. So they have a completely retrospective character."[96] When he writes that the need for a sufficient basis for the work of Christ in the person of Jesus allows that we can know or discover that basis and that preexistence can be that explanation, it certainly seems he affirms the doctrine. But then he says:

> The New Testament does not know of pre-existence as a speculative theme. A pre-existence *christology* understood as isolated, independent, atomized reflection on a divine being of Jesus Christ "in" or "alongside" God before the world, a sonship understood in metaphysical terms, is not the concern of the New Testament. On the contrary, such a pre-existence christology must be relativized in the light of the New Testament.[97]

Precisely what Kuschel appears to grant at one point he rejects at another,

---

[93]Karl-Josef Kuschel, *Born Before All Time?* trans. John Bowden (New York: Crossroad, 1992), p. 493.

[94]Ibid., p. 495.

[95]Ibid., p. 493.

[96]Ibid., pp. 491-92.

[97]Ibid., p. 491.

although Christian tradition would reject the language "isolated, independent, atomized" as an accurate statement of its position. Kuschel's statement that preexistence is not a speculative theme in the New Testament is a straw man argument. No one says that it is. In fact, Hurtado claims precisely what Kuschel says: "Moreover, in all New Testament references to the idea of Jesus' preexistence, the premise is not philosophical or mystical speculations; instead, they express the conviction that Jesus is the eschatological savior truly sent forth from God."[98] Showing that eschatological preexistence is similar to ideal preexistence, Kuschel says, "Though christological confessions may oscillate between predestination and pre-existence, in terms of content they express the same basic thought: what God has done in Christ for human salvation."[99] This just is not so. Predestination and preexistence are distinct concepts—unless we conceive of preexistence as ideal preexistence.

Preexistence in the Pauline and "deutero-Pauline" writings serves a functional, not an ontological role. It is not a statement about conditions within God, but a confessional statement made in the face of persecution and with the expectation of Christ's coming in final judgment. Kuschel draws the biblical exegesis to support such statements from the more radical continental New Testament scholarship. For example, writing about Colossians 1:15-20, he says, "This text does not provide any encouragement for a hypostatization of Christ so that he becomes an independent 'creator deity.' . . . So in this text Christ remains purely and simply the mediator of the creative activity of God—he is clearly distinguished from God the creator on the one hand and human beings, the creatures, on the other."[100] I know of no conservative exegete who would disagree with the first sentence, but I can think of no reason why that statement supports Kuschel's conclusion. As it stands Kuschel's portrayal of Christ sounds remarkably Arian. Later, Kuschel says the Colossians passage does not describe what Christ's preexistence looks like. "The author is not interested in any mythological elaboration of what is 'before' time. . . . 'It was the activity of Christ in creation, not his pre-existence that Paul emphasized.' "[101] What this says is true, but the conclusion Kuschel draws is not. It is because Paul invariably mentioned Christ's preexistence in the context of an argument he was making about another subject, assuming common consent to his preexistence language, that makes that language so significant.

[98]Hurtado, *Lord Jesus Christ,* p. 364.
[99]Kuschel, *Born Before All Time?* p. 363.
[100]Ibid., p. 332.
[101]Ibid., p. 334. Kuschel is quoting W. D. Davies.

In addition to biblical and historical objections, Kuschel introduces Spirit christology themes into his argument. "If we reason on the basis of Paul's theology, the pre-existence of Jesus is really that of the Pneuma . . . since it is possession of the Pneuma that constitutes the unique aspect of Jesus."[102] It is true Paul spoke of Jesus being filled with the Spirit, but this does not constitute his uniqueness. If it did, Paul's exhortations to believers to be filled with the Spirit would be nonsense—he would be calling us to a state only Jesus could enjoy! Kuschel also presents John's Gospel in terms we will see are characteristic of Spirit christology. "The Christological statements about pre-existence seek above all to secure the singularity of Jesus as the absolute and definitive bringer of salvation. . . . Now this singularity rests above all on the fact that God and his will for salvation became manifest in the man Jesus of Nazareth as never before."[103] The language of Christ's preexistence is but another way of saying God is proexistence, that he is and always has been there for us when we needed him. Jesus simply reveals this truth in a way it never has been revealed before. Such language trivializes what the New Testament says about Jesus' death for the sins of the world.

In evaluating the New Testament evidence, Kuschel concludes nearly three-fourths of the books call Jesus "the Son of God" without using the language of personal preexistence. Even those that do speak in terms of a personal preexistence provide a counterpoint that shows preexistence to be a secondary consideration. This is where Kuschel becomes confusing: sometimes he talks about real preexistence; other times he speaks of independent preexistence. Apparently, we are supposed to see these as similar if not identical terms, but they are not. No New Testament author wrote in terms of Christ's independent preexistence, but I would venture that far more than one-fourth of the books say something about a real (or personal) preexistence.

This same frustrating mix of legitimate and questionable language permeates Kuschel's discussion of John's Gospel. He writes, "So John is not concerned with the epiphany of a divine being, but with the incarnation of the Word of God himself; not with the miraculous transformation of a divine being among us, but with the manifestation of God in a historical human being." He continues, "John does not have an isolated pre-existence christology. . . but a sending and revelation christology, in which the statement about pre-existence . . . has the function of emphasizing the origin of the revealer Christ from God

---

[102]Wilhelm Thüsing and Karl Rahner, *A New Christology,* trans. David Smith (New York: Seabury, 1980), p. 171, quoted in Kuschel, p. 422.

[103]Franz Mussner, quoted in Kuschel, *Born Before All Time?* p. 390 (ellipses original).

and the unity of Jesus with God."[104] The key word here is *function*. Kuschel is saying Jesus plays a role and no more; he acts for God and that is the totality of his relationship with God. John, says Kuschel, did not investigate "the metaphysical nature and being of the pre-existent Christ." He was not concerned about the internal constitution of the Godhead or ontological relationships within the Godhead.[105] Pannenberg, looking at Kuschel's argument, suggests Kuschel is attempting to "purge the picture of Jesus of anything that might lead to the doctrine of the Trinity."[106]

Because we can express the relationship between God and the world only in temporal categories, we cannot avoid the concept of preexistence. It is necessary, says Kuschel, to hold together both Jesus' origin in time and his origin in the eternity of God.[107] Like Küng, Kuschel believes the christological development of the ecumenical councils was the result of a Hellenistic takeover of the church. And, as also happens with Küng, when it becomes necessary to speak clearly and concisely, Kuschel is obscure and equivocal.

From this point, however, Kuschel tries to walk a fine line. He recognizes Christ's preexistence constrains what Christianity can and cannot be, but he does not want this to interfere with his ecumenical interests. After all, if Jesus is the incarnation of the preexistent Son of God, Christianity certainly would seem to stand alone as the religion founded by God. He affirms Nicea's location of Christ on the side of the Creator rather than the creature, and this for soteriological reasons, but the preexistence Kuschel is most comfortable with appears to be an ideal preexistence.

In the dialogue between Christianity and other religions, Kuschel considers the doctrines of Christ's preexistence and incarnation to constitute a significant problem. He quotes with approval Hick's comment about the consequences if Christ's preexistence and incarnation are true and notes Hick has shown not only the close connection between the doctrines and the salvation of humanity but also what he calls the self-contradictory nature of the exclusivist soteriological claim.[108] Kuschel proceeds along two paths simultaneously in his advocacy of a pluralist soteriology. He argues the Catholic Church does not teach the ex-

---

[104]Kuschel, *Born Before All Time?* pp. 383-84.

[105]Ibid., p. 389.

[106]Wolfhart Pannenberg, *Systematic Theology,* trans. Geoffrey W. Bromiley (Grand Rapids: Eerdmans, 1994), 2:369-70 n. 134.

[107]Kuschel, *Born Before All Time?* p. 497.

[108]Karl-Josef Kuschel, "Christologie—unfähig zum interreligiösen Dialog? Zum Problem der Einzigartigkeit Christi in Gespräch mit den Weltreligionen," in *Christentum und nichtchristliche Religionen,* ed. Karl-Josef Kuschel (Darmstadt: Wissenschaftliche Buchgesellschaft, 1994), p. 138.

clusivist position and the New Testament does not teach the preexistence and incarnational doctrines in the way they have been developed by later theology. The historical Jesus is not the same as the Christ of the councils. Along the way he argues no religion, no revelation and no savior can fully represent the mystery of God; thus we must recognize Christianity can be no more than a part of religious reality. For Christians, Jesus can be the unique revelation or incarnation of God, but there are other equally valid and comprehensive revelations of God.[109] Kuschel makes his argument on the basis of a functional understanding of revelation, quoting Hick and Knitter.

Kuschel's goal is to find a way of retaining the preexistence and incarnation language without keeping the associated doctrines since these carry with them an exclusivist soteriology. He believes he has done so by interpreting the terms functionally, just as he does other elements of his christology. The functional approach allows him to relativize Christ's role without denying he was a significant and salvific figure. But he plays this role only for Christians; other religions have figures who play similar role for their adherents.

Hans Küng. Küng has described Christ as the way of salvation for those in the Christian tradition. The clear import of this statement is that for those from other religious traditions there are other ways of salvation. This means Küng must present a Jesus different from the Jesus of traditional Christianity. Küng says Christianity took a wrong turn when it shifted its focus from Jesus' death and resurrection to his divine preexistence and incarnation. Despite compelling evidence to the contrary, Küng insists this emphasis on Christ's origin was a product of what he calls the Hellenization of the church. Küng's complaint is in a way surprising because he is no more comfortable with the traditional interpretation of the resurrection than he is with the incarnation.

In *Christianity,* Küng traces the development of Christian doctrine, attempting to show where and how it has deviated from the biblical evidence over the centuries. Basically, he is trying to show why his theology is correct and that of the Catholic Church hierarchy is wrong. So Küng begins with the New Testament materials about Jesus, trying to demonstrate an evolutionary development of christology even within the New Testament but especially during the following three centuries. Neither Paul nor John, he asserts, shows a trace of any personal preexistence christology or concept of a triune God.[110] These ideas appeared during the second century when the early Christian apologists linked the Johannine concept of the Logos with the Greek metaphysics of the Logos, seek-

---

[109]Ibid., pp. 141-42.
[110]Hans Küng, *Christianity,* trans. John Bowden (New York: Continuum, 1995), p. 93.

ing to emphasize both the oneness of God and the universal significance of
Jesus. "The starting point had been shifted: from the earthly and exalted Christ
to the pre-existent Christ."[111]

Not even John's christology is about preexistence, it is about revelation. The
preexistence language serves the function of emphasizing Jesus' significance as
Redeemer and Messiah. "John does not investigate the metaphysical nature and
being of the pre-existent Christ. . . . This way of conceiving things is alien to
John."[112] In fact, John's christology remains entirely within the Jewish worldview
of his day. In sharp contrast to most biblical scholars, Küng even includes John
1:14 in this sweeping conclusion. He achieves this result by separating Jesus Christ
from the Logos of God: "It will be said that the basis for the pre-existence of Jesus
[sic] seems already to be laid in the famous prologue to the Gospel. But what kind
of pre-existence was this? The answer is that at least in the prologue, what is spoken of is not the pre-existence of the Son but that of the Logos, the Word."[113]

In the Hellenistic world that Christianity entered during its first century, Küng
believes the idea of preexistence was common. So it was a simple matter to apply this idea to Jesus; there was even material in the New Testament writings
that could be interpreted consistently with such an application. The problem
with this transference by the Apologists from emphasis on the historical Jesus
to the preexistent Son is that they submerged Christ's humanity in his deity.
"They combined christology with cosmology, but they were unable to link it
with soteriology."[114]

Küng has reached his conclusions as the result of an idiosyncratic reading
not only of the New Testament but also of the patristic material. Soteriology was
the impetus behind the church's christological thinking from its earliest days.
That was what all the arguments that led up to the fourth and fifth century conciliar statements were all about. Yes, it is true much of the New Testament language about Jesus was functional, but the functional language carried clear ontological implications, and some portions of the New Testament can only be
described as ontological. In emphasizing the Hellenization of the early church,
Küng has mistaken appearance for substance. It is true that patristic language
was Hellenistic, but the Hellenistic outlook appeared not in Christian orthodoxy
but in such early heresies as Arianism.

It was in the early 1960s that Küng first suggested the idea the world religions

---

[111]Ibid., p. 171.
[112]Ibid., pp. 90-91.
[113]Ibid., p. 89.
[114]Ibid., p. 171.

might be independently valid in their own right. Only in the 1980s, when he reconceived the history of Christian thought in terms of paradigm shifts (following Thomas Kuhn's scientific model), did Küng discover the tool that would allow him to legitimate a fundamental reordering of Christian doctrines without denying outright their truth. In *Christianity,* he described the history of Christian thought in terms of succeeding and overlapping paradigms; the final one (still in development) would situate Christianity as one among the major religions of the world and its founder as one of the great religious figures of world history.

In a series of books that began in the mid-1980s, Küng has sought to bridge the differences among the major world religions. As part of a dialogue about Christian and Muslim beliefs about Jesus, Küng attempted to find common ground. In doing so, he made several points relevant to the doctrine of Christ's preexistence. First, he described the New Testament sonship language as a post-Easter phenomenon. The resurrection made such an impression on the disciples that they concluded he had been "lifted up" to God, whom he had called "Father," so it was only appropriate to describe him as Son. Küng argued, however, that such sonship was purely functional, adoptive rather than ontological.[115] Second, he repeated the argument he has been making for more than two decades that the conception of Christ's sonship in ontological terms resulted from the Hellenization of the early church. Moreover, the incarnation should be seen in terms of a process rather than a point in time: "On no account should the 'incarnation' of the Son be connected exclusively to the 'mathematical' or 'mystical' point when Jesus was conceived or born; it must, rather, be linked up *with his entire life, death, and new life.*"[116] Third, he argued the New Testament's concern is with the functional and relational categories used to explain God's salvific activities. Thus "believing in the son of God means believing in the revelation of the one God in the man Jesus of Nazareth. In the New Testament, Jesus Christ is primarily viewed not as an eternal, intradivine hypostasis, but as a human, historical person concretely related to God." And believing in the Holy Spirit means "believing in God's power and might at work among human beings in this world."[117] Fourth, he said the dogmatic statements about the Trinity are a distant derivative of the original New Testament statements about Father, Son and Spirit. Although he did not say so, Küng implied that in the process of development the original, pure New Testament ideas were corrupted by alien

---

[115]Hans Küng et al., *Christianity and the World Religions,* trans. Peter Heinegg (Garden City, N.Y.: Doubleday, 1986), pp. 117-18. Küng describes the Old Testament model as legal and appointive in a way that seems best described in terms of ancient adoption practices.

[116]Ibid., p. 119.

[117]Ibid., pp. 120-21.

thought forms, especially those from Hellenistic philosophy. Fifth, the criterion for being a Christian is practical rather than doctrinal. This means our concern should be with imitating Christ, not wondering who he is.

The traditional doctrinal language about Christ, which includes his preexistence, constitutes a serious impediment to interreligious dialogue. Küng recognizes this, but because his life work has become dialogue and mutual acceptance among the world religions to the point where each is seen as a valid source of salvation in its own right, he is compelled to explain away Christ's pre-incarnate deity. As Hick noted, if that doctrine is true, then that is the end of the discussion—there is only one religion that has come directly from God himself. In emphasizing our imitation of Christ, it is inconceivable that Küng actually believes we should give no consideration to whom we are imitating.

The doctrine of Christ's preexistence makes meaningful beliefs that undermine the religious projects of Hick, Kuschel and Küng. This shows why they find the doctrine in its traditional form so objectionable. But the doctrine was no easier to accept in the church's first century than in its twentieth. Kasper reminds us, "The message of the exaltation and pre-existence of the crucified Jesus was an intolerable scandal to both Jews and Greeks."[118]

THE REVIVAL OF SPIRIT CHRISTOLOGY

The distinguishing feature of Spirit christology is its portrayal of Jesus of Nazareth as a man uniquely filled with the Spirit of God. In reminding us of this biblical truth, it performs a crucial role. Its weakness consists in its insistence that this is the whole truth about Jesus. Not only is Spirit christology a mixed bag in terms of systematic theology, it is no less so in regard to Christian spirituality. It affirms Christ's real humanity in an adoptionist way that denies his real deity. As a man filled with the Spirit of God, Jesus of Nazareth is an example to all Christians that they should be no less empowered by God's Spirit.

Spirit christology has been undergoing something of a revival among theologians after a period of virtual invisibility. Spirit christologies in the early church were uniformly adoptionist and therefore were rejected. While such theologians as Walter Kasper have been interpreted in terms of Spirit christology, I believe such a description confuses the meaning of Spirit christology. It is better to say that Kasper and others incorporate the Spirit more visibly into what is clearly a Chalcedonian christology. Spirit christology, properly under-

---

[118]Walter Kasper, *The God of Jesus Christ*, trans. Matthew J. O'Connell (New York: Crossroads, 1984), p. 174.

stood, is and only can be adoptionist. It is a christology that begins from below with Jesus of Nazareth and never gets beyond that point, however grandly it might portray Jesus' humanity.

Geoffrey Lampe says interpreting christology in terms of Jesus as a man inspired, indwelt and possessed by the Spirit of God "allows us to make the same affirmation while avoiding the metaphysical difficulties, both christological and trinitarian, of the classical formulation."[119] Lampe believes he can offer a Spirit christology uncontaminated by adoptionism, which he says always has been and should continue to be rejected. "A christology of inspiration and possession states no less clearly than a christology of substance that in the person of Jesus Christ God has taken human nature and from the moment of birth or before has made it his own."[120] Such a christology, Lampe believes, lets us do away with such "mythological concepts" as the preexistence of the Son and the descent from heaven of a personal being who is born as an infant. Christ is not "substantively" God, but he is "adverbially" or functionally God. The mutual interaction of God's Spirit and the human spirit in free response so completely establish a unity of will and action that in everything he did the man Jesus acted "divinely."[121]

Lampe believes the great value of Spirit christology is that it avoids the "pluralistic trinitarianism" required by incarnational christology and replaces it with one compatible with monistic theology without surrendering the acknowledgment of Christ's real humanity or the divine nature of his words and deeds.[122] Like many of the theologians we have examined in this chapter, Lampe believes preexistence doctrine undercuts Jesus' real humanity. So to claim absolute finality and infallible authority for Christ is to deny his humanity's reality and completeness.

Jesus' relationship with God comes from his being possessed by the preexistent Spirit of God and his relationship to other humans comes from his possessing the same essential humanity as the rest of us. There is no suggestion that other people have or may in the future enjoy the perfect presence of God's Spirit that Jesus did. Instead, the Christian hope is that the Spirit might reproduce within Jesus' followers the same character Jesus had. So those with the Spirit do not become competitors or adversaries of Jesus but instead seek themselves to be as much like Jesus as possible. "Wherever God's active presence moves and

---

[119]Geoffrey W. H. Lampe, "The Holy Spirit and the Person of Christ," in *Christ, Faith and History,* ed. S. W. Sykes and J. P. Clayton (Cambridge: Cambridge University Press, 1972), p. 125.
[120]Ibid., pp. 125-26.
[121]Ibid., p. 124.
[122]Ibid., p. 123.

informs the spirit of man by evoking his free cooperation, there is, in some measure, an incarnation of deity."[123]

Lampe's Jesus is not the divine Son who became incarnate to die and redeem fallen humanity. He is the bearer of God's Spirit who communicates that Spirit to others.

> His 'deity' is discerned in the fact that, because he is the central point of God's liberating and transforming contact with man, the pre-eminent meeting-point of God's grace with man's response, he cannot be interpreted adequately within the human dimension alone and without resort to "God" language as well as "man" language.[124]

Jesus differs in degree from other humans in the completeness of his relationship with God, but he does not differ in kind. Were it otherwise, he would not truly share in our humanity. Preexistence, descent from heaven and incarnational language are merely the early church's way of stating its belief that in Jesus people encounter God's active presence. "Pre-existence of Christ as God the Son . . . entails his difference in kind from all men. Deity, anthropologically conceived as the Son who condescended to become incarnate, cannot at the same time be said to be truly human."[125] Only in the man Jesus was the human reluctance to respond to God fully overcome, only in the man Jesus was God able to indwell completely and perfect his human spirit and personality.[126] According to Lampe, such a christological approach better allows us to describe Jesus as "the God-man" than does the traditional teaching of a hypostatic union.

Lampe recognizes that his Spirit christology would require a major restructuring of trinitarian doctrine. He is willing to retain the threefold distinction in God, but interprets it in a way that can only described as modalism: "We may properly use the traditional Trinitarian language in speaking of the creative, redemptive and sanctifying activity of the one God toward his human creation."[127] Traditional trinitarian doctrine Lampe describes as tritheistic. Similarly, the Holy Spirit is neither a divine intermediary or even a person, but "God himself considered in respect of his outreach and immanence."[128]

Lampe is able to discard Christ's personal preexistence, even as he acknowl-

---

[123]Geoffrey W. H. Lampe, "The Essence of Christianity—IV: A Personal View," *Expository Times* 87 (1976): 136.

[124]Ibid., p. 133.

[125]Ibid., p. 134.

[126]Ibid., p. 136.

[127]Lampe, "Holy Spirit," p. 129; see also his "Essence of Christianity," p. 135.

[128]Lampe, "The Essence of Christianity," p. 135. Lampe here places the Holy Spirit in quotation marks.

edges it is taught in much of the New Testament, because he considers Jesus' salvific work as exemplary. For a salvation by example we need only a human Jesus; actually, we do better with a Jesus who was only human. How could we ever hope to follow the example of a Jesus who was obviously divine in his actions? But we must ask Lampe if that is consistent with the biblical witness or even possible for humans in the fallen state in which we exist. Lampe's picture of human nature is far too optimistic. I have already argued that functional christology necessarily points beyond itself to ontology; Lampe simply assumes his "adverbial" understanding of Christ's divinity can stand on its own. It cannot. Further, Lampe asserts his Spirit christology says just as clearly as the traditional two-natures doctrine that in Jesus God has taken human nature from the beginning of a life and made it his own. Precisely what "made it his own" means is left undefined, but the traditional doctrine says much more than this. It clearly affirms that God cares enough about humanity's plight that he came himself to save us and did so at great cost to himself. These two affirmations are fundamental to the Christian understanding of God. But Lampe says none of this. His christology seems to say God picked out one human, the one who was most open to God, and made him bear the brunt of humanity's sin and rebellion. That sounds nothing like the God of the Bible, and it is not a god many would be comfortable loving or worshiping.

SPIRIT CHRISTOLOGY AND WORLD RELIGIONS

In making his argument for Spirit christology, Roger Haight joins concern about protecting Jesus' real humanity with a pluralistic approach to world religions. Modern historical consciousness, he assures us, requires christology begin with Jesus' humanity and continue throughout to emphasize that humanity. In terms of biblical studies this means beginning with the Synoptic Gospels instead of John. When we consider the New Testament picture of Jesus, we must start by acknowledging there "is no single coherent understanding or presentation of Christ which meets us after Easter."[129] The strongest candidate for explaining how God himself acted in and through Jesus is the Spirit. Word and Wisdom, to the extent they are personified and hypostatized, tend to present someone both distinct from and inferior to God incarnated in Jesus, no matter that it is called divine or "of God." Given Paul's, John's and Hebrews' insistent argument to the contrary, it is difficult to see how Haight has reached this conclusion apart from a very selective reading of the New Testament.

---

[129]Roger Haight, "The Case for Spirit Christology," *Theological Studies* 53 (1992): 271. Haight quotes James Dunn in support of his claim.

The same historical consciousness that requires we emphasize Jesus' real humanity precludes our admitting that humanity has for its center a divine person instead of a human one. Quoting Lampe, Haight says Spirit christology affirms Jesus' divinity "adverbially."[130] This also means that using preexistence language about Jesus is a denial of Chalcedon's teaching that Jesus is consubstantial with the rest of humanity—Haight says nothing about Chalcedon's equally strong affirmation of Jesus' consubstantiality with God. Despite this, he makes the amazing statement that "there is no reason why God's personal self-communication, presence, and activity in Jesus should not be understood as an ontological Incarnation, so long as Incarnation is not taken to mean that Jesus' humanity is negated."[131] Unless Haight is radically redefining the meaning of incarnation, this statement contradicts everything he has said. But for a traditional christology such a requirement creates no problem at all.[132] Says Haight, if Jesus' full humanity is to be protected, then his experience of the Spirit must be comparable to our own. Similarly, any qualitative difference between Jesus' union with God and that of other humans would show Jesus not to be consubstantial with us. At this point, we have a Jesus who differs from all other humans only in degree, not in kind. This undercuts any traditional understanding of Jesus' salvific role.

Haight acknowledges that "implicit in any conception of the person of Jesus lies a conception or at least a tacit view of the meaning of salvation."[133] His soteriology is revelational and exemplary, so Jesus saves "not only by mediating God as Spirit and thus empowering a saved life, but also, from the point of view of the Christian, by being followed."[134] All of this is true in traditional soteriology, but there it is only part of the story—and not the first part. For traditional Christianity there is the matter of human sinfulness and guilt to be accounted for, but this finds no place in Haight's model. He seems to think it is enough to know of Jesus' example in order to be able to follow it. Salvation began with God, Haight argues, not Jesus; Jesus saves by revealing God and the salvation he has accomplished as Spirit from the beginning.

Haight notes that by their worship of Jesus Christians revealed their attitude toward him "as toward a divine figure"; this was the setting out of which the conciliar doctrines emerged. This appears to be what Haight means by "adverbial" divinity, but as early as the New Testament, Christians proclaimed Christ

---

[130]Ibid., p. 275. The quote marks around "adverbially" are Haight's.
[131]Ibid., p. 277.
[132]See Weinandy, *Likeness of Sinful Flesh,* pp. 11ff.
[133]Haight, "Case for Spirit Christology," p. 265.
[134]Ibid., p. 278.

as God the Son, not one who was *like* a divine figure. This leads us to Haight's concern for world religions. Attempting to balance conciliar christology—which he says must be affirmed—with the validity of other world religions, Haight writes:

> In an historicist framework and on the basis of a Spirit Christology one also confesses that Jesus is an ontological mediation of God that is decisive, definitive, final, and even absolute, provided that these determinations are not construed exclusively, as negating the possibility that God as Spirit is at work in other religions.[135]

Haight appears to want to have it both ways. Taken as a whole his statement is incoherent; it requires an absolute that must be qualified. Further, the role of the Spirit in other religions is vague in this statement, yet Haight earlier wrote that "the explanation of the status of Jesus must be such that it not be exclusive. It must also allow for the possibility of other savior figures of equal status and who may also reveal something of God that is normative."[136] This presumes quite a substantial role for the Spirit in other religions and particularly in their founders. Haight rightly recognizes that traditional christology is inconsistent with the stronger second statement (though not necessarily with the first), so he argues that Spirit christology facilitates discussion of how Jesus relates to other historical religious figures and the religions they founded. The problems with this are that it is not the highest goal of Christianity, and Haight accomplishes his goal by removing from Christianity everything offensive to non-Christians.

Because God's Spirit is present to the human Jesus from the beginning of his existence, Haight considers his approach not to be adoptionist. It is not chronology but ontology that distinguishes adoptionism from traditional christology, however. *When* the Spirit of God enters Jesus is not the issue, but *that* the Spirit enters a Jesus who is essentially human and only adjectivally or adverbially deity. If adoptionism is an inappropriate description of Haight's Spirit christology, perhaps it relates better to the Ebionitism of early Jewish Christianity. In either case, despite his protestations, Haight's christology is incompatible with the conciliar statements of Nicea and Chalcedon, and does not adequately reflect the christological language of the New Testament. His rejection of the historic understanding of Christ's preexistence results not only in a different picture of Jesus, it reformulates the nature of God. No longer is God triune. Jesus is in no way deity but only human, and the Spirit is a divine force accomplishing God's work in creation.

---

[135]Ibid., p. 292.
[136]Ibid., p. 281.

Such a reconfiguration of Christian doctrine has practical consequences. Salvation becomes revelational and exemplary: Jesus tells us what God requires and shows us how to do it. This assumes we can do so, either in our own power or by turning to the Spirit for empowerment. Neither option reflects the biblical pessimism about the capacity of fallen humanity. And if this is all Jesus does, why not Socrates, Gautama, Muhammad or some current figure? So Haight's Spirit christology, with its rejection of Jesus' preexistent deity, has consequences for how we understand God, humanity, sin and salvation. One recent critic has challenged Haight's contention that preexistence makes Jesus different from other humans in a way contrary to the teaching of Chalcedon:

> On the question of preexistence, Haight argues that in order to assure that Jesus is thoroughly like us, one cannot "really think of a preexistence of Jesus," since that would demand that he be substantially different from us. As preexistent he would be a different kind of man. This argument misses the point entirely. The eternal Son, as God, preexists; not Jesus as man. . . . For Haight, if Jesus did preexist, he would necessarily preexist as a man, since within his Christology there is no preexistent divine Son.[137]

Weinandy's criticism applies no less to the others I have surveyed in this chapter who have expressed their rejection of preexistence because they believe it compromises Jesus' humanity. Christ's preexistence is not about his humanity but his deity. It does say something about his person, but it does not deny his real humanity. It is true Christianity presents Jesus' humanity as different from ours in an important way, but this does not derive from his preexistence. Unlike ours, Jesus' humanity is not corrupted and warped by sin. Jesus' humanity shows how God made us to be, intends us to be and one day will have restored us to be.

A SPIRIT-FILLED MAN

In probably the clearest and most consistent presentation of modern Spirit christology, Paul Newman calls on other advocates of Spirit christology to own up to the implications of their doctrine. Consistent Spirit christology, he says, requires a complete rethinking of Christian doctrine, and no one should be shy about admitting this fact. Newman's determining criterion seems to be the modern worldview. The knowledge explosion of this century has provided us information inconsistent with what since the fourth century has been the orthodox interpretation of Jesus. "For example, the traditional interpretations of the pro-

---

[137]Thomas Weinandy, "The Case for Spirit Christology: Some Reflections," *Thomist* 59 (1995): 184.

tological passages in the New Testament, those suggesting pre-existence of the Christ before the time of Jesus, are now seen to be mistaken."[138] According to Newman, these statements intend merely to recognize "the way of God's working in Jesus extends to all times and places."[139] Unfortunately, this statement is representative of the quality of Newman's work. Although his extensive bibliography includes a wide range of biblical scholars, he does not interact with those whose conclusions differ significantly from his own. Had he done so, he would not speak so absolutely. Similarly, his claim that "scholars from the whole spectrum of the Christian community ranging from conservative Protestant to conservative Roman Catholic have had to acknowledge that the christology of Incarnation, as defined in the Council of Chalcedon, is not well founded in the New Testament," is simply untrue.[140] Newman may mean the precise language of Chalcedon is not found in the New Testament—that is universally agreed— but he ignores many scholars who consider the christology of Chalcedon the legitimate interpretation of New Testament statements.

In arguing for a new understanding of Jesus as a man filled with the Spirit of God, Newman warns of the danger of circularity in hermeneutics. He says "this is particularly inevitable in the case of theologians who begin their christological work with some kind of commitment to the singular importance of Jesus. Their theories about the historical Jesus are liable to be 'value-laden.' "[141] Somehow Newman misses the equal and opposite possibility that those who have a commitment against any singular importance of Jesus can arrive at equally "value-laden" theories of Jesus. In fact, Newman's failure to exercise precisely this sort of self-criticism characterizes his entire project.

According to Newman the consensus of New Testament scholars is that Jesus was a man full of the Holy Spirit. This is probably true of the New Testament scholars, and it certainly is true biblically, but it is only part of the truth. Newman, however, presents it as the whole truth. The New Testament picture of the man Jesus is that he was filled continually with the Spirit, but the New Testament picture of Jesus goes beyond this Spirit-filled man at many points to present him as more than a man. This is affirmed even by some who reject Jesus' deity, despite Newman's claim that Jesus' deity is "not well founded in the New Testament."[142] He concludes, "It can be seen in general that if [the scripture passages used in support of claims for Jesus' deity] are approached with the theocentric

---

[138]Paul W. Newman, *A Spirit Christology* (Lanham, Md.: University Press of America, 1987), p. xi.
[139]Ibid., p. 170.
[140]Ibid., p. 7.
[141]Ibid., p. 55.
[142]Ibid., p. xii.

presuppositions of the Jewish authors there are very few, if any, that can be said
to support the idea of Jesus' deity."[143] Granted that Newman has so qualified this
statement that it can hardly be negated, he is still claiming an insight into the
minds of authors from two thousand years ago for which he can offer no support. Although the subtitle of his book, *Recovering the Biblical Paradigm of
Christian Faith,* claims to be offering *the* biblical paradigm, Newman's exegetical work is both weak and one-sided. He has not interacted with those biblical
scholars who might cause him to examine more closely his premises and exegetical conclusions.

Classic trinitarian doctrine, according to Newman, was a third-century innovation based on a misreading of New Testament preexistence language. The
early church remained faithful to its Jewish theological background. Jesus was
the Spirit-filled Messiah of God, but no one thought he was himself God. Only
as Christianity moved out into the polytheistic world of Hellenism was Jesus deified. Trinitarian doctrine developed in an attempt to preserve Jewish monotheism while proclaiming Jesus' deity. The church's substance christology misused
the protological language of the New Testament to create a myth about Christ
as a preexistent heavenly being who was with God and was God before he descended to earth—although this language sounds very much like John's first-
century prologue. The church also used ontological ideas drawn from Platonic
and Aristotelian philosophies to claim Jesus was deity because his substance
was essentially identical with God's. Origen and theologians after him drew on
middle Platonism to impose a "pre-existence philosophy" on the original scriptural language. The result is that ever since then the church has been stuck with
a preexistent Christ and a preexistent Trinity.[144] The trinitarian "paradigm" that
results from preexistence doctrine does not accurately reflect biblical teaching,
but this is not its greatest sin—it offends feminist sensibilities, and for that reason
alone it should be removed from the liturgy.[145]

Preexistence poses insurmountable problems for Jesus' humanity. Whether
or not the doctrine of the Trinity is based on Jesus' preexistence, the doctrine
presupposes that preexistence. That, for Newman, means the traditional understanding of the Trinity must go. While theologians have for centuries affirmed
Jesus' real humanity, very few have recognized its implications for their doctrine
of God. Those implications, according to Newman, include rejecting the doc-

---

[143]Ibid., p. 174.
[144]Ibid., pp. 141-42. Newman's interpretation of the history of doctrine has only a tenuous hold
    on reality. Its portrayals of a pure Judaism versus a pure Hellenism and of a period of chris-
    tological development where Jesus was a great man find no support in recent scholarship.
[145]Ibid., p. 201.

trine of the Trinity, the deity of Christ, and the personhood and deity of the Holy Spirit. Just as Jesus was a man particularly open to God's Spirit, that Spirit is merely a metaphorical way of describing God at work.

"Jesus' uniqueness was not ontological but vocational." God chose, anointed and sent him to be the Servant-Messiah. This and this alone is what gives him significance. God has exalted him and we honor him because he carried out his mission faithfully. Jesus enjoys soteriological significance only because of his fidelity to his mission, not because of any purported ontological affinity with God. Newman calls this a christology of agency rather than of substance and describes it as truer to Scripture than any substance christology. "Because of his God-given vocation as Christ, Jesus represents God with a degree of authenticity that no one else can have."[146]

The christology Newman proposes is classic adoptionism. This description does not concern Newman the way it does other theologians I have discussed. He says the church rejected an adoptionist concept of Jesus' sonship because of its concern about his salvific role. "If Jesus was a complete human being his relationship with God must have been of an adoptive nature like the relationship that other people have with God." Any other relationship—biological, substantial, ontological—would mean he was no longer fully human; he would have to have become at least partly divine. "If Jesus was human he could not at the same time be deity. His relationship with God had to be adoptive."[147]

Newman says *adoption* is a useful and appropriate term to describe the covenantal relationship between God and his children, including Jesus. Apart from Jesus this statement is indeed correct, and its accuracy presents great preaching opportunities. But the New Testament in its entirety is adamant that Jesus' relationship to God and our relationship to God are essentially different. The church rejected adoptionism because it understood adoptionism in terms of a contingent arrangement that somehow depends on Jesus' accomplishments. This means adoption could only take place if God finds someone already worthy of adoption, and this circumscribes God's salvific ability by the limits of human behavior. Newman does not offer an alternative explanation of adoptionism that avoids this flaw, however. The best he can do is to suggest a new look at Arianism because its view of salvation as

> processive rather than absolute or juridical is much more resonant with the contemporary thought world. So is the Arian view of Jesus as a complete human being who was "improvable" with limited knowledge, who had faith in God, who had

---

[146]Ibid., pp. 185-86.
[147]Ibid., pp. 216-17.

genuine freedom, and who received the grace of God by participation in God's Spirit, pioneering and perfecting the way of salvation for those who follow him in the way of God's deigning.[148]

Despite this, Newman claims Spirit christology can affirm everything Christian tradition says about how God functions in Jesus even though it cannot derive Jesus' deity from God's activity in him. Thus we see Newman's christological model is functional in a way that ignores that function necessarily implies ontology. "Certainly 'God was in Christ reconciling the world' but this was a functional identity of God with Jesus' person, not an ontological identity which requires the horrendously complicated trinitarian doctrine to avoid polytheism."[149] Spirit christology, he says, can acknowledge something traditional christology finds problematic. If Jesus was deity, then it makes no sense to speak of him as having faith in God the way ordinary people do, or so says Newman. This, however, is a variation on the problem Weinandy identifies in Haight's work—namely, confusing Jesus' humanity with his deity. If Jesus was fully human, then he could have faith, pray and do everything else real humans can do (except sin).

Newman's understanding of the soteriological consequences of his Spirit christology is that "the incarnation of God in Jesus is the model for God's incarnation in all people." He believes an exclusive incarnation in Jesus is inadequate to express the good news that "God as Spirit can come to be in any human being in the same way as God 'reigned' in Jesus."[150] For Newman, incarnation need signify no more than that God is present in a person's life and actions. The transformation of this simple teaching into the doctrine of the incarnation means that salvation became based on juridical presuppositions. It equally emphasized God's masculinity and entrenched a male hierarchy in control of the church. And it made the church and its leaders the exclusive agents of God's forgiveness so the possibility of salvation could no longer be conceived outside the church. In truth, God cannot be claimed to belong exclusively to Christians. There is one God of the universe who is known in Christ, but he is not *constituted* by Christ.

Few today would agree that any of these consequences is a product of Christ's preexistence and incarnation conceived in traditional terms. Even though the doctrine of Christ's preexistent deity requires Christianity be the revelation of God, it does not deny individuals outside the visible church might be saved, and it certainly does not equate Jesus with God. This is the point of

---

[148]Ibid., p. 214.
[149]Ibid., pp. 181-82.
[150]Ibid., p. 184.

the trinitarian doctrine Newman holds in such contempt. John wrote that the Word was God—not God was the Word—because there is more to God than Christ. And it certainly does not mean God belongs to Christians; the Christian claim is rather the reverse: Christians belong to God.

The express outcome of Newman's soteriology is that each of us can enjoy precisely the same relationship with God that Jesus enjoyed. Because Jesus was no more than a human filled with God's Spirit, he need not be unique as a dispenser of God's grace. Jesus is a way to God, not *the* way.

Traditional Christian beliefs about Jesus have created a barrier between Christians and "others who believe in God." Christian pretensions to have absolute doctrine and exclusive access to God are unscriptural, according to Newman. Instead, Christians should enter into dialogue with those of other religions with the premise that God is at least potentially active and present in all religions in such a way that other dialogue participants could have an authentic experience of God to share. This means Christians need to acknowledge Christian beliefs can make no stronger truth claims than can other religious beliefs. Our criteria for evaluating religious truth claims should be primarily practical.[151] All this is part of Newman's claim that modernity should provide the decisive criteria for evaluating Christian belief. In this case the criteria are those of pluralism (not plurality) and relativism. In such an environment, exclusive claims are anathema. Thus Newman claims that in practice Christians have developed their theology as if God's disclosure in Jesus Christ "were of an entirely different order and kind" from the ways God revealed himself elsewhere, and this is offensive to those who share Newman's sensibilities even though the Bible unequivocally affirms the truth of the Christian claim.

The norm for all Christian doctrinal expressions is the Bible. This is true for Catholics, Orthodox and Protestants. It is not true for Newman, however. He shows no reservations in affirming a modernistic worldview as his norm, and this despite his contempt for an early church he believes allowed itself to be corrupted by captivity to Hellenistic philosophical categories. When he describes the sources for his christological model, two of three are modern standards. The third is not Scripture but a particular interpretation of Scripture—"a theology of Spirit from the scriptures." He also says theological doctrines must be evaluated in terms of their socioethical consequences. "The ethical criterion for any christological model should ask not only what harm the model may do but what good contribution it might make to human healing and social justice." It is troubling that any reference to God is lacking from this statement.

---

[151]Ibid., p. 24.

When Newman does mention God, he says a christological model's fruitfulness must reflect its "religious adequacy in communicating the full meaning of God's saving work in Jesus."[152] The difficulty with this language that sounds so good is that Newman has said earlier that "God's saving work" is something different cultures understand and express differently. So how we are to measure this religious adequacy is unclear. But this confusion is typical of Newman's Spirit christology. I believe he is correct in saying this is how a full-blown Spirit christology will look, and that is why I believe Spirit christologies are inherently heterodox. Their denial of Christ's preexistent deity is at the heart of their error, and that error works itself out through the other aspects of Christian faith. That is why, I believe, other advocates of Spirit christology are unwilling to take it to its logical conclusion or acknowledge its implications.

CONCLUSION

Modern objections to the doctrine of Christ's preexistence overlap in their concerns, and each says the early church made a wrong turn under the influence of Hellenistic philosophy. We have examined the fear that belief in Christ's preexistence detracts from or denies his real humanity, arguments that the New Testament nowhere or only late teaches Christ's preexistence—normally linked to claims the only preexistence the New Testament teaches is an ideal preexistence—and concerns that the doctrine of Christ's preexistence disparages the truth and soteriological claims made by other religions.

Most of the authors we examined display more than one of these concerns. Many charged belief in Christ's preexistent deity was a late development brought on by the infiltration of Hellenistic thought into the church. The result, inevitably, was a docetic christology. In response, they suggest the earliest New Testament christology was either adoptionist or what we would call Ebionite. There is no convincing evidence for any of these claims. Their historical and exegetical provenance is dubious. Their consequences are serious.

The methodology underlying each of these objections is itself suspect. The presuppositions that being both fully human and deity are incompatible and that God could not have revealed himself surpassingly in only one religion are mere assertions and lack compelling arguments. In each case the conclusion appears to derive from presuppositions rather than evidence. Evidence is not carefully assessed before conclusions are offered. In fact, much relevant evidence is ignored or its value minimized. Some, like Dunn, build hypothesis upon hypothesis to attain sure conclusions. In setting Jesus' humanity against his pre-

---

[152]Ibid., p. 63.

incarnate deity, critics miss entirely the reason for holding them together. Unless the one we know as Jesus of Nazareth enjoyed preexistent deity, affirmations of his humanity lose their value.

> To uphold the complete humanity of Christ at the slightest expense to his divinity is to sabotage the very reason for Jesus' being fully human. In the Incarnation, the Church proclaims the complete divinity and humanity of Christ, not for their own sake but for the sake of the other. . . . Thus, if it is not the Son of God in the fullness of his divinity who is fully and completely man, then the whole point of Jesus' being totally human is lost. Paradoxically, to preserve the complete humanity of Jesus while sacrificing his divine personhood is to deprecate radically the relevance of the humanity.[153]

The modern rejection of Christ's preexistence is detrimental to Christian doctrine and practice. This is inevitable since the two are inextricably bound. The historic understandings of God and Christ are so transformed by the modern denial of Christ's preexistence that, even for those who wish otherwise, the doctrine of the Trinity is no longer viable in other than a modalistic form. For advocates of Spirit christology, the result necessarily becomes a form of unitarianism. It says humanity has an affinity for God and can respond to God's initiative through his Spirit, but God and humanity are so different that bringing them together in Jesus Christ is like mixing oil and water. As a result, sin cannot be a serious concern because the remedy is superficial. Jesus' salvific role is to reveal what God has accomplished and provide a model for humans to emulate. His vicarious atonement is inconsistent with a Jesus who is essentially human, for some even a sinful human. The Jesus who has been proclaimed as Savior of the world turns out to be a person just like us. Despite what our authors claim, such a one cannot be Savior, because he needs a savior no less than we do. For the most recent among our sources, this is part of the postmodern paradigm with its rejection of absolute claims. Their warning against Christian triumphalism is salutary, but triumphalism is not a necessary, and certainly not a proper, consequence of Chalcedonian christology.

Denial of Christ's preexistence leaves us unclear about who God is and what he is like. It provides a salvation insufficient to respond to our empirically obvious sinfulness. And despite claims to the contrary, it does not accurately reflect the teaching of the Bible, Old Testament and New, or the testimony of the Christian church in its creeds and confessions. All this is because an alien thought form has been permitted the ultimate authority due to the Bible alone.

---

[153]Weinandy, *Likeness of Sinful Flesh,* pp. 7-8.

10

Concluding Thoughts

Knowing the Son of God has entered into our world in Jesus of Nazareth is transformative knowledge. If it is true, we who believe it can never be the same again. Such belief is not merely a matter of our intellect—it must affect our thoughts, words and actions as well. That Christ is the preexistent Son of God is the basis for believing God has loved us and given himself to us and for us without reservation. To say anything less about Christ's relationship with God is to deny this claim. Because Jesus is the preexistent Son, we can be confident God is not too busy for us, unconcerned about us, or ignorant of what we face daily. Instead, we know God loves us, values us and has acted personally and decisively to restore our broken relationship with him. So our study of the doctrine of Christ's preexistence has been far more than an academic survey of a traditional Christian belief too often taken for granted. The doctrine of Christ's preexistent deity guarantees the incarnation was a world-changing event and the resurrection had true salvific value.

Christians have long said that if we want to know what God is like, we need only look at Jesus Christ. This is an attractive offer because we have four accounts of Jesus' earthly life that tell enough about him that we know how he deals with other people, have some sense of his psychological makeup, and can see how he reacted to ordinary and extraordinary stresses in his life. This belief that we can know God by looking at Jesus has characterized Christians from a wide range of theological backgrounds. The result is that we have been confronted by many Christs who show us equally many versions of God. This does not necessarily invalidate the claim that we can know what God is like by knowing what Jesus is like. But if Jesus does not share in the divine essence, the claim is untrue because God and Jesus would differ precisely in that which is needed if one is truly to show us the other. So Christ's preexistence has both salvific and revelational worth.

Thus despite claims to the contrary, the doctrine of Christ's preexistence is not about abstract and obscure details of theology. Often those theological arguments accused of irrelevance and nitpicking have turned out to be about serious theological matters. Far from being a trivial sidelight, the debate over Christ's preexistence is about the nature of reality and how we understand that reality. This is especially true with regard to the concern of some that the doctrine places Christianity in a special category vis-à-vis the other world religions.[1] It is no overstatement to say the modern challenge places historic Christianity, with its doctrines of God, Christ, the Trinity, humanity, creation, sin and salvation, in jeopardy. Yet the challenge was no less severe in Christian antiquity; that is why the early church took denials of the doctrine so seriously—they recognized the implications of any alteration of the teaching. They also recognized Christ's preexistence was not an abstract product of idle speculation but lay at the heart of the Christian hope of salvation. This does not mean our rational powers can comprehend the doctrine fully, however. We know this teaching because God has revealed it to us and we understand it only to the extent he has revealed it to us. In this teaching, God has graciously given us a measure of insight into the eternal existence of the Godhead.

The alternatives to the doctrine of Christ's real or personal preexistence are uniformly unsatisfactory. Ideal preexistence, adoptionism, the great man theory—none of these speaks to the harsh reality of the human condition, and none can offer a caring God who is involved directly in the redemption of a rebellious humanity. Advocates of these positions offer a variety of objections to the historic teaching: concern to protect Jesus' humanity, the worth of all world religions, Jewish background, Hellenistic influence, and biblical exegesis. While these objections each contain some legitimate concerns, the proffered solution in every case constitutes overkill. Instead of healing minor wounds, they would kill the patient. The alternatives I have named are all mutually compatible, but each stands in direct contradiction to the classic teaching of Christ's preexistence. The Christianity that would result from their acceptance would hardly be recognizable as even a distant relative of historic Christian orthodoxy.

---

[1]The postmodern world has in common with the world of the early church an interest in religiosity, but for both it is a tolerant religiosity that does not permit universal truth claims or doubts about the validity of others' beliefs. Philip Sampson describes the postmodern mood this way: "It is true that postmodernity is more open to religious accounts than was doctrinaire modernity, but the price of such openness is to demand that all accounts relinquish their claim to transcendent, unique truth" ("The Rise of Postmodernity," in *Faith and Modernity*, ed. Philip Sampson et al. [Oxford: Regium, 1994], pp. 3-4). This is Hick's objection, that the Christian claim of Christ's personal preexistence, if true, falsifies the claims of all other religions.

Where We Have Been

In previous chapters we examined the origin and development of the doctrine of Christ's preexistence. Beginning with the testimony of the New Testament writers, we then looked for the influence of Jewish and Hellenistic sources from the centuries preceding the birth of Jesus. We also sought background from the Old Testament writings and the culture of the time. Then we traced the development of postapostolic Christian thinking through the ecumenical councils and the Reformation to the age of the Enlightenment. Next, we looked at what the doctrine does and does not say, and saw where it fits into the systematic structure of Christian thought. Then we concluded by looking at modern objections to the doctrine.

The New Testament evidence consistently presents Jesus Christ as preexistent deity every time the subject arises. I. Howard Marshall describes contrary views as a "travesty of the facts."[2] H. R. Mackintosh thinks it quite possible that Jesus himself was the ultimate source of the teaching.[3] The earliest christology, found in Paul's letters, is no less high than the late christology of John. "The idea of the preexistence of Christ, found now so clearly in the letters of Paul, which may look like a tremendous advance on the more primitive Christologies, was in reality implicit in them all along."[4]

In Paul's letters the theme of Christ's preexistence always appears in support of some other point, usually regarding Christian practice, that Paul was trying to impress on his readers. Paul wrote as if the teaching was widespread and generally accepted. In the midst of his many controversies, Paul never defended this teaching. He assumed its truth. So it appears that belief in Christ's preexistence was far more widespread than the beliefs he used this teaching to defend. The most explicit statement of Christ's preexistence occurs in the hymn in Philippians 2, which presents Jesus Christ as enjoying preexistent deity before humbling himself first to become human and then to die a humiliating death before reclaiming his original glory and receiving the accolades of God himself.

Despite frequent claims to the contrary, the Synoptic Gospels, Acts and several of the general epistles contain allusions to or expressions of Christ's preexistence. This shows up in Jesus' sending language, his use of the Son of Man title, and his "I have come" statements. The language appears throughout Matthew, Mark and Luke, both in the common material and in the material unique

---

[2]I. Howard Marshall, *Jesus the Savior* (Downers Grove, Ill.: InterVarsity Press, 1990), pp. 175-76.
[3]H. R. Mackintosh, *The Doctrine of the Person of Christ,* 2nd ed. (Edinburgh: T & T Clark; 1913), p. 68.
[4]Gerald Hawthorne, *The Presence and the Power* (Dallas: Word, 1991), p. 41.

to each writer. In addition to Jesus' words, we have his actions. Jesus performed a variety of acts in the Gospels that strongly implied his deity, a deity that requires preexistence. The claim that Acts shows evidence of an early low christology with a strong adoptionist flavor is not borne out by the evidence. Passages read in isolation may appear this way, but passages must be read in their context, and the context shows the language to be quite compatible with preexistence doctrine. First Peter presents Jesus Christ as preexistent and other non-Pauline letters that deal with christology without mentioning preexistence are consistent with the teaching of Christ's preexistence. The letter to the Hebrews teaches Christ's personal preexistence throughout. Its opening verses cannot easily be read in any other way. This letter strongly emphasizes Christ's real humanity, but it does so in a way that shows humanity is not the full story about Jesus.

Few have questioned that John in his Gospel and letters taught Christ's preexistent deity. The preferred approach to this Gospel has been to challenge its authority because it appears so different from the Synoptics. John's Gospel begins with a clear statement of Christ's preexistent deity, beside which it affirms an equally real humanity. In this Gospel we see Jesus identifying himself as the one who has come down from heaven and using the same "I have come" language we saw in the Synoptics. The "I am" statements hint at preexistence through their connection to the divine name in Exodus 3:14, except for John 8:58, which unequivocally claims preexistence. On the eve of his execution Jesus asked God to restore him visibly to his preexistent glory. The preexistence theme we find in the Fourth Gospel continues in 1-2 John. Thus the New Testament testifies consistently to Christ's preexistence.

A christology that seeks to do justice to the breadth and depth of the New Testament evidence will always attempt to express two things at the same time: Jesus' origin in time and his origin in the eternity of God himself; Jesus' birth from a woman and at the same time his origin "from the Father"; Jesus' concrete historical existence and at the same time his transhistorical preexistence.[5] Only the traditional doctrine of Christ's real preexistent deity does this adequately.

When we examined the possible Jewish and Hellenistic backgrounds to the New Testament, it was clear the overwhelming influence was Jewish. Several Old Testament personifications, such as Wisdom and Word, prepare us to recognize complexity within the Godhead. The angel of the Lord was a real person whom Old Testament figures treated as deity. The mysterious "one like a Son of Man"

---

[5]Karl-Josef Kuschel, *Born Before All Time?* trans. John Bowden (New York: Crossroad, 1992), p. 497.

in Daniel 7:13 is a divine figure better understood individually than collectively. While not in themselves conclusive, each of these pieces of the story points beyond itself and prepares us for the preexistence language of the New Testament.

Superficially attractive as a source for New Testament teaching about Jesus, Hellenistic thought contains a worldview alien and hostile to that of the Bible. Most of the "parallels" are not true parallels, but where they are, the causal relation seems to flow from the New Testament to Hellenistic thought and not the reverse. The suggestion that New Testament christology derived its picture of Jesus from Hellenistic ideas about adoption and apotheosis into divine status is without foundation as well as incompatible with a New Testament authorship that was almost uniformly Jewish. Several authors may have sought to establish points of contact with Gentile readers and used language those readers could understand, but that language was infused with new content and meaning intended to transform the readers' worldview. The best reading of the evidence is that it was not the advocates of Christ's preexistent deity and incarnation who were infected with Hellenism but their post-Ebionite opponents.

One important consideration when seeking the origin of preexistence doctrine is early Christian worship of Jesus. This is visible even in the New Testament writings, including the hymns found in many of the canonical letters and possibly in John's prologue, all of which present Jesus as preexistent deity. This worship is also attested by hostile Roman witnesses. According to Witherington, when Wisdom hymn material was applied to the historical man Jesus, the natural result was the attribution to Jesus of preexistent deity and incarnation. This high christology seems to have been both widespread and popular well before the writing of the First Gospel.[6] Despite scattered objections, the clear and consistent direction of christological development was toward the orthodoxy of the conciliar decisions of the fourth and fifth centuries. Discussion of Christ's preexistence occurred not as a matter of speculation but out of concern to protect the certainty of the salvation accomplished by Jesus Christ. With only scattered opposition, postconciliar christology affirmed Christ's preexistent deity. Only with the Radical Reformation and the Enlightenment was this classic christological teaching called into question.

Modern objections have drawn from Enlightenment thought to question Christ's preexistence on several grounds. The most common concern is that such a doctrine denigrates Christ's real humanity, making him so unlike us that his salvific work must be ineffectual. A recent concern has been that considering Christ to be preexistent deity is contrary to the modern desire for religious plu-

---

[6]Ben Witherington III, *Jesus the Sage* (Minneapolis: Fortress, 1994), p. 290.

ralism with its recognition of the salvific potential of all religions. Supposed biblical objections to the doctrine derive from presuppositions brought to the texts regarding what they can and cannot be teaching. While these objections are superficially attractive when viewed individually, considering them together requires a massive reinterpretation of the biblical witness that contradicts traditional Christian exegesis of both Old and New Testaments. Associated with these objections we find drastically altered understandings of God, humanity and the nature of salvation.

When we looked at the nature of Christian theology, we saw such a reformulation of doctrine was necessary if Christ's preexistence were denied. Because the various Christian teachings are inextricably linked, any significant modification of one must be reflected in alterations of the others. Christology stands at the heart of Christian theology, so changing the traditional teaching requires major modifications of the other important Christian doctrines as well. With regard to the doctrine of Christ's preexistence, this means its denial so significantly affects other teachings that the result can only loosely be called Christianity.

WHAT WE HAVE LEARNED

The clear, consistent teaching of Christian orthodoxy is that before his incarnation as Jesus of Nazareth, God the Son existed from eternity as deity. This teaching is evident in the biblical documents, in the practice of the early church and that of succeeding centuries, and in the near uniform teaching of councils and theologians from the postapostolic age until the Enlightenment. Modern skepticism about this doctrine derives from a changed outlook, not from the discovery of new evidence. Skepticism about the supernatural is a modern development. Marcus Borg says:

> The reality of the other world deserves to be taken seriously. Intellectually and experientially, there is much to commend it. The primary intellectual objection to it flows from a rigid application of the modern worldview's definition of reality. Yet the modern view is but one of a large number of humanly constructed maps of reality.[7]

Recent discussions of Christ's preexistence acknowledge the crucial role played by worldviews. One school of modern biblical scholarship appears to have defined preexistence in such a way as to minimize any reference to the transcendent. This has influenced discussion of the concept in obvious ways.

---

[7]Marcus Borg, quoted in Ben Witherington III, *The Jesus Quest* (Downers Grove, Ill.: InterVarsity Press, 1995), p. 99.

"Where there is no clear understanding of existence as temporal, and as distinct from a non-temporal essence, there can be no idea of pre-existence. It would appear, therefore, that pre-existence belongs in the realm of discourse which is concerned with the world of reality other than the sense-perceptible world."[8] Mascall concludes that the result of the failure of theologians to take the supernatural seriously is that "we have frequently produced naturalistic explanations of the primordial Christian events which, purely as arguments, are less coherent and plausible than the traditional supernatural ones."[9] What Mascall means is that it often takes more faith to accept the nonsupernatural explanations of Jesus Christ than it does the supernatural ones. Os Guinness is concerned that the significance of worldviews is underappreciated: "English-speaking evangelicals are marked by a consistent failure to take presuppositions seriously, and also have a corresponding bias toward data, statistics, and factoids—always the trees rather than the forest, always facts rather than the framework in which they make sense."[10]

The recent popularity of ideal preexistence among some theologians is the product of a worldview unable to accept God's ability to take unto himself real and full humanity. The result has been a trivialized understanding of preexistence. That God himself has entered into our world gives meaning and purpose to history. It is no longer a series of accidents but fits within a larger framework of explanation. Kenneth Cragg, writing in the context of interreligious dialogue, says of this objection, "Theologians speak of 'the pre-existence of Christ.' They do not thereby jeopardize the real humanness of Jesus."[11]

It is a terrifying thought that God could find one and only one human so good that he could be raised up to become the Son of God. For the rest of us this is not a source of encouragement but of despair. And if one human could be good enough to earn salvation, why should God treat the rest of us by a different standard? That God the preexistent Son has entered into our history in order to redeem it and us can only be a comfort and encouragement, however. This affirms the covenant faithfulness of God proclaimed throughout the Bible.

It is possible to have Christ's preexistence without his deity (as the Arians did), but it is not possible to have the deity without the preexistence. Christianity has defined itself in part as requiring belief in Christ's full deity. The debate about Jesus Christ, which focused on his incarnation in the 1970s, has now be-

[8]R. G. Hamerton-Kelly, *Preexistence, Wisdom, and the Son of Man* (Cambridge: Cambridge University Press, 1973), pp. 5-6.
[9]E. L. Mascall, *Theology and the Gospel of Christ* (London: SPCK, 1977), p. 1.
[10]Os Guinness, *Dining with the Devil* (Grand Rapids: Baker, 1993), p. 44.
[11]Kenneth Cragg, *Jesus and the Muslim* (London: George Allen & Unwin, 1985), p. 204.

gun to consider his preexistence. The outcome, the decision whether he is God incarnate or merely an elect, Spirit-filled human who serves as God's agent to the world, is about the essential nature and purpose of Christianity. Ideal preexistence tries improperly and unsuccessfully to remove the tension inherent in any human interpretation of the biblical evidence. Some of those we have read have charged that the early church's christological debates were either hopelessly abstract or the vehicle of political power struggles. According to Raymond E. Brown, however, "These debates show that instinctively Christians realized how important it was that nothing be allowed to obscure the true divinity and true humanity of Jesus."[12]

WHAT IT MEANS

The doctrine of Christ's real preexistence is not the product of intellectual curiosity. Neither did it derive from the desire to honor Jesus as a great teacher and moral example after his unfortunate demise. The doctrine was the product of serious consideration of the biblical and historical evidence and a concomitant concern to protect the certainty of Christ's salvific work. It also has important implications for how we should understand God, ourselves and the created order, and thus for how we who call Jesus our Savior should live our lives. Our acceptance or rejection of Christ's personal preexistence has significant consequences for both our faith and our practice.

Such major theologians as Athanasius and Anselm of Canterbury presupposed Christ's preexistence because they argued only a Christ who was fully deity and fully human could provide a sure salvation. They were correct, and the doctrine of preexistence allows for both his deity and his humanity.

What we conclude about Christ's preexistence determines what we can say about God and human salvation. But as important as our salvation is to us—and to God—the doctrine tells us something even more important about God. The God who came himself instead of sending an emissary is a God who loves us and shows his love by his actions. This is an extremely important message for the modern world that sees itself adrift in a vast, impersonal, uncaring universe. There is a personal God who takes a personal interest in each of his creatures and even took upon himself our nature and condition in order to reveal himself to us and to save us. If Jesus was no more than God's agent, our confidence in God's concern for and involvement in our world must be called into question. As Weinandy so aptly comments, "In a world racked with so much injustice and war and in the pain of sin and death that inflicts our personal life we need a

---

[12]Raymond E. Brown, *New Testament Essays* (Milwaukee: Bruce, 1965), p. 98.

God who does more than provide us moral encouragement."[13]

The biblical God is involved in his creation on a continuing basis. He is no deistic god who, having put the world together, walked away to let us work out our own problems by ourselves. Because he cares, the God of the Bible entered into the creation to become as involved in its activities as any of his creatures ever has been. God's intervention in our world reminds us this world is not all there is. We are but a part of the created order, yet to God we are a very important part.

The doctrine of Christ's preexistence involves two ethical concerns. One deals with us creatures, and the other deals with God himself. Paul never hesitated to point out to his readers the great sacrifice Christ had made on their behalf. This sacrifice did not consist solely in Christ's death on the cross, although that was the extremity of his humiliation and suffering. Several times Paul noted Christ humbled himself simply by becoming human. Arguing from the greater to the lesser, Paul wrote that if Christ loved us enough to become incarnate, surely we can love each other. God never calls upon us to do more than he has done already.

This leads us to the ethical charge some have brought against God. They have said they never could believe in a God who required the sacrifice of an innocent person to propitiate his anger. But surely this is to misunderstand the incarnation (and the atonement). The doctrine of Christ's preexistence affirms that it was not some poor innocent who was victimized by God's decision; it was God himself who chose and suffered. Yes, God did decree that sin is a capital offense because it is rebellion against God. But God himself chose to pay the price, first by becoming incarnate and then by living a blameless human life and being executed in our place for our sin. Substitutionary atonement may be a horrible doctrine, but its horror lies in the human sin that made it necessary, not because God is a mean, unfeeling deity who condemns the innocent to death.

By itself, preexistence is not enough. The one who preexisted must also be deity, and there must be a real incarnation. The Arian crisis of the fourth century reminds us of this. Preexistence remains the best explanation of the evidence. Despite his resistance to a personal preexistence, even John Knox admits this is the case. While isolated portions of the biblical witness can be interpreted in other ways, only the doctrine of Christ's personal preexistence is consistent with the evidence taken as a whole. The heart of the problem is that we are con-

---

[13]Thomas Weinandy, "The Case for Spirit Christology: Some Reflections," *Thomist* 59 (1995): 188.

vinced we know how God ought to act and we insist on seeing his behavior the way we think it ought to be rather than how God himself tells us it really is.[14]

Rejection or reformulation of the doctrine of Christ's preexistence would eviscerate Christianity. The result would be nothing like that which has grown and spread for nearly two thousand years. Every distinctive Christian belief would have to be discarded, from the doctrine of God and a realistic picture of human sinfulness to the ethical expectations and promise of divine grace. The modern attempt to make Christianity relevant by removing one of its more challenging teachings would end by making Christianity irrelevant and even destroying it.

> What would be the result if the prior eternity of Christ were invalidated? Simply that the Christian faith as we know it would cease to exist. Without the preexistent Son entering time there would be no Trinity. The God of the Bible and the church would vanish. Deny Christ's prior existence and there would be no incarnation of the Word. Negate preexistence and there would be no ultimate revelation of the Father. . . . For good reasons, then, the eternal existence of Jesus Christ has been upheld as a key doctrine of Christianity.[15]

Removing the doctrine of Christ's preexistent deity from the deposit of faith does not make Christianity realistic and relevant; it trivializes it and makes it irrelevant. We are left with a Jesus who, "however open to the will of God, cannot possibly carry the weight of significance which is still attributed to him."[16]

The Christian doctrine of Christ's preexistent deity confirms the glory of God's love and justifies the consolation and confidence of Christians. It says God so loved the world that he sent his only begotten Son to save it. It should elicit from us thanksgiving, worship and commitment.

---

[14]Leon Morris, *Reflections on the Gospel of John* (Grand Rapids: Baker, 1986), 2:244.
[15]Brian Hebblethwaite, "The Appeal to Experience in Christology," in *Christ, Faith and History,* ed. S. W. Sykes and J. P. Clayton (Cambridge: Cambridge University Press, 1972), p. 264.
[16]Bruce A. Demarest, *Jesus Christ* (Wheaton, Ill.: Victor, 1978), p. 20.

BIBLIOGRAPHY

This list does not include commentaries on books of the Bible, which may be found in the chapter footnotes.

Aldwinckle, Russell F. *More than Man: A Study in Christology.* Grand Rapids: Eerdmans, 1976.

———. "Myth and Symbol in Contemporary Philosophy and Theology: The Limits of Demythologizing." *Journal of Religion* 34 (1954): 267-79.

Anderson, Norman. *The Mystery of the Incarnation.* Downers Grove, Ill.: Inter-Varsity Press, 1978.

Anderson, Ray S. "The Incarnation of God in Feminist Christology: A Theological Critique." In *Speaking the Christian God: The Holy Trinity and the Challenge of Feminism*, edited by Alvin F. Kimel Jr. Grand Rapids: Eerdmans, 1992.

Badham, Paul. "The Meaning of the Doctrine of the Incarnation in Christian Thought." In *Christology: The Center and the Periphery*, edited by Frank K. Flinn. New York: Paragon, 1989.

Barbour, R. S. "Creation, Wisdom, and Christ." In *Creation, Christ and Culture: Essays in Honor of T. F. Torrance,* edited by R. W. A. McKinney. Edinburgh: T & T Clark, 1976.

Barclay, William. "Great Themes of the New Testament—I. Philippians ii. 1-11." *Expository Times* 70 (1958): 4-7, 40-44.

Barnard, L. W. "God, the Logos, the Spirit and the Trinity in the Theology of Athenagoras." *Studia Theologica* 24 (1970): 70-92.

Barr, James. "Christ in Gospel and Creed." *Scottish Journal of Theology* 8 (1955): 225-37.

———. "The Word Became Flesh: The Incarnation in the New Testament." *Interpretation* 10 (1956): 16-23.

Barrett, C. K. "Myth and the New Testament: How Far Does Myth Enter into the

New Testament?" *Expository Times* 68 (1957): 359-62.

———. "The Prologue of Saint John's Gospel." In *New Testament Essays*. London: SPCK, 1972.

Barth, Karl. *Church Dogmatics*. Translated by Geoffrey Bromiley et al. Edinburgh: T & T Clark, 1975-1977.

Bauckham, Richard. *God Crucified: Monotheism and Christology in the New Testament*. Grand Rapids: Eerdmans, 1998.

———. "The Sonship of the Historical Jesus in Christology." *Scottish Journal of Theology* 31 (1978): 245-60.

———. "The Worship of Jesus in Apocalyptic Christianity." *New Testament Studies* 27 (1981-1982): 323-41.

Berg, J. van den. "The Idea of the Pre-existence of the Soul of Christ: An Argument in the Controversy Between Arian and Orthodox in the Eighteenth Century." In *Tradition and Re-interpretation in Jewish and Early Christian Literature: Essays in Honor of Jürgen E. H. Lebram,* edited by J. W. Van Heuten et al. Leiden: E. J. Brill, 1986.

Berkey, Robert F., and Sarah A. Edwards, eds. *Christology in Dialogue*. Cleveland: Pilgrim, 1993.

Berkouwer, G. C. *The Person of Christ,* translated by John Vriend. Grand Rapids: Eerdmans, 1954.

Betz, Hans Dieter. "Jesus as Divine Man." In *Jesus and the Historian,* edited by F. Thomas Trotter. Philadelphia: Westminster Press, 1968.

Black, Matthew. "The Christological Use of the Old Testament in the New Testament." *New Testament Studies* 18 (1971-1972): 1-14.

Bloesch, Donald G. *Essentials of Evangelical Theology*. Vol. 1, *God, Authority, and Salvation*. San Francisco: Harper & Row, 1978.

———. *Jesus Christ: Savior and Lord*. Downers Grove, Ill.: InterVarsity Press, 1997.

Blomberg, Craig L. *The Historical Reliability of John's Gospel: Issues & Commentary*. Downers Grove, Ill.: InterVarsity Press, 2001.

Bockmuehl, Markus. *This Jesus: Martyr, Lord, Messiah*. Downers Grove, Ill.: InterVarsity Press, 1996.

Boers, Hendrikus. "Jesus and the Christian Faith: New Testament Christology since Bousset's *Kyrios Christos.*" *Journal of Biblical Literature* 89 (1970): 450-56.

Bornkamm, Günther. *Jesus of Nazareth,* translated by Irene and Fraser McLuskey with James M. Robinson. New York: Harper & Brothers, 1960.

———. "On Understanding the Christ-Hymn: Philippians 2:6-11." In *Early Christian Experience,* translated by Paul L. Hammer. New York: Harper & Row, 1969.

Brady, James R. *Jesus Christ: Divine Man or Son of God?* Lanham, Md.: University Press of America, 1991.

Bray, Gerald. *Creeds, Councils and Christ.* Downers Grove, Ill.: InterVarsity Press, 1984.

Brown, David. *The Divine Trinity.* LaSalle, Ill.: Open Court, 1985.

Brown, Graham. "Identity Statements and the Incarnation." *Heythrop Journal* 22 (1981): 261-77.

Brown, Raymond E. *The Birth of the Messiah: A Commentary on the Infancy Narratives in Matthew and Luke.* Garden City, N.Y.: Doubleday, 1977.

———. *Jesus, God and Man: Modern Biblical Reflections.* New York: Macmillan, 1967.

———. "The Theology of the Incarnation in John." In *New Testament Essays.* Milwaukee: Bruce, 1965.

———. *The Virginal Conception and Bodily Resurrection of Jesus.* New York: Paulist, 1973.

Bruce, F. F. "History and the Gospel." In *Jesus of Nazareth: Savior and Lord,* edited by Carl F. H. Henry. Grand Rapids: Baker, 1967.

Brunner, Emil. *The Christian Doctrine of Creation and Redemption: Dogmatics.* Vol. 2. Translated by Olive Wyon. Philadelphia: Westminster Press, 1952.

———. *The Mediator: A Study of the Central Doctrine of the Christian Faith,* translated by Olive Wyon. Philadelphia: Westminster Press, 1947.

Bulman, James M. "The Only Begotten Son." *Calvin Theological Journal* 16 (1981): 56-79.

Bultmann, Rudolf. "The Christological Confession of the World Council of Churches." In *Essays Philosophical and Theological,* translated by James C. G. Greig. New York: Macmillan, 1955.

———. *Jesus Christ and Mythology.* New York: Charles Scribner's Sons, 1958.

———. "New Testament and Mythology." In *Kerygma and Myth: A Theological Debate,* edited by Hans Werner Bartsch; translated by Reginald H. Fuller. London: SPCK, 1954.

Burney, C. F. "Christ as the APXH of Creation." *Journal of Theological Studies* 27 (1925-1926): 160-77.

Buzzard, Anthony F. "The Nature of Preexistence in the New Testament." *A Journal from the Radical Reformation* 6 (1996): 15-23.

Byrne, Brendan. "Christ's Pre-existence in Pauline Soteriology." *Theological Studies* 58 (1997): 308-30.

Caird, G. B. "The Development of the Doctrine of Christ in the New Testament." In *Christ for Us Today,* edited by Norman Pittinger. London: SCM Press, 1968.

———. "Son by Appointment." In *The New Testament Age: Essays in Honor of*

Bo Reicke. Vol. 1. Edited by William C. Weinrich. Macon, Ga.: Mercer University Press, 1984.

Campbell, J. C. "In a Son: The Doctrine of the Incarnation in the Epistle to the Hebrews." *Interpretation* 10 (1956).

Campenhausen, Hans von. *The Virgin Birth in the Theology of the Ancient Church.* Studies in Historical Theology. Translated by Frank Clarke. Naperville, Ill.: Alec R. Allenson, 1964.

Carnley, Peter. "The Poverty of Historical Scepticism." In *Christ, Faith and History: Cambridge Studies in Christology,* edited by S. W. Sykes and J. P. Clayton. Cambridge: Cambridge University Press, 1972.

Casey, R. P. "The Earliest Christologies." *Journal of Theological Studies,* n.s. 9 (1958): 253-77.

Ceroke, Christian P. "The Divinity of Christ in the Gospels." *Catholic Biblical Quarterly* 24 (1962): 125-39.

Charlesworth, James H. "From Jewish Messianology to Christian Christology: Some Caveats and Perspectives." In *Judaisms and Their Messiahs at the Turn of the Christian Era,* edited by Jacob Neusner. Cambridge: Cambridge University Press, 1987.

———. *Jesus Within Judaism: New Light from Exciting Archaeological Discoveries.* Garden City, N.Y.: Doubleday, 1988.

———. "The Jewish Roots of Christology: The Discovery of the Hypostatic Voice." *Scottish Journal of Theology* 39 (1986): 19-41.

———, ed. *The Messiah: Developments in Earliest Judaism and Christianity.* The First Princeton Seminar on Judaism and Christian Origins. Minneapolis: Fortress, 1992.

Cheeseman, Graham. "Dynamic Christology." *Themelios* 8, no. 1 (1982): 10-15.

Conzelmann, Hans. *Grundriss der Theologie des Neuen Testaments.* Munich: Chr. Kaiser, 1968.

Cook, Robert R. "The Psychology of Incarnation." *Themelios* 5, no. 1 (1979): 13-17.

Cotter, Anthony C. "The Divinity of Jesus Christ in Saint Paul." *Catholic Biblical Quarterly* 7 (1945): 259-89.

Craddock, Fred B. "The Poverty of Christ: An Investigation of II Corinthians 8:9." *Interpretation* 22 (1968): 158-70.

———. *The Pre-existence of Christ in the New Testament.* Nashville: Abingdon, 1968.

Cranfield, C. E. B. "Some Comments on Professor J. D. G. Dunn's *Christology in the Making* with Special Reference to the Evidence of the Epistle to the Romans." In *The Glory of Christ in the New Testament: Studies in Christology,* edited by L. D. Hurst and N. T. Wright. Oxford: Oxford University Press, 1987.

————. "The Witness of the New Testament to Christ." In *Essays in Christology for Karl Barth,* edited by T. H. L. Parker. London: Lutterworth, 1956.

Crawford, Robert G. *The Saga of God Incarnate.* Pretoria: University of South Africa, 1985.

Cullmann, Oscar. *The Christology of the New Testament.* Rev. ed. Translated by Shirlie C. Guthrie and Charles A. M. Hall. Philadelphia: Westminster Press, 1963.

————. "The Reply of Professor Cullman to Roman Catholic Critics," translated by Robert P. Meye. *Scottish Journal of Theology* 15 (1962): 36-43.

Dahl, Nils Alstrup. *Jesus the Christ: The Historical Origins of Christological Doctrine,* edited by Donald H. Juel. Minneapolis: Fortress, 1991.

Dalferth, Ingolf U. "Der Mythos vom inkarnierten Gott und das Thema der Christologie." *Zeitschrift für Theologie und Kirche* 84 (1987).

Daly, Mary. *Beyond God the Father: Toward a Philosophy of Women's Liberation.* Boston: Beacon, 1985.

Davenport, S. F. *Immanence and Incarnation.* Cambridge: Cambridge University Press, 1925.

Davies, P. E. "The Projection of Pre-existence." *Biblical Research* 12 (1967): 28-36.

Davies, W. D. *Paul and Rabbinic Judaism: Some Rabbinic Elements in Pauline Theology.* 4th ed. Philadelphia: Fortress, 1980.

Davis, Stephen T. *Risen Indeed: Making Sense of the Resurrection.* Grand Rapids: Eerdmans, 1993.

————, ed. *Encountering Jesus: A Debate on Christology.* Atlanta: John Knox, 1988.

Davis, Stephen T., Daniel Kendall and Gerald O'Collins, eds. *The Incarnation: An Interdisciplinary Symposium on the Incarnation of the Son of God.* Oxford: Oxford University Press, 2002.

De Kruijf, T. "The Glory of the Only Son." *Studies in John: Presented to J. N. Sevenster.* Supplement to *Novum Testamentum* 24 (1970): 111-23.

De Lacey, D. R. "Image and Incarnations in Pauline Christology—A Search for Origins." *Tyndale Bulletin* 30 (1979): 3-28.

Demarest, Bruce A. *Jesus Christ: The God-Man.* Wheaton, Ill.: Victor, 1978.

Denney, James. *Studies in Theology: Lectures Delivered in Chicago Theological Seminary: By the Rev. James Denney, D.D.* 5th ed. New York: A. C. Armstrong, 1897.

Dumbrell, William. "Grace and Truth: The Progress of the Argument of the Prologue of John's Gospel." In *Doing Theology for the People of God: Studies in*

Honor of J. I. Packer, edited by Donald Lewis and Alister McGrath. Downers Grove, Ill.: InterVarsity Press, 1996.

Dunn, James D. G. *Christology in the Making: A New Testament Inquiry into the Origins of the Doctrine of the Incarnation.* Philadelphia: Westminster Press, 1980.

————. "How Controversial Was Paul's Christology?" In *From Jesus to John: Essays on Jesus and New Testament Christology in Honour of Marinus de Jonge,* edited by Martinus C. DeBoer. JSNT Supplement Series 8. Sheffield: Sheffield Academic Press, 1993.

————. "The Making of Christology: Evolution or Unfolding?" In *Jesus of Nazareth: Lord and Christ: Essays on the Historical Jesus and New Testament Christology,* edited by Joel B. Green and Max Turner. Grand Rapids: Eerdmans, 1994.

————. "Was Christianity a Monotheistic Faith from the Beginning?" *Scottish Journal of Theology* 35 (1982): 303-36.

Dupuis, Jacques, *Who Do You Say I Am? Introduction to Christology.* Maryknoll, N.Y.: Orbis, 1994.

Dwyer, John C. *Son of Man & Son of God: A New Language for Faith.* New York: Paulist, 1983.

Elert, Werner. *Der christliche Glaube: Grundlinien der lutherischen Dogmatik.* 5th ed. Hamburg: Furche, 1956.

Erickson, Millard J. *The Word Became Flesh: A Contemporary Incarnational Christology.* Grand Rapids: Baker, 1991.

Evans, C. Stephen. *The Historical Jesus and the Christ of Faith: The Incarnational Narrative as History.* Oxford: Oxford University Press, 1996.

————. "The Incarnational Narrative as Myth and History." *Christian Scholar's Review* 23 (1994): 387-407.

————. "Mis-using Religious Language: Something about Kierkegaard and 'The Myth of God Incarnate.'" *Religious Studies* 15 (1979): 139-57.

Fairweather, Eugene R. "The 'Kenotic' Christology." In *A Commentary on the Epistle to the Philippians,* edited by F. W. Beare. Harper's New Testament Commentaries. New York: Harper & Row, 1959.

Farrer, Austin. *Interpretation and Belief.* London: SPCK, 1976.

Feenstra, R. J., and Cornelius Plantinga, eds. *Trinity, Incarnation, and Atonement: Philosophical and Theological Essays.* Notre Dame, Ind.: University of Notre Dame Press, 1989.

Feinberg, Paul D. "The Kenosis and Christology: An Exegetical-Theological Analysis of Phil. 2:6-11." *Trinity Journal,* no. 1 (1988): 21-46.

Fennema, D. A. "John 1:18: 'God the Only Son.'" *New Testament Studies* 31 (1985): 124-35.

Fitzmyer, Joseph A., *Scripture and Christology: A Statement of the Biblical Commission with Commentary*. New York: Paulist, 1986.

Fortman, Edmund J. *The Triune God: A Historical Study of the Doctrine of the Trinity*. Grand Rapids: Baker, 1972.

Forsyth, P. T. *The Person and Place of Jesus Christ: The Congregational Union Lecture for 1909*. Boston: Pilgrim, 1909.

France, R. T. "Development in New Testament Christology." *Themelios* 18 (1992): 4-8.

————. *Jesus and the Old Testament*. London: Tyndale, 1971.

————. *Matthew: Evangelist and Teacher*. Exeter: Paternoster, 1989.

————. "The Uniqueness of Christ." *Evangelical Review of Theology* 17 (1993): 9-28.

Franks, Robert S. *The Doctrine of the Trinity*. London: Gerald Duckworth, 1960.

Fredriksen, Paula. *From Jesus to Christ: The Origins of the New Testament Images of Jesus*. New Haven, Conn.: Yale University Press, 1988.

Freed, Edwin D. "Who or What Was Before Abraham in John 8:58?" *Journal for the Study of the New Testament* 17 (1983): 52-59.

Frei, Hans. *The Identity of Jesus: The Hermeneutical Basis of Dogmatic Theology*. Philadelphia: Fortress, 1975.

Fuller, Reginald H. *The Foundations of New Testament Christology*. London: Fontana, 1965.

————. *He That Cometh: The Birth of Jesus in the New Testament*. Harrisburg, Penn.: Morehouse, 1990.

————. "Pre-Existence Christology: Can We Dispense With It?" *Word & World* 2 (1982): 29-32.

————. "Theology of Jesus or Christology?" *Semeia* 30 (1985): 105-16.

Fuller, Reginald H., and Pheme Perkins. *Who Is This Christ? Gospel Christology and Contemporary Faith*. Philadelphia: Fortress, 1983.

Galot, Jean. *Who Is Christ? A Theology of the Incarnation*. Chicago: Franciscan Herald Press, 1981.

Garrett, James Leo, Jr. *Systematic Theology: Biblical, Historical, and Evangelical*. Vol. 1. Grand Rapids: Eerdmans, 1990.

Gese, Hartmut. "Wisdom, Son of Man, and the Origins of Christology: The Consistent Development of Biblical Theology." *Horizons in Biblical Theology* 3 (1981): 23-57.

Gieschen, Charles A. *Angelomorphic Christology: Antecedents and Early Evidence*. Leiden: Brill, 1998.

Glasson, T. Francis. "Two Notes on the Philippians Hymn (II:6-11)." *New Testament Studies* 21 (1974-1975): 133-39.

————. "The Uniqueness of Christ: The New Testament Witness." *Evangelical Quarterly* 43 (1971): 25-35.

Goppelt, Leonhard. *Theologie des Neuen Testaments: Zweiter Teil: Vielfalt und Einheit des apostolischen Christuszeugnisses.* Herausgeben von Jürgen Roloff. Göttingen: Vandenhoeck & Ruprecht, 1976.

Goulder, Michael, ed. *Incarnation and Myth: The Debate Continued.* Grand Rapids: Eerdmans, 1979.

Grant, Robert M. "The Christ at the Creation." In *Jesus in History and Myth,* edited by R. Hoffman and G. Larue. Buffalo: Prometheus, 1986.

Green, Michael, ed. *The Truth of God Incarnate.* Grand Rapids: Eerdmans, 1977.

Grenz, Stanley J. *Theology for the Community of God.* Nashville: Broadman & Holman, 1994.

Grillmeier, Aloys. *Christ in Christian Tradition.* Vol. 1: *From the Apostolic Age to Chalcedon (451).* 2nd ed. Translated by John Bowden. Atlanta: John Knox, 1975.

Gruenler, Royce G. *New Approaches to Jesus and the Gospels: A Phenomenological and Exegetical Study of Synoptic Christology.* Grand Rapids: Baker, 1982.

Gunton, Colin E. "And in One Lord Jesus Christ . . . Begotten not Made." *Pro Ecclesia* 10 (2001): 261-74.

————. *Christ and Creation.* Grand Rapids: Eerdmans, 1992.

————. *Yesterday & Today: A Study of Continuities in Christology.* Grand Rapids: Eerdmans, 1983.

Guthrie, Donald. *New Testament Theology.* Downers Grove, Ill.: InterVarsity Press, 1981.

Haag, Herbert. "'Son of God' in the Language and Thinking of the Old Testament." *Concilium* 153 (1982): 31-36.

Habermann, Jürgen. *Präexistenzaussagen in Neuen Testament.* Frankfurt am Main: Peter Lang, 1990.

Hahn, Ferdinand. *The Titles of Jesus in Christology: Their History in Early Christianity.* Translated by Harold Knight and George Ogg. London: Lutterworth, 1969.

Haight, Roger, "The Case for Spirit Christology." *Theological Studies* 53 (1992): 257-87.

Hall, Francis J. *The Kenotic Theory: Considered with Particular Reference to Its Anglican Forms and Arguments.* New York: Longmans, Green, 1898.

Hamerton-Kelly, R. G. *Pre-existence, Wisdom, and the Son of Man: A Study in the Idea of Pre-existence in the New Testament.* Cambridge: Cambridge University Press, 1973.

Hanson, A. T. *Grace and Truth: A Study in the Doctrine of the Incarnation.* London: SPCK, 1975.

———. *The Image of the Invisible God.* London: SCM Press, 1982.

———. *Jesus Christ in the Old Testament.* London: SPCK, 1965.

———. "Two Consciousnesses: The Modern Version of Chalcedon." *Scottish Journal of Theology* 37 (1984): 471-83.

Harnack, Adolf von. *History of Dogma.* 7 vols. Translated by Neil Buchanan. New York: Dover, 1961.

Harris, Murray J. *Jesus as God: The New Testament Use of Theos in Reference to Jesus.* Grand Rapids: Baker, 1992.

Hart, Thomas N. *To Know and Follow Jesus: Contemporary Christology.* New York: Paulist, 1984.

Harvey, A. E. *Jesus and the Constraints of History.* Philadelphia: Westminster Press, 1982.

———, ed. *God Incarnate: Story and Belief.* London: SPCK, 1981.

Hawthorne, Gerald. *The Presence & the Power.* Dallas: Word, 1991.

Hebblethwaite, Brian. *The Incarnation: Collected Essays in Christology.* Cambridge: Cambridge University Press, 1987.

Helland, Roger. "The Hypostatic Union: How Did Jesus Function?" *Evangelical Quarterly* 65 (1993): 311-27.

Helminiak, Daniel. *The Same Jesus: A Contemporary Christology.* Chicago: Loyola University Press, 1986.

Hengel, Martin. "Christological Titles in Early Christianity." In *The Messiah: Developments in Earliest Judaism and Christianity,* edited by James H. Charlesworth. Minneapolis: Fortress, 1992.

———. "Christology and New Testament Chronology." In *Between Jesus and Paul: Studies in the Earliest History of Christianity.* Philadelphia: Fortress, 1983.

———. "Hymns and Christology." In *Between Jesus and Paul: Studies in the Earliest History of Christianity.* London: SCM Press, 1983.

———. "'Logos, Image, Son': Some Models and Paradigms in Early Christology." In *Creation, Christ, and Culture: Studies in Honour of T. F. Torrance,* edited by R. W. A. McKinney. Edinburgh: T & T Clark, 1976.

———. *The Son of God: The Origin of Christology and the History of Hellenistic-Jewish Religion.* Philadelphia: Fortress, 1976.

———. *Studies in Early Christology.* Edinburgh: T & T Clark, 1995.

Heron, Alasdair. "Article Review: Doing Without the Incarnation." *Scottish Journal of Theology* 31 (1978): 51-71.

Hick, John. "The Logic of God Incarnate." *Religious Studies* 25 (1989): 409-23.

———. *The Metaphor of God Incarnate.* Louisville: Westminster/John Knox, 1993.

————, ed. *The Myth of God Incarnate*. Philadelphia: Westminster Press, 1977.

Hill, David. "The Relevance of the Logos Christology." *Expository Times* 78 (1967): 136-39.

Hodgson, Leonard. *The Doctrine of the Trinity: Croall Lectures, 1942-43*. Digswell Place, U.K.: James Nisbit, 1943.

Holladay, Carl R. "New Testament Christology: A Consideration of Dunn's *Christology in the Making*." *Semeia* 30 (1985): 65-82.

————. "New Testament Christology: Some Considerations of Method." *Novum Testamentum* 25 (1983): 257-78.

Hooker, Morna D. "Christology and Methodology." *New Testament Studies* 17 (1971): 480-87.

————. "The Christology of the New Testament: Jesus and the Son of Man." In *The Finality of Christ,* edited by Dow Kirkpatrick. Nashville: Abingdon, 1966.

————. "Philippians 2:6-11." In *Jesus und Paulus: Festschrift für W. G. Kümmel,* edited by E. Earle Ellis and Erich Grässer. Göttingen: Vandenhoeck & Ruprecht, 1976.

Hoover, Roy W. "The Harpagmos Enigma: A Philological Solution." *Harvard Theological Review* 64 (1971): 95-119.

Houlden, J. L. "The Doctrine of the Trinity and the Person of Christ." *Church Quarterly Review* 169 (1968): 4-18.

————. "The Place of Jesus." In *What About the New Testament? Essays in Honor of Christopher Evans,* edited by Morna Hooker and Colin Hickling. London: SCM Press, 1975.

Howard, George. "Phil 2:6-11 and the Human Christ." *Catholic Biblical Quarterly* 40 (1978): 368-87.

Hudson, D. F. "A Further Note on Philippians ii:6-11." *Expository Times* 77 (1965-1966): 29.

Hurst, L. D. "The Christology of Hebrews 1 and 2." In *The Glory of Christ in the New Testament: Studies in Christology,* edited by L. D. Hurst and N. T. Wright. Oxford: Oxford University Press, 1987.

————. "Re-enter the Pre-existent Christ in Philippians 2:5-11?" *New Testament Studies* 32 (1986): 449-57.

Hurtado, Larry W. *Lord Jesus Christ: Devotion to Jesus in Earliest Christianity*. Grand Rapids: Eerdmans, 2003.

————. "New Testament Christology: A Critique of Bousset's Influence." *Theological Studies* 40 (1979): 306-17.

————. "New Testament Christology: Retrospect and Prospect." *Semeia* 30 (1985): 15-27.

————. *One God, One Lord: Early Christian Devotion and Ancient Jewish Monotheism.* Philadelphia: Fortress, 1988.

————. "The Origins of the Worship of Christ." *Themelios* 19, no. 2 (1994): 4-8.

————. "Pre-existence." In *Dictionary of Paul and His Letters,* edited by Gerald F. Hawthorne and Ralph P. Martin. Downers Grove, Ill.: InterVarsity Press, 1993.

Iersel, B. van. "'Son of God' in the New Testament." *Concilium* 153 (1982): 37-48.

Jenson, Robert W. *Systematic Theology.* Vol. 1: *The Triune God.* Oxford: Oxford University Press, 1997.

Jewett, R. *Christology and Exegesis: New Approaches.* Semeia 30. Decatur, Ga.: Society of Biblical Literature, 1985.

Johnson, Marshall D. "Reflections on a Wisdom Approach to Matthew's Christology." *Catholic Biblical Quarterly* 36 (1974): 44-64.

Jonge, Marinus de. *Christology in Context: The Earliest Christian Response to Jesus.* Philadelphia: Westminster Press, 1988.

Juel, Donald. "Incarnation and Redemption: A Response to Reginald H. Fuller." *Semeia* 30 (1985): 117-21.

Kasper, Walter. *The God of Jesus Christ,* translated by Matthew J. O'Connell. New York: Crossroad, 1984.

————. *Jesus the Christ,* translated by V. Green. New York: Paulist, 1976.

Kelly, Balmer, H. "Word of Promise: The Incarnation in the Old Testament." *Interpretation* 10 (1956): 3-15.

Kelly, J. N. D. *Early Christian Creeds.* 3rd ed. Burnt Mill, U.K.: Longmans, 1972.

————. *Early Christian Doctrines.* 2nd ed. New York: Harper & Row, 1960.

Kim, Seyoon. *The Origin of Paul's Gospel.* 2nd ed. Tübingen: J. C. B. Mohr, 1984.

Knox, John. *Christ the Lord: The Meaning of Jesus in the Early Church.* Chicago: Willett, Clark, 1945.

————. *The Humanity and Divinity of Christ: A Study of Pattern in Christology.* Cambridge: Cambridge University Press, 1967.

————. *Jesus, Lord and Christ.* New York: Harper & Brothers, 1958.

Knox, Wilfred L. "The 'Divine Hero' Christology in the New Testament." *Harvard Theological Review* 41 (1948): 229-49.

Kramer, Werner R. *Christ, Lord, Son of God,* translated by Brian Hardy. Naperville, Ill.: A. R. Allenson, 1966.

Küng, Hans. *Christianity: Essence, History, and Future,* translated by John Bowden. New York: Continuum, 1995.

————. *The Incarnation of God: An Introduction to Hegel's Theological Thought as a Prolegomena to Future Christology,* translated by J. R. Stephenson. New York: Crossroad, 1987.

─────. *On Being a Christian,* translated by Edward Quinn. Garden City, N.Y.: Doubleday, 1977.

Kuschel, Karl-Josef. *Born Before All Time? The Dispute Over Christ's Origin,* translated by John Bowden. New York: Crossroad, 1992.

Lampe, G. W. H. "The Holy Spirit and the Person of Christ." In *Christ, Faith and History: Cambridge Studies in Christology,* edited by S. W. Sykes and J. P. Clayton. Cambridge: Cambridge University Press, 1972.

Laymon, Charles M. *Christ in the New Testament.* New York: Abingdon, 1958.

Lewis, C. S. "Modern Theology and Biblical Criticism." In *Christian Reflections,* edited by Walter Hooper. Grand Rapids: Eerdmans, 1967.

─────. "Myth Become Fact." In *God in the Dock,* edited by Walter Hooper. Grand Rapids: Eerdmans, 1970.

Loader, William. *The Christology of the Fourth Gospel: Structure and Issues.* Beiträge zur biblischen Exegese und Theologie 23. Frankfurt: Peter Lang, 1989.

Lonergan, Bernard. *The Way to Nicea: The Dialectical Development of Trinitarian Theology,* translated by Conn O'Donovan. Philadelphia: Westminster Press, 1976.

Longenecker, Richard N. *The Christology of Early Jewish Christianity.* Grand Rapids: Baker, 1970.

─────. "The Foundational Conviction of New Testament Christology: The Obedience/ Faithfulness/Sonship of Christ." In *Jesus of Nazareth: Lord and Christ: Essays on the Historical Jesus and New Testament Christology,* edited by Joel B. Green and Max Turner. Grand Rapids: Eerdmans, 1994.

─────. "Some Distinctive Early Christological Motifs." *New Testament Studies* 14 (1967-1968): 529-45.

Löser, Werner. "Jesus Christus—Gottes Sohn, aus dem Vater geboren vor aller Zeit. Zur Deutung der Präexistenzaussagen in der gegenwärtigen Theologie." *Internationale Katholische Zeitschrift* 6 (1977): 31-45.

Machen, J. Gresham. *The Virgin Birth of Christ.* New York: Harper & Row, 1930.

Mack, Burton L. "Wisdom, Myth and Mytho-logy: An Essay in Understanding a Theological Tradition." *Interpretation* 24 (1970): 46-60.

Mackey, James P. *Jesus the Man and the Myth: A Contemporary Christology.* New York: Paulist, 1979.

MacKinnon, Donald M. "Prolegomena to Christology." *Journal of Theological Studies* 33 (1982).

─────. "The Relation of the Doctrines of the Incarnation and the Trinity." In *Creation, Christ, and Culture,* edited by R. W. A. McKinney. Edinburgh: T & T Clark, 1976.

———. Review of *Christology in the Making* by James D. G. Dunn. *Scottish Journal of Theology* 35 (1982).

Mackintosh, H. R. *The Doctrine of the Person of Christ.* 2nd ed. Edinburgh: T & T Clark, 1913.

Macleod, Donald. *The Person of Christ.* Downers Grove, Ill.: InterVarsity Press, 1998.

Macquarrie, John. *Christology Revisited.* Harrisburg, Penn.: Trinity Press, 1998.

———. *Jesus Christ in Modern Thought.* London, SCM Press, 1990.

———. "The Pre-existence of Jesus Christ." *Expository Times* 77 (1965-1966): 199-202.

Marsh, John. "Christ in the Old Testament." In *Essays in Christology for Karl Barth,* edited by T. H. L. Parker. London: Lutterworth, 1956.

Marshall, I. Howard. "The Christ-Hymn in Philippians 2:5-11." *Tyndale Bulletin* 19 (1968): 104-27.

———. "The Development of Christology in the Early Church." *Tyndale Bulletin* 18 (1967): 77-93.

———. "The Divine Sonship of Jesus." *Interpretation* 21 (1977): 87-103.

———. *Jesus the Savior: Studies in New Testament Theology.* Downers Grove, Ill.: InterVarsity Press, 1990.

———. *The Origins of New Testament Christology.* Downers Grove, Ill.: InterVarsity Press, 1976.

———. "Palestinian and Hellenistic Christianity: Some Critical Comments." *New Testament Studies* 19 (1972-1973): 271-87.

Martin, Ralph P. *Carmen Christi: Phil. 2:5-11 in Recent Interpretation and in the Setting of Early Christian Worship.* 2nd ed. Cambridge: Cambridge University Press, 1983.

———. *Worship in the Early Church.* Grand Rapids: Eerdmans, 1974.

Mascall, Eric L. *He Who Is: A Study in Traditional Theism.* London: Longmans, 1962.

———. *Jesus: Who He Is—And How We Know Him.* London: Darton, Longman & Todd, 1986.

———. *Theology and the Gospel of Christ: An Essay in Reorientation.* London: SPCK, 1977.

Matthews, W. R. *The Problem of Christ in the Twentieth Century.* London: Oxford University Press, 1950.

Mauser, Ulrich. "Image of God and Incarnation." *Interpretation* 24 (1970): 336-56.

McCormick, Scott, Jr. *Behold the Man: Re-reading Gospels, Re-humanizing Jesus.* New York: Continuum, 1994.

McDermott, Brian O. *The Personal Unity of Jesus and God According to Wolfhart Pannenberg*. St. Ottilien, Germany: EOS, 1973.

McDermott, J. M. "Jesus and the Son of God Title." *Gregorianum* 62 (1981): 277-319.

McDonald, H. D. "The Person of Christ in Contemporary Speculation and Biblical Faith." *Vox Evangelica* 11 (1979): 5-17.

McGrath, Alister E. *Understanding Jesus: Who Jesus Christ Is and Why He Matters*. Grand Rapids: Zondervan, 1987.

McIntyre, John. *The Shape of Christology*. Philadelphia: Westminster Press, 1966.

Mealand, David L. "The Christology of the Epistle to the Hebrews." *Modern Churchman*, no. 22 (1979): 180-85.

Meijering, E. P. *God Being History: Studies in Patristic Philosophy*. Amsterdam: North-Holland, 1975.

Merklein, Helmut. "Zur Entstehung der urchristlichen Aussage vom präexistenten Sohn Gottes." In *Zur Geschichte des Urchristentums*, edited by Gerhard Dautzenberg et al. Quaestiones Disputatae 87, edited by Karl Rahner and Heinrich Schlier. Freiburg: Herder, 1979.

Meynell, Hugo. "On Believing in the Incarnation." *Clergy Review* 64 (1979): 210-16.

Miller, E. L. "'The *Logos* was God.'" *Evangelical Quarterly* 53 (1981): 65-77.

Moberly, Walter. "God Incarnate: Some Reflections from an Old Testament Perspective." *Churchman* 98 (1983): 44-59.

Molnar, Paul D. *Divine Freedom and the Doctrine of the Immanent Trinity: In Dialogue with Karl Barth and Contemporary Theology*. London: T & T Clark, 2002.

Moore, R. "Pre-existence." In *Encyclopedia of Religion and Ethics*, edited by James Hastings. Edinburgh: T & T Clark, 1918.

Morris, Leon. "The Emergence of the Doctrine of the Incarnation." *Themelios* 8, no. 1 (1982): 14-19.

———. *Jesus Is the Christ: Studies in the Theology of John*. Grand Rapids: Eerdmans, 1989.

———. *The Lord from Heaven: A Study of the New Testament Teaching on the Deity and Humanity of Jesus Christ*. 2nd ed. Downers Grove, Ill.: InterVarsity Press, 1974.

Morris, Thomas V. *The Logic of God Incarnate*. Ithaca, N.Y.: Cornell University Press, 1986.

———. "Reduplication and Representational Christology." *Modern Theology* 2 (1986): 319-27.

Moulder, James. "Is Chalcedonian Christology Coherent?" *Modern Theology* 2 (1986): 285-307.

Moule, C. F. D. *The Birth of the New Testament*. 3rd ed. San Francisco: Harper & Row, 1982.

————. "Further Reflections on Philippians 2:5-11." In *Apostolic History and the Gospel: Biblical and Historical Essays Presented to F. F. Bruce,* edited by W. W. Gasque and R. P. Martin. London: Paternoster, 1970.

————. "The Influence of Circumstances on the Use of Christological Terms." *Journal of Theological Studies,* n.s. 10 (1959): 247-63.

————. "The New Testament and the Doctrine of the Trinity: A Short Report on an Old Theme." *Expository Times* 88 (1976): 16-20.

————. *The Origin of Christology*. Cambridge: Cambridge University Press, 1977.

————. "The Pre-existence of Christ in the Light of the Experience of New Testament Christians." *Theologia Evangelica* 8 (1975): 137-50.

————. Review of *Christology in the Making: An Inquiry into the Origins of the Doctrine of the Incarnation* by James D. G. Dunn. *Journal of Theological Studies,* no. 33 (1982): 258-63.

Mowinckel, Sigmund. *He That Cometh,* translated by G. W. Anderson. Nashville: Abingdon, 1956.

Mühlenberg, E. "The Divinity of Jesus in Early Christian Faith." *Studia Patristica* 17, pt. 1. Edited by Elizabeth A. Livingstone. Oxford: Pergamon, 1982.

Murphy-O'Conner, J. "Christological Anthropology in Phil. II, 6-11." *Revue Biblique* 83 (1976): 25-50.

Neill, Stephen. "Jesus and Myth." In *The Truth of God Incarnate,* edited by Michael Green. Grand Rapids: Eerdmans, 1977.

Neusner, Jacob. *The Incarnation of God: The Character of Divinity in Formative Judaism*. Philadelphia: Fortress, 1988.

————. *Judaisms and Their Messiahs at the Turn of the Christian Era*. Cambridge: Cambridge University Press, 1987.

Newman, Paul W. *A Spirit Christology: Recovering the Biblical Paradigm of Christian Faith*. Lanham, Md.: University Press of America, 1987.

Nock, Arthur Darby. *Early Gentile Christianity and its Hellenistic Background*. New York: Harper & Row, 1964.

————. Review of *Paulus: Die Theologie des Apostels im Lichte der jüdischen Religionsgeschichte* by Hans-Joachim Schoeps. *Gnomon* 33 (1961): 581-90.

Norris, R. A., Jr. "The Problem of Human Identity in Patristic Christological Speculation." In *Studia Patristica* 17, pt. 1. Edited by Elizabeth A. Livingstone. Oxford: Pergamon, 1982.

Norris, Richard A., Jr., ed. and trans. *The Christological Controversy*. Philadelphia: Fortress, 1980.

O'Collins, Gerald. *Christology: A Biblical, Historical, and Systematic Study of Jesus Christ.* New York: Oxford University Press, 1995.

———. *Interpreting Jesus.* Ramsey, N.J.: Paulist, 1983.

Oden, Thomas C. *The Word of Life: Systematic Theology.* Vol. 2. San Francisco: Harper & Row, 1989.

Ogden, Schubert M. *Christ Without Myth: A Study Based on the Theology of Rudolf Bultmann.* Dallas: SMU Press, 1991.

O'Neill, J. C. "The Prologue to St. John's Gospel." *Journal of Theological Studies,* n.s. 20 (1969): 41-52.

———. *Who Did Jesus Think He Was?* Leiden: E. J. Brill, 1995.

Oppenheimer, Helen. *Incarnation and Immanence.* London: Hodder & Stoughton, 1973.

Owen, H. P. "The New Testament and the Incarnation: A Study in Doctrinal Development." *Religious Studies* 8 (1972): 221-32.

Page, Ruth. *The Incarnation of Freedom and Love.* London: SCM Press, 1991.

Pannenberg, Wolfhart. *Jesus: God and Man.* 2nd ed. Translated by Lewis L. Wilkins and Duane A. Priebe. Philadelphia: Westminster Press, 1977.

———. *Systematic Theology.* Vol. 2. Translated by Geoffrey W. Bromiley. Grand Rapids: Eerdmans, 1994.

Payne, Philip B. "Jesus' Implicit Claim to Deity in His Parables." *Trinity Journal* 2 (1981): 3-23.

Perrin, Norman. *A Modern Pilgrimage in New Testament Christology.* Philadelphia: Fortress, 1974.

Pinnock, Clark. *Flame of Love: A Theology of the Holy Spirit.* Downers Grove, Ill.: InterVarsity Press, 1996.

Piper, Otto A. "The Virgin Birth: The Meaning of the Gospel Accounts." *Interpretation* 18 (1964): 131-48.

Plantinga, Cornelius, Jr. "Trinity." In *International Standard Bible Encyclopedia,* edited by Geoffrey W. Bromiley. Vol. 4. Grand Rapids: Eerdmans, 1988.

Pollard, T. E. "Cosmology and the Prologue of the Fourth Gospel." *Vigiliae Christianae* 12 (1958): 147-53.

———. *Johannine Christology and the Early Church.* Cambridge: Cambridge University Press, 1970.

———. "Logos and Son in Origen, Aruis, and Athanasius." In *Studia Patristica.* Vol. 2, pt. 2. Edited by Kurt Aland and F. L. Cross. Berlin: Akademie-Verlag, 1957.

Prestige, G. L. *God in Patristic Thought.* 2nd ed. London: SPCK, 1952.

Quick, O. C. *Doctrines of the Church.* London: Nisbet, 1938.

Rahner, Karl. *The Content of Faith: The Best of Karl Rahner's Theological Writing,* edited by Karl Lehmann and Albert Raffelt; translated by Harvey D. Egan. New York: Crossroad, 1993.

———. "Current Problems in Christology." *Theological Investigations.* Vol. 1. New York: Seabury, 1961.

———. "On the Theology of the Incarnation." *Theological Investigations.* Vol. 4. New York: Seabury, 1966.

Ramm, Bernard L. *An Evangelical Christology: Ecumenic & Historic.* Nashville: Thomas Nelson, 1985.

Rawlinson, A. E. J. *Essays on the Trinity and the Incarnation.* London: Longmans, 1928.

Reese, James M. "Christ as Wisdom Incarnate: Wiser than Solomon, Loftier than Lady Wisdom." *Biblical Theology Bulletin* 11 (1981): 44-47.

Richter, G. "Die Fleischwerdung des Logos im Johannesevangelium." *Novum Testamentum* 13 (1971): 81-126; 14 (1972): 256-76.

Ridderbos, Herman. *Paul: An Outline of His Theology.* Translated by John Richard DeWitt. Grand Rapids: Eerdmans, 1975.

———. *Paul and Jesus: Origin and General Character of Paul's Preaching of Christ,* translated by David H. Freeman. Nutley, N.J.: Presbyterian & Reformed, 1957.

Riesenfeld, H. "The Mythological Background of New Testament Christology." In *The Gospel Tradition: Essays by H. Riesenfeld.* Philadelphia: Fortress, 1970.

Riesner, Rainer. "Präexistenz und Jungfraugeburt." *Theologische Beiträge* 12 (1981): 177-87.

Robinson, James M. "Jesus as Sophos and Sophia: Wisdom Tradition and the Gospels." In *Aspects of Wisdom in Judaism and Early Christianity,* edited by R. L. Wilken. Notre Dame, Ind.: University of Notre Dame Press, 1975.

Robinson, John A. T. *Can We Trust the New Testament?* Grand Rapids: Eerdmans, 1977.

———. "The Fourth Gospel and the Church's Doctrine of the Trinity." In *Twelve More New Testament Studies.* London: SCM Press, 1984.

———. *The Human Face of God.* London: SCM Press, 1973.

———. *The Priority of John,* edited by J. F. Coakley. London: SCM Press, 1985.

———. "The Use of the Fourth Gospel for Christology Today." In *Twelve More New Testament Studies.* London: SCM Press, 1984.

Rowdon, H. H., ed. *Christ the Lord: Studies in Christology Presented to Donald Guthrie.* Downers Grove, Ill.: InterVarsity Press, 1982.

Runia, Klaas. *The Present-Day Christological Debate.* Downers Grove, Ill.: InterVarsity Press, 1984.

Sabourin, Leopold. *Christology: Basic Texts in Focus.* New York: Alba House, 1984.

———. "Christ's Pre-existence." *Religious Studies Bulletin* 4 (1984): 22-29.

Sanders, E. P. *Jesus and Judaism.* Philadelphia: Fortress, 1985.

———. "Jesus in Historical Context." *Theology Today* 50 (1993): 429-48.

Sanders, J. A. "Dissenting Deities and Philippians 2:1-11." *Journal of Biblical Literature* 88 (1969): 279-90.

Sandmel, Samuel. "Parallelomania." *Journal of Biblical Literature* 81 (1962): 1-13.

Schillebeeckx, Edward. *Christ: The Experience of Jesus as Lord,* translated by John Bowden. New York: Crossroad, 1980.

———. *Jesus: An Experiment in Christology,* translated by Hubert Hoskins. New York: Seabury, 1979.

Schimanowski, Gottfried. *Weisheit und Messias: Die jüdischen Voraussetzungen der urchristlichen Präexistenzchristologie.* Tübingen: J. C. B. Mohr, 1985.

Schleiermacher, Friedrich. *The Christian Faith,* translated by H. R. Mackintosh and J. S. Stewart. Philadelphia: Fortress, 1976.

Schnackenburg, Rudolf. *Jesus in the Gospels: A Biblical Christology,* translated by O. C. Dean Jr. Louisville: Westminster/John Knox, 1995.

———. "The Origin and Nature of the Johannine Concept of the Logos." In *The Gospel of John.* Vol. 1. Translated by Kevin Smyth. New York: Herder & Herder, 1968.

———. "Pre-existence." In *The Gospel of John.* Vol. 1. Translated by Kevin Smyth. New York: Herder & Herder, 1968.

Schneider, Gerhard. "Christologische Präexistenzaussagen im Neuen Testament." *Internationale Katholische Zeitschrift* 6 (1977): 21-30.

———. "Präexistenz Christi: Der Ursprung einer neutestamentlichen Vorstellung und das Problem ihrer Auslegung." In *Neues Testament und Kirche: Für Rudolf Schnackenberg,* edited by J. Gnilka. Freiburg: Herder, 1974.

Schneider, H. "'The Word Was Made Flesh': An Analysis of the Theology of Revelation in the Fourth Gospel." *Catholic Biblical Quarterly* 31 (1969): 344-56.

Schoonenberg, Piet, *The Christ: A Study of the God-Man Relationship in the Whole of Creation and in Jesus Christ,* translated by Della Couling. New York: Herder & Herder, 1971.

Schüssler Fiorenza, Elisabeth. "Wisdom Mythology and the Christological Hymns of the New Testament." In Aspects of Wisdom in Judaism and Early Christianity, edited by Robert L. Wilken. Notre Dame, Ind.: University of Notre Dame Press, 1975.

Schütz, Paul. "Existenz—Praeexistenz—Postexistenz." *Zeitschrift für Religions und Geistesgeschichte* 9 (1957): 103-15.

Schwarz, Hans. *Responsible Faith: Christian Theology in the Light of 20th-Century Questions*. Minneapolis: Augsburg, 1986.

Schweizer, Eduard. "Die Herkunft der Präexistenzvorstellung bei Paulus." *Evangelische Theologie* 19 (1954): 65-70.

———. *Jesus*. Translated by David E. Green. Atlanta: John Knox, 1971.

———. "The Sending of the Pre-existent Son of God." In *Theological Dictionary of the New Testament*. Vol. 8. Grand Rapids: Eerdmans, 1971.

———. "What Do We Mean When We Say, 'God Sent His Son'?" In *Faith and History: Essays in Honor of Paul W. Meyer,* edited by J. Carroll et. al. Atlanta: Scholars Press, 1990.

———. "Zum religionsgeschichtlichen Hintergrund der 'Sendungsformel' Gal 4:4f. Rm 8:3f. Joh 3:16f. I Joh 4:9." *Zeitschrift für die Neutestamentliche Wissenschaft und die Kunde der älteren Kirche* 57 (1966): 199-210.

Seeberg, Reinhold. *Text-Book of the History of Doctrines*. 2 vols. Translated by Charles E. Hay. Philadelphia: Lutheran Publication Society, 1905.

Segal, Alan. "Pre-existence and Incarnation: A Response to Dunn and Holladay." *Semeia* 30 (1985): 83-95.

———. *Two Powers in Heaven: Early Rabbinic Reports about Christianity and Gnosticism*. Leiden: E. J. Brill, 1977.

Skarsaune, Oskar. *Incarnation: Myth or Fact?* translated by Trygve R. Skarsten. St. Louis: Concordia, 1991.

Stead, Christopher. *Divine Substance*. Oxford: Oxford University Press, 1977.

———. *Philosophy in Christian Antiquity*. Cambridge: Cambridge University Press, 1994.

Stein, Robert H. *The Method and Message of Jesus' Teaching*. Philadelphia: Westminster Press, 1978.

Strimple, Robert B. "Philippians 2:5-11 in Recent Studies: Some Exegetical Conclusions." *Westminster Theological Journal* 41 (1979): 247-68.

Studer, Basil. "Das Christusdogma der Alten Kirche und das neutestamentliche Christusbild." *Münchener Theologische Zeitschrift* 44 (1993): 13-20.

———. Trinity and Incarnation: The Faith of the Early Church, edited by Andrew Louth; translated by Matthias Westerhoff. Collegeville, Minn.: Liturgical Press, 1993.

Sturch, Richard. *The Word and Christ: An Essay in Analytic Christology*. Oxford: Oxford University Press, 1991.

Styler, G. M. "Stages in Christology in the Synoptic Gospels." *New Testament Studies* 10 (1963-1964): 398-409.

Suggs, M. Jack. *Wisdom, Christology and Law in Matthew's Gospel*. Cambridge, Mass.: Harvard University Press, 1970.

Swinburne, Richard. "Could God Become Man?" In *The Philosophy in Christianity,* edited by Godfrey N. Vesey. Cambridge: Cambridge University Press, 1989.

Sykes, S. W., and J. P. Clayton, eds. *Christ, Faith and History: Cambridge Studies in Christology.* Cambridge: Cambridge University Press, 1972.

Talbert, Charles H. "'And the Word Became Flesh': When?" In *The Future of Christology: Essays in Honor of Leander E. Keck,* edited by Abraham J. Malherbe and Wayne A. Meeks. Minneapolis: Fortress, 1993.

———. "The Myth of a Descending-Ascending Redeemer in Mediterranean Antiquity," *New Testament Studies* 22 (1975-1976): 418-40.

———. "The Problem of Pre-existence in Philippians 2:6-11." *Journal of Biblical Literature* 86 (1967): 141-53.

Tavard, George H. *Images of the Christ: An Enquiry into Christology.* Washington, D.C.: University Press of America, 1982.

Taylor, Vincent. "Does The New Testament Call Jesus 'God'?" *Expository Times* 73 (1962): 116-18.

———. *The Names of Jesus.* London: Macmillan, 1953.

———. *The Person of Christ in New Testament Teaching.* London: Macmillan, 1958.

Teeple, Howard. "The Origin of the Son of Man Christology." *Journal of Biblical Literature* 84 (1965): 213-50.

Thompson, Marianne Meye. *The Incarnate Word: Perspectives on Jesus in the Fourth Gospel.* Peabody, Mass.: Hendrickson, 1993.

Thompson, William M. *The Jesus Debate: A Survey and Synthesis.* New York: Paulist, 1985.

———. *The Struggle for Theology's Soul: Contesting Scripture in Christology.* New York: Crossroad, 1996.

Thrall, Margaret E. "Alternative Visions of Christian Faith." *Expository Times* 88 (1977): 115-19.

———. "The Origin of Pauline Christology." In *Apostolic History and the Gospel: Biblical and Historical Essays Presented to F. F. Bruce on His 60th Birthday,* edited by W. Ward Gasque and Ralph P. Martin. Grand Rapids: Eerdmans, 1970.

Tiede, David L. *The Charismatic Figure as Miracle Worker.* Missoula, Mont.: Scholars Press, 1972.

Tillich, Paul. *Systematic Theology.* Vol. 2: *Existence and the Christ.* Chicago: University of Chicago Press, 1957.

Torrance, Thomas F. *The Christian Doctrine of God, One Being Three Persons.* Edinburgh: T & T Clark, 1996.

————. *The Doctrine of Jesus Christ.* Eugene, Ore.: Wipf & Stock, 2002.

————. *Space, Time, and Incarnation.* London: Oxford University Press, 1969.

————. *Theology in Reconciliation: Essays Towards Evangelical and Catholic Unity in East and West.* Grand Rapids: Eerdmans. 1975.

————. *The Trinitarian Faith: The Evangelical Theology of the Ancient Catholic Church.* Edinburgh: T & T Clark, 1995.

————, ed. *The Incarnation: Ecumenical Studies in the Nicene-Constantinopolitan Creed, A.D. 381.* Edinburgh: Handsel, 1981.

Trakatellis, Demetrius Christ. *The Pre-existence of Christ in the Writings of Justin Martyr.* Missoula, Mont.: Scholars Press, 1976.

Tuckett, Christopher. "Christology and the New Testament." *Scottish Journal of Theology* 33 (1980): 401-16.

Turner, H. E. W. *Jesus the Christ.* London: Mowbrays, 1976.

Turner, Nigel. "St. John's Eternal Word." *Evangelical Quarterly* 22 (1950): 243-48.

Unnik, W. C. van. "Jesus the Christ." *New Testament Studies* 8 (1961-1962): 101-16.

Vawter, Bruce. *This Man Jesus: An Essay Toward a New Testament Christology.* Garden City, N.Y.: Doubleday, 1973.

Vermes, Geza. *Jesus the Jew: A Historian's Reading of the Gospels.* London: Collins, 1973.

Wainwright, A. T. "The Confession 'Jesus Is God' in the New Testament." *Scottish Journal of Theology* 10 (1957): 274-99.

————. *The Trinity in the New Testament.* London: SPCK, 1962.

Wainwright, Geoffrey. "'Son of God' in Liturgical Doxologies." *Concilium* 153 (1982): 49-54.

————, ed. *Keeping the Faith: Essays to Mark the Centenary of Lux Mundi.* Philadelphia: Fortress, 1988.

Walter, Nikolaus. "Geschichte und Mythos in der urchristlichen Präexistenzchristologie." In *Mythos und Rationalität,* edited by Hans Heinrich Schmid. Gütersloh: Gerd Mohn, 1988.

Wanamaker, Charles Arthur. "Christ as Divine Agent in Paul." *Scottish Journal of Theology* 39 (1986): 517-28.

————. "Philippians 2:6-11: Son of God or Adamic Christology?" *New Testament Studies* 33 (1987) 179-93.

Watson, Francis. "Is John's Christology Adoptionist?" In *The Glory of Christ in the New Testament: Studies in Christology,* edited by L. D. Hurst and N. T. Wright. Oxford: Oxford University Press, 1987.

Weber, Otto. *Foundations of Dogmatics.* Vol. 2. Translated and annotated by Darrell L. Guder. Grand Rapids: Eerdmans, 1983.

Welch, Claude, ed. and trans. *God and Incarnation in Mid-Nineteenth Century German Theology: G. Thomasius, I. A. Dorner, A. E. Biedermann.* New York: Oxford University Press, 1965.

Wells, David F. *The Person of Christ: A Biblical and Historical Analysis of the Incarnation.* Westchester, Ill.: Crossway, 1984.

Werther, David. "The Temptation of God Incarnate." *Religious Studies* 29 (1993): 47-50.

White, Vernon. *Atonement and Incarnation: An Essay in Universalism and Particularity.* Cambridge: Cambridge University Press, 1991.

Wiles, Maurice. *The Christian Fathers.* New York: Oxford University Press, 1982.

———. *Explorations in Theology* 4. London: SCM Press, 1979.

———. "Person or Personification? A Patristic Debate about Logos." In *The Glory of Christ in the New Testament: Studies in Christology,* edited by L. D. Hurst and N. T. Wright. Oxford: Oxford University Press, 1987.

———. *The Remaking of Christian Doctrine: The Hulsean Lectures 1973.* London: SCM Press, 1974.

———. "Some Reflections on the Origins of the Doctrine of the Trinity." *Journal of Theological Studies* 8 (1957): 92-106.

Willet, Michael E. *Wisdom Christology in the Fourth Gospel.* San Francisco: Mellen Research University Press, 1992.

Williams, George Huntston. *The Radical Reformation.* Philadelphia: Westminster Press, 1962.

Williamson, Ronald. "The Incarnation of the Logos in Hebrews." *Expository Times* 95 (1983): 4-8.

———. "Philo and New Testament Christology." *Expository Times* 90 (1979): 361-65.

Witherington, Ben, III. *The Christology of Jesus.* Minneapolis: Fortress, 1990.

———. *The Jesus Quest: The Third Search for the Jew of Nazareth.* Downers Grove, Ill.: InterVarsity Press, 1995.

———. *Jesus the Sage: The Pilgrimage of Wisdom.* Minneapolis: Fortress, 1994.

Wong, T. Yai-chow. "The Problem of Pre-existence in Philippians 2:6-11." *Ephemerides Theologicae Lovanienses* 62 (1986): 267-82.

Wright, N. T. *The Climax of the Covenant: Christ and the Law in Pauline Theology.* Edinburgh: T & T Clark, 1991.

———. "'Constraints' and the Jesus of History." *Scottish Journal of Theology* 39 (1986): 189-210.

———. *Jesus and the Victory of God: Christian Origins and the Question of God.* Vol. 2. Minneapolis: Fortress, 1996.

———. *The New Testament and the People of God.* Minneapolis: Fortress, 1992.

———. *Who Was Jesus?* Grand Rapids: Eerdmans, 1992.

Young, Frances. *The Making of the Creeds.* Philadelphia: Trinity Press, 1993.

Subject Index

Adam christology, 9, 74, 77, 78, 99, 103, 275-76, 278

adoptionism, 14, 28, 57, 75, 89-90, 107, 118-19, 121, 125-26, 134, 136, 187, 207, 223, 232, 237, 256, 261, 264, 267, 274, 282, 284, 294-95, 299, 303

Against Heresies, 215-16

Against Marcion, 218

Against Praxeas, 217-18

angel of the Lord, 85, 180-81, 219, 231, 246, 311

angels, 68, 130, 171, 175, 177, 179, 180-81, 184, 196, 211, 216-17, 219, 232

anthropomorphism, 183, 186

Antiochene christology, 250

apotheosis, 187, 189, 205

Arianism, 15, 16 n. 13, 69, 178, 187, 196, 221-24, 262, 303, 314

atonement, 22, 118-19, 129, 133, 227, 232, 307, 316

Chalcedon, Council of, 226, 249

Chalcedon, Definition of, 226, 228, 243, 248-49, 269-71, 285, 298, 300-301

christology, high, 45, 87, 111, 118, 123, 126, 161, 171, 202-3, 233, 310, 312

christology, low, 87, 118, 202

contextualization, 49, 193-94, 208, 259, 261

creation, 82-86, 101-2, 128-29, 142, 146, 176-79, 249, 253, 316

deification, 189

deism, 20, 232-33

Dialogue with Trypho, 213

Docetism, 144, 191, 196, 214, 257, 265, 306

Ebionitism, 29, 71, 170, 223, 262

Enlightenment, the, 14, 20-21, 23-24, 46-47, 233, 259, 312

First Enoch, 174-75

functional language, 14, 37-39, 53-55, 101, 109, 205, 246-48, 258, 265, 273, 279, 288, 290, 293, 304

Gnosticism, 27, 76, 126, 146, 153, 163, 167-68, 188-89, 190-92, 196, 215, 223

God, 12, 17, 24-25, 29, 33, 35, 46, 57, 67, 86, 92, 112, 129, 140-41, 172, 185, 196, 219, 250-52, 281, 287, 299, 307, 308

God the Father, 59, 82, 109, 116, 141-42, 144, 147, 149, 150, 210, 212, 214-15, 217-19, 225, 243, 250, 265, 269, 287

Hellenism, 48-49, 132, 143, 180, 185, 187, 196, 214, 221, 233, 312

hellenization of doctrine, 14, 43, 48-49, 53, 99, 187, 221, 271, 290-91, 302, 306

hermeneutics, 41-43, 46-49, 301

Holy Spirit, 9, 31, 87, 103, 112-13, 203-4, 218, 221, 226, 235, 239, 241, 245, 268, 293, 296, 299, 301, 303

hymns, 45, 74, 141, 201, 203, 205, 207, 312

incarnation, 9, 14-15, 18, 26 n. 36, 35, 40, 45, 74, 81, 96, 116, 133, 141, 143-44, 156, 159-60, 166,

185, 193, 195, 198, 210, 213, 215-17, 221, 226-29, 231, 234, 237-38, 240, 245-46, 250-51, 264, 267-68, 277, 284, 289, 291, 307, 316

intermediary figures, 171-72, 202

Jehovah's Witnesses, 13 n. 7, 235

Jesus

deity of, 63, 68, 80, 87, 151, 158, 160, 200, 202, 206, 227, 262, 270, 272, 285, 307, 315

God-man, 13, 16 n. 14, 227, 241-42, 245, 252, 259, 271, 280, 285, 296

humanity of, 14-15, 17, 23, 28, 88, 92, 124, 130, 168-69, 200, 202, 212, 227, 236, 242, 245-46, 257-59, 262-63, 267-70, 272, 282, 295, 297, 300, 302, 307, 314-15

preexistence of, 16, 133, 228, 237, 241-44, 300

John, reliability of, 36-37, 135-39

Judaism, Hellenistic, 125, 182-84

Judaism, Rabbinic, 171, 173-75, 181 n. 63, 183, 185 n. 78, 186, 194

Judaism, Second Temple, 51, 67-68, 92, 133, 170-72, 178, 180-81, 185 n. 78, 186

Kyrios. See Lord

Letter to Diognetus, The, 211

Logos. See Word of God

Lord, 63-64, 84, 86, 112, 124, 168, 188, 190, 214, 226

love (of God), 9, 17, 68-69, 74, 145, 158, 233, 245-46, 248, 251-52, 308-9, 315-17

mediator, 72, 85-86, 110,

176-78, 181, 188, 214, 264,
268, 273-74, 279, 312
wisdom christology, 45, 82-
84, 203, 275
Wisdom of Solomon, 179
Word (of God), 15, 62-63,
140-42, 144, 156, 171, 178-

81, 184, 188, 209-10, 213-
15, 217, 220, 225, 228,
239-41, 244, 268, 270, 274,
281, 289, 292
world religions, 18, 28, 255-
56, 282-86, 292-94, 299,
309

worldview, 19-22, 23-26,
29-30, 53 n. 28, 254, 256,
313-14
worship, 45, 60, 101 n. 124,
129, 180, 201, 203-7, 212,
221, 227, 255, 284, 298,
312